SEASONAL FREEZER COOKBOOK

SEASONAL FREEZER COOKBOOK

Caroline Ellwood
Clare Ferguson
Carole Handslip
Jeni Wright

CONTENTS

INTRODUCTION

SPRING

SUMMER

AUTUMN

WINTER

REFERENCE SECTION

Freezer information by Jeni Wright
Starters & vegetable recipes by Caroline Ellwood
Main-courses by Clare Ferguson
Desserts & baking recipes by Carole Handslip

Photography by Paul Williams

This edition first published in 1984 by
Octopus Books Limited, 59 Grosvenor Street, London W1

© 1983 Octopus Books Limited

ISBN 0 86273 159 3

Produced by Mandarin Publishers Ltd., Hong Kong
Printed in Hong Kong

Seasonal Freezer Cookbook was originally published
by Octopus Books Limited in 1983 in hardback

INTRODUCTION

What could be nicer than having your own private store of each season's goodies? To have peas from the garden on Christmas Day, a fresh raspberry mousse for New Year and lychees all the year round!

Stop thinking of your freezer as an emergency storecupboard, a refuge for burgers, bangers and beans. Whether you grow your own produce in the garden, snap up bargains at the local market or farm, you need to know how to make the most of Nature's bounty. In this book, each season has an A to Z of the best fresh produce for the time of year, when and how to harvest, prepare and pack it for the freezer, how long to store and thaw. Plus a selection of some of the most mouthwatering recipes ever written – all of them tried and tested with detailed freezing and thawing instructions.

This section provides all of the technical information you will need: advice on which type of freezer to buy, how to look after it, run it economically and what to do in an emergency. Plus guidelines on packaging and equipment, freezing terms and techniques.

How a Freezer Works

Quite simply, to freeze food is to turn it from a liquid or pliable food to a solid state by lowering its temperature. At a temperature of −18°C/0°F food becomes frozen solid, but in order to preserve its original properties and to be safe to eat, it needs to be frozen quickly – at a lower temperature than this: at −25° to −30°C/−13° to −22°F.

As food freezes, the water content separates from the food and converts into ice crystals inside and between the tissue cells. The slower the freezing process, the larger the ice crystals and therefore the greater the damage to the structure of the food. Fast-freezing gives small ice crystals.

Freezing does not kill the enzymes and micro-organisms present in food, it simply slows down their activity to such a rate that little or no changes take place in the food while it is in the freezer. Fast-freezing halts the action of these bodies as rapidly as possible. Recommended storage times for foods are calculated according to the rate of enzyme and micro-organism activity inside the freezer, and it is therefore wise to follow them. Remember also that enzymes and micro-organisms resume their activity on thawing and that thawed foods have a tendency to spoil faster than fresh – this is why thorough reheating is essential.

Choosing a Freezer

There are three main types of freezer – chest, upright and combination refrigerator/freezer. All freezers work on the same basic principle and all are capable of freezing down fresh food at a temperature of −25° to −30°C/−13° to −22°F and storing it at −18°C/0°F or below. All freezers in the U.K. must display a 4-star symbol ✸✸✸✸ to indicate that they can freeze down

fresh food. Ice-making compartments of refrigerators are not cold enough to freeze down fresh foods, but they can store ready-frozen food.

When deciding which freezer to buy, consider the available space, cost (both purchase price and running costs), the size of your family and the purpose for which you require the freezer. As a general guide, allow a minimum of 56 litres/2 cu ft of freezer space for each member of the family, remembering that 28 litres/1 cu ft should hold about 9 kg/20 lb of food. If you intend to freeze down seasonal produce, batch cook and bulk buy, you will need a greater cubic capacity than this. However, do not be tempted to buy a freezer that is far too large for your needs as the running costs of a freezer which has lots of empty space inside are extremely high, and what you can save by growing your own produce or by buying in bulk will be lost in high electricity bills.

Chest Freezers Chest freezers with top-opening hinged lids vary in size from as small as 125 litres/4 cu ft to as large as 775 litres/25 cu ft. There is a wider range of large chests to choose from than uprights, which are not generally available over 370 litres/13 cu ft. Chest models are less expensive to buy than uprights per litre/cu ft; they are also less expensive to run because they use less electricity – when the lid of a chest freezer is opened there is minimal loss of cold air (cold air is heavier than warm so it does not rise up and escape through the open top). In economical terms, therefore, a chest freezer is the best buy.

Disadvantages of chest freezers are that in small, modern kitchens they take up more valuable floor space than uprights, and they cannot be conveniently fitted under a work surface because the lid needs to be raised to get inside. Packages tend to get 'lost' in their hidden depths and unless you are tall, it is not always easy to delve around inside. Investing in removable baskets is a great help, so too is a colour coding system (see page 10). Remember also that chest freezers are rather more difficult to defrost than uprights, although they do not need defrosting quite so often.

Upright Freezers Upright freezers are available from about 60 litres/2 cu ft up to 370 litres/13 cu ft. They tend to be more expensive to buy and run than chest freezers, but they are more convenient to use in kitchens – some are even small enough to stand on top of units or other appliances. Most upright freezers take up the same amount of floor space as a refrigerator.

Running costs are high because every time the door is opened a relatively large volume of warm air is allowed into the freezer. Look for a model with shelf shields which help minimize this problem, or for one with shelves on runners to make it easier and therefore quicker to find things. Another problem arising from the door opening in upright freezers is

that there is a tendency for a more rapid build-up of frost around the door than there is in chest freezers. Some (more expensive) upright models have useful built-in defrosting units.

Combination Refrigerator/Freezer If your kitchen is small, this is an ideal model to buy because the two units together take up only the floor space of one – either the refrigerator stands on top of the freezer or vice versa. Combination fridge/freezers are available in a variety of sizes, but the maximum cubic capacity of the freezer is usually around 170 litres/6 cu ft.

When buying a combination unit, check whether there are two separate compressors as one compressor is unlikely to be able to cope with the different temperature requirements of both refrigerator and freezer – the temperature of the refrigerator is likely to be too frosty.

Siting a Freezer

A full freezer is an extremely heavy object, so check that the floor is strong enough to support its weight. Garages and other outhouses, if available, are convenient places to keep freezers, in that they do not use up valuable space inside the house. They must however be well-ventilated and not damp, or the cabinet will quickly become rusty. Check the electricity supply to such buildings and, as a wise precaution, have any wire grounded.

If your freezer is to be kept in a garage, make sure that it can be locked. If necessary, fit a simple padlock to the freezer or keep the door of the outhouse itself locked. A lock prevents small children climbing into the freezer as well as guarding against theft.

The kitchen is the most convenient site for a freezer if you can spare the space, although a freezer in a warm kitchen will cost slightly more to run than one in a cold garage. Make sure plenty of air can circulate all around the freezer and avoid siting it next to any direct source of heat, such as the cooker.

Whichever position you choose for your freezer, it is wise to tape over the freezer plug and its socket, to guard against possible removal or switching off. Also check that in the event of the freezer breaking down (see below) you will notice before is it too late – do not obscure the temperature warning light.

Insurance

Most new freezers carry a one-year guarantee which covers the freezer and its contents, plus the cost of labour and materials in case of a breakdown, but after the first year it is wise to take out your own freezer insurance. Most insurance policies cover the cost of repairs, labour and food spoiled through mechanical breakdown or electrical fault, but spoilage of food caused by accidental switching off or leaving the lid or door open may not be covered in a normal policy – check the small print!

Emergency Procedures

A breakdown is an unusual circumstance with a freezer, but it is wise to be prepared. If the freezer is out of order for no more than 12 hours and the lid or door has been firmly shut during this time, the food inside should still be frozen. No two freezers or its contents are alike, but a freezer that is full of tightly packed food will stay frozen longer than one which is half empty. If the breakdown is not due to a simple electrical fault or a power cut, resist the temptation to open the freezer and contact your service engineer or the maintenance department of the freezer supplier or manufacturer.

If the engineer cannot repair your freezer immediately, or if there is an extended power cut which may last more than 12 hours, then you will have to take your own emergency action. It is advisable *not* to open the freezer, but if you are unsure when the freezer was last working, you may have to check the contents to ascertain this. Do so quickly – press packages in your hand and if you can feel ice crystals, then the food can be safely refrozen. You may find that food at the top of the freezer is thawed and food at the bottom is still frozen solid, in which case remove the thawed items quickly, pack the empty spaces with newspapers and close the freezer again.

If you are unsure when the freezer will be in working order again, you will have to find an alternative place to store food that is still frozen – the ice-making compartment of the refrigerator can take some items, otherwise 'borrow' freezer space from friends. If you have a freezer centre service contract, they will probably store the frozen food at their depot or provide you with a temporary freezer while yours is being repaired.

Food that has started to thaw or has already thawed is highly perishable. If you are in any doubt, throw it away. The best procedure is to cook all raw produce (meat, fish, poultry, fruit and vegetables) as quickly as possible, then eat or cool quickly and freeze immediately. It is safe to refreeze in this case, as long as the food is thoroughly cooked and cooled, and the freezer is in full working order again. Ready-cooked and made-up dishes which have been thawed tend to be more perishable; they should therefore be reheated thoroughly and eaten immediately – on no account must they be refrozen.

When the freezer is in working order again, switch it on to 'fast-freeze' or the equivalent coldest setting and leave it on this setting for at least 6 hours or overnight. Fresh and frozen food can be safely replaced in the cabinet after this time.

Cleaning

An empty new freezer or one that has been defrosted should be cleaned before being loaded. Never clean the inside with soap powder, detergent or any abrasive cleaning agent. Simply wipe the inside of the cabinet with a cloth rinsed out in water to which bicarbonate of soda has been added (dilute 2 teaspoons in approximately 1.2 litres/2 pints water). Rinse with fresh water, then dry thoroughly.

Maintenance

There is very little maintenance involved with a freezer. Check frequently that all controls are working and check the internal temperature occasionally by placing a freezer thermometer in several different positions inside the cabinet: it should read −18° to −20°C/0° to −4°F to be running economically. If not, adjust the temperature control. If a freezer is consistently registering a higher or lower temperature than this, call in a service engineer.

Frost – which tends to build up around the opening of the freezer – must be removed regularly. This is more of a problem with upright models than chest freezers. As soon as the frost is as thick as 5 mm/¼ inch, simply scrape it off with a plastic or wooden spatula. Never use a metal spatula for scraping because this may damage the lining of the walls.

Defrosting

Regular defrosting is essential if the freezer is to run efficiently. It is impossible to say exactly how often this is necessary, but on average it should be two or three times a year for an upright, once or twice for a chest. As a general guide, when the ice has built up to a thickness of more than 5 mm/¼ inch inside the cabinet, it is time to defrost. Some freezers have built-in defrosting devices.

Defrost when stocks are low and the weather is cold (evening time is best in summer), according to the following procedure:

1. Switch off and remove plug from mains. Remove food and baskets, plus shelves if possible. Put some food in the ice making compartment of the refrigerator, then wrap the remainder in newspapers and place in the main body of the refrigerator, or pack in insulated bags if available. Excess items should be well wrapped in newspaper, blankets or rugs and put in the coldest possible place.

2. Line the bottom of the freezer with a thick layer of paper or towels, placing some paper on the floor in front of the freezer if it is an upright. Put several bowls of very hot water inside the freezer and close the lid or door.

3. As soon as the ice starts to melt, scrape it off with a plastic or rubber spatula. Do not wait too long or the ice will melt and water in the bottom of a chest freezer is very difficult to remove. As the ice falls onto the paper, it can be removed easily.

4. Replace the hot water in the bowls as soon as it cools down. Repeat as necessary until all the ice has been removed.

5. Wash with bicarbonate of soda solution (see Cleaning above), then rinse and dry.

6. Close the lid or door, reconnect the plug and 'fast-freeze' for 30 minutes. Wash and dry baskets and shelves during this time. Check for faulty packaging and freezer burn (see page 11) and take this opportunity of bringing records up to date and rotating stock.

7. Return baskets/shelves and food to freezer and close again. Keep on fast-freeze for at least 6 hours or overnight until internal temperature is −18°C/0°F, then return to normal setting.

Packaging Materials

Correct packaging is essential in the freezer to preserve the quality of the food. Packaging protects food from moisture and cold air, thus avoiding dehydration, freezer burn and oxidation (see pages 10 to 12). It also protects foods from damaging each other, and avoids cross-flavouring. Packaging must be strong, moisture proof, vapour proof and non-toxic.

Special packaging materials for the freezer can be quite costly, but at the same time inadequate packaging will mean money lost if food is damaged. The main types of freezer packaging available are listed below. Packaging materials not suitable for the freezer include greaseproof paper, unwaxed cartons and expanded polystyrene.

Freezer Bags Bags are sensible for the freezer, because they take up no more room than the food inside them. Exclusion of air and sealing (see page 12) are extremely important. Polythene bags (sometimes also called polybags or freezer bags) are the most common type, but they must be of heavy-duty polythene suitable for use in the freezer (ie between 120 and 150 gauge), or they will not protect food sufficiently and may split or burst in low temperature conditions. Available in a wide range of sizes, some with gussets which are useful for large and awkwardly-shaped foods, polythene bags are re-usable. Wire ties for sealing are usually included, although some bags are self-sealing and some have labels printed on them.

Coloured polythene bags are available in many colours for easy identification of different foods in the freezer (see colour coding – page 10). Extra-large coloured bags are known as *batching bags* for holding several smaller bags of the same colour together. Coloured bags and batching bags are particularly useful in chest freezers.

Boil-in-bags or *boil-a-bags* are made of high density polythene (usually 200 gauge) so they can withstand both freezing and boiling temperatures. They are extremely useful for sauces, soups, casseroles and vegetables, which can be frozen down in them, then reheated straight from the freezer in boiling water. Sealing is very important with these bags, or water may enter during boiling. They are re-usable, and suitable for use in pressure cookers and microwave ovens. *Boil-a-bag* tubing is also available which enables you to make any size bag – this is particularly convenient if used in conjunction with a heat sealing unit (see page 9).

Roasting bags or *roast-in-bags* can be used for freezing down and for cooking in both a conventional and a microwave oven. Meat, poultry and fish can all be frozen in roasting bags, then put straight in the oven from the freezer – thus conserving all juices and flavour and keeping the oven clean.

Foil-lined freezer bags are made of stiffened paper lined with foil. Ideal for sauces, soups and casseroles, they should not be used for foods with a high acid content and they are not re-usable.

Rigid Containers Rigid containers or boxes, made from rigid polythene, are suitable for foods which need more protection than polythene bags can provide, although they do take up extra room in the freezer. Rigid containers are useful for all types of food, but are especially good for decorated items such as cakes and gâteaux to prevent crushing. They can also be used as preformers in conjunction with polythene bags (see preforming – page 12).

The best kind of rigid containers for the freezer are those with airtight lids. Although expensive to buy, they are re-usable and will last for many years. They are available in many different sizes, shapes and colours and in stacking sets which make for compact storage in the freezer.

It is possible to use cleaned cartons from foods such as cottage cheese, cream and yogurt for freezer storage, but they are not as sturdy as the rigid containers and do not have self-sealing airtight lids. These improvised containers are therefore best reserved for short-term storage and overwrapped in a polythene bag to be on the safe side.

Waxed cartons are available for freezer storage. They stack easily and are useful for purées, soups, sauces and stocks. Their main disadvantage is that hot foods must always be cooled before being packed in them otherwise the wax melts. Another disadvantage is that these cartons are not re-usable.

Freezer Foil Heavy duty aluminium foil, also called freezer foil, is ideal for wrapping food for the freezer, especially if it is an awkward shape such as a joint of meat on the bone. Foil is also useful for padding protruding bones and for interleaving. Ordinary kitchen foil can be used double if freezer foil is not available. After wrapping an item in foil, always overwrap in a polythene bag to protect against puncturing. Foil is not suitable for use in a microwave.

Cling Film This is a good freezer wrapping because it quite literally clings to the surface of food, thus excluding all air. Only use heavy-gauge freezer cling film, and always overwrap. Use for wrapping any item, but particularly those which are awkwardly shaped. Do not re-use. Cling film can also be used for interleaving.

Interleaving Sheets Special interleaving sheets of paper-thin waterproof or waxed tissue are available. These are most useful for separating slices, etc, from each other in a pack, so that they can be removed individually.

Foil Containers These are available in a wide variety of sizes and shapes, including pie dishes, plates and pudding basins. Food can be frozen down, reheated and served in the same foil container. Freezer dishes and plates are re-usable, but this is not true of the cardboard lids frequently supplied with them. When re-using, foil covering may be used as a substitute.

Freezer-To-Oven-To-Table Dishes Many manufacturers of earthenware, ceramic dishes and toughened glassware now make dishes which are both freezer-proof and ovenproof. These are extremely useful, as the food can be frozen down, reheated and served in the same dish. Follow manufacturer's instructions carefully; some freezer/ovenproof dishes cannot be placed straight in the oven from the freezer. To avoid storing such dishes in the freezer for long periods of time, they can be used as preformers (see page 12).

Glass Containers Most non-toughened glass tends to shatter at low temperatures so it is not the ideal packaging medium. It is therefore wise to use only those glass containers which are designated freezer-proof. Leave room for the contents to expand on freezing and always pack glass in a polythene bag as an additional precaution. Never freeze bottles of milk or alcohol.

Microwave Cookware A range of dishes, trays, basins and plates, etc, is available which is suitable for both freezer storage and reheating in a microwave. Plastic is the most common material used. All microwave containers need to be overwrapped in polythene bags for storage in the freezer, but remember to remove the bag before putting the container in the microwave.

Packaging Accessories

Labels are essential for identification purposes. Some freezer bags have labels printed on them, but plain bags and rigid containers, etc, should be identified with special adhesive freezer labels. Ordinary adhesive labels are not suitable as they do not adhere at very low temperatures. Always write on labels with a *chinagraph* or *waxed pencil* or a *felt tip pen* which is not water-based (water-based pens run and lead pencils fade away in the freezer).

State the contents of the package, quantity, weight or number of servings, date of freezing and any special thawing or reheating instructions. Polythene bags can be sealed with *wire closures* or *ties* or special *freezer tape*, or with a special heat sealing unit (see opposite). Some wire closures are combined with labels, which makes them doubly useful. Labels, ties and tape can be colour matched with bags and containers to make an extremely efficient freezer storage system.

Other Useful Freezer Equipment

Blanching Basket A blanching basket is essential for freezing down fresh vegetables – the basket ensures that water penetrates individual vegetables. Buy one complete with its own blanching pan that will hold at least 4 litres/7 pints water. The pan should have a good-quality thick ground base to ensure maximum heat retention so that water quickly returns to the boil after vegetables are added – this way they will not become overblanched.

Fast-Freeze Trays Although foil-lined baking trays can be used for open freezing, specially designed fast-freeze trays are available. Usually made of rigid plastic, the best ones are those which stack on top of each other without crushing delicate items such as piped rosettes of whipped cream or soft fruit.

Freezer Diary A diary is useful for keeping an accurate record of freezer contents and to ensure efficient rotation of stock. Record each item in the diary at the time it is put in the freezer – state content of package, quantity, weight or number of servings, position in freezer and date by when it should be eaten, plus thawing and reheating instructions. Don't forget to cross off items when they are taken out of the freezer. Always keep your diary near the freezer.

Freezer Knives Ordinary knives are liable to break when cutting through frozen foods, so a specially toughened freezer knife is a must. If you are planning to buy meat in bulk, it is also wise to invest in a freezer saw, which will cut through bone as well as frozen meat. A meat cleaver is also useful for dividing up joints and large pieces of meat.

Freezer Pump A mechanical vacuum pump is one of the most efficient and hygienic ways to remove air from polythene bags. Simple to use, and much more effective than trying to squeeze air out by hand.

Freezer Thermometer To check the internal temperature of the freezer occasionally. Normal storage temperature should be −18°C/0°F, fast-freeze temperature when freezing down fresh food should be −25° to −30°C/−13°F to −22°F. Thermometers that clip onto shelves or baskets are most convenient. Test several positions in the freezer to be accurate.

Heat Sealing Unit Electrically operated units for sealing polythene bags are expensive, but worthwhile if you intend to freeze a lot of produce. The unit comes complete with polythene tubing so that you can make bags any size to fit individual requirements. The seal is airtight, which prevents dehydration, freezer burn and oxidation (see pages 10 to 12), and some units have a variable temperature control of different gauges of polythene.

Spatula Most freezers are sold complete with a plastic spatula for removing build-up of frost around the freezer door periodically, and for defrosting, but these can also be bought separately.

Freezing Terms and Techniques

Batch Cooking This means to cook a 'batch' or large quantity of the same dish, then to divide it into smaller, usable quantities to freeze for future use. You can either set aside a time for batch cooking special dishes for the freezer, or make up an extra quantity when cooking a meal that is to be eaten fresh. Batch cooking is sensible in that it saves time, money and fuel, and provides your feezer with a convenient supply of ready-cooked foods. A fan-assisted oven is particularly good for batch baking because of its even heat distribution. If your oven is not fan-assisted, exchange trays between the oven shelves once or twice during baking to ensure even browning and cooking – especially for biscuits and cakes.

The best times for batch cooking are when you have bought in bulk, and when seasonal fruit and vegetables are plentiful. Ideal dishes for batch cooking are: soups and sauces, casseroles and stews, pastry-based dishes such as quiches, pies and tarts, pâtés and terrines, pizzas and pasta dishes, cakes, bread and biscuits. Special coloured batching bags are available from freezer equipment suppliers to make identification easier (see page 8).

Blanching This procedure is essential for many vegetables to preserve their quality in the freezer, and when specified in freezing instructions it should not be disregarded. Blanching is necessary to retard the activity of natural enzymes present in vegetables; if it is not carried out the enzymes will continue to work in the freezer with consequent deterioration of colour, texture, flavour and nutritive value. If vegetables are not blanched, their freezer storage life is therefore considerably shortened.

To blanch vegetables: fill a blanching basket with no more than 500 g/1 lb prepared vegetables. Immerse in a large pan containing about 4 litres/7 pints rapidly boiling water (lemon juice is added to prevent discoloration in some cases – see individual vegetable freezing instructions). Return quickly to the boil, then calculate the blanching time accurately, from the moment the water comes to the boil at this stage. Immediately blanching time is up, remove the basket from the pan and refresh in a bowl of iced water for same length of time as blanching, then drain and pack. Blanching water can be used several times over (as many as 6 or 7 times) before replacing; this helps to increase vitamin C retention.

Blast Freezing A commercial method of freezing in which large quantities of food are frozen very quickly at the lowest possible temperatures, to minimize loss of flavour, appearance and nutritive value. Some butchers who specialize in freezer orders will blast freeze meat for you so that it is in peak condition to go into your freezer.

Brick Freezing A method of packing food for the freezer in 'brick' shapes, which makes for compact storage. The food may be frozen in suitable quantities in a preformer container (see page 12), or open frozen in a large block until solid, then cut into 'brick' shapes of usable quantity and packed individually. A freezer knife is essential for this method. Brick freezing is ideal for sauces, soups, purées, casseroles and stews which have been batch cooked in large quantities, and for re-packing bulk frozen purchases in usable quantities.

Bulk Buying Buying food in large quantities for the freezer saves time and money. Meat, fish, vegetables and fruit can be bought in bulk; ready-prepared foods, such as ice cream and yogurts, are also sold in large quantities at freezer centres and supermarkets.

Look for fruit and vegetable bargains at local markets, nurseries, pick-your-own farms and farm-shops. Some of the largest savings can be made by buying meat in bulk from butchers, specialist farms etc. For instructions on freezing cuts of meat see pages 196 to 199. When buying any food in bulk, always look for good quality.

Butcher's Wrap A method of wrapping irregularly shaped foods, such as awkward joints of meat. Place the item on a corner of a large square sheet of foil or polythene. Fold the corner over the meat, then roll the food in the sheet to the middle. Fold the sides over the food and continue rolling to the opposite corner. Press to exclude air, then seal with freezer tape.

Chain Cooking A useful technique used in conjunction with bulk buying, or at times when there is a glut of fresh seasonal produce. As with batch cooking (see above), large quantities of food are prepared for the freezer, but with chain cooking the same basic ingredients are used to start the 'chain', then the mixture is divided up and different ingredients are added to each part to make a selection of different dishes. For example, onions, garlic and minced beef can start the 'chain', which can then be turned into a variety of dishes such as bolognese sauce, moussaka, lasagne, chilli con carne, curry, etc.

Colour Coding This is a useful system of packaging for the freezer. Different-coloured containers, bags, labels, ties and tapes are used to identify different categories of food such as meat, fish, poultry, pastry-based dishes, etc. An extremely efficient system, especially with large chest freezers in which things tend to get 'lost'. Keep the key to the colour coding stuck to the outside of the freezer door.

Cooling This is one of the most vital stages in the preparation of cooked food for the freezer. Food that is placed in the freezer must be as cold as possible to prevent moisture being trapped inside packages. If the food is warm when packaged and frozen, it will cause large ice crystals to form within the food which will damage its cell structure. All cooked food should be cooled as quickly as possible, to prevent contamination by harmful bacteria, and to slow down the natural enzyme activity present in the food itself.

When freezing instructions and recipes specify 'cool quickly', this means to immerse the pan or container of food in a bowl of iced water and to keep it there until the food is cold, changing the water as frequently as possible. Chilling food in the refrigerator before packing and sealing for the freezer also helps accelerate the freezing down process.

Cross-Flavouring Strong-smelling foods such as garlic and onions, and dishes containing herbs and spices can often cause the problem of cross-flavouring, ie their aroma and flavour pass into other more delicate foods in the freezer and thus spoil them. Cross-flavouring is easily prevented by careful sealing of all packages before freezing. As an added precaution with items which may give cause for concern, overwrapping (see below) is advised.

Defrosting See thawing (below) and page 7.

Dehydration Food may become dehydrated in the freezer if it is incorrectly or inadequately wrapped, or if the package has burst or come open during storage. When food is exposed to the extreme cold of the air in the freezer, it loses its moisture and thus becomes dehydrated. Meat and poultry are particularly susceptible to dehydration, so be sure they are properly wrapped – severe cases can lead to freezer burn (see below), which makes food look grey and unappetizing.

Speed in preparation is also an absolute must to minimize the length of time food is exposed to air. When open freezing do not leave food for longer than 4 to 6 hours before wrapping. Overwrapping (see page 12) is also a wise precaution to prevent dehydration.

Discoloration Certain foods discolour when exposed to air (see oxidation – page 12), and this should be prevented both by speedy preparation of food for freezing and by correct packaging. The flesh of white fish and some vegetables is particularly prone to discoloration, sprinkling with lemon juice helps avoid this problem. Vegetables which discolour easily should have lemon juice added to their blanching water. Fruits are particularly susceptible – especially those with a low vitamin C content such as apricots, peaches and pears. Freezing fruit in sugar packs helps prevent discoloration; adding an anti-oxidant, such as ascorbic acid, is a further preventative measure. See also oxidation and sugar packs (page 12).

Drug Store Pack A method of wrapping food which has a regular shape (ideally rectangular) in a sheet of foil or polythene. Place the item square in the centre of a large sheet of wrapping, then bring two opposite edges to meet in the centre over the food. Fold over, then continue folding these edges until the wrapping is pressed tightly to the food and all air is excluded. Fold over the ends in the same way, then seal with freezer tape and overwrap.

Dry Pack The term used to describe the packaging of fruit without sugar or sugar syrup. Most suitable for dark-coloured fruits with a high vitamin C content which do not suffer from discoloration, such as juicy blackberries, strawberries and raspberries, currants, cherries and gooseberries. In a dry pack, whole raw fruit can be placed directly in a polythene bag or container, or it can be open frozen until solid, then stored as a free-flow pack.

Dry Sugar Pack See sugar packs (page 12).

Fast-Freezing Fast-freezing is essential to suspend enzyme activity quickly when freezing down fresh food, and to ensure formation of small ice crystals which do not damage food tissues. It also helps to prevent food that is already frozen and stored in the freezer becoming partially thawed by having non-frozen food placed next to it. Freezers vary in their methods of fast-freezing: some have special compartments or shelves, others have an override fast-freeze or 'super-freeze' switch. This switch activates the motor to run continuously to lower the temperature in the cabinet to a freezing down temperature of between −25° to −30°C/−13° to −22°F as opposed to its normal storage temperature of −18°C/0°F.

Consult freezer manufacturer's handbook for exact fast-freezing procedure, but as a general guide do not fast-freeze if only a few small items are being put in the freezer at one time (simply place them near the coldest part of the freezer − the floor or against the walls of a chest, close to the evaporator tubes in an upright). With larger quantities of vegetables and cooked foods, switch on to fast-freeze about 4 hours before and after putting in the freezer; with meat, 6 hours before and 24 hours after. All freezers are capable of freezing down at least one-tenth of their total storage capacity in 24 hours, but check with the handbook, your freezer may take more. It is important not to exceed this freezing capacity.

Flash Freezing See open freezing (page 12).

Free-Flow Pack This is a pack of frozen food that has been open frozen (see page 12) so that individual items freeze separately and are free-flowing. Vegetables (eg peas, beans, Brussels sprouts) and fruit (eg blackberries, cherries, raspberries) are most often packed in this way for convenience. Simply shake out the exact number you require.

Freezer Burn Greyish-white and brown patches that appear on the surface of food in the freezer − particularly meat and poultry − are referred to as 'freezer burn'. This is not actually a burn, but spoilage of the food due to loss of moisture (see dehydration above). Freezer burn is caused by inadequate or faulty packaging; it is not harmful to eat food which has patches of freezer burn, but it does look unsightly and unpalatable, so is best cut off before cooking. To avoid freezer burn, use correct freezer packaging and seal securely. Overwrap all packages and check them regularly for damage.

Headspace This refers to the space which is left between the surface of a liquid and the lid of a container. Because liquids expand with freezing, headspace is essential to prevent the lid of the container being forced off, which would lead to dehydration and eventual freezer burn (see above). When pouring liquids into a rigid container, simply leave a space of 2 cm/¾ inch at the top of the container, slightly more than this if the container is a narrow one.

Ice Glazing A method of freezing whole fish that does not damage its skin as conventional freezer wraps might − used most often for whole salmon where presentation is important. Gut and clean the fish, then open freeze on fast-freeze control until solid. Dip in cold water, open freeze again, then repeat these two stages over and over again until a layer of ice about 5 mm/¼ inch thick has built up all around the fish. Wrap tightly in cling film, polythene or foil, then overwrap and seal before storing.

Interleaving Separating slices or portions of food in one pack with sheets of freezer tissue (known as

interleaving sheets), cling film or foil. It is a sensible way to pack items such as hamburgers or slices of cake, meat loaf, etc, so that individual pieces can be taken out as required.

Open Freezing There are three methods of open freezing – sometimes also called 'flash freezing' – but the basic principle is the same: food is frozen without wrappings for a short time until solid, then wrapped and sealed for the freezer. Always open freeze quickly on fast-freeze control and do not open freeze for longer than 4 to 6 hours, or dehydration (see page 10) may occur.

1. Open freezing individual items: this technique is used to produce free-flow packs of fruit and vegetables which are convenient to use, and to keep items such as meringues and piped rosettes of whipped cream and duchesse potatoes separate so they do not become squashed during storage. Line a baking tray with foil or greaseproof, then spread out individual items on it so they are not touching each other. Freeze on fast-freeze control until solid. Remove from the tray with a palette knife, then pack and seal and return to the freezer. Delicate items such as cream rosettes should be packed interleaved in rigid containers.

2. Open freezing large items: this protects delicate decorations such as piping on gâteaux and cheesecakes from damage due to wrappings. Stand the cake on a tray, open freeze on fast-freeze control until solid, then carefully remove from tray and pack in a rigid container for storage in the freezer. Remove from container and stand on serving plate before thawing, or decoration may be spoiled.

3. Open freezing casseroles, bakes, mousses, etc: immensely useful for re-using the dish in which food has been prepared. Open freeze the food in its dish until solid, then turn out (dip the base of the dish in hot water if turning out is difficult). Wrap and seal the food, then store in the freezer. For serving, unwrap and return food to its original dish, then thaw or reheat.

Overwrapping This is used to prevent cross-flavouring of strong-smelling foods such as garlic, onions and fish; to cushion food against puncturing from heavy handling; to pad bones in meat and poultry to prevent them from bursting through packaging. To overwrap, pack items in the normal way, then wrap again in foil or in a polythene bag. Stockinette is sometimes used as an overwrap for fish.

Oxidation Oxygen is absorbed from the air into food and causes two types of 'oxidation' in the freezer:
1) In the fat cells of foods – especially meat and fish – oxidation causes 'off' smells and flavours, and eventually results in the food turning rancid. Guard against it by excluding as much air as possible from packages and by wrapping adequately.
2) In pale-coloured fruits and those with a low vitamin C content, such as apricots, peaches and pears, oxidation causes discoloration. To prevent this, fruit should be stored either in a dry sugar pack or a sugar syrup pack, and the addition of an anti-oxidant will also help (see sugar packs opposite).

Preforming A way of packaging food for the freezer that makes economic use of freezer space and containers. Pour liquid food such as soup, stocks, stews and casseroles into a rigid container lined with a polythene bag, open freeze until solid, then remove the bag from the container; seal and store in the freezer. The container (known as the preformer) can be any shape or size, even a casserole dish. The obvious advantage of preforming is that the container can be used again and again.

Refreezing Refreezing food that has thawed is not recommended because it can be harmful and is certainly likely to spoil the quality of food. Meat, fish, poultry and made-up dishes containing them should *never* be refrozen once they have thawed. However, if the meat or poultry is raw, it can be cooked after thawing, then quite safely refrozen in its cooked form – as long as it is thawed, cooked, cooled and refrozen as quickly as possible, to avoid the possibility of harmful bacteria. Dairy produce of all kinds (and dishes containing them) should not be refrozen.

Refreshing In freezing terms, this has two meanings:
1) To immerse blanched vegetables in iced water immediately after blanching. This stops cooking immediately, and helps preserve the colour of vegetables. Refreshing time should be the same as blanching time.
2) To reheat thawed baked goods such as cakes, pastries and biscuits in the oven to give them a crisp 'just baked' look and flavour. Refreshing time varies according to individual recipes.

Reheating see thawing.

Rotation of Stock Food in the freezer needs a constant turnover if it is to be enjoyed at its best within recommended storage times. For efficient rotation, record-keeping is really essential (see freezer diary – page 8).

Sealing One of the most important freezer techniques. As much air as possible should be excluded from all packages, containers and bags before sealing, to protect food from air and possible damage due to freezer burn and oxidation.

Rigid containers with airtight snap-on or clip-on lids are ideal for freezer storage, and wrapping solid objects using a butcher's wrap or drug store pack (see page 10) presents no problem, but the exclusion of air from polythene bags is rather more tricky and can be done in several ways. Either squeeze out as much air as possible with your hands, working from the bottom of the bag upwards, or suck out the air with a clean drinking straw, or use a freezer pump (see page 9).

Sterilizing As a precaution against harmful bacteria, it is a good idea to sterilize all containers before re-using for the freezer. Immerse in boiling water, or better still, in a chemical sterilizing solution such as Milton. Sterilization also avoids cross-flavouring if strong-smelling foods have been stored in containers.

Storage Times Storage times recommended in freezing instructions and recipes and by manufacturers of commercial goods err on the safe side. Food will not normally be harmful if eaten shortly after the recommended date, but the quality in terms of colour, flavour and texture will not be as good, so it makes sense to follow the recommended storage times. The maximum storage time given in this book is 12 months, which in the case of fruit and vegetables is the time it takes for the crop to come again, but to use your freezer economically it is wiser to eat food within 3 months.

Sugar Packs There are two kinds of sugar packs used for freezing fruit and they are used as an alternative to a dry pack (see page 10), for fruit with a low vitamin C content which discolours easily.

Dry Sugar Pack: Suitable for most soft, juicy fruits, except apricots, peaches and pears which are more liable to discoloration and best packed in a sugar syrup pack with ascorbic acid added (see below). Pack prepared sliced or diced fruit in a rigid container, sprinkling each layer with sugar and allowing 125 to 175 g/4 to 6 oz sugar to 500 g/1 lb fruit, according to taste. Leave 2 cm/¾ inch headspace before sealing. An alternative method is to toss fruit and sugar together in a bowl with 1 teaspoon water added, cover and leave for about 2 hours before packing.

Sugar Syrup Pack: For hard, non-juicy fruits and those with a low vitamin C content which discolour easily, such as apricots, peaches and pears – the syrup forms a barrier between the fruit and the air, thus preventing oxidation and subsequent discoloration (see page 10). To make a sugar syrup for the freezer, bring the water to the boil in a covered pan, add the sugar and stir to dissolve, then boil for 2 minutes. Cool and chill in the refrigerator, then pour over prepared fruit in rigid container, or half fill container with syrup and drop in the fruit as it is prepared. Leave 2 cm/¾ inch headspace and fill the gap with crumpled greaseproof before sealing. The strength of syrup varies according to taste and future use of fruit as well as variety of fruit, so individual freezing instructions should be followed. As a general guide a light or weak syrup uses 125 g/4 oz sugar to 600 ml/1 pint water, a medium syrup used 350 g/12 oz sugar, and a heavy syrup uses 500 g/1 lb.

White granulated sugar is normally used; honey can be substituted, but its flavour is very strong; brown sugar causes the fruit to darken. If discoloration is likely to be a problem, an anti-oxidant must be added to the sugar syrup before use: this can be in the form of lemon juice or citric acid, but ascorbic acid (available in powder and tablet form from chemists) is more effective – it also has the added advantage of increasing the vitamin C content of the fruit. Use ¼ teaspoon powdered ascorbic acid to 600 ml/1 pint sugar syrup.

Always make and chill plenty of sugar syrup in advance of preparing fruit for the freezer, to prevent delay in packaging. As a general guide, you will need approximately 300 ml/½ pint syrup for every 500 g/1 lb fruit.

Thawing The words defrosting and thawing tend to be used interchangeably in freezing, although defrosting usually refers to the de-icing of the freezer itself (see defrosting – page 7) and thawing is more often applied to the process whereby food is brought from a frozen solid state to an unfrozen pliable one. Thawing times and conditions vary tremendously from one item to another, therefore individual thawing instructions should be followed, but there are a few general rules:

● Always eat or cook food as soon as possible after thawing as it is just as perishable and susceptible to spoilage from bacteria and micro-organisms as fresh food, if not more so.

● Certain foods retain their texture better if they are cooked from frozen – eg vegetables, fish fillets and steaks, uncooked pastry dishes and burgers.

● Fruit is best thawed in the refrigerator and served while still slightly icy – this way it tends to keep more shape and texture.

● Many cooked dishes such as sauces, soups and casseroles can be thawed quickly by reheating from frozen, either on top of the stove or in the oven. As they are liable to stick, frequent stirring is essential and sometimes extra liquid is necessary.

● Thaw baked goods (cakes, breads and biscuits) quickly at room temperature, remembering to unwrap any that are decorated before thawing. Eat as soon as possible as they quickly become stale after thawing.

● Always thaw poultry completely at room temperature before cooking. If birds are insufficiently thawed, cooking may not completely destroy any food poisoning organisms present, especially inside the carcass.

● Always thaw whole fish completely in the refrigerator, for the same reason as with poultry above.

● Meat cooked from frozen will suffer less shrinkage, loss of flavour and moisture. Boned and rolled joints are the exception, since heat may not penetrate right through to the centre of the joint. Such joints should be thawed overnight in the refrigerator before cooking.

NOTES ON USING THE RECIPES
Standard spoon measurements are used in all recipes
1 tablespoon = one 15 ml spoon
1 teaspoon = one 5 ml spoon
All spoon measures are level

Fresh herbs are used unless otherwise stated. If unobtainable substitute a bouquet garni of the equivalent dried herbs, or use dried herbs instead but halve the quantities stated.

Size 3 eggs should be used unless otherwise stated.

Ovens should be preheated to the specified temperature.

For all recipes, quantities are given in both metric and imperial measures. Follow either set but not a mixture of both, because they are not interchangeable.

Serving Without Freezing
To serve food immediately without freezing, observe the following guidelines *except* where specific instructions are given in the recipe introduction.

If food is to be served hot, simply follow the basic method and serving instructions, omitting the cooling and freezing instructions.

If the food is to be served cold, follow the method and serving instructions; omit freezing instructions.

SPRING

Spring is a good season for the freezer. A time to be thinking of the year ahead, sowing the seeds and planting out for the summer and autumn harvests later on. A time to be looking at the old stock in the freezer and planning to replenish it in the coming months. So take a look not only at this spring section, but also at the later sections in the book and plan your fruit and vegetable gardens accordingly. 'Springclean' the freezer by defrosting it ready to take the new year's supply of fresh garden produce, and to restock it with some of the made-up dishes suggested here for spring. Your efforts will be amply rewarded in the months to come.

VEGETABLES IN SEASON

Artichoke,
   Jerusalem
Asparagus*
Beetroot*
Broad beans*
Broccoli
Cabbage, Spring*
Carrot*
Cauliflower
Celery
Cucumber
Kohlrabi
Leek
Lettuce
Mushroom
Onion
Parsnip
Potato, new
Radish
Spinach*
Swede
Swiss chard*
Tomato
Turnip

FRUIT IN SEASON

Apple
Avocado
Banana*
Gooseberry*
Grape
Grapefruit
Guava*
Lemon
Lime
Lychee
Mango
Orange
Papaya*
Passionfruit*
Pear
Pineapple
Rhubarb*
Strawberry

*Freezing instructions given in this section

15

Asparagus

Asparagus is rarely an inexpensive vegetable, due to the fact that it is quite difficult to grow – it dislikes extremes of temperature and prefers a warm, sunny climate. It is essentially only a springtime vegetable and therefore worth freezing to extend that short season.

To be at its best when thawed, asparagus must be frozen soon after picking. Imported asparagus is therefore not worth freezing, it is invariably expensive, and since it has travelled some distance, it can never be as fresh as home-produced varieties.

Although asparagus connoisseurs claim that it is only worth freezing homegrown asparagus directly after cutting, there is no reason why absolutely fresh local produce should not be frozen successfully. The English asparagus season is very short – May 1st is the 'official' date when it makes its first appearance, and experts claim that it should not be cut after the end of June, although with imported growing techniques and good weather conditions, this season is sometimes extended at either end. Most English asparagus is grown in the south where conditions are milder. The best areas in which to buy the freshest and least expensive varieties are Essex, Norfolk, Suffolk and the Vale of Evesham.

Selecting for freezing: Homegrown asparagus from the garden should only be harvested after its third year of growth. Harvest it when the spears are about 10 to 15 cm/4 to 6 inches tall, making a clean cut with a sharp knife 5 to 10 cm/2 to 4 inches below the surface of the soil.

When buying asparagus for freezing, look for neat bundles with tight heads or tips in which the spears are not too thick. Asparagus is usually sold in bundles rather than by weight, and is graded as Super, Extra, Select and Choice, according to the thickness of the stems. Colour can vary from white to bright green according to the different varieties. The whitest, thicker stems are obviously the most highly prized, but take care when buying these that they are not old and woody. Look for 'sprue' asparagus which is often a good buy for the freezer; this is the thinnest variety, which is considerably less expensive than the graded asparagus – simply because its shape and size is not so good. Sprue asparagus is excellent when used in made-up dishes for the freezer, where appearance is not important, because its flavour is just as good as the graded varieties.

Preparation for freezing: Once the asparagus is cut, it is important to keep it in a cool place and to freeze it as soon as possible. First cut off the hard, woody ends of the stems, then, with a potato peeler or small sharp knife, scrape away any fibrous scales, working downwards from tip to base. Work carefully so that the tender, delicate tips are not damaged. Rinse gently in a bowl of fresh, cold water to which a pinch of salt has been added, then sort into bundles of similar thickness and length, trimming the ends if necessary.

To freeze: For short-term storage, asparagus can be frozen unblanched, but if storing in the freezer for longer than 1 month it should be blanched before freezing. Blanch stems of the same thickness together in boiling water, allowing 4 minutes for thick stems, 3 minutes for medium, 2 minutes for thin and 1 minute for sprue asparagus. Drain after blanching, cool quickly in iced water, then drain and dry thoroughly on kitchen paper. Pack in rigid containers lined with moisture-proof freezer paper, keeping the same sizes together, alternating the tips and separating the layers with paper. Do not pack in polythene bags as frozen asparagus is very fragile and breaks easily. Seal, label and freeze.

To thaw and serve: If serving whole asparagus with melted butter or a sauce such as Hollandaise or mousseline, always use from frozen to avoid over-cooking. Plunge the frozen asparagus into boiling salted water, bring back to the boil and simmer for 2 to 4 minutes according to thickness of stems. Drain and serve immediately. For use in made-up dishes, unpack and thaw at room temperature until stems will separate easily – then use as for fresh asparagus in soups, quiches, vol-au-vents, omelettes, hors d'oeuvres and salads. See also Asparagus and Smoked Salmon Quiche (page 25) and Cream of Asparagus Soup (page 54).

Beetroot

Of the many different varieties of beetroot grown, the red or globe beetroot, *beta vulgaris*, is the most common in this country. One of the easiest vegetables to grow, it is worth freezing if you have a bumper crop in the garden.

Although beetroot keeps well and is available all year round, young springtime beetroot is best for tenderness and flavour; apart from pickling, which limits its uses, freezing is the best means of preserving these qualities. If left in the ground or stored by other means, beetroot quickly becomes woody, fibrous and unpalatable. Even commercially grown beetroot is worthwhile freezing in spring, because it is all home-grown (mostly in southern England) and is therefore usually still reasonably fresh by the time it reaches shops and markets. Served as a fresh vegetable, beetroot has a high nutritional value.

Selecting for freezing: Harvest beetroot from the garden in springtime while still small – no more than about 7.5 cm/3 inches in diameter. Pull them out of the ground with your hands – taking care not to damage the skins or roots.

The new season's beetroot appears in greengrocers and markets at the end of May. For freezing, always buy the fresh uncooked variety with leaves attached. Avoid beetroot with limp, yellow leaves and blemished skin, and never buy ready-cooked beetroot for freezing – there is no telling how or when it was cooked. As a general rule, choose the smallest, youngest 'baby beets'; even-sized and spherical, these tend to freeze better than the long, tapering maincrop varieties.

Preparation for freezing: Prepare beetroot for freezing as soon as possible after harvesting or purchase. Twist, do not cut, off the leaves, or the skin will be broken and cause 'bleeding' during cooking which leads to loss of colour, flavour and nutrients. Wash carefully under cold running water to remove excess soil, etc., taking care not to damage skins or root and stem ends.

To freeze: Always cook beetroot before freezing. Sort into groups of the same size so that cooking time can be calculated accurately, then place in a pan of cold water to which 1 teaspoon vinegar has been added (this helps prevent 'bleeding'). Extra flavour can be given by adding 1 or 2 bay leaves and a few black peppercorns to the water. Bring to the boil, then lower the heat, cover and simmer for 10 to 20 minutes, according to size. To test if beetroot are tender, remove from the water with a slotted spoon, leave for a minute or two until cool enough to handle, then squeeze gently with the fingers to tell if the skin will rub off easily; never prick with a fork. When tender, drain carefully, then rinse under cold running water and rub off the skins with your fingers. Leave until cold (do not soak in iced water).

Pack small whole beetroot in rigid containers; larger beetroot can be sliced or diced before packing in the same way. (Beetroot packed in polythene bags is likely to become damaged in the freezer – it can also be messy!). Seal, label and freeze for up to 6 months.

To thaw and serve: Thaw beetroot in container at room temperature for at least 4 hours before use. Use cold in salads as for fresh beetroot, particularly with grated horseradish or horseradish dressing, or with oranges. Serve hot as a vegetable dish with a plain béchamel sauce, or with a teaspoon of horseradish added. Use in stews and soups to add colour. See also Creamed Beetroot (page 36).

Broad Beans

The broad bean is spring's first pod vegetable to appear, and one of the first homegrown vegetables in the shops after the winter. Yet at a time when there is little choice in fresh vegetables, the broad bean is sadly neglected. One of the main reasons for this is that broad beans are often left too long in the pod until they become large and leathery. Broad beans freeze extremely well; if picked young, fresh and small, they can be amongst the most delicious of all frozen

vegetables. Rich in protein, iron, vitamin C and dietary fibre, they provide a useful source of nutrients.

Selecting for freezing: If you are growing broad beans in the garden, there are three possibilities for freezing:

Broad bean tips can be eaten before the pod begins to form; break them off when they are about 7.5 cm/3 inches long, after the flowers have started to become embryo pods.

One of the most delicious ways of eating broad beans is whole in their pods. Pick them right at the beginning of the season just as the beans are beginning to form in the pods, but before they are swollen enough to be visible. Test them with your fingers and pick them when you can feel the tiny seeds forming – they will look and feel similar to mangetout.

If you prefer broad beans shelled, leave them until the beans are properly formed, but don't allow the pods to become stringy and leathery, or the beans to appear bulbous and swollen.

Selecting broad beans for freezing at the greengrocer or market is more difficult. Buy them as soon as they first appear; it is hardly worthwhile waiting for late bargains as these rarely come until the beans are old and stringy and past their best for freezing. Choose the smallest, brightest green pods you can find, before they have had a chance to become starchy. If possible, squeeze the pods to check that they are still tender.

Preparation for freezing: Wash broad bean tips and pods thoroughly under cold running water. If freezing shelled beans, remove from the pods and deal with them as quickly as possible. Discard any broad beans

ABOVE: Freezing broad beans
OPPOSITE: Freezing asparagus

that have a thick, leathery outer skin – these are simply not worth freezing.

To freeze: Sort tips and whole pods into usable quantities of the same size, then plunge into boiling water, to which a little lemon juice has been added, and blanch for 2 minutes only. Drain, cool quickly in iced water, then drain and pat dry with kitchen paper. Pack in polythene bags, seal, label and freeze for up to 12 months.

Blanch shelled beans in boiling water for 1½ minutes only, drain, cool and dry as for tips and pods above. Open freeze on trays until solid, then transfer to polythene bags to make 'free-flow' packs so that beans do not freeze in a solid mass. Seal, label and return to the freezer for up to 12 months.

To thaw and serve: Never thaw tips, pods or beans before cooking. Simply plunge into boiling salted water, bring back to the boil and simmer for 3 to 5 minutes according to size. Drain and serve hot, tossed in melted butter and herbs, or coated with parsley sauce. Cooked, shelled broad beans are also good in salads: toss them in a vinaigrette dressing while still warm; this allows the dressing to penetrate the beans and give them more flavour. See also Watercress and Broad Bean Soup (page 24), Stir-Fried Summer Vegetables (page 87), Broad Beans au Gratin (page 36), Spring Vegetable Curry (page 38) and Vegetable Lasagne (page 38).

Cabbage, Spring

Although cabbage has been eaten in Britain since it was introduced here by the Romans, it can never really be described as a popular vegetable. It is much maligned due to the fact that it is rarely cooked properly — boiled in copious amounts of water for an indeterminate length of time rids cabbage of its most important nutrients and reduces this crisp, bright green vegetable to a limp mass. Cabbage should be cooked for the shortest possible time, particularly when it has been frozen.

There are so many different varieties of cabbage available all year round that it may seem a waste of valuable freezer space to store it, but if spring cabbage is one of your favourites, you may wish to freeze some.

Selecting for freezing: Spring cabbage from autumn sowing falls into two main types — spring greens which are young unhearted cabbages, and spring cabbage which is the hearted variety, often conical or pointed in the centre.

Hearted spring cabbages are right for harvesting from the garden at the end of May. Unhearted spring greens can be picked much earlier than this, according to individual preference. Pick only when the leaves are bright or dark green and still very crisp — these will be the most tender after freezing and cooking. Young, small cabbages are most successful in the freezer. Cut immediately before you intend to freeze them; avoid keeping them for even an hour before freezing.

Cabbage from the greengrocer or market is usually homegrown English cabbage, although some varieties are imported from Holland. Choose the best quality, freshest-looking cabbage, preferably buying in the early morning before the leaves show signs of wilting.

Preparation for freezing: Do not freeze whole cabbages. Separate the leaves of the cabbage and wash each thoroughly under cold running water. Discard any tough or damaged outer leaves. Trim the stalks, cutting off any hard ends. Leave whole or cut the leaves into strips, about 1 cm/½ inch wide.

To freeze: Blanch in boiling water to which 1–2 tablespoons vinegar has been added (this helps cabbage retain its colour) for 1½ minutes only. Drain thoroughly, then plunge into iced water and cool quickly. Drain thoroughly, then pack in usable quantities in polythene bags. As a precaution, double wrapping is advisable, to avoid the possibility of cabbage odour tainting other foods in the freezer. Seal, label and freeze for up to 6 months.

To thaw and serve: Frozen cabbage is not suitable for serving uncooked; neither should this vegetable be thawed before cooking. Plunge frozen cabbage into a pan, containing enough boiling salted water to just cover the bottom, and bring back to the boil. Simmer, uncovered, for a maximum of 5 minutes, stirring frequently. Drain thoroughly and serve immediately as a vegetable accompaniment with melted butter and plenty of freshly ground black pepper. Thawed whole cabbage leaves can also be stuffed (e.g. with minced meat mixtures, rice and other vegetables), then rolled and baked in the oven.

Carrot

A member of the parsley family, the carrot is a rich source of valuable nutrients, especially carotene. It also provides useful amounts of vitamin C, minerals and dietary fibre.

The young, sweet baby carrots that appear in late spring with their characteristic feathery green tops are well worth freezing — especially for use in the winter months when old carrots are woody and lacking in colour and flavour. Commercially grown carrots are stored during the winter months in earth 'clamps' or sheds; this method prevents them from rotting, but does not preserve their colour and texture particularly well. Freezing is the most reliable and successful method of preserving carrots for use all year.

Selecting for freezing: It is only worthwhile freezing young spring carrots — available from heated frames in April, from cold frames in May — until the main crop arrives in July. After lifting the roots from the ground with a fork, cut off the feathery tops to within 1 cm/ ½ inch of the carrot root and shake off excess soil. Discard any damaged carrots.

Commercially grown carrots are best bought in bunches with their tops intact to ensure maximum freshness. Look for even-shaped carrots — no thicker than a man's thumb — with smooth skins. Avoid those with green patches around crown or stem end as this is a sure sign they have surfaced too early. Check whether the carrots are homegrown — imported ones will not be as fresh as English varieties.

Preparation for freezing: Slice the tops off, then wash the carrots thoroughly under cold running water. Because there is a concentration of vitamins close beneath the skin, it is best to scrub them with a stiff vegetable brush, rather than peel them. Alternatively, scrape with a vegetable peeler or small sharp knife.

To freeze: If the carrots are very young and small they are best frozen whole. Grade into sizes and pack straight into polythene bags for short-term storage of up to 6 months. Blanching is essential for longer storage: plunge into boiling water and blanch for 3 minutes, drain, then plunge into iced water and cool quickly. Drain again, then dry with kitchen paper. Pack in usable quantities in polythene bags or open freeze on trays until solid, then store as free-flow packs. Seal, label and freeze for up to 12 months.

Larger carrots can be sliced or diced before freezing. Blanch, cool and dry as for whole carrots, allowing only 2 minutes blanching time. Sliced and diced carrots are most useful in free-flow packs.

To thaw and serve: Plunge frozen carrots into boiling salted water, bring back to the boil and simmer until just tender — 4 to 5 minutes according to size. Drain, toss in melted butter and seasonings and serve hot as a vegetable accompaniment. Or cook from frozen without water in a heavy-based pan with melted butter and herbs or spices; parsley and caraway are suitable. Sliced or diced carrots can be added frozen to casseroles, or used in making soups. Frozen carrots are not satisfactory for grating or use in salads. See also Cream of Carrot Soup (page 25), Carrots with Herbs (page 36) and Spring Vegetable Curry (page 38).

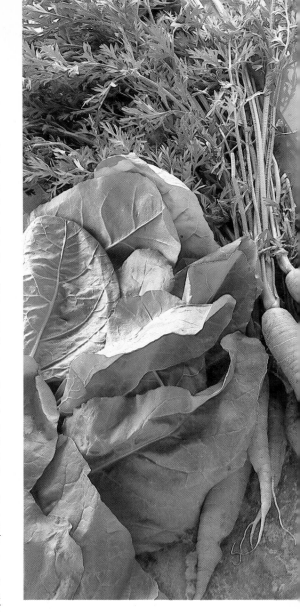

Spinach

There are two different types of spinach — the winter or prickly-seeded spinach and summer or round-seeded spinach. To confuse matters Swiss Chard (opposite), and New Zealand spinach, which are not varieties of this vegetable are nevertheless often sold as spinach, especially in the hot summer months. The optimum time for freezing true spinach is in March and April. In the longer days of summer, spinach is liable to bolt.

Raw spinach contains valuable quantities of vitamins and mineral salts, especially iron, but these are quickly spoiled if spinach is cooked incorrectly — for a long time in copious amounts of water. Spinach should be cooked with only the water clinging to its leaves after washing, for the shortest possible time.

Selecting for freezing: Pick young homegrown spinach from the garden as soon as the leaves are of usable size. Pick in the early morning when spinach is at its freshest and before any hot mid-day sun causes its leaves to wilt. Twist, do not cut, off the outer leaves at the base — constant picking of small amounts of spinach in this way promotes growth and discourages the

Freezing carrots and spinach

commercially on a wide scale, but is easy to grow in the garden and well worthwhile freezing as an alternative to spinach and cooked celery. The most common Swiss chard is the green *Beta vulgaris cicla*, although there is a red variety called ruby or rhubarb chard, which is most often grown for ornamental use in the garden. Do not confuse Swiss chard with seakale, a vegetable which is rather like a cross between rhubarb and celery.

Selecting for freezing: Harvest Swiss chard in the early spring from seed sown at the end of the previous summer, or in the late summer and early autumn from seed sown the previous spring. Do not cut the leaves, but twist gently to release them. To encourage further growth, strip only the outer leaves away, leaving the inner leaves intact. Pick while young and fresh-looking before the leaves have grown too large and the stalks become tough.

Preparation for freezing: Work in a cool kitchen and prepare and freeze as soon as possible after picking. Wash each leaf individually under cold running water to remove all dirt, then carefully strip the leaves away from the central stalk. Discard any damaged or blemished leaves. Trim the stalks at each end, then cut into 5 cm/2 inch lengths, dividing them lengthways if they are very wide. Pull off any stringy parts.

To freeze: Plunge the leaves into boiling water, small quantities at a time, and blanch for 2 minutes, moving the pan frequently to prevent the leaves from sticking together. Drain thoroughly, plunge into iced water, then drain again and pat dry with kitchen paper or squeeze dry. Pack the leaves in usable quantities in polythene bags, seal, label and freeze for up to 12 months.

Blanch, cool, dry and pack the stalks as for the leaves, allowing 3 minutes blanching time and adding a little lemon juice to the blanching water. As Swiss chard stalks tend to discolour easily, it is often a good idea to combine them with a béchamel or cheese sauce after blanching, then pack in a rigid container and freeze as a made-up dish.

To thaw and serve: Cook leaves from frozen for about 5 minutes in a heavy-based pan with melted butter and seasonings; ground mace and freshly grated nutmeg are the perfect spices. Serve hot as a vegetable accompaniment, or use in any recipe as a substitute for spinach, particularly in quiches and soups, remembering that Swiss chard has a stronger flavour and therefore you will need to use a smaller quantity.

Plunge frozen sliced stalks into boiling salted water, bring back to the boil, cover and simmer for about 7 minutes. Drain, coat with a white or cheese sauce and serve au gratin, as a vegetable accompaniment like celery. Alternatively simply toss in butter, lemon juice, herbs and seasonings. If stalks have been frozen in a sauce, reheat from frozen in a preheated moderately hot oven (190°C/375°F/Gas Mark 5) for 30 minutes or until bubbling. Sprinkle with freshly grated Parmesan and grill until golden brown.

plants from going to seed. Never strip an entire spinach plant.

Only buy spinach for freezing where you know it is absolutely fresh, and buy early in the morning. Avoid any spinach which has yellow, damaged or wilted leaves, flower heads, large fibrous stalks and heavy midribs, or if you can see large amounts of grass amongst the spinach leaves.

Preparation for freezing: Work in a cool kitchen and prepare and freeze as soon as possible after picking or purchase. Snap off stalks, then wash each leaf individually under cold running water to remove all dirt. Leaves can be left whole or torn.

To freeze: Plunge the leaves into boiling water, small quantities at a time, and blanch for 2 minutes. Move the pan frequently to prevent leaves sticking together. Drain thoroughly, pressing the leaves with the back of a wooden spoon to extract as much moisture as possible. Cool quickly, then pack in usable quantities in polythene bags. (Remember that spinach reduces to half its original weight during cooking and that 250 g/ 8 oz raw spinach is an average serving.) Seal, label and freeze for up to 12 months.

To thaw and serve: Cook spinach from frozen for about 5 minutes in a heavy-based pan with melted butter and seasonings; ground mace or freshly grated nutmeg is traditional. Spinach can be roughly chopped or puréed in an electric blender or food processor, after thawing. Serve hot as an accompaniment with cream and/or grated Parmesan. Or use in quiches, soups and dishes, such as Spinach Triangles (page 39).

Swiss Chard

Swiss chard, also known as seakale beet or spinach beet, is a type of beet which is grown for its edible leaves rather than its root. A little-known vegetable in Britain, it deserves to be used more often because it is in fact two vegetables in one. The glossy green leaves are cooked and eaten like spinach, although they grow larger and their flavour is stronger. The yellowish white midrib stalks are cooked separately because they are coarser than those of spinach, and take longer to cook than the leaves.

Most Swiss chard is grown in southern England, and is available from late spring right through the summer to late autumn. It is not a vegetable that is grown

Banana

Although available all year round, bananas are at their best – and at their least expensive – during spring and early summer. At other times of the year the fruits are liable to damage from frost. Most bananas come here from the West Indies, but the fruit is grown throughout the world's tropics. Although they cannot be frozen whole, bananas can be frozen in pulp form and in made-up dishes, such as Iced Banana Whip (page 40), Rhubarb and Banana Fool (page 54), and Banana and Honey Teabread (page 51).

Selecting for freezing: Choose firm, ripe fruit with deep yellow skins and just a few spots of brown, indicating they are in peak condition. Avoid fruit which is still green, or marked with larger brown patches. If in doubt, choose under-ripe fruit and ripen in a warm dry place for a few days.

Preparation for freezing: Bananas cannot be frozen whole in their skins, because they lose their texture, and discolour easily. It is essential to process the peeled fruit quickly and in small quantities.

Banana pulp: After peeling, immediately mash the bananas with lemon juice and sugar to taste. On average, allow 3 tablespoons lemon juice and 125 g/ 4 oz sugar for every 6 to 8 bananas, depending on size.

Bananas in chocolate sauce: Peel the fruit, then halve lengthways. Pack usable quantities in rigid containers and cover immediately with a cooled, homemade chocolate sauce; see Profiteroles (page 46).

To freeze: *Banana pulp:* Pack immediately in usable quantities in rigid containers, leaving 2 cm/¾ inch headspace. Seal, label and freeze for up to 6 months.

Bananas in chocolate sauce: Seal containers, label and freeze for up to 6 months.

To thaw and serve: *Banana pulp:* Thaw in container in the refrigerator for 5 to 6 hours. Use immediately after opening container as a sandwich filling, or for making bread, cakes and whipped desserts.

Bananas in chocolate sauce: Thaw in container as for banana pulp, then transfer to individual serving dishes and serve immediately, with cream or ice cream.

Gooseberry

This traditional English fruit is one of the first to appear in the spring. It has become extremely popular and many varieties are grown in Britain today, particularly in the Midlands and the North where the fruit is best suited to the cooler climate.

Gooseberries are categorized by their colour – green, yellow and red. Some varieties (mostly yellow) are suitable only as a dessert fruit, others (green varieties) for cooking, bottling and jam-making, and some (red ones) can be used both raw and cooked. As a general rule, only the cooking varieties are really successful in the freezer.

Levellers are the most common type of gooseberry grown both commercially and by the home gardener; these are the large, sweet, juicy fruit, yellowish in colour, suitable for eating raw as a ripe dessert fruit, but not for freezing. It is important to check the variety before purchasing. If you intend growing gooseberries in the garden for freezing, choose Careless or Whinham's, both of which are also good for bottling and jam-making; these varieties are generally available from greengrocers and market stalls, and also from 'pick your own' farms.

Gooseberries show little sign of deterioration in the freezer and, after cooking, are hardly distinguishable from the fresh fruit. In times of glut they can also be stored in the freezer in the more compact forms of cooked and stewed fruit or puréed and sieved pulp, which is immensely useful for making quick desserts.

Selecting for freezing: Fresh gooseberries are only available for 2 to 3 months in spring and early summer, so watch for their appearance in the shops during May, and buy when they are at their best.

The hard, green cooking gooseberry, most suitable for the freezer, is one of the earliest varieties to be harvested. Pick while still small, firm and slightly under-ripe – soft, juicy berries will disintegrate to a pulp in the freezer. When harvesting or buying Careless or Whinham's gooseberries for freezing, they must be green in colour.

Preparation for freezing: According to the intended use, gooseberries can be frozen in different forms:

Whole gooseberries: Wash thoroughly in iced water immediately after picking or purchase. Discard any damaged fruit. Topping and tailing is not necessary if freezing in a free-flow pack as tops and tails rub off more easily when the fruit is frozen. Top and tail if freezing in a dry sugar or sugar syrup pack.

Stewed gooseberries: Wash thoroughly, top and tail, then poach whole fruit gently with water and sugar to taste. Add a few elderflower heads tied in a muslin bag to the pan for a unique flavour. Remove the bag and cool quickly.

Gooseberry pulp: Wash thoroughly, but do not top and tail. Poach whole fruit with the minimum amount of water (with elderflower heads tied in muslin, if liked). Cool slightly, then purée in an electric blender or food processor and sieve to remove tops, tails and skins. Sweeten to taste if liked, but unsweetened purée is often more convenient; sugar can be added on thawing. Leave until cold.

To freeze: *Whole gooseberries:* These can be frozen as free-flow, dry sugar or syrup packs.

Free-flow pack: Open freeze on trays until solid, then pack in polythene bags. Seal, label and return to the freezer for up to 12 months.

Dry sugar pack: Pack in usable quantities in rigid containers, sprinkling each layer with sugar; allow 125 to 175 g/4 to 6 oz sugar to 500 g/1 lb fruit, according to taste. Seal, label and freeze for up to 12 months.

Sugar syrup pack: Pack in usable quantities in rigid containers and cover with a medium sugar syrup made from 350 g/12 oz sugar to 600 ml/1 pint water. Leave 2 cm/¾ inch headspace, seal, label and freeze for up to 12 months.

Stewed gooseberries: Pack in usable quantities in rigid containers, leaving 2 cm/¾ inch headspace. Seal, label and freeze for up to 12 months.

Gooseberry pulp: Pour into rigid containers in usable quantities, leaving 2 cm/¾ inch headspace. Seal, label and freeze for up to 12 months.

To thaw and serve: *Whole gooseberries:* Rub off tops and tails from free-flow packs while still frozen. Use frozen free-flow and dry sugar packs in pies, puddings and crumbles and for poaching, allowing a little extra cooking time for thawing. For preserves and jam-making, spread fruit from free-flow packs on trays and thaw at room temperature for 1 hour before use. Poach fruit in sugar syrup pack gently from frozen.

Stewed gooseberries: Reheat from frozen in a heavy-based pan. Stir frequently to prevent sticking, adding a little water if necessary. Taste for sweetness before serving.

Gooseberry pulp: Thaw in a containers overnight in the refrigerator or at room temperature for about 3 hours. Use as for fresh pulp – for making fools, soufflés, mousses, ice creams, sorbets, sauces, cheesecake toppings and tart fillings. See also Guard of Honour with Cape Gooseberries (page 35), Gooseberry Crunch (page 44) and Iced Gooseberry Soufflé (page 43).

Rhubarb

Rhubarb was originally grown for the medicinal properties of its roots, then later as an ornamental plant. It was not until the 19th century that it was cultivated for its edible stalks. The leaves should not be eaten – they contain poisonous quantities of oxalic acid.

Rhubarb freezes successfully, and it can be stored in several different forms as well as in made-up dishes, both sweet and savoury. Most of the rhubarb available in Britain is grown in Cheshire and Yorkshire. Forced rhubarb, available from the late winter through to early spring, is the pale pink type. It is 'forced' by being

lifted from outside in the autumn, then grown indoors through the winter so that it can be harvested before the outdoor varieties. The stalks are thin, tender and sweet; they are perfect for freezing because of their texture and colour, but forced rhubarb is the most expensive variety.

Outdoor or 'natural' rhubarb is the second crop of the year, appearing in shops and gardens in May; it is stronger in flavour and coarser in texture than forced rhubarb. It is easy to grow in the garden, and one or two crowns will be quite prolific – constant picking will encourage growth. Outdoor rhubarb is perfectly suitable for freezing, providing it is not allowed to become too coarse and woody.

Selecting for freezing: When buying early forced rhubarb for freezing, choose the palest colour and the thinnest stems. Forced rhubarb is rarely found at bargain prices, but it is generally less expensive once the season is well under way. There are two grades, thick and thin; both can be frozen. Avoid any bruised or blemished stalks.

Selecting outdoor or garden rhubarb for freezing is more difficult; by the time it reaches shops and markets it is often well past its best. If possible buy in May or June, avoiding the thick stalks which have large, unwieldy leaves. Check that stalks are not stringy and that leaves are not wilted. Depending on the variety, some rhubarb stalks are green, others red – both are suitable for freezing.

To harvest homegrown rhubarb, pull the sticks gently from the crown as soon as it first appears, using a twisting action (do not cut). This encourages growth and ensures tenderness for freezing.

Preparation for freezing: Immediately after purchase or harvesting, cut off the leaves and root ends, then wash the stalks thoroughly under cold running water. Outdoor rhubarb which shows signs of being tough and stringy may need to be peeled – discard any very woody specimens.

Cut rhubarb stalks: Chop prepared stalks into short lengths, about 2.5 to 5 cm/1 to 2 inches long.

Stewed rhubarb: Cut prepared stalks into short lengths as above, then poach gently in a minimum amount of water with sugar to taste. Rhubarb cooks very quickly so take care that pieces remain whole and do not disintegrate. Spices such as ginger or cinnamon, or a little finely grated orange rind and juice, can be added for extra flavour if liked. Cool quickly.

Rhubarb purée: This is an ideal way to store rhubarb in the freezer if you are short of space. Poach as for stewed rhubarb above, cool slightly, then purée in an electric blender or food processor. Sweeten to taste if liked, or leave unsweetened at this stage and add sugar after thawing according to individual recipes. Leave until cold.

To freeze: *Cut rhubarb stalks:* Rhubarb stalks should preferably be blanched before freezing to preserve colour, and to make them less bulky and therefore easier to pack. Plunge cut stalks into boiling water, blanch for 1 minute only, drain, then cool quickly in iced water. Drain again, then dry with kitchen paper.

Free-flow pack: Open freeze on trays until solid, then pack in polythene bags. Seal, label and return to the freezer for up to 12 months.

Dry sugar pack: Pack in usable quantities in rigid containers, sprinkling each layer with sugar; allow 125 to 175 g/4 to 6 oz sugar to 500 g/1 lb fruit according to taste. Seal, label and freeze for up to 12 months.

Sugar syrup pack: Pack blanched or unblanched stalks in rigid containers and cover with a medium sugar syrup made from 300 g/10 oz sugar and 600 ml/1 pint water. Leave 2 cm/¾ inch headspace, seal, label and freeze for up to 12 months.

Stewed rhubarb: Pack in rigid containers in usable quantities, leaving 2 cm/¾ inch headspace. Seal, label and freeze for up to 12 months.

Rhubarb purée: Pour into rigid containers in usable quantities, leaving 2 cm/¾ inch headspace. Seal, label and freeze for up to 12 months.

To thaw and serve: *Cut rhubarb stalks:* Use free-flow and dry sugar packs in pies, puddings and crumbles, and for poaching, allowing a little extra cooking time for thawing. For jam-making, spread out fruit from free-flow packs on trays and thaw at room temperature for 1 hour before use. Poach rhubarb in sugar syrup pack gently from frozen.

Stewed rhubarb: Use as a dessert with custard, cream or ice cream, or as a pie filling. Thaw in container at room temperature for about 3 hours. Taste for sweetness before serving.

Rhubarb purée: Use to make fools, soufflés, mousses, ice creams and sorbets. Thaw in container in the refrigerator overnight or at room temperature for about 3 hours. Use as for fresh rhubarb purée, adding sugar to taste, according to individual recipes. See also Rhubarb and Orange Cream (page 43), and Rhubarb and Banana Fool (page 54).

Freezing gooseberries and rhubarb

TROPICAL FRUIT

Spring is a particularly good season to buy tropical guavas, papayas and passionfruit, because home produced fruits are in limited supply at this time of the year. Imported supplies of these exotic fruits therefore tend to be better during spring.

Guava

A tropical fruit which has a high vitamin C content, the guava can vary in size from as small as a cherry to as large as an apple. At one time, guavas were grown in English greenhouses,. but all those on sale in Britain today are imported.

The flavour of the guava itself is almost impossible to describe, since it varies considerably from one variety to another – some taste a little like melons, others like strawberries (there is a highly prized variety

known as the strawberry guava). Its soft pulpy flesh ranges in colour from white through to yellow, pink and even crimson.

Fresh guavas can be eaten raw sprinkled with sugar or, as in India, with salt and chilli powder, but the raw fruit is something of an acquired taste, since it can be sour and contains many hard seeds. You will probably find guavas more palatable cooked in pies, or simply poached in a compote, or made into ice cream. Guavas also make excellent preserves, and guava jelly, which is not unlike quince jelly, is renowned for its compatability with roast meats.

Look out for guavas in West Indian food stores and markets or in specialist greengrocers throughout spring; they are unlikely to be inexpensive, but are worth buying for freezing if you are particularly fond of their flavour.

Selecting for freezing: Buy only firm, young fruit with shiny, unblemished skin that is not discoloured or bruised. Some retailers display a few cut guavas so that customers can see the seedy insides. Check that seeds are fresh and not bad, asking the greengrocer to cut one open for you if necessary.

Preparation for freezing: Peel, cut in half lengthways and scoop out seeds with a sharp-edged teaspoon. Leave as halves or cut flesh into thin slices, if preferred.

To freeze: _Guava halves and slices: These can be_ frozen in dry sugar or syrup packs.

Dry sugar pack: Put halves or slices in usable quantities in rigid containers, sprinkling each layer with sugar to taste. Seal, label and freeze for up to 6 months.

Sugar syrup pack: Pack halves or slices in usable quantities in rigid containers and cover with a light sugar syrup made from 125 g/4 oz sugar and 600 ml/

Freezing guavas, papayas and passionfruit

<u>Guava purée:</u> Thaw in covered container in refrigerator overnight and serve cold as a dessert sauce or use in making ice creams, sorbets, soufflés and mousses. Or reheat from frozen in a heavy-based pan, stirring frequently to prevent sticking and adding a little water if necessary. Serve hot as an accompaniment to rich meats and oily fish, as a substitute for apple or gooseberry sauce.

Papaya

Papaya or pawpaw is a large tropical fruit native to Central America, the West Indies and Pacific islands, and south-east Asia. Imported into Britain in spring, it is available fresh in West Indian shops and markets, and specialist greengrocers. In its country of origin, papaya can grow to a huge size, weighing up to 9 kg/20 lb, but imported papayas are usually around the 500 g/1 lb mark, similar in size to melons.

The skin of the papaya is thin, smooth and edible (green when under-ripe, yellow when ripe), while the juicy flesh varies from yellow to orange and is sweet-tasting, some say like a cross between apricots, peaches and melons! In the centre of the flesh is a cavity containing black seeds. In tropical countries, ripe papaya is eaten raw for its refreshing qualities, on its own or in fruit salads. Papaya juice makes a refreshing drink in hot climates.

Apart from vitamins, papaya also contains the enzyme papain which digests protein, thus giving the fruit tenderizing properties. In the tropics, the leaves are wrapped around meat to tenderize it; the juice is rubbed into the meat for the same reason. Slices of green under-ripe papaya can be cooked and frozen with meat in casseroles.

Selecting for freezing: Look for reasonably-priced fresh papaya in good markets and greengrocers. Both green and yellow-skinned varieties are available in spring, so select fruit according to intended use. (Green papaya will ripen and turn yellow if left in a warm place for a few days.) Choose fruit with firm, unblemished skin.

Preparation for freezing: Peel, cut in half lengthways and scoop out seeds with a sharp-edged teaspoon. Cut flesh into thin slices.

To freeze: *Papaya slices:* Under-ripe papaya slices can be frozen in casseroles. See also Pork Chops Pacific (page 32). Ripe uncooked slices can be frozen in syrup. *Sugar syrup pack:* Put slices in usable quantities in rigid containers and cover with a medium sugar syrup made from 350 g/12 oz sugar to 600 ml/1 pint water with 2 teaspoons lemon juice added. Leave 2 cm/¾ inch headspace, seal, label and freeze for up to 6 months. *Papaya purée:* Work slices in an electric blender or food processor to a purée with sugar and lemon juice to taste. Pour usable quantities into rigid containers, leaving 2 cm/¾ inch headspace. Seal, label and freeze for up to 6 months.

To thaw and serve: Casseroles containing under-ripe papaya can be reheated from frozen in the usual way.

<u>Sugar syrup pack slices:</u> Thaw in covered container at room temperature for 1 to 2 hours, then use in fresh fruit salads in place of peaches or apricots.

<u>Papaya purée:</u> Thaw in covered container in the refrigerator overnight. Taste and adjust sweetness if necessary. Serve chilled as a refreshing drink (diluted if preferred), or use for making ice creams, sorbets, soufflés and mousses.

Passionfruit

This tropical fruit comes from the climbing plant *passiflora edulis*. Native to Brazil, it is now grown extensively in south-east Asia and Australia. Varieties of climbing *passiflora* grown in Britain will produce flowers in summer, but unless artificially fertilized and grown in hothouses, will not bear fruit.

The fruit itself has a thick purple skin which is not edible. When first picked, this skin is smooth and firm, but as it ripens it becomes wrinkled and soft, and it is not until it reaches this stage that the fruit is really edible. The simplest way to enjoy passionfruit is to cut it in half, scoop out the pulp with a teaspoon and eat it straight away. Its juice is also made into a refreshing drink and beautiful-tasting liqueurs and preserves.

Passionfruit is immensely popular in Australia, where it is used in pavlova, the sweet meringue dessert filled with tropical fruits and cream. It is also used as a topping for gâteaux, in fruit salads, ice creams and other desserts (it goes particularly well with bananas).

Fresh passionfruit is imported into Britain during the spring and summer months. Its pulp freezes well and is extremely good for adding a tropical look and flavour to all kinds of desserts and cakes apart from pavlova, especially in the winter when soft fruits are scarce. The pulp can be frozen raw or used to make exotic Passionfruit Ice Cream (see page 41). It can also be frozen in meat dishes such as Pork Chops Pacific (page 32).

Selecting for freezing: Look for ripe passionfruit in specialist markets and greengrocers from May onwards. The skin should be soft and slightly wrinkled and purple in colour; if possible, squeeze the fruit gently with your fingers to ascertain the softness of the pulp and hold the fruit in your hand – it should feel quite heavy for its size and have a sweet aroma. Buy for freezing early in the season; as the fruit becomes older the skin takes on a shrivelled, dry appearance and the pulp loses it juiciness – at this stage it will feel very light in your hand. The best test is to ask the greengrocer to cut one open for you.

Preparation for freezing: Cut the fruit in half with a sharp knife and scoop out the pulp with the seeds, using a teaspoon.

To freeze: Weigh the pulp and mix with half its weight of sugar. Stir and leave until the sugar has dissolved, then pack in usable quantities in rigid containers, leaving 2 cm/¾ inch headspace. Seal, label and freeze for up to 12 months.

To thaw and serve: Thaw in covered container at room temperature for about 1½ hours. Stir gently, then pour over ice cream or fruit salads, or use as a topping for any fruit or meringue dessert.

1 pint water. Leave 2 cm/¾ inch headspace, seal, label and freeze for up to 6 months.

<u>Guava purée:</u> Cook slices in a light sugar syrup made from 125 g/4 oz sugar and 600 ml/1 pint water for about 30 minutes until tender, mashing the fruit with a wooden spoon. Leave to cool. Purée in an electric blender or food processor, then sieve. Pour into a rigid container, seal, label and freeze for up to 6 months.

To thaw and serve: <u>Dry sugar pack guavas:</u> Use frozen halves or slices in pies and flans, mixing with other fruit if liked. Allow a little extra cooking time for thawing.

<u>Sugar syrup pack guavas:</u> Cook from frozen in a heavy-based pan until tender. Stir frequently to prevent sticking, adding a little water if necessary and taking care not to crush the fruit. Taste for sweetness. Serve hot or chilled as a dessert with pouring cream, or use chilled in fresh fruit salads.

WATERCRESS AND BROAD BEAN SOUP

The subtle flavours of watercress and broad beans complement each other extremely well, and the texture of this soup is wonderfully smooth and velvety. Serve with garlic croûtons (see below), or hot crusty French bread.

40 g/1½ oz butter
2 onions, peeled and chopped
1 tablespoon plain flour
1.2 litres/2 pints homemade chicken stock
500 g/1 lb broad beans, shelled, or 250 g/8 oz frozen
  broad beans
1 bouquet garni
250 g/8 oz watercress, trimmed and roughly chopped
salt and freshly ground black pepper
TO SERVE
2 eggs yolks
150 ml/¼ pint double cream
CROÛTONS
4 tablespoons vegetable oil
3 garlic cloves, peeled but left whole
4 slices white bread, crusts removed and diced
TO GARNISH
watercress or thyme sprigs

Melt the butter in a pan, add the onions and cook for 5 minutes without browning. Add the flour and cook for a further 2 minutes, stirring all the time. Gradually stir in the stock, bring to the boil, then lower the heat and simmer for 2 minutes, stirring occasionally. Add the broad beans and bouquet garni. Bring to the boil, then lower the heat, cover and simmer for 10 minutes until the beans are tender. Add the watercress and cook for a further 5 minutes. Season to taste with salt and pepper.

Remove the bouquet garni, leave the soup to cool slightly, then work to a purée in an electric blender or food processor. Leave to cool completely.
To freeze: Pour the soup into a rigid container, leaving 2 cm/¾ inch headspace, then seal, label and freeze for up to 6 months.
To thaw and serve: Leave to stand in container at room temperature for 3 to 4 hours.
To make the croûtons: Heat the oil in a pan, add the garlic and diced bread and fry until the bread is browned on all sides. Remove from the pan with a slotted spoon, discard the garlic, then drain the croûtons on kitchen paper.

Transfer the soup to a pan and bring to the boil, stirring frequently. Lower the heat. Blend the egg yolks and cream together in a bowl until smooth, then stir in a little of the hot soup. Stir the egg mixture back into the pan and heat through gently without boiling. Taste and adjust the seasoning.

Pour into individual soup bowls and top with the croûtons. Garnish with watercress or thyme sprigs and serve immediately.
Serves 6

MUSHROOM AND MUSTARD SOUP

The flavour of this soup depends largely on the type of mushrooms used: button mushrooms give a more delicate taste, whereas field mushrooms impart a stronger, but delicious, flavour. Serve with hot buttered toast.

75 g/3 oz butter
1 large onion, peeled and chopped
500 g/1 lb mushrooms, trimmed and roughly chopped
600 ml/1 pint homemade chicken stock
4 tablespoons dry sherry
2 tablespoons French mustard
1 tablespoon chopped fresh thyme
salt and freshly ground black pepper
TO SERVE
150 ml/¼ pint double cream

Melt the butter in a pan, add the onion and fry gently for 5 minutes without browning. Add the mushrooms and cook for a further 10 minutes until tender. Stir in the stock and sherry, bring to the boil, then lower the heat and simmer for 5 minutes. Stir in the mustard, thyme and salt and pepper to taste. Leave to cool slightly, then work to a purée in an electric blender or food processor. Leave to cool completely.
To freeze: Pour the soup into a rigid container, leaving 2 cm/¾ inch headspace, then seal, label and freeze for up to 4 months.

To thaw and serve: Leave to stand in container at room temperature for 3 to 4 hours, then transfer to a pan and bring to the boil, stirring frequently. Lower the heat, stir in the cream and heat through gently without boiling. Taste and adjust the seasoning. Serve hot.
Serves 4 to 6

OPPOSITE: *Asparagus and Smoked Salmon Quiche*
BELOW: *Watercress and Broad Bean Soup; Cream of Carrot Soup*

ASPARAGUS AND SMOKED SALMON QUICHE

This special occasion quiche is not quite as extravagant as it seems! Use the very thin sprue asparagus, which is least expensive, and smoked salmon off-cuts.

PASTRY
175 g/6 oz plain flour
salt
125 g/4 oz butter
2 tablespoons grated Parmesan cheese
1 egg yolk
about 1 tablespoon iced water
FILLING
175 g/6 oz asparagus
125 g/4 oz smoked salmon pieces
3 eggs
200 ml/⅓ pint double cream
squeeze of lemon juice
1 teaspoon chopped thyme
1 teaspoon chopped parsley
freshly ground black pepper
TO SERVE
lemon or lime slices
parsley or chervil sprigs

To make the pastry: Sift the flour and a pinch of salt into a bowl. Rub in the butter until the mixture resembles fine breadcrumbs. Stir in the Parmesan and the egg yolk, and enough water to mix to a fairly stiff dough. Turn onto a floured surface, knead lightly until smooth, then roll out and use to line a 23 cm/9 inch flan tin. Chill in the refrigerator for 30 minutes.

Prick the base and sides of the dough and line with foil and baking beans. Bake 'blind' in a preheated moderately hot oven (200°C/400°F/Gas Mark 6) for 10 minutes, then remove the foil and beans and return to the oven for a further 5 minutes. Remove from the oven and set aside. Reduce the oven temperature to moderate (180°C/350°F/Gas Mark 4).

To make the filling: Steam the asparagus for 5 minutes and pat dry with kitchen paper.

Place the smoked salmon pieces on the base of the pastry, then arrange the asparagus in a circle on top, with the spears radiating out towards the edge.

Beat the eggs in a bowl with the cream, lemon juice, herbs and salt and pepper to taste. Pour gently into the flan, taking care not to disturb the position of the asparagus. Bake in the oven for 20 to 25 minutes, until the filling is golden brown and just set. Leave to cool.

To freeze: Open freeze the quiche until solid, then remove carefully from the tin and wrap in foil. Seal, label and return to the freezer for up to 4 months.

To thaw and serve: Unwrap and place on a wire rack; leave to stand at room temperature for 2 to 3 hours until thawed completely. Serve cold, or reheat in a preheated moderate oven (180°C/350°F/Gas Mark 4) for 15 minutes and serve warm, garnished with lemon or lime slices and parsley or chervil.

Serves 6

CREAM OF CARROT SOUP

This soup has a very fresh flavour with a real promise of spring. It can be served chilled rather than hot, in which case use 3 to 4 tablespoons oil instead of the butter. Thaw overnight in the refrigerator, then whisk vigorously before stirring in the cream.

50 g/2 oz butter
2 large onions, peeled and grated
2 garlic cloves, peeled and crushed
1 tablespoon plain flour
500 g/1 lb carrots, peeled and grated
salt and freshly ground black pepper
900 ml/1 ½ pints homemade chicken stock
TO SERVE
300 ml/½ pint double cream
4 tablespoons soured cream
1 carrot, peeled and grated

Melt the butter in a pan, add the onions and garlic and fry gently for 5 minutes without browning. Add the flour and cook for a further 2 minutes, stirring all the time.

Add the grated carrots, season well with salt and pepper, then stir in the stock. Bring to the boil, stirring occasionally, then lower the heat, cover and simmer for 30 minutes.

Leave to cool slightly, then work to a purée in an electric blender or food processor, or pass through a sieve. Leave to cool completely.

To freeze: Pour the soup into a rigid container, leaving 2 cm/¾ inch headspace, then seal, label and freeze for up to 4 months.

To thaw and serve: Reheat gently from frozen in a heavy-based pan, stirring frequently, then stir in the double cream. Pour into a warmed tureen or individual soup bowls, spoon the soured cream into the centre of the soup, then sprinkle the grated carrot on top. Serve immediately.

Serves 4 to 6

SALMON MOUSSE

Take advantage of the fresh salmon available in the spring to make this light mousse. At other times of the year, make it on the day it is required with frozen salmon, which should be thawed before use.

300 ml/½ pint milk
1 bay leaf
1 small onion
1 carrot
1 celery stick
1 bouquet garni
500 g/1 lb fresh salmon
150 ml/¼ pint dry white wine
salt and freshly ground black pepper
40 g/1½ oz butter
25 g/1 oz plain flour
15 g/½ oz (1 envelope) powdered gelatine
150 ml/¼ pint water
1 tablespoon lemon juice
1 tablespoon wine vinegar
150 ml/¼ pint mayonnaise
150 ml/¼ pint double cream
TO SERVE
cucumber slices
few cooked unpeeled prawns
parsley or chervil sprigs

Put the milk and bay leaf, onion, carrot, celery and bouquet garni into a pan and bring to the boil. Remove from the heat and leave to infuse until cold. Strain the milk and reserve.

Put the salmon into an overproof dish, pour over the wine and sprinkle with salt and pepper to taste. Dot with 15 g/½ oz butter, then cover with foil. Cook in a preheated moderate oven (180°C/350°F/Gas Mark 4) for 15 to 20 minutes until the fish is cooked. Leave until cold, then remove the fish from the cooking liquid. Flake the fish, discarding the skin and bones, then pound the flesh until smooth.

Melt the remaining butter in a pan, add the flour and cook for 2 minutes, stirring all the time. Remove from the heat and gradually add the reserved infused milk, beating vigorously after each addition. Return to the heat and bring to the boil, stirring constantly. Lower the heat and simmer for 2 minutes, then add salt and pepper to taste. Cover the surface closely with cling film to prevent a skin forming. Leave to cool.

Dissolve the gelatine in the water, then stir in the lemon juice and vinegar. Quickly stir the gelatine mixture into the cold sauce, then mix in the salmon and mayonnaise. Whip the cream until it will stand in soft peaks, then fold evenly into the mousse.

Spoon the mixture into 6 individual dishes and chill in the refrigerator until set.

To freeze: Cover each dish with cling film or foil, then place in individual polythene bags. Seal, label and freeze for up to 2 months.

To thaw and serve: Unwrap and leave to stand at room temperature for 2 to 3 hours. Garnish with cucumber slices, prawns and parsley or chervil sprigs before serving.
Serves 6

CRABMEAT ON CROÛTES

In the spring, fresh crabs are at their best – and reasonably priced. If you cannot buy fresh crabs use frozen crabmeat which must be thawed before use.

250 g/8 oz crabmeat, flaked
125 g/4 oz peeled prawns
squeeze of lemon juice
25 g/1 oz butter
25 g/1 oz plain flour
300 ml/½ pint milk
2 tablespoons dry sherry
½ teaspoon French mustard
½ teaspoon dried mixed herbs
salt and freshly ground black pepper
2 tablespoons double cream
4 slices white bread, crusts removed
vegetable oil, for shallow frying
TO SERVE
chervil or parsley sprigs

Place the crabmeat, prawns and lemon juice in a bowl and mix together gently.

Melt the butter in a pan, add the flour and cook for 2 minutes, stirring all the time. Remove from the heat and gradually add the milk, beating vigorously after each addition. Return to the heat and bring to the boil, stirring constantly. Lower the heat and simmer for 2 minutes, then add the sherry, mustard, herbs and salt and pepper to taste. Simmer for a further 2 minutes, then remove from the heat and fold in the cream and crabmeat mixture. Leave to cool.

Cut each slice of bread into a circle or attractive shape. Heat the oil in a frying pan, add the croûtes and fry until golden brown on each side. Leave to drain and cool on kitchen paper.

To freeze: Spoon the crabmeat mixture into a rigid container, seal, label and freeze for up to 3 months. Open freeze the croûtes until solid, then pack into a separate rigid container. Seal, label and return to the freezer for up to 3 months.

To thaw and serve: Reheat the crabmeat mixture gently from frozen in a heavy-based pan. When thawed completely, cook for 10 minutes. Meanwhile, place the croûtes on a baking sheet and reheat from frozen in a preheated hot oven (220°C/425°F/Gas Mark 7) for 10 minutes.

Arrange the croûtes on individual plates, spoon the crabmeat mixture over and garnish with sprigs of chervil or parsley. Serve immediately.

Serves 4

OLD-FASHIONED FRENCH PÂTÉ

This is a traditional French pâté which can be made at any time of year, but is particularly good when using very fresh herbs in spring or summer. Serve with hot buttered toast.

350 g/12 oz chicken livers, roughly chopped
250 g/8 oz belly pork, rinds and bones removed and thinly sliced
125 g/4 oz sausagemeat
8–10 rashers streaky bacon, rinds removed
MARINADE
6 tablespoons brandy
1 tablespoon port
2 tablespoons dry sherry
1 garlic clove, peeled and thinly sliced
1 tablespoon chopped thyme
1 bouquet garni
pinch of grated nutmeg
salt and freshly ground black pepper

First, put the marinade ingredients into a large bowl with salt and pepper to taste and mix well. Add the chicken livers, belly pork and sausagemeat and turn to coat in the marinade. Cover and leave to marinate in the refrigerator for 24 hours, turning occasionally.

Stretch the bacon rashers with the flat of a knife blade, then use to line the base and sides of a 750 g to 1 kg/1½ to 2 lb loaf tin. Spoon the marinated mixture into the tin, discarding the bouquet garni, and level the top. Cover with greaseproof paper and foil, then stand in a bain-marie (roasting tin half-filled with hot water). Bake in a preheated hot oven (220°C/425°F/Gas Mark 7) for 1¾ to 2 hours, until cooked through. Remove from the bain-marie and leave until completely cold, then place heavy weights on top of the pâté and chill in the refrigerator until firm.

To freeze: Turn the pâté out of the tin, then wrap in cling film and overwrap in a polythene bag. Seal, label and freeze for up to 4 months.

To thaw and serve: Unwrap the pâté and place on a serving plate. Cover loosely and leave to stand at room temperature for about 6 hours before serving.
Serves 6 to 8

MUSHROOMS AND CELERY À LA GRÈCQUE

Choose the smallest button mushrooms you can buy for this marvellous all-year-round starter. When leeks are in season, substitute them for the celery, using two small ones and slicing them thinly. Serve with hot French bread or toast.

3 tablespoons olive oil
1 onion, peeled and finely chopped
1 garlic clove, peeled and thinly sliced
6 tomatoes, skinned, seeded and chopped
150 ml/¼ pint dry white wine
1 bouquet garni
salt and freshly ground black pepper
500 g/1 lb button mushrooms
4 celery sticks, chopped
1 tablespoon tomato purée
1 tablespoon chopped thyme
TO SERVE
lime twists

Heat the oil in a pan, add the onion and garlic and fry gently for 7 to 8 minutes until lightly browned.

Add the tomatoes, wine, bouquet garni and salt and pepper to taste and bring to the boil. Lower the heat and simmer, uncovered, for 15 minutes until the tomatoes have cooked to a pulp.

Add the mushrooms, stir well to coat in the sauce, then simmer for 5 minutes. Add the celery, simmer for a further 10 minutes, then stir in the tomato purée. Remove from the heat, discard the bouquet garni and leave until cold. Stir in the chopped thyme.

To freeze: Spoon the mixture into a rigid container, seal, label and freeze for up to 6 months.

To thaw and serve: Leave to thaw in container in the refrigerator overnight. Stir gently, taste and adjust the seasoning, then pile into a serving dish and garnish with lime twists. Serve chilled.
Serve 6

Mushrooms and Celery à la Grècque;
Crabmeat on Croûtes; Salmon Mousse

SOLE AND PARMA PARCELS

This is a delicious dish, combining the flavours of fish and Parma ham. Ask the fishmonger to skin the sole and remove 2 double fillets from each; ask for the skin and bones to make the fish stock. To serve this dish immediately, without freezing, cook in a preheated moderately hot oven (190°C/375°F/Gas Mark 5) for 20 minutes. Top with the shallot butter just before serving.

2 Dover soles, each about 625 g/1 ¼ lb, skinned and
  filleted
250 g/8 oz coley fillets, skinned and boned
300 ml/½ pint water
4 parsley stalks
salt and freshly ground white pepper
125 g/4 oz Parma ham
2 tablespoons chopped parsley
4 tablespoons soured cream
SHALLOT BUTTER
150 g/5 oz butter, softened
2 shallots, peeled and finely chopped
2 tablespoons chopped parsley
few drops of lemon juice
TO SERVE
few watercress sprigs

Put the skin and bones from the sole in a pan with the coley, water, parsley stalks and salt and pepper to taste. Bring to the boil and simmer for 12 to 15 minutes, then strain, reserving the coley. Return the stock to the rinsed-out pan and boil rapidly until reduced to 6 tablespoons. Remove from the heat and set aside.

Chop and mince the coley, or work in an electric blender or food processor until smooth. Set aside 8 long strips of Parma ham for tying the parcels; shred the rest and mix with the coley, chopped parsley and salt and pepper to taste to make the filling.

Place the 4 sole fillets, skinned side up, on a board. Divide the filling equally amongst them, placing it in the centre. Fold over the ends of each fillet to enclose the filling. Use 2 strips of ham to 'tie' each fillet like a parcel and secure with wooden cocktail sticks. Place the fillets in a single layer in an ovenproof dish lined with a large sheet of foil. Mix 4 tablespoons of the reduced stock with the soured cream and pour over the fish.

To make the shallot butter: Melt 25 g/1 oz butter in a pan, add the shallots and fry gently for 5 minutes without browning. Beat into the remaining butter with the parsley, lemon juice, the remaining reduced stock and salt and pepper to taste. Shape into a cylinder, chill in the refrigerator until firm, then cut into 4 slices.

To freeze: Open freeze the fish and sauce until solid, then remove from the dish in the foil and fold over the foil to make a tight parcel. Pack in polythene bags, seal, label and return to the freezer for up to 3 months. Open freeze the shallot butter separately until solid, then pack in a rigid container, separating each portion with foil. Seal, label and return to the freezer for up to 2 months.

To thaw and serve: Unwrap the fish and return to the original dish. Cover with foil, place in an unheated oven and bake from frozen at moderately hot (190°C/375°F/Gas Mark 5) for 50 minutes. Remove the foil, put 1 slice frozen shallot butter on top of each fish parcel and bake for a further 10 minutes. Garnish with the watercress and serve hot.
Serves 4

CURRIED BEIGNETS OF WHITEBAIT

An unusual way of preparing these tiny fish. Already fried, they are a boon for the hostess, as they are quickly served from a hot oven. Cook the batter as soon as the egg whites and fish are added, otherwise it loses its lightness.

500 g/1 lb whitebait, washed and dried
BEER BATTER
175 g/6 oz self-raising flour
2 teaspoons curry powder
salt and freshly ground black pepper
2 eggs, separated
300 ml/½ pint beer
vegetable oil, for shallow frying
TO SERVE
150 ml/¼ pint mayonnaise
½ teaspoon curry powder
½ teaspoon chilli powder
½ teaspoon paprika
parsley sprigs

To make the batter: Sift the flour into a bowl with the curry powder and salt and pepper to taste. Make a well in the centre, add the egg yolks and beer and whisk to a smooth batter, gradually drawing in the flour from the sides of the bowl. Whisk the egg whites until stiff, then fold into the batter. Carefully fold in the whitebait.

Drop 3 heaped tablespoons of the mixture into hot shallow oil, spacing them well apart, and fry over moderate heat for 1 minute on each side or until golden brown. Remove with a slotted spoon and drain on kitchen paper while frying the remainder in similar small batches. Leave to cool.

To freeze: Pack the beignets into a rigid container, separating the layers with interleaving sheets or foil. Seal, label and freeze for up to 1 month.

To thaw and serve: Put frozen beignets on a baking sheet and reheat in a preheated hot oven (220°C/425°F/Gas Mark 7) for 20 minutes. Meanwhile, mix the mayonnaise with the curry powder, chilli powder and paprika. Serve the beignets hot, garnished with parsley. Hand the spiced mayonnaise separately.
Makes 12

SEA BREAM MATELOTE

If you are fortunate enough to buy really fresh sea bream in the spring, prepare this interesting dish and store it in your freezer ready for effortless entertaining. This recipe gives all the pleasure of eating a fish dish in almost its original shape – but without the bones! Ask the fishmonger to skin the sea bream and remove the bone, leaving 2 fillets.

1 sea bream, about 1.5 kg/3–3½ lb, skinned and filleted
salt and freshly ground black pepper
1 tablespoon vegetable oil
25 g/1 oz butter
3 shallots or 1 medium onion, peeled and sliced
2 celery sticks, sliced
50 g/2 oz mushrooms, sliced
300 ml/½ pint Chablis or other dry white wine
1 teaspoon cornflour
1 tablespoon water
150 ml/¼ pint single cream
TO SERVE
1 stale croissant, crumbled
3 tablespoons chopped parsley

Sprinkle the fish fillets with salt and pepper, then place 1 fillet, skinned side down, in an ovenproof dish lined with a large sheet of foil. Heat the oil and butter in a pan, add the vegetables and fry gently for 5 minutes without browning. Spread over the fish and cover with the second fillet, skinned side up. Pour the wine over and bake in a preheated moderately hot oven (190°C/375°F/Gas Mark 5) for 15 minutes.

Drain the liquid from the fish into a pan and boil rapidly to reduce by half. Mix the cornflour to a paste with the water, add to the pan and boil for 1 minute, stirring constantly. Cool a little, stir in the cream and pour over the fish. Cool completely.

To freeze: Open freeze the fish and sauce until solid, then remove from the dish in the foil and fold over the foil to make a tight parcel. Pack in a polythene bag, seal, label and return to the freezer for up to 2 months.

To thaw and serve: Unwrap and return to the original dish. Cover with the foil, place in an unheated oven and reheat from frozen at moderate (180°C/350°F/Gas Mark 4) for 1 hour 20 minutes. Mix together the crumbled croissant and parsley and sprinkle in a line on top of the fish. Increase the oven temperature to hot (220°C/425°F/Gas Mark 7) and bake for a further 10 minutes. Serve hot.

Serves 4

RAINBOW TROUT WITH FENNEL

To avoid damaging this fragile fish, so delicious in the spring months, line the cooking dish with foil and open freeze until solid, then it can be lifted out safely. To serve immediately, without freezing, bake in a preheated moderately hot oven (190°C/375°F/Gas Mark 5) for about 20 minutes.

4 rainbow trout, cleaned
salt and freshly ground black pepper
2 bulbs (about 500 g/1 lb) fennel
6 spring onions, trimmed
50 g/2 oz butter
8 tablespoons water
250 g/8 oz unpeeled cooked prawns

Wash and dry the trout and sprinkle inside and out with salt and pepper. Set aside. Trim the feathery fronds from the fennel and reserve. Thinly slice the fennel and 2 spring onions.

Melt the butter in a pan, add the sliced fennel and spring onions and fry gently for 5 minutes without browning. Add the water and salt and pepper to taste, cover and simmer for 5 minutes. Leave to cool slightly, then work to a smooth purée in an electric blender or food processor. Cool completely.

Pour the purée into an ovenproof dish lined with a large sheet of foil. Chop the white parts of the remaining spring onions finely, then mix with the reserved fennel fronds. Stuff this mixture inside each trout, dividing it equally between them. Reserve 4 whole prawns and peel the remainder. Put the peeled prawns inside the trout, then place the trout on the fennel purée and place an unpeeled prawn on top of each one.

To freeze: Open freeze the trout until solid, then remove from the dish in the foil and fold over the foil to make a tight parcel. Pack in a polythene bag, seal, label and return to the freezer for up to 2 months.

To thaw and serve: Unwrap the fish and return to the original dish. Cover with the foil, place in an unheated oven and bake from frozen at moderately hot (190°C/375°F/Gas Mark 5) for 1 hour. Transfer the fish to a warmed serving platter with a fish slice, then coat with the purée and re-arrange the prawns. Serve hot.

Serves 4

ABOVE: Rainbow Trout with Fennel; Sea Bream Matelote
OPPOSITE: Curried Beignets of Whitebait; Sole and Parma Parcels

DANDYPRAT RABBIT

A light-hearted way to serve tender rabbit joints: mustard-coated and crumbed, then frozen raw ready for deep-fat frying at short notice. The sharp-flavoured sauce is frozen separately. To serve immediately, without freezing, deep-fry for 6 to 8 minutes.

1 oven-ready rabbit, about 1.25 kg/2½ lb, cut into
    8 pieces
3 tablespoons Dijon mustard
1 egg yolk
125 g/4 oz dried breadcrumbs
1 tablespoon ground ginger
2 tablespoons dry mustard
1½ teaspoons salt
HOT TARTARE SAUCE
25 g/1 oz butter
25 g/1 oz potato flour (fécule)
1 tablespoon Dijon mustard
25 g/1 oz gherkins, sliced, 1 tablespoon brine reserved
2 tablespoons cider or white wine vinegar
25 g/1 oz stoned green olives, sliced
1 tablespoon chopped parsley
1 spring onion, trimmed and chopped
4 tablespoons single cream
TO SERVE
vegetable oil, for deep frying
150 ml/¼ pint milk

Pat the rabbit pieces dry with kitchen paper. Mix together the Dijon mustard and egg yolk and brush over each piece of rabbit. Mix the breadcrumbs, ginger, dry mustard and salt together and spread out on a flat plate. Toss the rabbit in this mixture, pressing on the crumbs until each piece is thoroughly and evenly coated.

To make the tartare sauce: Melt the butter in a pan. Mix the potato flour and mustard in a bowl. Mix the reserved brine from the gherkins with the vinegar and make up to 150 ml/¼ pint with water. Stir into the potato flour mixture, then add to the butter. Cook for 2 minutes, stirring constantly, then stir in the gherkins and the remaining ingredients. Remove from the heat and leave to cool.

To freeze: Open freeze the rabbit until solid, then pack in a rigid container, separating the layers with interleaving sheets or foil. Seal, label and return to the freezer for up to 2 months. Freeze the sauce in a separate rigid container, leaving 2 cm/¾ inch headspace.

To thaw and serve: Heat 7.5 cm/3 inches of oil to 180°C/350°F in a deep-fat fryer. Put in half the rabbit pieces and deep-fry from frozen for 10 to 12 minutes or until cooked through. Remove with a slotted spoon and drain on kitchen paper while frying the remaining rabbit. Meanwhile, put the frozen sauce into a heavy-based pan with the milk and reheat gently, whisking occasionally to make a smooth sauce. Serve the rabbit immediately, accompanied by the hot sauce.

Serves 4 to 6

VENEZUELAN DUCK

Duck with a difference: the banana and red pepper braised with the duck are later puréed to form an unusual sauce accompaniment.

1 oven-ready duck, about 1.5 kg/3–3½ lb, cut into
    quarters
1 tablespoon vegetable oil
15 g/½ oz butter
1 medium onion, peeled and sliced
2 pieces stem ginger, drained and sliced, with
    2 teaspoons syrup reserved
2 bananas, peeled and sliced
1 large red pepper, cored, seeded and cut into rings
150 ml/¼ pint dry cider
salt and freshly ground black pepper
TO SERVE
1 banana, peeled and sliced
squeeze of lemon juice

Wipe the duck quarters, dry thoroughly with kitchen paper, then flatten them as much as possible.

Heat the oil and butter in a large flameproof casserole, add the duck and fry until well browned on all sides. Remove from the pan with a slotted spoon and drain on kitchen paper. Add the onion and sliced ginger to the pan and fry gently for 5 minutes without browning. Add the bananas, red pepper, reserved ginger syrup and the cider and bring to the boil.

Return the duck to the pan, add salt and pepper to taste, then lower the heat, cover and simmer for about 45 minutes or until the duck is tender. Cool quickly.

To freeze: Transfer the duck and sauce to a rigid container, seal, label and freeze for up to 3 months.

To thaw and serve: Leave to stand in container at room temperature for about 2 hours, then transfer to the original casserole, cover and reheat gently for about 30 minutes until the duck is really hot. Transfer the pieces of duck to a warmed serving dish with a slotted spoon and keep hot.

Work the sauce to a purée in an electric blender or food processor, or through a sieve. Taste and adjust the seasoning, reheat if necessary, then pour over the duck. Garnish with the banana slices dipped in lemon juice and serve immediately.

Serves 4

ELIZABETHAN CAPON PIE

Cooked and frozen within its own serving dish, this grand and stylish pie uses prime poultry, meats, fruit and seasonal herbs. Eaten cold, it will grace any picnic or party table.
Prepare the puff pastry as for Tarte Française (page 140).

1 oven-ready capon, about 1.5 kg/3–3½ lb, boned
salt and freshly ground black pepper
350 g/12 oz minced veal
5 tablespoons chopped parsley
500 g/1 lb minced pork
3 spring onions, trimmed and chopped
8 stoned prunes
1 tablespoon snipped chives
350 g/12 oz puff pastry (total weight)
1 egg, beaten, to glaze

Put the capon, skin side down, on a board and sprinkle liberally with salt and pepper.

Season the veal and spread over the capon. Add 3 tablespoons chopped parsley to the pork with the spring onions and salt and pepper to taste, and mix well to combine. Form into a cylinder shape around the prunes and place in the centre of the capon. Roll up tightly, making a compact shape. Secure with a skewer underneath.

Place the capon in a roasting tin and bake in a preheated moderately hot oven (200°C/400°F/Gas Mark 6) for 50 minutes. Pour off the juices from the tin, skim off the fat and reserve the juices. Cool the capon quickly, remove the skewer, then fit it into a pie dish just large enough to hold the bird. Mix the reserved juices with the remaining parsley and the chives and pour into the bottom of the dish.

Roll out the pastry thinly on a lightly floured surface and cut into 1 cm/½ inch strips. Brush the pastry strips, bird and rim of the dish with beaten egg. Fit strips of pastry around the rim of the dish and place strips of pastry, glazed side up, over the capon in a criss-cross pattern. Press firmly to seal onto the rim, then with the end of a small pastry brush handle, press firmly where each 2 pieces of pastry cross to seal them together.

Bake in a preheated hot oven (220°C/425°F/Gas Mark 7) for 25 minutes or until the pastry is well risen and golden brown. Cool the pie quickly.
To freeze: Put the capon pie in a polythene bag, seal, label and freeze for up to 3 months.
To thaw and serve: Unwrap and place on a wire rack; leave to stand at room temperature for 12 hours or until thawed completely. Serve cold, cut into slices.
Serves 6 to 8

POUSSINS IN THYME BUTTER

Tiny young chickens, particularly delicious in spring, are easily prepared and cooked before freezing for effortless serving later.

4 oven-ready single poussins, each about 500 g/1 lb
salt and freshly ground black pepper
juice of 1 lemon
STUFFING
4 rashers streaky bacon, derinded and chopped
125 g/4 oz chicken livers, halved if large
4 tablespoons chopped parsley
THYME BUTTER
50 g/2 oz butter, softened
4 teaspoons chopped fresh thyme
finely grated rind of 1 lemon

Wash and dry the poussins and sprinkle inside and out with salt and pepper.
To make the stuffing: Fry the chopped bacon in a dry pan until the fat runs, then add the chicken livers and cook until lightly browned. Add the parsley and salt and pepper to taste. Divide the stuffing equally between the birds.
To make the thyme butter: Place the butter in a bowl and beat in the thyme and lemon rind until thoroughly incorporated.

Put the poussins side by side in an ovenproof dish or roasting tin lined with a large sheet of foil. Spread the thyme butter over them, then roast in a preheated moderately hot oven (200°C/400°F/Gas Mark 6) for 35 to 40 minutes or until cooked (the juices should run clear when the thickest part of the flesh is pierced with a skewer). Stir the lemon juice into the liquid from the poussins and baste the birds well. Cool quickly.
To freeze: Remove the poussins from the dish in the foil and fold over the foil to make a tight parcel. Pack in a polythene bag, seal, label and freeze for up to 3 months.
To thaw and serve: Remove the poussins from the polythene bag. Return the parcel to the original dish and loosen the foil. Reheat from frozen in a preheated moderately hot oven (200°C/400°F/Gas Mark 6) for 20 minutes, then open the foil, baste the poussins with the cooking juices and cook for a further 10 minutes. Serve hot.
Serves 4

LEFT: Elizabethan Capon Pie
OPPOSITE: Poussins in Thyme Butter

VEAL KIDNEYS MADEIRA

Enjoy veal kidneys at their young spring best in this quick recipe, which is as easy to serve as it is to make. If veal kidneys are unobtainable, replace them with 8 lamb's kidneys.

1 tablespoon olive oil
40 g/1½ oz butter
6 veal kidneys, fat and cores removed, very thinly sliced
6 shallots or 2 small onions, peeled and sliced
175 g/6 oz button mushrooms, sliced
2 tablespoons chopped basil
6 tablespoons dry Madeira
TO SERVE
salt and freshly ground black pepper
basil leaves

Heat the oil and butter in a frying pan, add the sliced kidneys and fry over brisk heat for 1 minute, stirring constantly. Remove the kidneys from the pan with a slotted spoon and put into a rigid container. Add the shallots and mushrooms to the pan, fry quickly without browning until softened, then transfer with the slotted spoon to the container. Sprinkle with the basil.

Pour the Madeira into the pan and stir vigorously, scraping up the pan juices to deglaze, then pour over the kidneys and vegetables. Cool quickly.
To freeze: Transfer to a rigid container, seal, label and freeze for up to 3 months.
To thaw and serve: Leave to stand in container at room temperature for 3 hours, then transfer to a pan and reheat gently for 6 to 8 minutes until really hot, stirring frequently. Add salt and pepper to taste and serve immediately, garnished with basil leaves.
Serves 4

VEAL IN VERMOUTH

A hearty dish which has a particularly aromatic garnish of orange, garlic and fresh rosemary added at serving time. Shin of veal pieces on the bone are used to make the classic Italian dish osso buco, and butchers often sell the cut under this name. Each piece of veal is about 5 cm/2 inches thick and consists of a piece of bone with marrow in the centre, surrounded by meat.

1.5 kg/3½ lb shin of veal pieces on the bone
2 tablespoons plain flour
salt and freshly ground black pepper
2 tablespoons olive oil
4 medium carrots, scraped
4 medium onions, peeled and sliced
300 ml/½ pint sweet white vermouth
TO SERVE
finely grated rind of ½ orange
1 garlic clove, peeled and finely chopped
1 teaspoon chopped rosemary

Toss the pieces of veal in the flour seasoned with salt and pepper. Heat the oil in a large flameproof casserole, add the veal and fry over brisk heat until browned on all sides. Add the carrots, onions and vermouth, stirring well. Bring to the boil, then lower the heat, cover and simmer for 1½ hours, turning the veal once during this time. Cool quickly.
To freeze: Transfer the veal and vegetables to a rigid container, seal, label and freeze for up to 3 months.
To thaw and serve: Leave to stand in container at room temperature for 3 hours, then return to the original casserole. Reheat gently for about 30 minutes, turning once. Taste and adjust the seasoning of the sauce, then transfer veal and sauce to a warmed serving dish. Mix together the orange rind, garlic and chopped rosemary and sprinkle over the veal. Serve immediately.
Serves 4

GLAZED GAMMON STEAKS

As suitable for brunches and barbecues as suppers, these individual, foil-wrapped gammon steaks form their own delicious aromatic glaze as they cook. Piquant Carrots and Leeks (see page 36) makes an excellent accompaniment. To serve immediately without freezing, cook as below, but for only 10 minutes before opening the foil.

4 unsmoked gammon steaks, each weighing about 175 g/6 oz
2 teaspoons vegetable oil
8 juniper berries, crushed
50 g/2 oz dark soft brown sugar
4 tablespoons clear honey
4 tablespoons lemon juice
1 medium onion, peeled and thinly sliced

Snip through the rind and fat of the gammon steaks with kitchen scissors to prevent them from curling up during cooking. Heat the oil in a large frying pan, add 2 gammon steaks and brown quickly on both sides. Remove from the pan with a slotted spoon and repeat with the other 2 steaks.

Cut 4 pieces of foil, each one large enough to enclose a gammon steak. Mix together the juniper berries and sugar and sprinkle half over the pieces of foil. Place a gammon steak on each piece of foil, then sprinkle with the remaining juniper berries and sugar. Mix together the honey, lemon juice and onion and pour over the top.
To freeze: Fold the foil around each steak to make a tight parcel. Pack in a polythene bag, seal, label and freeze for up to 3 months.
To thaw and serve: Remove the parcels from the polythene bag, put them on a baking sheet and loosen the foil. Cook from frozen in a preheated moderately hot oven (200°C/400°F/Gas Mark 6) for 30 minutes, then open the foil and cook for a further 15 minutes. Serve hot.
Serves 4

PORK CHOPS PACIFIC

Pork chops combined with two unexpected seasonal fruits, papaya and passionfruit, for tenderness and a specially fragrant sauce.

2 teaspoons vegetable oil
4 pork chops
2 garlic cloves, peeled and chopped
1 cm/½ inch piece ginger root, peeled and chopped
4 fresh passionfruit
1 under-ripe papaya, peeled, seeded and sliced
4 tablespoons water
salt and freshly ground black pepper

Heat the oil in a large flameproof casserole, add the pork chops and fry over moderate heat until browned on both sides. Add the garlic and ginger root and fry for a further 1 minute.

Cut the passionfruit in half, scoop out the pulp and seeds, and add to the casserole with the papaya, water and salt and pepper to taste. Cover with a lid and simmer for 30 minutes or until the chops are tender. Cool quickly.
To freeze: Transfer the chops and sauce to a rigid container, seal, label and freeze for up to 3 months.
To thaw and serve: Leave to stand in container at room temperature for 2 hours, then transfer to a pan and reheat gently for 30 minutes. Taste and adjust the seasoning of the sauce and serve hot.
Serves 4

PORK WITH APPLES

2 tablespoons oil
4 pork chops
250 g/8 oz button onions
1 garlic clove, chopped
2 dessert apples, peeled, cored and cut into rings
salt and freshly ground black pepper
300 ml/½ pint cider
TO SERVE
4 tablespoons double cream

Heat the oil in a large flameproof casserole, add the chops and fry until browned on both sides. Remove from the pan, add the onions and garlic and fry for 3 minutes. Replace the chops and lay the apples on top. Season to taste and pour on the cider. Cover and simmer for 30 minutes. Cool quickly.
To freeze: Transfer to a rigid container, seal, label and freeze for up to 3 months.
To thaw and serve: Leave to stand at room temperature for 2 hours, then transfer to a pan and reheat gently for 30 minutes. Stir in the cream and heat through. Serve immediately.
Serves 4

Veal Kidneys Madeira; Veal in Vermouth; Pork Chops Pacific

Beef Vedette

Bake these pastry-wrapped beef fillets 35 to 45 minutes before sitting down to eat – the pre-freezer preparation ensures a rare and taste-packed treat.

Make the shortcrust pastry as for Individual Prawn Quiches (page 104). To serve immediately, without freezing, glaze the pastry parcels with beaten egg and bake as below but for only 15 to 20 minutes.

4 thick slices from small end of beef fillet, each
  weighing about 125 g/4 oz
125 g/4 oz chicken livers
2 tablespoons olive oil
3 tablespoons red wine
1 garlic clove, peeled and crushed
1 onion, peeled and sliced
½ teaspoon dried thyme
15 g/½ oz butter
salt and freshly ground black pepper
500 g/1 lb shortcrust pastry (total weight)
1 egg, beaten, to glaze
TO SERVE
parsley sprigs

Put the beef and livers in a bowl. Mix together half the oil with the wine, garlic, onion and thyme and pour over the meat. Turn to coat all sides, cover and leave to marinate for about 1 hour.

Remove the steaks from the marinade. Heat the remaining oil and the butter in a frying pan, add the steaks and fry for 1 minute on each side for rare steaks, longer for medium steaks. Remove from the pan with a slotted spoon, sprinkle with salt and pepper to taste and set aside on a plate.

Remove the livers and onion from the marinade with a slotted spoon and reserve the marinade. Add the livers and onion to the frying pan and fry quickly, then remove with the slotted spoon to another plate. Pour the reserved marinade into the pan, scraping up the sediment in the bottom of the pan. Boil to reduce to 1 tablespoon, then add to the livers and onion with salt and pepper to taste.

Reserve a small piece of pastry for decorating. Cut the remaining pastry into 4 equal pieces and roll out into circles. Divide the liver mixture equally between the circles, then top each one with a steak. Brush the pastry edges with egg, fold over the steaks to make parcels and seal. Turn the parcels over and decorate with the reserved pastry, cut into shapes. Brush with the remaining egg. Leave until cold.

To freeze: Open freeze the steak parcels until solid, then pack in a single layer in a rigid container. Seal, label and return to the freezer for up to 2 months.

To thaw and serve: Place the frozen parcels on a baking sheet and bake from frozen in a preheated moderately hot oven (200°C/400°F/Gas Mark 6) for 35 to 45 minutes. Serve immediately, garnished with parsley.

Serves 4

Burgundy Beef with Black Olives

Individually stuffed pieces of beef in a rich red wine sauce which mellows deliciously after freezing.

750 g/1½ lb beef topside, in 1 piece
2 tablespoons plain flour
salt and freshly ground black pepper
12 black olives, stoned
12 blanched and skinned almonds
2 tablespoons vegetable oil
15 g/½ oz butter
1 large onion, peeled and sliced
250 g/8 oz back bacon, derinded and cut into pieces
1 bay leaf
300 ml/½ pint Burgundy or other red wine
TO SERVE
parsley sprigs

Cut the topside into 12 pieces, each about 5 cm/ 2 inches square. Toss the beef in the flour seasoned with salt and pepper, until evenly coated. Stuff each olive with an almond, make a small hole in the centre of each piece of beef, then press the stuffed olives into the holes.

Heat the oil and butter in a large flameproof casserole, add the onion and fry gently for 5 minutes without browning. Add the beef and brown well on all sides. Add the bacon and bay leaf, then stir in the wine. Bring to the boil, then lower the heat, cover and simmer for 1½ hours or until the beef is tender. Discard the bay leaf. Cool quickly.

To freeze: Transfer the beef and sauce to a rigid container, seal, label and freeze for up to 3 months.

To thaw and serve: Leave to stand in container at room temperature for 2½ hours, then return to the original casserole. Reheat gently for about 30 minutes. Taste and adjust the seasoning of the sauce. Serve hot, garnished with parsley.

Serves 4

GUARD OF HONOUR WITH CAPE GOOSEBERRIES

Cape gooseberries are tiny, yellow tropical fruit, encased in thin papery husks. They are sweet in flavour, with a slightly acid aftertaste. During their short spring season, they are delicious combined with spring lamb in this sophisticated dinner party dish, which comes straight from the freezer to the oven to the table. If you find cape gooseberries difficult to obtain, use ordinary gooseberries instead.
To serve straight away, without freezing, cover just the tips of the bones with foil and roast in a preheated moderate oven (180°C/350°F/Gas Mark 4) for about 50 minutes.

2 × 7-bone pieces prepared best end of neck of lamb,
  each about 500 g/1 lb
salt and freshly ground black pepper
GLAZE
175 g/6 oz cape gooseberries, husks removed,
  chopped
finely grated rind and juice of 1 orange
1 tablespoon vegetable oil
STUFFING BALLS
125 g/4 oz fresh breadcrumbs
1 small onion, peeled and finely chopped
3 tablespoons chopped parsley

Interlace the exposed lamb bones and tie or skewer them together securely, using a trussing needle and fine string. Sprinkle liberally with salt and pepper. Cover the exposed bones with a thick wad of foil. Put onto a baking sheet or freezer tray, lined with a large sheet of foil.
To make the glaze: Work the chopped cape gooseberries to a smooth purée in an electric blender or food processor, then stir in the orange rind and juice and the oil. Brush half of this glaze evenly over the meat.
To make the stuffing balls: Mix the breadcrumbs, onion and parsley together in a bowl. Add the remaining glaze to bind the mixture. Shape into 12 compact balls and put around the meat.
To freeze: Open freeze the meat and stuffing balls until solid, then wrap in the foil to make a tight parcel. Pack in a polythene bag, seal, label and return to the freezer for up to 3 months.
To thaw and serve: Remove the polythene bag, put the foil parcel in a roasting tin and loosen the foil. Roast from frozen in a preheated moderate oven (160°C/ 325°F/Gas Mark 3) for 1 hour, then open the foil and roast for a further 15 minutes. Serve hot, with young carrots and new potatoes.
Serves 4 to 6

LEFT: Burgundy Beef with Black Olives; Beef Vedette
RIGHT: Guard of Honour with Cape Gooseberries

BRAISED LEG OF SPRING LAMB

Young lamb, piquantly seasoned and braised, is frozen in the same convenient roasting bag in which it is later reheated, thus preserving juices and minimizing time and cooking utensils.

1 leg of young spring lamb, about 1.5 kg/3–3½ lb
salt and freshly ground black pepper
2 tablespoons vegetable oil
25 g/1 oz butter
150 ml/¼ pint medium-dry white wine
500 g/1 lb baby carrots, scraped and halved lengthways
2 medium onions, peeled and quartered
HACHIS
4 garlic cloves, peeled and crushed
1 tablespoon snipped chives
1 tablespoon chopped tarragon
1 small onion, peeled and very finely chopped
finely grated rind of ½ lemon

Make long diagonal incisions in the lamb about 1 cm/ ½ inch deep and at 2.5 cm/1 inch intervals. Mix together the hachis ingredients, then press a little hachis into each incision. Sprinkle the surface of the lamb liberally with salt and pepper.

Heat the oil and butter in a large flameproof casserole, add the lamb and fry over brisk heat until browned on all sides. Pour in the wine and bring to the boil, then lower the heat, cover and simmer for 1½ hours, adding the vegetables for the last 15 minutes. Cool quickly.
To freeze: Wrap the bone end of the lamb in a thick wad of foil. Put the lamb, vegetables and cooking liquid into a roasting bag, seal, label and freeze for up to 3 months.
To thaw and serve: Open the roasting bag, cut a few small holes in the top, then loosely seal the open end. Put into a roasting tin and reheat from frozen in a preheated moderate oven (160°C/325°F/Gas Mark 3) for 1½ hours. Taste and adjust the seasoning of the sauce and serve hot.
Serves 4 to 6

PIQUANT CARROTS AND LEEKS

In this quick and unusual vegetable dish, the carrots and leeks are cooked from frozen and added to a soured cream sauce just before serving.

500 g/1 lb frozen whole young carrots
250 g/8 oz frozen sliced leeks
TO SERVE
15 g/½ oz butter
1 garlic clove, peeled and thinly sliced
150 ml/¼ pint soured cream
1 tablespoon chopped parsley
salt and freshly ground pepper
½ teaspoon French mustard
2 tablespoons sesame seeds, lightly toasted

Steam the whole carrots over a pan of boiling water for 10 minutes, add the sliced leeks and steam for a further 7 to 8 minutes, until the vegetables are just tender.

Meanwhile, melt the butter in a pan, add the garlic and fry gently for 1 to 2 minutes until lightly browned. Stir in the soured cream, parsley, mustard and salt and pepper to taste and heat through gently without boiling. Remove from the heat, add the vegetables and toss well to coat in the sauce. Transfer to a warmed serving dish and sprinkle with the sesame seeds. Serve immediately.
Serves 4 to 6

CARROTS WITH HERBS

In this recipe, frozen carrots are used with fresh and dried herbs to give a subtle and unusual springtime flavour.

750 g/1½ lb frozen whole young carrots
TO SERVE
25 g/1 oz butter
2 onions, peeled and finely chopped
15 g/½ oz plain flour
150 ml/¼ pint dry white wine
5 tablespoons well-flavoured chicken stock
1 tablespoon chopped parsley
1 teaspoon dried thyme
salt and freshly ground black pepper
parsley sprigs

Melt the butter in a pan, add the onions and fry gently for 10 minutes until golden. Add the flour and cook for a further 2 minutes, stirring all the time. Gradually stir in the wine and stock, bring to the boil, then lower the heat. Add the herbs and salt and pepper to taste and simmer gently for 8 minutes, stirring frequently.

Meanwhile, cook the carrots in boiling salted water for 5 minutes until just tender. Drain, stir into the sauce and heat through for 2 to 3 minutes. Taste and adjust seasoning. Serve immediately, garnished with parsley.
Serves 4 to 5

ITALIAN MUSHROOMS

This is an excellent accompaniment to grills and roasts; it can also be served – either hot or cold – with Melba toast as a starter.

2 tablespoons olive oil
15 g/½ oz butter
2 garlic cloves, peeled and finely sliced
500 g/1 lb button mushrooms, thinly sliced
3–4 tablespoons Marsala wine
1 bouquet garni
3 anchovy fillets, soaked in milk for 15 minutes, rinsed and dried, then finely chopped
freshly ground black pepper
TO SERVE
1 tablespoon finely chopped spring onions

Heat the oil and butter together in a pan, add the garlic and fry gently for 1 minute without browning. Add the mushrooms and cook for 5 minutes until soft. Add the Marsala and bouquet garni, increase the heat and cook for 5 minutes. Remove from heat, discard bouquet garni, then stir in the anchovies and pepper to taste.
To freeze: Transfer to a rigid container, cool quickly, then seal, label and freeze for up to 2 months.
To thaw and serve: Leave to stand in container at room temperature for 3 to 4 hours, then transfer to a pan and reheat gently, stirring occasionally. Taste and adjust the seasoning, then serve hot, garnished with spring onions.
Serves 4 to 6

CREAMED BEETROOT

Beetroot is a much-forgotten vegetable; it should be used more often than simply in salads or for pickling.

25 g/1 oz butter
1 onion, peeled and finely chopped
2 tablespoons plain flour
300 ml/½ pint milk
2 tablespoons double cream
1 teaspoon dried mixed herbs
salt and freshly ground black pepper
500 g/1 lb cooked beetroot, skinned and diced
1 tart dessert apple, peeled, cored and diced
TO SERVE
2 tablespoons chopped parsley

Melt the butter in a pan, add the onion and fry gently for 5 minutes without browning. Add the flour and cook for a further 2 minutes, stirring all the time. Remove from the heat and gradually add the milk, beating vigorously after each addition. Return to the heat and bring to the boil, stirring constantly. Lower the heat and simmer for 2 minutes, stirring occasionally, then stir in the cream, herbs and salt and pepper to taste. Fold in the beetroot and apple and simmer for a further 5 minutes, stirring occasionally.

Remove from the heat and leave to cool, stirring occasionally to prevent a skin forming.
To freeze: Transfer the beetroot and sauce to a rigid container, seal, label and freeze for up to 5 months.
To thaw and serve: Leave to stand in container at room temperature for 4 hours, then transfer to a pan and reheat gently for 10 minutes, stirring occasionally. Taste and adjust the seasoning, then serve hot, sprinkled with parsley.
Serves 4 to 6

BROAD BEANS AU GRATIN

This dish is also delicious made from the whole young broad beans in their pods. In this case the quantity of beans should be halved.

50 g/2 oz butter
1 large onion, peeled and sliced
4 spring onions, trimmed and chopped
1 garlic clove, peeled and crushed
40 g/1½ oz plain flour
300 ml/½ pint chicken stock or milk
300 ml/½ pint single cream
125 g/4 oz Gruyère cheese, grated
50 g/2 oz mature Cheddar cheese, grated
1 teaspoon French mustard
salt and freshly ground black pepper
1.25 kg/2½ lb broad beans, shelled
TO SERVE
4 tablespoons dried breadcrumbs
3 tablespoons grated Parmesan cheese
4 rashers streaky bacon, rinds removed, crisply fried and crumbled

Melt the butter in a pan, add the onion and fry gently for 5 minutes without browning. Add the spring onions and garlic and fry for a further 2 minutes. Add the flour and cook for a further 2 minutes, stirring all the time. Remove from the heat and gradually add the stock or milk, beating vigorously after each addition. Return to the heat and bring to the boil, stirring constantly. Lower the heat, add the cream, cheeses, mustard and salt and pepper to taste and simmer, stirring, until the cheese has melted. Add the shelled beans and simmer for a further 3 minutes.
To freeze: Pour the beans and sauce into a rigid container, cool quickly, then seal, label and freeze for up to 4 months.
To thaw and serve: Leave to stand in container at room temperature for 4 hours, then transfer to an ovenproof dish. Sprinkle over the breadcrumbs and Parmesan cheese and reheat in a preheated moderately hot oven (200°C/400°F/Gas Mark 6) for 35 minutes. Sprinkle over the crispy bacon and bake for a further 5 minutes. Serve immediately.
Serves 4 to 6

Italian Mushrooms; Carrots with Herbs; Piquant Carrots and Leeks; Broad Beans au Gratin

VEGETABLE LASAGNE

This is a perfect dish to keep in the freezer for entertaining friends. Serve as a lunch or supper with fresh French bread and butter or hot garlic bread.

4 tablespoons olive oil
3 large onions, peeled and sliced
2 garlic cloves, peeled and crushed
500 g/1 lb tomatoes, skinned, seeded and chopped
150 ml/¼ pint dry white wine
2 teaspoons chopped basil
2 teaspoons chopped parsley
2 teaspoons chopped oregano
salt and freshly ground black pepper
1 tablespoon tomato purée
350 g/12 oz courgettes, trimmed and sliced
250 g/8 oz shelled broad beans
125 g/4 oz shelled fresh peas
SAUCE
600 ml/1 pint milk
2 carrots, peeled and roughly chopped
1 leek, trimmed and roughly chopped
1 small onion, peeled and roughly chopped
1 bay leaf
few peppercorns
50 g/2 oz butter
50 g/2 oz plain flour
2 teaspoons French mustard
175 g/6 oz mature Cheddar cheese, grated
50 g/2 oz Gruyère cheese, grated
1 tablespoon Parmesan cheese, grated
500 g/1 lb spinach or egg lasagne
TO SERVE
parsley sprigs

Heat half the oil in a pan, add the onions and garlic and fry gently for 7 to 8 minutes until lightly browned. Add the tomatoes and wine, bring to the boil, then simmer uncovered for 20 minutes. Add the herbs and salt and pepper to taste. Cook for a further 5 minutes, then stir in the tomato purée, courgettes, broad beans and peas and cook for a further 5 minutes. Remove from the heat and leave to cool.

To make the sauce: Put the milk, carrots, leek, onion, bay leaf, salt and peppercorns in a pan. Bring to the boil, then remove from the heat and leave to infuse until cold. Strain the milk and reserve.

Melt the butter in a clean pan, add the flour and cook for 2 minutes, stirring all the time. Remove from the heat and gradually add the infused milk, beating vigorously after each addition. Return to the heat and bring to the boil, stirring constantly. Lower the heat, add the mustard and cheeses and simmer, stirring, until the cheese has melted. Taste and adjust seasoning.

Cook the lasagne in batches in boiling salted water with the remaining olive oil for 10 minutes. Drain and cool under cold running water, then drain well again.

Arrange a layer of pasta in the base of a lightly greased ovenproof dish. Spoon over some of the vegetable mixture, then top with another layer of pasta and cover with a layer of cheese sauce. Continue with these layers until all the ingredients are used up, finishing with cheese sauce. Leave until cold.

To freeze: Open freeze, then remove from the dish and wrap in foil. Pack in a polythene bag, seal, label and return to the freezer for up to 6 months.

To thaw and serve: Unwrap and return to the original dish. Thaw at room temperature for 6 hours, then reheat in a preheated moderately hot oven (200°C/400°F/Gas Mark 6) for 40 minutes until bubbling and golden. Serve immediately, garnished with parsley.

Serves 6

SPRING VEGETABLE CURRY

Any available vegetables can be used in this dish, which can be served as a vegetarian main course with rice and poppadoms or chappatis.

2 tablespoons vegetable oil
1 large onion, peeled and roughly chopped
2 garlic cloves, peeled and thinly sliced
2 teaspoons cumin seeds
2 teaspoons ground coriander
1 teaspoon chilli powder
½ teaspoon ground turmeric
500 g/1 lb mixed vegetables (e.g. broad beans, carrots, onions, spring cauliflower, potatoes), prepared and cut into small pieces
2–3 tomatoes, skinned, seeded and chopped
300 ml/½ pint chicken stock
salt

Heat the oil in a pan, add the onion and garlic and fry gently until lightly browned. Add the cumin seeds and fry for 1 minute, then stir in the coriander, chilli and turmeric and fry for a further 2 minutes.

Add the mixed vegetables, tomatoes and stock and bring to the boil. Lower the heat, add salt to taste, then cover the pan and simmer for 15 minutes until the vegetables are just tender.

To freeze: Transfer the curry to a rigid container, leaving 2 cm/¾ inch headspace. Cool quickly, then seal, label and freeze for up to 4 months.

To thaw and serve: Leave to stand in container at room temperature for 3 to 4 hours, then transfer to a pan and reheat gently for 10 minutes, stirring occasionally. Taste and adjust the seasoning before serving.

Serves 4 to 6

SPINACH TRIANGLES

These Greek pastries are made from filo pastry, a fine strudel-type of pastry available from Greek shops. It is important to keep the pastry wrapped in cling film as it dries out very quickly, so work with one sheet at a time.

250 g/8 oz filo pastry
50 g/2 oz butter, melted
FILLING
500 g/1 lb fresh spinach
15 g/½ oz butter
50 g/2 oz curd cheese
25 g/1 oz Gruyère cheese, grated
1 tablespoon grated Parmesan cheese
2 tablespoons double cream
1 egg
1 egg yolk
pinch of freshly grated nutmeg
salt and freshly ground black pepper
TO SERVE
a little melted butter
coriander leaves

For the filling: Cook the spinach in a covered saucepan, with just the water clinging to the leaves after washing, for 6 to 8 minutes until tender. Drain, and squeeze dry, then chop the spinach finely. Melt the 15 g/½ oz butter in a pan, stir in the spinach and heat through gently. Remove from the heat and beat in the cheeses, cream, eggs, nutmeg, and salt and pepper to taste.

Cut 1 sheet of filo pastry lengthways into 7.5 cm/ 3 inch wide strips. Brush 1 strip with melted butter, put a rounded teaspoon of filling about 2.5 cm/1 inch in from one end, then fold the corner over the filling to make a triangle. Fold the remaining pastry strip over and over to make a little fat triangular package. Continue this process with the remaining pastry, melted butter and filling.

Place the triangles on a baking sheet. Brush with the remaining melted butter and bake in a preheated moderately hot oven (200°C/400°F/Gas Mark 6) for 15 to 20 minutes until golden brown. Transfer to a wire rack to cool.

To freeze: Open freeze the triangles until solid, then pack carefully in rigid containers, separating the layers with interleaving sheets or foil. Seal, label and return to the freezer for up to 4 months.

To thaw and serve: Place the frozen triangles on a baking sheet and brush with a little melted butter. Reheat in a preheated moderate oven (160°C/325°F/ Gas Mark 3) for 25 to 30 minutes until crisp and thoroughly heated. Garnish with coriander leaves and serve immediately.

Serves 6 to 8

LEFT: Spinach triangles; Watercress and Spring Onion Quiche
RIGHT: Vegetable Lasagne

WATERCRESS AND SPRING ONION QUICHE

Watercress is particularly good in the spring, as the leaves are light-coloured and less bitter. It cannot be frozen raw for use as a salad vegetable, however, because its high water content causes it to become limp. Made into a soup, or used as a quiche filling, its flavour is just as good as when it is fresh.
If you prefer, the watercress can be replaced by 250 g/ 8 oz blanched and chopped fresh spinach.

175 g/6 oz plain flour
salt
50 g/2 oz margarine
25 g/1 oz lard
75 g/3 oz mature Cheddar cheese, grated
2 tablespoons grated Parmesan cheese
a little iced water
FILLING
25 g/1 oz butter
8 large spring onions, trimmed and chopped
1 large bunch watercress, thick stems removed and
  roughly chopped
3 eggs
150 ml/¼ pint double cream
1 teaspoon French mustard
pinch of dried mixed herbs
125 g/4 oz mature Cheddar cheese, grated
cayenne pepper
TO SERVE
few watercress sprigs
few spring onions, trimmed and sliced

Sift the flour and a pinch of salt into a bowl. Rub in the fats until the mixture resembles fine breadcrumbs. Stir in the cheeses and enough water to mix to a fairly stiff dough. Turn the dough onto a floured surface. Knead lightly until smooth, then roll out and use to line a 20 cm/8 inch flan ring (about 1″ deep) placed on a baking sheet. Chill in the refrigerator for 30 minutes.

To make the filling: Melt the butter in a pan, add the spring onions and fry gently for 3 minutes without browning. Stir in the watercress and cook for 1 minute until just soft, then remove from the heat and leave to cool.

Beat the eggs, cream, mustard and herbs together in a bowl. Stir in the cheese, then season to taste with salt and cayenne.

Prick the base and sides of the dough and line with foil and baking beans. Bake 'blind' in a preheated moderately hot oven (200°C/400°F/Gas Mark 6) for 10 minutes, then remove the foil and beans and return to the oven for a further 5 minutes. Spoon the spring onions and watercress over the base, pour over the egg and cream mixture and bake in the oven for 25 minutes, until the filling is well risen and golden brown. Leave to cool.

To freeze: Open freeze the quiche until solid, then remove carefully from the flan ring and wrap in foil. Pack in a polythene bag, seal, label and return to the freezer for up to 4 months.

To thaw and serve: Unwrap and place on a wire rack; leave to stand at room temperature for 2 to 3 hours until thawed completely. Serve cold, or reheat in a preheated moderate oven (180°C/350°F/Gas Mark 4) for 15 minutes and serve warm. Garnish with watercress and spring onions before serving.

Serves 4 to 6

ICED BANANA WHIP

Bananas are at their best and most plentiful in late spring and early summer, but this dessert can be made at any time of year. Serve with crisp biscuits, such as Golden Curls (see page 146).

4 bananas
1 egg white
50 g/2 oz light soft brown sugar
150 ml/¼ pint double cream
2 tablespoons Tia Maria or other coffee liqueur
TO SERVE
4 tablespoons double cream, whipped
banana slices (optional)

Peel the bananas and mash to a smooth purée. Whisk the egg white until stiff, then whisk in the sugar a little at a time. Whip the cream until it will stand in soft peaks. Fold the banana purée into the meringue mixture together with the cream and liqueur. Spoon the banana whip into individual freezerproof dishes and level the surface.

To freeze: Open freeze the desserts until solid, then wrap individually in cling film or foil and overwrap in polythene bags. Seal, label and return to the freezer for up to 2 months.

To thaw and serve: Unwrap and transfer the banana whips to the refrigerator 20 minutes before serving to soften. Pipe a swirl of whipped cream on each dessert and decorate with banana slices if preferred. Serve immediately.

Serves 6

COFFEE AND BRANDY ICE CREAM

Serve this delicious ice cream with crisp, sweet biscuits such as Lacy Almond Wafers (see page 146).

3 eggs
75 g/3 oz caster sugar
300 ml/½ pint single cream
3 tablespoons instant coffee powder
300 ml/½ pint double cream
3 tablespoons brandy

Beat the eggs and sugar together until smooth. Bring the single cream and coffee just to the boil in a small pan, then stir into the egg mixture. Transfer to the top of a double boiler, or to a heatproof bowl over a pan

of simmering water. Cook gently, stirring constantly, until the custard is thick enough to coat the back of a spoon. Strain into a bowl and leave to cool, stirring occasionally to prevent a skin forming.

Whip the double cream until it will stand in soft peaks, then fold into the cold custard with the brandy. Pour into a rigid container, cover and freeze for 2 to 3 hours until half-frozen. Remove from the freezer and stir well, then return to the container.

To freeze: Seal, label and return to the freezer for up to 3 months.

To thaw and serve: Transfer the ice cream to the refrigerator 30 minutes before serving to allow it to soften. Scoop into chilled glasses or dishes and serve immediately.

Serves 6 to 8

PASSIONFRUIT ICE CREAM

This is a very creamy ice cream that does not need to be softened after removing from the freezer. It can be served in scoops directly from the freezerproof container, but for a dinner party, it looks more attractive if prepared in a mould, then served whole and decorated.

2 eggs, separated
125 g/4 oz caster sugar
8 ripe passionfruit
1 teaspoon lemon juice
300 ml/½ pint double cream
TO SERVE
pulp and seeds of 1 passionfruit
4 tablespoons double cream, whipped (optional)

Put the egg yolks and half the sugar in a bowl and whisk with an electric beater until thick and mousse-like. Cut the passionfruit in half and scoop out the pulp into a sieve over a bowl. Press through the sieve, to extract as much juice as possible, discarding the seeds. Stir the lemon juice into the passionfruit.

Whisk the egg whites until stiff, then whisk in the remaining sugar. Whip the cream until it will stand in soft peaks. Fold the egg whites into the egg yolk mixture with the passionfruit juice and the cream. Spoon into a 1 litre/1¾ pint loaf tin or mould and level the surface.

To freeze: Cover the mould with foil, wrap in a polythene bag, then seal, label and freeze for up to 3 months.

To thaw and serve: Unwrap the mould and invert onto a serving plate. Rub with a cloth wrung out in very hot water until the ice cream drops out. Spoon the passionfruit pulp along the centre of the ice cream and decorate with piped whipped cream if liked. Serve immediately.

Serves 6

LEFT: Iced Banana Whip; Coffee and Brandy Ice Cream
RIGHT: Biscuit Tortoni; Passionfruit Ice Cream

BISCUIT TORTONI

This bombe was first made at Tortoni's famous restaurant in Paris in the 19th century. It is given this unusual name because it is served cut into thin slices to look like biscuits.

300 ml/½ pint double cream
300 ml/½ pint whipping cream
4 tablespoons sweet sherry
3 tablespoons icing sugar, sifted
50 g/2 oz ratafias, crushed
TO SERVE
40 g/1½ oz ratafias

Put all the ingredients except the ratafias in a bowl and whisk until the mixture forms soft peaks. Fold in the crushed ratafias until evenly incorporated. Spoon into a 1 kg (2 lb) loaf tin and level the surface.

To freeze: Cover the tin with foil, wrap in a polythene bag, then seal, label and freeze for up to 2 months.

To thaw and serve: Unwrap the loaf tin and invert onto a serving plate 45 minutes before serving. Rub with a cloth wrung out in very hot water until the ice cream drops out. Leave at room temperature for 10 minutes. Set aside 8 ratafias for decoration if liked. Crush the remaining ratafias and press them evenly onto the top and sides of the bombe. Leave in the refrigerator for 30 minutes. Decorate with the whole ratafias, if reserved, before serving.

Serves 8

MANGO FOOL

If you are making this fool to eat straight away, frozen and thawed mango purée can be used instead of fresh mangoes suggested here. Serve with crisp biscuits.

2 mangoes
125 g/4 oz icing sugar, sifted
juice of ½ lime
300 ml/½ pint double cream
TO SERVE
6 lime slices

Cut the mangoes in half lengthways, scrape out the flesh and place in an electric blender or food processor. Add the icing sugar and lime juice and work until smooth.

Whip the cream until it will stand in soft peaks, then fold in the mango purée. Pour into a freezerproof serving dish or individual soufflé dishes and chill in the refrigerator for about 1 hour or until set.

To freeze: Cover the dish(es) with cling film, wrap in polythene bag(s), then seal, label and freeze for up to 3 months.

To thaw and serve: Leave to stand in wrappings in the refrigerator overnight (or for about 4 hours for individual dishes). Unwrap, decorate with slices of lime and serve chilled.
Serves 6

ICED GOOSEBERRY SOUFFLÉ

500 g/1 lb gooseberries
150 ml/¼ pint water
125 g/4 oz granulated sugar
2 heads elderflower, tied in muslin (optional)
4 eggs, separated
125 g/4 oz caster sugar
300 ml/½ pint double cream
few drops of green food colouring (optional)
TO SERVE
4 tablespoons double cream, whipped
few kiwi fruit slices (optional)

Tie a band of foil very tightly around a 900 ml/1½ pint soufflé dish, to stand 5 cm/2 inches above the rim.

Put the gooseberries in a pan with the water, granulated sugar and elderflower (if using). Cover and simmer gently for 15 minutes until tender. Discard the elderflower (if used) and leave the gooseberries to cool. Work in an electric blender or food processor until smooth, then work through a nylon sieve to remove the tops and tails.

Put the egg yolks and caster sugar in a bowl and whisk with an electric beater until thick and mousse-like. Whip the cream until it will stand in soft peaks, then fold in the gooseberry purée. Fold the goose-

Mango Fool; Iced Gooseberry Soufflé; Rhubarb and Orange Cream

berries and cream into the egg mixture, with the food colouring if using. Whisk the egg whites until stiff, carefully fold 1 tablespoon into the gooseberry mixture, then fold in the remainder. Spoon into the prepared soufflé dish and level the surface.

To freeze: Open freeze the soufflé until solid, then wrap in a polythene bag. Seal, label and return to the freezer for up to 2 months.

To thaw and serve: Unwrap and place in the refrigerator 45 minutes before serving to soften. Remove the foil carefully and pipe a cream border around the top of the soufflé. Decorate the centre with kiwi fruit if preferred, and serve immediately.
Serves 6 to 8

RHUBARB AND ORANGE CREAM

500 g/1 lb rhubarb, cut into 2.5 cm/1 inch lengths
175 g/6 oz caster sugar
finely grated rind and juice of 1 orange
4 tablespoons water
15 g/½ oz (1 envelope) powdered gelatine, dissolved
   in 4 tablespoons water
150 ml/¼ pint double cream, whipped
TO SERVE
120 ml/4 fl oz double cream, whipped
finely shredded orange rind

Put the rhubarb in a bowl, cover with the sugar and leave for 1 hour to draw out the juices. Turn into a saucepan, add the orange rind and juice and the water. Bring to the boil, lower the heat, cover and simmer gently for 30 minutes until the rhubarb is very soft.

Mix with a fork to break up the rhubarb, then stir in the dissolved gelatine over low heat. Allow to cool, then fold in the whipped cream. Pour into an oiled 750 ml/1¼ pint mould and level the surface. Chill in the refrigerator for 2 to 3 hours or until set.

To freeze: Cover with cling film, wrap in a polythene bag, then seal, label and freeze for up to 3 months.

To thaw and serve: Leave to stand in wrappings in the refrigerator overnight, then unwrap and turn out onto a serving plate. Decorate with the whipped cream and orange shreds. Serve immediately.
Serves 6

CHOCOLATE MINT ICE

3 egg yolks
125 g/4 oz caster sugar
300 ml/½ pint single cream
few drops of green food colouring
½ teaspoon peppermint essence
300 ml/½ pint double cream
125 g/4 oz plain chocolate, finely chopped

Place the egg yolks in a bowl with the sugar and beat until pale and creamy. Bring the single cream to just below boiling point in a small pan, then stir thoroughly into the egg mixture. Transfer to the top of a double

boiler, or to a heatproof bowl over a pan of simmering water, and cook gently, stirring constantly, until the custard is thick enough to coat the back of a spoon. Strain into a bowl and leave to cool, stirring occasionally to prevent a skin forming, then stir in the colouring and peppermint essence.

Whip the double cream until it will stand in soft peaks then fold in the custard. Pour into a rigid container, cover, seal and freeze for about 3 hours until half-frozen. Remove from the freezer, add the chocolate and stir thoroughly.

To freeze: Return to the container, seal and label. Return to the freezer for up to 3 months.

To thaw and serve: Transfer to the refrigerator 20 minutes before serving to soften. Scoop into chilled glasses to serve.
Serves 8

CHOCOLATE MERINGUE SURPRISE

CHOCOLATE MERINGUE
250 g/8 oz caster sugar
4 tablespoons cocoa powder
4 egg whites
FILLING
4 egg whites
125 g/4 oz caster sugar
300 ml/½ pint double cream
finely grated rind of 2 oranges
2 tablespoons Tia Maria or other coffee liqueur
TO SERVE
150 ml/¼ pint double cream, whipped
1 orange, cut into segments

Line 2 baking sheets with non-stick silicone paper or baking parchment. With a pencil draw two 23 cm/9 inch circles on the paper.

Sift the sugar and cocoa powder together. Whisk the egg whites until stiff, then whisk in the sugar mixture, 1 tablespoon at a time. Continue whisking until the meringue is very stiff and holds its shape. Spoon into a piping bag fitted with a 1 cm/½ inch plain nozzle and pipe into the circles marked on the paper.

Bake in a preheated very cool oven (110°C/225°F/Gas Mark ¼) for 2 hours until crisp. Peel the paper carefully off the meringues, then place on a wire rack and leave to cool.

Make the filling: Whisk the egg whites until stiff, then gradually whisk in the sugar until the mixture is very stiff. Whip the cream with the orange rind and coffee liqueur until stiff, then fold in the egg white mixture.

Sandwich the meringues together with the cream, pressing down well so that the filling extends to the edge of the meringue.

To freeze: Open freeze until solid, then pack in a rigid container, seal, label and return to the freezer for up to 3 months.

To thaw and serve: Unwrap the gâteau and place on a serving plate. Decorate with piped whipped cream and orange segments.
Serves 8 to 10

APRICOT LATTICE TART

Drained canned apricots may be used instead of fresh ones. Alternatively, dried apricots – presoaked in cold water – can be used. Serve this dessert with pouring cream.

250 g/8 oz plain flour
2 teaspoons ground mixed spice
175 g/6 oz butter
25 g/1 oz caster sugar
1 egg, separated
about 1 tablespoon iced water
FILLING
750 g/1 ½ lb apricots, stoned
juice of ½ a lemon
1 tablespoon clear honey
2 tablespoons water
3 tablespoons cornflour
TO SERVE
1 egg yolk mixed with 1 teaspoon water, to glaze

Sift the flour and spice into a bowl. Rub in the butter until the mixture resembles fine breadcrumbs. Stir in the caster sugar, the egg yolk and enough water to mix to a fairly stiff dough.

Turn the dough onto a floured surface, knead lightly until smooth, then roll out and use to line a 20 cm/ 8 inch flan ring. Reserve the pastry trimmings. Chill the flan case and pastry trimmings in the refrigerator for 30 minutes.

Prick the base and sides of the dough and line with foil and baking beans. Bake 'blind' in a preheated moderately hot oven (200°C/400°F/Gas Mark 6) for 15 minutes, then remove the foil and beans. Brush the base with the egg white and return to the oven for a further 3 minutes.

Make the filling: Place the apricots in a pan with the lemon juice and honey. Cover and simmer gently for 5 to 10 minutes or until softened. Cool slightly, then work in an electric blender or food processor until smooth. Return to the pan.

Blend the cornflour to a smooth paste with the water and add to the apricot purée. Cook over low heat for 2 to 3 minutes until thickened, stirring constantly. Allow to cool, then turn into the pastry case and level the surface.

Roll out the reserved pastry trimmings and cut into strips. Make a lattice pattern over the fruit, attaching the pastry with a little water.

To freeze: Open freeze the tart until solid, then wrap in cling film and overwrap in a polythene bag. Seal, label and return to the freezer for up to 3 months.

To thaw and serve: Unwrap and place on a baking sheet. Brush the pastry lattice with the egg glaze, then bake from frozen in a preheated moderately hot oven (200°C/400°F/Gas Mark 6) for 35 to 40 minutes until golden brown. Cover the rim of the pastry with foil if it appears to brown too quickly during cooking.

Serve hot or cold, with pouring cream if liked.

Serves 6

GOOSEBERRY CRUNCH

If the dessert is to be served immediately rather than frozen, sweetened gooseberry purée from the freezer (see page 20), made from 500 g/1 lb gooseberries and 75 g/3 oz sugar, can be used instead of the fresh gooseberries and sugar used here. Thaw the purée before use.

125 g/4 oz ginger nuts, crushed
50 g/2 oz hazelnuts, chopped and lightly toasted
500 g/1 lb gooseberries
75 g/3 oz granulated sugar
2 heads elderflower, tied in muslin (optional)
1 egg white
50 g/2 oz caster sugar
150 ml/¼ pint double cream
TO SERVE
6 tablespoons double cream, whipped

Mix together the biscuits and hazelnuts and set aside.

Put the gooseberries in a pan with the sugar and elderflower (if using). Cover and simmer gently for 15 minutes until tender. Discard the elderflower (if used), then leave the gooseberries to cool. Work in an electric blender or food processor until smooth, then work through a nylon sieve to remove tops and tails.

Whisk the egg white until stiff, then gradually whisk in the caster sugar. Continue whisking until the mixture stands in stiff peaks. Whip the cream until it will stand in soft peaks. Fold the gooseberry purée into the egg whites with the cream. Place half the fruit mixture in a freezerproof serving dish and cover with half the biscuit mixture. Repeat the layers.

To freeze: Cover with cling film, wrap in a polythene bag, then seal, label and freeze for up to 3 months.

To thaw and serve: Remove the polythene bag and leave to stand in the refrigerator overnight. Remove the cling film, then pipe the cream around the edge of the dish. Serve immediately.

Serves 6

CHOCOLATE AND ORANGE CHEESECAKE

50 g/2 oz butter or margarine
125 g/4 oz digestive biscuits, finely crushed
25 g/1 oz demerara sugar
175 g/6 oz plain chocolate, broken into small pieces
250 g/8 oz full-fat soft cheese
finely grated rind of 2 oranges
75 g/3 oz caster sugar
2 eggs, separated
150 ml/¼ pint whipping cream
1 teaspoon powdered gelatine, dissolved in
    1 tablespoon water
TO SERVE
150 ml/¼ pint double cream, whipped
2 oranges, peeled and thinly sliced

Melt the butter or margarine in a small pan, then mix in the biscuit crumbs and demerara sugar. Press the mixture over the base of a lightly oiled 20 cm/8 inch springform cake tin; chill in the refrigerator for about 15 minutes until firm.

Melt the chocolate in a heatproof bowl over a pan of hot water. Beat the soft cheese, orange rind, caster sugar and egg yolks together until thoroughly blended. Whip the cream until it will stand in soft peaks. Fold the warm chocolate into the cheese mixture with the dissolved gelatine, then fold in the cream.

Whisk the egg whites until fairly stiff and quickly fold into the chocolate mixture. Spoon over the biscuit base, level the surface and chill in the refrigerator for 1 to 1½ hours or until set.

To freeze: Open freeze the cheesecake until solid, then carefully remove from the tin and place on a cake board. Wrap in a polythene bag, seal, label and return to the freezer for up to 1 month.

To thaw and serve: Unwrap, place on a serving plate and leave to stand in the refrigerator overnight. Pipe a decorative border of whipped cream around the edge of the cheesecake and decorate with the orange slices. Serve chilled.

Serves 6

VARIATION

To make a plain chocolate cheesecake, omit the orange rind from the cheesecake mixture and decorate the cheesecake, after thawing, with chocolate curls instead of orange slices.

To make chocolate curls, use a potato peeler to shave thin layers from a block of plain chocolate.

OPPOSITE: Gooseberry Crunch
BELOW: Apricot Lattice Tart; Chocolate and Orange Cheesecake

PROFITEROLES

These profiteroles are frozen individually, so you can take out a few at a time if you prefer.

CHOUX PASTRY
50 g/2 oz butter
150 ml/¼ pint water
65 g/2½ oz plain flour, sifted
2 eggs, lightly beaten
CHOCOLATE SAUCE
175 g/6 oz plain chocolate, broken into small pieces
120 ml/4 fl oz water
75 g/3 oz sugar
TO SERVE
175 ml/6 fl oz double cream, whipped

To make the choux pastry: Put the butter and water in a pan and bring to the boil. Remove from the heat and immediately beat in the flour all at once. Beat well until the mixture leaves the sides of the pan clean. Cool slightly, then add the eggs a little at a time, beating thoroughly between each addition.

Spoon the dough into a piping bag fitted with a 1 cm/½ inch plain nozzle and pipe about 25 to 30 small mounds on dampened baking sheets, spacing them well apart. Bake in a preheated hot oven (220°C/425°F/Gas Mark 7) for 10 minutes, then reduce the temperature to moderately hot (190°C/375°F/Gas Mark 5) and bake for a further 20 minutes until well risen and golden brown. Make a slit in the side of each profiterole with the point of a sharp knife, then leave to cool on a wire rack.

Meanwhile, make the sauce: put all the ingredients in a small heavy-based pan and heat gently until the chocolate has melted and the sugar dissolved. Bring to the boil, then lower the heat and simmer gently for 10 minutes, stirring frequently. Remove from the heat and leave to cool.

To freeze: Open freeze the profiteroles until solid, then pack in polythene bags, seal, label and return to the freezer for up to 3 months. Pour the chocolate sauce into a rigid container, seal, label and freeze for up to 3 months.

To thaw and serve: Unwrap the profiteroles and place on baking sheets. Reheat from frozen in a preheated moderate oven (180°C/350°F/Gas Mark 4) for 10 to 15 minutes. Transfer to a wire rack and leave to cool completely. Reheat the chocolate sauce from frozen in a small heavy-based pan over a very low heat, stirring occasionally; do not allow to boil. Pipe a little whipped cream into each profiterole, pile them on a serving dish and pour over the warm chocolate sauce. Serve immediately.

Serves 4 to 6

COFFEE MERINGUES

These meringues need not be piped. If you prefer, you can simply spread the mixture into the marked circles with a palette knife.

---

2 egg whites
125 g/4 oz caster sugar
1 tablespoon instant coffee powder
FILLING AND TOPPING
250–300 ml/8–10 fl oz double cream
2 tablespoons Tia Maria or other coffee-flavoured liqueur

Line 2 baking sheets with non-stick silicone paper or baking parchment. With a pencil, draw six 7.5 cm/3 inch circles and six 5 cm/2 inch circles on the paper.

Whisk the egg whites until stiff, then whisk in the sugar 1 tablespoon at a time. Add the cooled coffee and continue whisking until the meringue is very stiff and holds its shape. Spoon into a piping bag fitted with a 1 cm/½ inch plain nozzle and pipe over the circles.

Bake in a preheated cool oven (120°C/250°F/Gas Mark ½) for 2 hours until crisp. Peel the paper carefully off the meringues, then cool on a wire rack.

Whip the cream and liqueur together in a bowl until stiff. Spoon into a piping bag fitted with a large fluted nozzle and pipe three-quarters of the cream onto the larger meringue circles. Top with the small circles, then pipe a whirl on each one with the remaining cream.

To freeze: Open freeze the meringues until solid, then pack carefully in a rigid container, separating each one with an interleaving sheet or foil. Seal, label and return to the freezer for up to 3 months.

To thaw and serve: Place the meringues on a serving plate and leave to stand at room temperature for 2 hours. Serve as soon as possible.

Serves 6

GÂTEAU GANACHE

4 egg whites
275 g/9 oz caster sugar
few drops of vanilla essence
1 teaspoon vinegar
125 g/4 oz hazelnuts, ground and toasted
FILLING
75 g/3 oz plain chocolate, broken into small pieces
3 tablespoons water
300 ml/½ pint double cream
TO SERVE
25 g/1 oz plain chocolate

Grease two 20 cm/8 inch sandwich tins, line the bases with greaseproof paper, then grease the paper.

Whisk the egg whites until stiff, then whisk in the sugar 1 tablespoon at a time. Continue whisking until the meringue is very stiff and holds its shape. Carefully fold in the vanilla essence, vinegar and hazelnuts.

Turn the mixture into the prepared tins and level the surface. Bake in a preheated moderate oven (180°C/350°F/Gas Mark 4) for 45 to 50 minutes.

Loosen the meringues from the tins with a sharp knife, turn out and carefully peel off the paper. Place on a wire rack and leave to cool.

Melt the chocolate with the water in a heatproof bowl over a pan of hot water, remove from the heat and leave to cool. Whip the cream until it begins to thicken, then whisk in the cooled chocolate and continue whisking until stiff. Sandwich the meringue rounds together with the chocolate cream.

To freeze: Open freeze the gâteau until solid, then pack carefully in a rigid container. Seal, label and return to the freezer for up to 3 months.

To thaw and serve: Remove from the container, place on a serving plate and leave to stand at room temperature for 3 to 4 hours. Melt the chocolate in a heatproof basin over a pan of hot water, then allow to cool. Put the cooled chocolate in a greaseproof piping bag, snip off the tip, then drizzle the chocolate across the top of the meringue. Leave to set. Serve as soon as possible.

Serves 6 to 8

Profiteroles; Coffee Meringues; Gâteau Ganache

CHOCOLATE MINT CAKE

The combination of chocolate and mint in this cake is perfect for serving with the coffee and liqueurs after a dinner party. Chocolate vermicelli can be used instead of grated chocolate if you prefer.

125 g/4 oz butter or margarine, softened
125 g/4 oz caster sugar
2 tablespoons cocoa powder, blended with
    2 tablespoons hot water
2 eggs, beaten
125 g/4 oz self-raising flour, sifted
BUTTER ICING
150 g/5 oz butter, softened
350 g/12 oz icing sugar, sifted
2 tablespoons milk
few drops of green food colouring
few drops of peppermint essence
TO DECORATE
125 g/4 oz plain chocolate

Grease a 30 × 20 cm/12 × 8 inch Swiss roll tin, line with greaseproof paper, then grease the paper.

Cream the butter or margarine and sugar together until light and fluffy, then beat in the slightly cooled cocoa mixture. Beat in the eggs a little at a time, adding 1 tablespoon flour after each addition. Carefully fold in the remaining flour with a metal spoon.

Turn the mixture into the prepared tin and level the surface. Bake in a preheated moderately hot oven (190°C/375°F/Gas Mark 5) for 20 to 25 minutes until the cake springs back when lightly pressed in the centre. Turn out onto a wire rack, carefully peel off the lining paper, turn the cake the right way up and leave to cool.

Make the butter icing: Beat the butter with half the icing sugar until smooth. Add the remaining icing sugar with the milk, colouring and flavouring and beat again until creamy.

Slice the cake vertically into 3 equal pieces, 20 × 10 cm (8 × 4 inches). Sandwich them together with one third of the icing. Cover the sides of the cake with a thin layer of icing. Grate 75 g/3 oz of the chocolate and use to coat the sides. Use one quarter of the remaining icing to cover the top of the cake and smooth with a palette knife.

Break the remaining chocolate into small pieces and melt in a heatproof bowl over a pan of hot water. Put the warm chocolate into a greaseproof piping bag, leave to cool slightly, then snip off the tip. Drizzle the chocolate across the top of the cake, then leave to set. Put the remaining icing in a piping bag fitted with a fluted nozzle and pipe a border on top of the cake.

To freeze: Open freeze the cake until solid, then place in a rigid container, seal, label and return to the freezer for up to 2 months.

To thaw and serve: Place the cake on a serving plate and leave to stand at room temperature for 4 hours. Serve as soon as possible.

Serves 8

HAZELNUT GÂTEAU

A delicious gâteau for a special occasion. If you find it difficult to obtain ground hazelnuts, buy whole hazelnuts and grind them yourself in a rotary grater. Toast them under the grill after grinding.

4 eggs
175 g/6 oz caster sugar
75 g/3 oz plain flour, sifted
75 g/3 oz ground hazelnuts, lightly toasted
1 tablespoon vegetable oil
CRÈME AU BEURRE
3 egg whites
175 g/6 oz icing sugar, sifted
175 g/6 oz unsalted butter, softened
2 tablespoons coffee and chicory essence
PRALINE POWDER
50 g/2 oz unblanched almonds
50 g/2 oz caster sugar

Grease two 20 cm/8 inch sandwich tins, line the bases with greaseproof paper, then grease the paper. Dust the insides of the tins lightly with flour.

Put the eggs and caster sugar in a bowl and whisk with an electric beater until thick and mousse-like. Carefully fold in the flour, hazelnuts and oil, then turn the mixture into the tins and level the surface.

Bake in a preheated moderately hot oven (190°C/375°F/Gas Mark 5) for 25 to 30 minutes until the cakes spring back when lightly pressed in the centre. Turn out onto a wire rack, carefully peel off the lining paper, turn the cakes the right way up and leave to cool. Slice each cake in half horizontally.

Make the crème au beurre: Whisk the egg whites until stiff, then gradually whisk in the icing sugar. Cream the butter until soft, then whisk in the meringue mixture a little at a time. Flavour with the coffee essence.

Make the praline: Place the almonds and sugar in a heavy pan and cook over the lowest possible heat until the sugar has melted. Watch carefully and shake the pan frequently or the edges will brown before the centre has melted. When the mixture turns a nut colour, pour it onto an oiled baking sheet. Leave until cold, then crush to a coarse powder.

Mix 2 tablespoons of the praline into one-quarter of the crème au beurre, then use this mixture to sandwich the cakes together.

Spread more crème au beurre thinly around the side of the cake, then spread a thicker layer over the top and mark into a swirl design with a palette knife. Press the remaining crushed praline around the side of the cake, then pipe the remaining crème au beurre in a border around the top edge.

To freeze: Open freeze the gâteau until solid, then place in a rigid container, seal, label and return to the freezer for up to 2 months.

To thaw and serve: Place the gâteau on a serving plate and leave to stand at room temperature for 4 hours. Serve as soon as possible.

Serves 10

BAKED RICOTTA CHEESECAKE

This cheesecake is delicious served with coffee, but can also be topped with canned cherry pie filling and served as a dessert.

25 g/1 oz butter or margarine
75 g/3 oz digestive biscuits, crushed
250 g/8 oz ricotta cheese
2 eggs, separated
50 g/2 oz ground almonds
finely grated rind of 1 lemon
150 ml/¼ pint single cream
50 g/2 oz caster sugar
TO SERVE
a little icing sugar

Melt the butter in a small pan, then mix in the biscuit crumbs. Press the mixture over the base of a lightly oiled 20 cm/8 inch springform cake tin; chill in the refrigerator for about 15 minutes until firm.

Beat the soft cheese with the egg yolks, almonds and lemon rind until smooth, then gradually stir in the cream. Whisk the egg whites until stiff, then whisk in the sugar a little at a time. Carefully fold into the cheese mixture, then spoon over the biscuit base and level the surface.

Bake in a preheated moderate oven (160°C/325°F/Gas Mark 3) for 1 to 1¼ hours until firm. Turn off the heat and leave the cheesecake in the oven until cold.

To freeze: Open freeze the cheesecake until solid, then remove from the tin and place on a cake board. Wrap in a polythene bag, seal, label and return to the freezer for up to 1 month.

To thaw and serve: Unwrap, place on a serving plate and leave to stand in the refrigerator overnight. Sift icing sugar over the top of the cheesecake just before serving. Serve chilled.

Serves 8

VARIATION

To make a firmer baked cheesecake, without a crumb base, cream together 75 g/3 oz butter, 125 g/4 oz sugar and the grated rind of 1 lemon, until light and fluffy. Gradually beat in 300 g/10 oz ricotta or curd cheese, then add 2 egg yolks and beat thoroughly.

Fold in 50 g/2 oz ground almonds, 25 g/1 oz semolina and the juice of 1 lemon. Whisk 2 egg whites until stiff and carefully fold into the cheese mixture.

Spoon the mixture into a lined and greased 20 cm/8 inch loose-bottomed cake tin and bake in a preheated moderate oven (180°C/350°F/Gas Mark 4) for 50 to 60 minutes. Turn off the heat and leave the cheesecake in the oven until cold.

Freeze the cheesecake as above, for up to 1 month. Unwrap and thaw as above. Sift icing sugar over the top of the cheesecake just before serving.

Chocolate Mint Cake; Baked Ricotta Cheesecake; Hazelnut Gâteau

DANISH PASTRIES

Danish pastries are absolutely delicious taken straight from the freezer, but take a long time to make, so it is a good idea to make a large quantity and take out a few at a time as you need them. You can use other fillings if you prefer, such as apples or crème patissière.

Apricot glaze can be used instead of glacé icing. To serve pastries immediately rather than freeze all of them, leave to prove for 20 to 30 minutes after shaping and filling. Glaze, bake and serve as below.

25 g/1 oz fresh yeast
150 ml/¼ pint tepid water
500 g/1 lb plain flour
50 g/2 oz lard
2 tablespoons caster sugar
2 eggs, beaten
300 g/10 oz butter
beaten egg
FILLINGS
almond paste
apricot or raspberry jam
canned apricots, drained
TO SERVE
beaten egg to glaze
50 g/2 oz icing sugar, sifted
2 teaspoons hot water
toasted flaked almonds, to decorate

Cream the yeast with the water and leave in a warm place for 10 minutes until frothy. Sift the flour into a warm bowl and rub in the lard until the mixture resembles very fine breadcrumbs. Stir in the sugar. Make a well in the centre, pour in the yeast mixture and the eggs and mix to a soft dough, adding a little more water if necessary.

Turn the dough onto a floured surface and knead until smooth and elastic. Wrap in a polythene bag and chill in the refrigerator for 15 minutes. Beat the butter to soften it to a similar consistency to the dough, then form into an oblong shape about 1 cm (½ inch) thick on a sheet of greaseproof paper.

Roll out the dough on a floured surface to an oblong 3 times the size of the butter. Place the butter in the centre, flour it lightly and fold the dough over to enclose it. Seal the open sides by pressing them firmly with a rolling pin.

Turn the dough so that the folds are to the sides and roll it out to a rectangle 3 times as long as it is wide. Fold the top third of the dough down over the centre third then fold the lower third up over the top. Press the edges together.

Return the dough to the polythene bag and chill for a further 15 minutes. Roll and fold twice more, turning the dough each time; sprinkle with flour any patches where the butter may break through. Chill again for 15 minutes.

Roll out the dough thinly and cut into 10 cm/4 inch squares. Shape and fill the pastry squares, choosing from any of the following suggestions:

Stars: Place 1 teaspoon jam or almond paste in the centre of each square. Make a cut from each corner to within 1 cm/½ inch of the centre. Fold alternate points to the centre and secure the tips with beaten egg.

Triangles: Place a little almond paste in the centre of each square, dampen the edges with beaten egg and fold into a triangle.

Crossovers: Make a right-angled cut 1 cm/½ inch in from the edge of 2 opposite corners, extending three quarters of the way along each side. Place an apricot half in the centre and fold over one of the cut corners to meet the cut on the opposite side; secure with beaten egg. Repeat with the opposite corner.

To freeze: Open freeze the pastries until solid, then pack in rigid containers, separating each pastry with an interleaving sheet or piece of foil. Seal, label and return to the freezer for up to 6 months.

To thaw and serve: Place the pastries on a baking sheet and leave to stand at room temperature for about 2 hours until thawed and proved. Brush with beaten egg to glaze and bake in a preheated hot oven (220°C/425°F/Gas Mark 7) for 15 to 20 minutes until golden. Meanwhile, mix the icing sugar with the water to make a smooth, thin glacé icing.

Transfer the pastries to a wire rack and, while still warm, brush with glacé icing and sprinkle with almonds. Serve warm.

Makes 20 to 22

ABOVE: Shaping Danish Pastries: stars and crossovers
RIGHT: Swiss Tartlets; Palmiers

BANANA AND HONEY TEABREAD

This teabread is ideal for using up over-ripe, discoloured bananas. It will keep beautifully moist and fresh for 4 to 5 days after thawing.

125 g/4 oz butter or margarine
50 g/2 oz soft brown sugar
2 tablespoons clear honey
2 eggs, beaten
2 large bananas
175 g/6 oz self-raising flour
1 teaspoon ground mixed spice

Grease a 1 kg/2 lb loaf tin, line with greaseproof paper, then grease the paper.

Cream the butter or margarine, sugar and honey together until light and fluffy. Beat in the eggs a little at a time, adding 1 tablespoon flour after each addition. Peel and mash the bananas, then stir into the creamed mixture. Sift the flour and mixed spice together, then fold into the creamed mixture carefully until evenly incorporated.

Pour into the prepared tin, level the surface and bake in a preheated moderate oven (180°C/350°F/ Gas Mark 4) for 1¼ to 1½ hours until firm to the touch. Leave to cool in the tin for 1 minute, then turn out onto a wire rack and carefully peel off the lining paper. Turn the cake the right way up and leave to cool completely.

To freeze: Wrap the teabread in a polythene bag, seal, label and freeze for up to 2 months.

To thaw and serve: Unwrap the teabread and leave to stand at room temperature for 4 hours. Serve sliced, with butter.

Serves 6 to 8

SWISS TARTLETS

This mixture can also be piped into fingers on a baking sheet and sandwiched together with jam when cool. The ends can then be dipped in melted chocolate.

175 g/6 oz butter or margarine
50 g/2 oz icing sugar
½ teaspoon vanilla essence
50 g/2 oz cornflour
125 g/4 oz plain flour
TO SERVE
a little icing sugar
1 tablespoon redcurrant jelly

Cream the butter or margarine, icing sugar and vanilla together until light and fluffy. Sift in the cornflour and plain flour and work the ingredients together until a paste is formed. Add a little extra plain flour if the mixture is very soft. Spoon into a piping bag fitted with a 2 cm/¾ inch fluted nozzle.

Put 12 paper cases into patty tins and pipe a whirl of the mixture into each paper case. Chill for 30 minutes.

Bake in a preheated moderate oven (180°C/350°F/ Gas Mark 4) for 20 to 25 minutes until golden brown. Leave in the tins for 5 minutes, then transfer to a wire rack and leave to cool.

To freeze: Pack the tartlets in a rigid container, separating the layers with interleaving sheets or foil. Seal, label and freeze for up to 6 months.

To thaw and serve: Leave to stand in the container at room temperature for 20 minutes, then sift icing sugar lightly over the tops of the tartlets and put a dot of redcurrant jelly in the centre of each one. Serve as soon as possible.

Makes 12

PALMIERS

Fresh strawberries or jam can be used for the filling instead of raspberries. If using jam, spread or pipe the cream onto half the palmiers, and spread jam over the remaining half. Sandwich together in pairs.

250 g/8 oz puff pastry (total weight)
75 g/3 oz granulated sugar
TO SERVE
150 ml/¼ pint double cream, whipped
125 g/4 oz raspberries
a little icing sugar

Roll out the pastry on a well-sugared surface to a 30 × 25 cm/12 × 10 inch rectangle. Sprinkle with the sugar and press in with the rolling pin. Take the shorter edge of the pastry and roll it up to the centre. Roll up the other side to meet at the centre. Brush with water and press together to join the rolls.

Cut into 1 cm/½ inch slices and place well apart on a dampened baking sheet. Flatten slightly with the palm of your hand. Bake in a preheated hot oven (220°C/ 425°F/Gas Mark 7) for 10 to 12 minutes. Turn the palmiers over when they begin to brown, so that both sides caramelize. Cool on a wire rack.

To freeze: Open freeze the palmiers until solid, then pack in a rigid container, separating each one with an interleaving sheet or foil. Seal, label and return to the freezer for up to 3 months.

To thaw and serve: Leave to stand in the container at room temperature for 15 minutes. Pipe swirls of whipped cream onto half the palmiers, place the fruit on top, then cover with the remaining palmiers. Sift over the icing sugar and serve as soon as possible.

Makes 6

CHOCOLATE CHIP COOKIES

These quick and easy family favourites provide a useful standby in your freezer.

125 g/4 oz butter or margarine
50 g/2 oz soft brown sugar
1 egg, beaten
150 g/5 oz self-raising flour
125 g/4 oz plain chocolate, finely chopped

Cream the butter or margarine and sugar together until light and fluffy. Beat in the egg, then sift in the flour and add the chocolate pieces. Mix thoroughly.

Put 25 teaspoonfuls of the mixture slightly apart on a greased baking sheet and bake in a preheated moderate oven (180°C/350°F/Gas Mark 4) for 15 to 20 minutes until golden brown. Leave on the baking sheet for 1 minute, then transfer to a wire rack and leave to cool.

To freeze: Pack the cookies in a rigid container, separating the layers with interleaving sheets or foil. Seal, label and freeze for up to 6 months.

To thaw and serve: Leave the cookies to stand in the container at room temperature for 20 minutes. Serve as soon as possible.

Makes 25

CHOCOLATE NUT SHORTIES

These delicious little biscuits are best stored in the freezer to keep them away from the family until you need them!

125 g/4 oz butter or margarine
50 g/2 oz caster sugar
125 g/4 oz self-raising flour
1 tablespoon cocoa powder
50 g/2 oz shelled hazelnuts, chopped

Cream the butter or margarine and sugar together until light and fluffy. Sift in the flour and cocoa powder, then add the nuts, reserving a few for decoration. Mix to a firm dough.

Divide the dough into 24 even pieces and roll into small balls with your hands. Place slightly apart on a baking sheet and flatten with a damp fork. Sprinkle the reserved nuts over the top of the biscuits and press in lightly.

Bake in a preheated moderately hot oven (190°C/375°F/Gas Mark 5) for 10 to 15 minutes until golden brown. Leave on the baking sheet for 1 minute, then transfer to a wire rack and leave to cool.

To freeze: Pack the biscuits in a rigid container, separating the layers with interleaving sheets or foil. Seal, label and freeze for up to 6 months.

To thaw and serve: Leave the biscuits to stand in the container at room temperature for 15 minutes. Serve as soon as possible.

Makes 24

MACAROONS

These traditional almond biscuits, with their slightly soft, sticky centres are delicious served with coffee and ices.

250 g/8 oz caster sugar
150 g/5 oz ground almonds
1 tablespoon ground rice
2 egg whites
20 split almonds, to decorate

Mix together the sugar, ground almonds and ground rice. Beat the egg whites lightly, add the dry ingredients and mix to a smooth, firm consistency. Leave to stand for 30 minutes.

Divide the mixture into 20 even pieces. Roll into small balls and place slightly apart on a baking sheet lined with rice paper. Flatten slightly with the palm of your hand, then lightly press a split almond into the top of each one.

Bake in a preheated moderate oven (180°C/350°F/Gas Mark 4) for 15 to 20 minutes. Cool on the baking sheet, then carefully peel off the rice paper.

To freeze: Pack the macaroons in a rigid container, separating the layers with interleaving sheets or foil. Seal, label and freeze for up to 3 months.

To thaw and serve: Leave to stand in the container at room temperature for 20 minutes. Serve as soon as possible.

Makes 20

HAZELNUT OATIES

After thawing, these nutty fingers will keep for 7 to 10 days in an airtight tin.

120 ml/4 fl oz vegetable oil
3 tablespoons malt extract
2 tablespoons soft brown sugar
250 g/8 oz rolled oats
50 g/2 oz shelled hazelnuts, chopped

Pour the oil into a pan, add the malt extract and sugar and heat gently, stirring, until the sugar has melted. Remove from the heat, add the remaining ingredients and mix thoroughly.

Press the mixture into a greased 30 × 20 cm (12 × 8 inch) Swiss roll tin and smooth the top with a palette knife. Bake in a preheated moderate oven (180°C/350°F/Gas Mark 4) for 25 to 30 minutes. Cool in the tin for 2 minutes, then cut into 20 fingers. Cool completely before removing from the tin.

To freeze: Pack the fingers in a rigid container, separating the layers with interleaving sheets or foil. Seal, label and freeze for up to 2 months.

To thaw and serve: Place the hazelnut fingers on a serving plate and leave to stand at room temperature for about 1 hour.

Makes 20

COCONUT FINGERS

These delicious, chewy cakes are quick to thaw and are therefore ideal to keep in the freezer for unexpected guests. If you may need only a few coconut fingers at a time, separate the individual slices with foil or interleaving sheets, so they can easily be removed a few at a time.

125 g/4 oz butter or margarine, softened
125 g/4 oz caster sugar
2 eggs, beaten
125 g/4 oz self-raising flour, sifted
1 tablespoon boiling water
TOPPING
2 egg whites
75 g/3 oz demerara sugar
75 g/3 oz desiccated coconut

Grease a 28 × 18 cm/11 × 7 inch Swiss roll tin, line with greaseproof paper, then grease the paper.

Cream the butter or margarine and sugar together until light and fluffy. Beat in the eggs a little at a time, adding 1 tablespoon flour after each addition. Carefully fold in the remaining flour with a metal spoon, then fold in the water. Turn the mixture into the prepared tin and level the surface.

To make the topping: Whisk the egg whites until stiff. Carefully fold in the sugar and desiccated coconut until evenly incorporated. Spread evenly over the sponge mixture with a fork to give a rough surface.

Bake in a preheated moderate oven (180°C/350°F/Gas Mark 4) for 30 to 35 minutes until the cake springs back when lightly pressed in the centre. Turn out onto a wire rack, carefully peel off the lining paper, turn the cake the right way up and leave to cool. Cut into 20 fingers using a sharp knife.

To freeze: Pack the fingers in a rigid container, separating the layers with interleaving sheets or foil. Seal, label and freeze for up to 2 months.

To thaw and serve: Unwrap the coconut fingers and place them on a serving plate. Leave to stand at room temperature for 20 to 25 minutes. Serve as soon as possible after thawing.

Makes 18 to 20

Chocolate Nut Shorties; Hazelnut Oaties; Chocolate Chip Cookies; Coconut Fingers

EASTER MENU

If you're entertaining family and friends for the Easter weekend, prepare ahead and freeze away a few things to give you time to relax and enjoy the holiday as much as your guests. In the weeks leading up to Easter, all the baking can be taken care of, so that over the weekend you can simply take things from the freezer as and when you want them.

Choose a selection of bakes from this book like scones, breads and biscuits and, if you've time, make your own hot cross buns. Alternatively, buy these festive treats early in the week to avoid later queues at the local bakers, and store them wrapped in foil in the freezer – they taste just as good as fresh hot cross buns after warming through in a preheated oven for a few minutes.

With a little forethought, all the weekend's meals can be taken from the freezer; the secret is to combine both fresh and frozen food so your guests can't tell one from the other – they'll only wonder how you manage to produce such amazing meals without spending time in the kitchen!

The following suggestion for a three-course meal for six people makes an ideal Easter Sunday or Monday lunch. Cream of asparagus soup makes one of the prettiest starters for Spring, with its subtle colouring and delicate flavour. The first English asparagus begins to appear in the shops and markets just in time for Easter. No Easter menu would be complete without English lamb; in this menu it's given an unusual Eastern Mediterranean flavour with cumin, cinnamon, tomatoes and yogurt – perfect with a selection of fresh seasonal vegetables like carrots, potatoes and broad beans, or a Mediterranean pilaf. A light rhubarb fool rounds off the meal perfectly.

CREAM OF ASPARAGUS SOUP

The thin green 'sprue' asparagus is perfectly good for soup-making, and is far less expensive than the bundles of white spears – it also tends to have a slightly stronger flavour. For a more substantial soup float a few croûtons on top just before serving.

25 g/1 oz butter
1 small onion, peeled and chopped
750 g/1½ lb fresh asparagus, trimmed and cut into
   2.5 cm/1 inch pieces
1.2 litres/2 pints well-flavoured homemade chicken
   stock
salt and freshly ground white pepper
125 g/4 oz Brie or Camembert cheese, rind removed
   and diced
few drops of green food colouring (optional)
TO SERVE
150 ml/¼ pint single cream
few slices cooked asparagus (optional)

Melt the butter in a large pan, add the onion and cook gently for 5 minutes without browning. Add the asparagus and cook for 1 to 2 minutes. Pour in the stock, add salt and pepper to taste and bring to the boil. Lower the heat, cover and simmer for about 25 minutes until the asparagus is tender.

Remove from the heat and leave to cool slightly, then work the soup to a purée with the diced cheese in an electric blender or food processor, in batches if necessary. Taste and adjust the seasoning, then add green food colouring to taste, if liked. Leave to cool completely.

To freeze: Pour the soup into a rigid container, leaving 2 cm/¾ inch headspace. Seal, label and freeze for up to 1 month.

To thaw and serve: Leave to stand in container at room temperature for 3 to 4 hours. Transfer soup to a pan and bring to the boil, stirring frequently. Taste and adjust the seasoning, then pour into a warmed soup tureen or individual soup bowls. Swirl the cream on the top and garnish with asparagus slices, if obtainable. Serve immediately.
Serves 6

CYPRUS SPRING LAMB

This is delicious served with a pilaf of rice – made by combining boiled rice with chopped olives, pine nuts and chopped coriander – and a Greek salad of shredded lettuce and cabbage tossed in an olive oil and lemon juice dressing.

2 tablespoons olive oil
2 kg/4½ lb leg of lamb, boned and cut into large cubes
1 large onion, peeled and sliced
2 garlic cloves, peeled and crushed
2 teaspoons ground cumin
500 g/1 lb tomatoes, skinned, seeded and chopped
2 tablespoons red wine vinegar
250 ml/8 fl oz white wine
1 cinnamon stick
salt and freshly ground black pepper
TO SERVE
few coriander leaves
150 ml/¼ pint natural yogurt

Heat the oil in a large flameproof casserole, add the lamb and fry over brisk heat until sealed on all sides. Remove from the pan with a slotted spoon and set aside.

Add the onion and garlic to the pan with the cumin and fry for 5 minutes, stirring frequently. Add the tomatoes, wine vinegar and wine, and bring to the boil, stirring to break up the tomatoes.

Lower the heat, return the lamb to the pan and add the cinnamon and salt and pepper to taste. Cover the casserole with foil, then with a lid and bake in a preheated moderate oven (170°C/325°F/Gas Mark 3) for 2 hours or until the lamb is tender. Cool quickly, then discard the cinnamon.

To freeze: Transfer the lamb mixture to a rigid container, seal, label and freeze for up to 3 months.

To thaw and serve: Leave to stand in the container at room temperature for 4 to 5 hours, then transfer to a large casserole. Cover and reheat in a preheated moderately hot oven (190°C/375°F/Gas Mark 5) for about 50 minutes until bubbling. Taste and adjust the seasoning. Garnish with coriander and hand the yogurt separately.
Serves 6

RHUBARB AND BANANA FOOL

The sharpness of a rhubarb purée, contrasting with a creamy custard and banana, makes a delicate spring dessert.

750 g/1½ lb rhubarb, trimmed and cut into 2.5 cm/
   1 inch lengths
2 tablespooons water
125–175 g/4–6 oz sugar
4 teaspoons custard powder
300 ml/½ pint milk
2 bananas
150 ml/¼ pint double cream
TO SERVE
150 ml/¼ pint double cream, whipped
1–2 bananas, peeled and thinly sliced

Put the rhubarb in a large pan with the water and sugar to taste. Cover and simmer gently for 30 minutes or until the rhubarb is very soft. Remove from the heat and cool slightly, then work to a purée in an electric blender or food processor.

Mix the custard powder to a paste with a little of the milk. Bring the remaining milk to just below boiling point, then add to the custard paste, stirring. Return to the pan and cook, stirring constantly, until thick. Fold into the rhubarb purée. Leave until cold, stirring occasionally.

Peel and mash the bananas, then fold into the rhubarb mixture. Whip the cream until it will stand in soft peaks, then fold into the rhubarb mixture. Taste for sweetness, adding a little more sugar if necessary.
To freeze: Transfer the rhubarb fool to a rigid container, seal, label and freeze for up to 3 months.
To thaw and serve: Leave to stand in the container at room temperature for 4 hours. Whisk thoroughly, then spoon into 6 serving dishes. Chill in the refrigerator for about 30 minutes before serving; decorate with whipped cream and banana slices.
Serves 6

Cream of Asparagus Soup; Cyprus Spring Lamb served with a rice pilaf

SUMMER

Summer is the busiest season for freezing, so plan to set aside as much time as you can during these three months to stock up your freezer with sunny summer fruits and vegetables – they'll cheer you up later in the year. This is the season when you'll wish you had more freezer space – and may even think of buying a larger freezer, but beware not to invest in one that you can't fill all year round, or you'll find it false economy in high electricity bills.

If your freezer is on the small side, simply freeze away a few of summer's luxuries for later winter treats – apricots, cherries, peaches and strawberries will remind you of long summer days, as will fresh garden peas, beans, courgettes, and fresh herbs – all so expensive and difficult to obtain at other times of the year.

VEGETABLES IN SEASON

Artichoke, Globe*	Cucumber*
Aubergine*	Herbs*
Beetroot	Horseradish*
Bean, broad	Lettuce*
Bean, French*	Marrow
Bean, runner*	Mushroom
Broccoli, sprouting*	Okra*
	Onion
Cabbage	Pea*
Carrot	Pepper*
Cauliflower*	Potato*
Celery	Radish
Courgette*	Sweetcorn
	Tomato*

FRUIT IN SEASON

Apple	Lemon
Apricot*	Lime
Avocado*	Loganberry*
Banana	Mango
Blackberry	Melon*
Cherry*	Nectarine*
Currant: black, red and white*	Orange
	Papaya
Date	Peach*
Fig	Pear
Gooseberry	Persimmon*
Grape*	Pineapple
Grapefruit	Plum
Greengage	Raspberry*
Kiwi fruit	Strawberry*

*Freezing instructions given in this section

Artichoke, Globe

The globe artichoke was introduced into Britain from Europe and, until recently, has been considered a vegetable for the wealthy. It is a member of the thistle family, and there are three main varieties. The green artichoke is the one most commonly grown in this country (particularly in southern England). The purple variety, which is also grown in England, is similar to the green, but has purple tinges on its leaves. With both these varieties, only the heart and the fleshy part at the base of the leaves are eaten. Poivrades are very small tender artichokes which are eaten whole. They are mostly grown in France and Italy and are not generally available in Britain, although you may see some imported ones in specialist markets.

Globe artichokes can be grown in the garden, particularly in the warmer southern counties. If you do not grow your own, look for them in the shops and markets from the end of May; they should be at their best for freezing during July and August.

Selecting for freezing: Gather artichokes from the garden just as they begin to open and before they become so large that mauve tufts appear. Remove the central artichoke first to encourage the side ones to mature, cutting about 13 cm/6 inches down the stalk.

Only the best quality artichokes are worth freezing, so select first-class artichokes from a reputable green-grocer or market gardener. Imported varieties from Europe and America are available, but look for English artichokes for freshness. The leaves should be stiff, and only just slightly open. Avoid any that are fully open, discoloured or with fuzzy leaves. A good test is to pick them up – they should weigh heavy, an indication that the leaves are tightly packed.

Preparation for freezing: Once cut, artichokes do not keep at all well, so freeze immediately after harvesting or purchase, and work quickly in a cool kitchen. If you are freezing a large quantity and they begin to wilt, soak in iced water for an hour or so to revive them.

Pull off the coarse, outer leaves then, with a sharp knife, trim the stalk level with the base and cut off the pointed top (do not remove chokes at this stage – it is easier to do this when the artichoke has been boiled). Cut off the spiky tops of the leaves with kitchen scissors. Immediately wash or soak in cold water to remove grit between leaves, drain, then rub all cut surfaces with lemon to prevent discoloration.

To freeze: Globe artichokes may be frozen whole, or as artichoke hearts.

Whole artichokes: Grade artichokes into sizes, then plunge 4 to 6 at a time into a large pan of boiling water to which a little lemon juice has been added. Blanch for 5 to 7 minutes according to size. Drain, cool quickly in iced water, then drain thoroughly by standing upside-down. Pack the artichokes into rigid containers. Seal, label and freeze for up to 12 months.

Artichoke hearts: Cook whole prepared artichokes in boiling water with salt and lemon juice until tender (between 20 and 40 minutes depending on size). Drain, leave until cool enough to handle, then pull off the leaves and discard the choke to reveal the heart. Leave to cool completely, then pack in rigid containers, separating the layers with interleaving sheets or foil. Seal, label and freeze for up to 6 months.

To thaw and serve: *Whole artichokes:* Plunge frozen artichokes into a large pan of boiling salted water, bring back to the boil and simmer for 5 to 10 minutes according to size, until the base feels tender when pierced with a skewer and the leaves will pull away easily. Drain thoroughly, then serve immediately as a starter with melted butter or Hollandaise sauce. Or serve hot or cold with a vinaigrette dressing. Alternatively remove the chokes and inner leaves, fill the cavity with a savoury stuffing and bake in the oven.

Artichoke hearts: Leave to thaw in covered container at room temperature for about 4 hours. Serve cold as a starter with a vinaigrette or other cold dressing, or use in salads, casseroles, omelettes, quiches and baked dishes (artichoke hearts go particularly well with cheese sauce). Alternatively fry in butter and serve hot as a vegetable accompaniment.

Freezing globe artichokes and French beans

Aubergine

Otherwise known as eggplant or eggfruit because of its shape, the aubergine has only recently become a popular vegetable in Britain.

The aubergine most frequently grown and imported into Britain is the most common type – glossy and purple-skinned, shaped rather like an overgrown egg – but there are many other shapes and sizes, from the thin, elongated 'slim jim' which is streaky purple and white in appearance, to the rarer white eggplant. All varieties need long hours of sunshine if they are to ripen and are best grown in shelter under glass in this country. Some aubergines are grown commercially here – in hothouses – but the majority on sale are imported from the Canary Islands, Kenya, Holland, Israel and the southern Mediterranean countries.

All aubergine varieties are suitable for freezing. They may be frozen raw (sliced), but owing to their high water content, they are often more successful frozen in made-up dishes such as moussaka and ratatouille – see also Aubergines with Capers (page 77), Turkish Stuffed Aubergines (page 87), Ratatouille Tarts (page 88) and Algerian Lamb (page 82).

Aubergines are now sold in most supermarkets and greengrocers, and on market stalls. For freezing, look for best-quality homegrown and imported ones in July and August – there is often a glut and bargains are to be had; these are well worth freezing for the winter when aubergines become prohibitively expensive.

Selecting for freezing: If you grow your own aubergines, gather them when they are fully coloured, but still slightly soft – they should feel 'springy' when gently pressed with the fingers. Don't be tempted to leave them too long on the plant just to obtain larger ones – they will become dry and hard.

Select aubergines for the freezer at your greengrocer or market with care. Choose only those with smooth, shiny skins and a firm feel; any that are wizened, dry or wrinkled, or that have brown or bruised patches are well past their best. July and August are the best months for aubergines, in terms of both quality and price. By September they may be less expensive, but they are usually bitter in flavour.

Preparation for freezing: Young aubergines can be left unpeeled; older ones may be peeled, according to taste. Prepare and freeze them in a cool kitchen as soon as possible after harvesting or purchase – they soon become soft and wrinkled, especially if kept in a warm atmosphere. Wash under cold running water, dry thoroughly on kitchen paper, then slice off the stalk end (including the green cap) with a sharp stainless steel knife. Work quickly, preparing only a few aubergines at a time as the flesh quickly turns brown.

For freezing raw, aubergine flesh can be cut into slices or diced, according to intended future use. Slicing is the usual method for freezing: cut either diagonally or horizontally across to make ovals or rounds, about 1 to 2 cm/½ to ¾ inch thick. Diced flesh should be the same thickness as slices. Immediately after slicing or dicing, the aubergines must be degorged. This draws out the bitter juices from the flesh and helps prevent it absorbing too much oil when fried. To degorge aubergines, put slices or diced flesh in a colander and sprinkle each layer lightly with salt. Cover with a plate, put heavy weights on top and leave to stand for about 30 minutes. Rinse under cold running water, drain and dry thoroughly on kitchen paper.

To freeze: Immediately after preparation, plunge into boiling water to which a little lemon juice has been added and blanch diced flesh for 3 minutes, slices for 4 minutes. Drain, cool quickly in iced water, then drain again thoroughly and pat dry with kitchen paper. Open freeze slices until solid, then pack in polythene bags or in rigid containers, separating layers with interleaving sheets or foil. Seal, label and return to the freezer for up to 9 months. Diced aubergines can be packed straight into polythene bags without open freezing; storage time is the same.

To thaw and serve: Leave to thaw in wrappings at room temperature until just beginning to soften; care must be taken not to leave them too long or they will discolour. As soon as they feel soft, unpack them and pat as dry as possible with kitchen paper. Frying in oil is the usual cooking method, and aubergines will absorb less oil if they are first coated in seasoned flour or batter. Serve hot as a vegetable accompaniment or use in other made-up dishes.

Bean, French

Until recent years, the French beans available in this country were mostly imported from Europe and regarded as something of a luxury vegetable, but they are now grown here commercially on quite a large scale, especially in East Anglia. The fact that they freeze so well makes them one of the best vegetables to grow in the garden, and even the smallest plot will produce a substantial quantity of beans because they are such heavy croppers. Most varieties are suitable for freezing, from dwarf to kidney, so called because of the kidney shape of its seeds. Stringless varieties such as Sprite are particularly good for freezing, so too are the round-podded ones nicknamed 'bobbi' beans. All French beans freeze successfully raw, but for convenience they can also be frozen in made-up dishes, for example with sauces and other vegetables – see French Bean and Tomato Casserole (page 86) and Stir-Fried Summer Vegetables (page 87).

Selecting for freezing: Homegrown French beans are in season from June to September. Pick them from the garden when they are young and tender; they should be a maximum length of 10 cm/4 inches. Any longer than this and they will be dry and stringy. Beans for freezing should snap cleanly when you break them open, and the insides of the pods should be juicy, with small seeds.

Imported French beans are available in good supermarkets and specialist greengrocers for most of the year, but these are generally expensive; for home freezing, buy English varieties, available from June and throughout the summer months. Shop early in the season to be sure of buying the youngest, freshest beans and select the thinnest possible as these are more likely to be stringless and tender.

Preparation for freezing: Freeze as soon as possible after picking or purchase. Young and tender French beans can be left whole. Top and tail them, then wash thoroughly under cold running water. Larger beans should be sliced before freezing; after topping, tailing and washing, cut them diagonally into 2.5 cm/1 inch lengths, removing any strings as you work.

To freeze: Grade whole beans into sizes if necessary, and deal with whole beans and slices separately. Plunge into boiling water and blanch for 3 minutes for whole beans, 2 minutes for slices. Drain, cool quickly in iced water, then drain and pat dry with kitchen paper. Open freeze on trays until solid, then transfer to polythene bags to make 'free-flow' packs. Seal, label and return to the freezer for up to 12 months.

To thaw and serve: Plunge frozen beans into boiling salted water, bring back to the boil and simmer for 7 minutes for whole beans, 5 minutes for sliced beans. Drain, then serve immediately tossed in melted butter, herbs and seasonings according to taste. Alternatively cook the beans from frozen in a melted butter and herb mixture without first boiling in water, if a crunchier texture is preferred.

Bean, Runner

Nicknamed 'scarlet' runners because of their pretty red flowers and 'stick' beans because they twine themselves naturally up long poles or sticks, runner beans have been grown in England since the 17th century. Nowadays runner beans are one of the most popular vegetables for the home gardener, and the heaviness of their crop to ground space makes them perfect candidates for freezing. Most varieties are suitable for freezing, but Enorma, Streamline, Scarlet Emperor, Kelvedon Marvel and Crusader are amongst the most successful, so too are the white-flowered White Achievement and the pink-flowered Sunset, both of which tend to go stringy less quickly.

Commercially grown runner beans start appearing in the shops and markets early in July; these are the homegrown varieties which come mostly from the Home Counties and East Anglia. Imported runner beans are also available at other times of the year from Cyprus and Kenya, Egypt and Spain, but these are invariably expensive and hardly worthwhile buying for freezing.

Selecting for freezing: Pick runner beans from the garden before they have become too long and stringy, and before the seeds are visible through the pod. To encourage new flowers and subsequently more beans, it is essential to pick as frequently as possible. It is therefore best to pick and freeze in small batches continually throughout the summer months. Do not freeze end-of-season tough beans or ones which have been attacked by frost.

Buy runner beans for freezing from the beginning of July. Look for young, fresh beans which snap cleanly when you break them open with your fingers; the seeds inside should be small and succulent-looking. Avoid any beans which have slug damage, and those which are old, tough and leathery. Although they are available all over Britain in greengrocers and markets, the best place to buy fresh runner beans for freezing is at pick-your-own farms, then you can be sure of their freshness.

Preparation for freezing: As soon as possible after picking or purchase, top and tail, then wash thoroughly under cold running water. Remove strings on either side by peeling lengthways with a vegetable peeler or small sharp knife (very young beans may not need stringing). Young, small beans can be left whole, but most beans are best sliced. Cut into slices about 2.5 cm/1 inch thick, either horizontally or diagonally.

To freeze: Grade young whole beans into sizes if necessary. Plunge into boiling water and blanch for 3 minutes for whole beans, 2 minutes for sliced ones. Drain, cool quickly in iced water, then drain and pat dry with kitchen paper. Open freeze on trays until solid, then transfer to polythene bags to make 'free-flow' packs. Seal, label and return to the freezer for up to 12 months.

To thaw and serve: Plunge frozen beans into boiling, salted water, bring back to the boil and simmer for 7 minutes for whole beans, 5 minutes for sliced beans. Drain, then toss immediately in melted butter, with herbs and seasonings according to taste.

Broccoli, sprouting (calabrese)

Of all the different types of broccoli, only the green sprouting variety known as calabrese is really successful in the freezer. Calabrese is the least hardy of the broccolis. Grown from seed in late March or early April, it is extremely susceptible to frost, so is best kept under glass until planting out in June for a summer harvest. Best varieties for freezing are Express Corona and Green Comet.

Calabrese comes into the shops in July and is then widely available until the winter when it is killed off by frost. Most supplies are homegrown, although some are imported from the continent, particularly Italy. For freezing, it is best to buy homegrown calabrese as this is likely to be the least expensive.

Selecting for freezing: Pick at frequent intervals from July onwards to encourage growth right through until October. Harvest central heads first to promote development of side shoots. Snap the shoots off with your hands when they are no longer than about 30 cm/12 inches. Buy only best-quality calabrese for freezing. There should be no wilted, yellow or damaged leaves, the stalks should be no more than 2.5 cm/1 inch thick and snap cleanly. Buy early in the morning when the heads are fresh, from a farm shop if possible.

Preparation for freezing: As soon as possible after picking or purchase, cut away outer leaves and trim any thick or woody stems. Wash thoroughly in salted water, then rinse under cold running water.

To freeze: Grade sprigs according to thickness and freeze in batches. Plunge into boiling water and blanch for 4 minutes for thick stems, 3 minutes for medium and 2 minutes for thin. Drain, cool quickly in iced water, then drain and pat dry with kitchen paper. Pack in rigid containers, alternating heads (do not pack in polythene bags as frozen calabrese is very fragile). Seal, label and freeze for up to 12 months.

To thaw and serve: Plunge frozen stems into boiling, salted water, bring back to the boil and simmer for 3 to 7 minutes according to size; do not overcook, broccoli should still be slightly crisp. Drain, then serve immediately tossed in butter, lemon juice and freshly ground black pepper. Or coat in a cheese sauce.

Cauliflower, summer

There are two main types of cauliflower grown in Britain, summer cauliflower which is in season from June to November, and winter cauliflower in season from October to June; it is therefore an all-year-round vegetable and, some would say, hardly worth freezing. However cauliflowers freeze well, and if there is a glut in your garden or in the shops, they are certainly worth freezing – especially in made-up dishes.

Both summer and winter cauliflowers are suitable for freezing and are virtually identical except that the summer varieties tend to have slightly more open curds. Best summer varieties for freezing are Alpha, Snow King, Snowball and All Year Round. If seedlings are planted out in the garden in March or April, the cauliflowers should be ready for harvesting in June or July. Pick them for freezing early morning. For freezing instructions, see Cauliflower, winter (page 154).

Courgette

Often known by their Italian name of zucchini, courgettes are miniature marrows. They were created as recently as the 1950's and have become increasingly popular. Home produced supplies of courgettes are plentiful from June through to September and October, but the produce best for freezing, with the firmest flesh and best flavour, is most abundant early in the season. Courgettes have a high water content, which limits their possibilities for the freezer. Any large fruits are best frozen ready cooked in such dishes as ratatouille or with a well-flavoured stuffing. See also Iced Courgette Soup (page 74), Ratatouille Tarts (page 88), Stir-Fried Summer Vegetables (page 87), Courgette Cheesecake (page 89).

Given plenty of sun, shelter and water, courgettes are easy to grow and crop heavily at home; both green and yellow varieties are available. Some farms offer pick-your-own courgettes at very reasonable prices.

Selecting for freezing: Harvest or buy only small, very young courgettes, since these have the best flavour and lowest water content. Ideally, cut young courgettes from the garden which still have their yellow flowers attached – the more you cut them the heavier the crop will be. For all courgettes, check that the skins are firm and shiny all over, and free from blemishes.

Preparation for freezing: Prepare and freeze courgettes within 24 hours of picking or purchase. Wipe them or wash, if necessary, then trim the ends but do not peel them. They can then be left whole or cut in half lengthways. Large courgettes are best cut into 1 cm/½ inch slices or chunks; they can also be frozen as a purée: slice thinly, boil in a little salted water until tender, then work in an electric blender or food processor until smooth.

To freeze: *Whole courgettes, halves, chunks and slices:* Plunge whole courgettes into boiling water, blanch for 2 minutes, then drain and plunge into iced water to cool quickly. Drain again, then dry with kitchen paper. Pack in usable quantities in polythene bags, seal, label and freeze for up to 9 months. Treat halves, chunks and slices in the same way, blanching for 1 minute.
Courgette purée: Pack in usable quantities in rigid containers, leaving 2 cm/¾ inch headspace. Seal, label and freeze for up to 6 months.

To thaw and serve: *Whole courgettes, halves, chunks and slices:* Thaw in wrappings at room temperature for about 2 hours. Slice whole ones, then sauté slices and chunks in butter and oil to make an excellent vegetable accompaniment, either alone or sprinkled with herbs and seasonings, or coated in a batter. Courgette chunks and slices can also be added from frozen to a ratatouille base of tomatoes, onions and aubergines, or to any casserole near the end of cooking time. Halves can be stuffed and baked.
Courgette purée: Thaw in wrappings at room temperature for 2 hours, then heat through gently in a pan with a knob of butter, herbs and seasonings to taste.

Freezing sprouting broccoli (calabrese) and courgettes

Cucumber

Once considered a gourmet's treat, the 'cow cumber' as it was known, only became widely available – in Victorian times. Both outdoor 'ridge' cucumbers and the greenhouse varieties can be home grown for freezing. Because of its high water content, the cucumber does not freeze successfully untreated. When sautéed quickly in butter and/or made into a purée for later use in soups and sauces, however, it can be frozen. Freeze as instructed below, or in a ready-made dish such as Cucumber and Mint Sorbet (page 75) or Poacher's Salmon (page 79).

Selecting for freezing: Choose cucumbers for freezing in July and August when the crop is at its peak. Select firm produce with no soft or mouldy patches. For ease of preparation, choose cucumbers that are as straight as possible, but look out for good misshapen bargains which are ideal for freezing if firm and undamaged.

Preparation for freezing: Peel the cucumbers using a sharp knife or potato peeler, then chop them and work to a purée in an electric blender or food processor, or pass them through a vegetable mill.

To freeze: Pack cucumber purée in usable quantities in rigid containers, leaving 2 cm/¾ inch headspace. Seal, label and freeze for up to 2 months.

To thaw and serve: Thaw in container at room temperature for several hours, then use in hot or cold soups and sauces.

Horseradish

Horseradish is an aromatic, highly flavoured root which is easily grown in even the poorest garden soil. Horseradish freezes well, but if freezer space is short, it will keep in the refrigerator if grated and packed in screw-top jars with sugar and vinegar.

Selecting for freezing: Dig only roots of the current year's growth – old ones are liable to be woody. Avoid very gnarled or damaged roots.

Preparation for freezing: Trim, clean thoroughly using a scrubbing brush under cold running water, then grate. Sprinkle immediately with white wine vinegar.

To freeze: Pack in usable quantities in rigid containers, seal, label and freeze for up to 6 months.

To thaw and serve: Thaw in the container, either in the refrigerator overnight or at room temperature for about 3 hours. To make horseradish sauce, mix with soured or whipped double cream and add salt, pepper and sugar to taste. As well as beef, horseradish goes well with smoked mackerel, shellfish and cabbage; it can also be used in salads.

Lettuce

Lettuce is available in a wide range of forms from the soft round types such as Arctic King and Buttercrunch to crisp Iceberg and the crunchy long-leaved Cos. Because lettuce has a very high water content and loses its crispness when frozen, it cannot be frozen for later use in salads. However, tender hearts may be frozen for use in soups – if you have excess garden supplies. It is not worth buying lettuce for freezing.

Selecting for freezing: Select perfect quality, tight lettuce hearts, preferably of a crisp, crunchy variety. Check that the leaves show no traces of brown and have not been attacked by garden pests.

Preparation for freezing: Trim off any wilted, loose or damaged leaves.

To freeze: Plunge into boiling water and blanch for 2 minutes, then drain, plunge into iced water and cool quickly. Drain again, gently squeezing out as much water as possible. Pack in usable quantities in polythene bags, seal, label and freeze for up to 6 months.

To thaw and serve: Lettuce is best used straight from the freezer. Add the frozen hearts to soups and sauces, puréeing the mixture in an electric blender or food processor once the lettuce has thawed. Lettuce soup flavoured with dill is particularly good.

Okra

Okra is a green seed-filled pod vegetable native to Africa. It is also called 'lady's fingers' because of its delicately pointed shape, and known as bhindi in Asia, where it is a popular curried vegetable. Fresh okra is becoming more widely available in Britain, and is most plentiful in June, July and August. Most supplies are imported from the Mediterranean and Middle East, but okra can be grown here in a greenhouse. It freezes well both raw and in made-up dishes such as Rosy Bacon with Okra (page 84).

Selecting for freezing: Choose small pods, 5 cm/2 inches long at the most. The pods must not be damaged – if they are split the juices may leak out during freezing. Avoid any shrunken pods or those marked with brown patches.

Preparation for freezing: Simply trim the stems with sharp kitchen scissors or a knife, taking care to avoid piercing the main part of the pod.

To freeze: Blanch the pods by plunging them into boiling water for 3 minutes. Drain, cool quickly in iced water, then drain again and pat dry with kitchen paper. Pack the pods in usable quantities in rigid containers or polythene bags, then seal, label and freeze for up to 12 months.

To thaw and serve: Okra can be used from frozen in casseroles, curries and soups. It is particularly good in hot, spicy mixtures. Alternatively, simmer from frozen for 6 to 8 minutes until tender, and serve them on their own as a vegetable accompaniment.

Pea

Peas are justly one of the most popular of all vegetables – particularly in frozen form. Along with many other vegetables, they were introduced to Britain by the Romans.

Most of the peas on sale in Britain are home grown and come from Worcestershire, Yorkshire and the East of England. July is the peak freezing month for homegrown peas, but the season lasts from June to October and imported peas are available at other times of year. Freeze podded peas as free-flow packs (below) or in made-up dishes such as casseroles and soups. See also Purée Clamart (page 86). Early in the season, peas are available for eating in the pod. These flat mangetout peas, also known as snow or sugar peas, specially cultivated for their taste, also freeze exceptionally well – see Stir-Fried Summer Vegetables (page 87) and French-Style Mangetouts (page 86).

All kinds of peas are easy to grow in the garden, and are increasingly available from pick-your-own farms. Sometimes farm shops sell fresh peas shelled and ready for freezing. Good varieties to grow yourself or to look out for are Kelvedon Wonder and Little Marvel, both of which are early croppers, and Lord Chancellor which is a marrowfat maincrop pea. Oregon Sugar Pod is an excellent mangetout variety.

Selecting for freezing: _Podded peas:_ It is vital to freeze produce that is young and tender. For this reason pick young pods which are slightly plump but not tight and overfull, and avoid any brown, yellow, shrivelled or damaged pods. When buying peas, make certain they have been freshly picked that morning, otherwise they will most probably have lost their sweetness. Buy them from pick-your-own farms or farm shops for guaranteed freshness.

Mangetout: Choose pods that are flat and shiny, with no large peas inside, and no brown or soft patches. Break a pod in half to check that it snaps cleanly and that its sides are not stringy. It is perfectly acceptable to buy mangetout for freezing from a reliable retailer, since they do not deteriorate so quickly as other peas.

Preparation for freezing: _Podded peas:_ To preserve flavour, it is essential to prepare and freeze them as soon as they have been picked. Shell the peas, popping the pods at the pointed end for ease.

Mangetout: On the day of picking or purchase, top and tail the pods with kitchen scissors if necessary.

To freeze: _Podded peas:_ Blanch immediately after shelling by plunging them into boiling water for 1 minute. During blanching shake the basket well to ensure even heat distribution. Drain, cool quickly in iced water, then drain again thoroughly. Open freeze on trays until solid, then pack in polythene bags as 'free-flow' packs. Seal, label and return to the freezer for up to 12 months.

Mangetout: Blanch by plunging into boiling water for 30 to 60 seconds. Drain, cool quickly in iced water, then drain again. Pat dry with kitchen paper, then pack in usable quantities in polythene bags. Seal, label and freeze for up to 12 months.

To thaw and serve: _Podded peas:_ To serve as a vegetable accompaniment, cook from frozen in boiling salted water for 4 minutes until tender. The addition of herbs or spices, such as mint or nutmeg, will enhance their flavour. For use in soups and casseroles, peas can be used from frozen. Add to a casserole 15 minutes before the end of the cooking time, to prevent them going mushy.

Mangetout: Cook from frozen in boiling salted water for about 3 minutes, then serve with freshly ground black pepper and a knob of butter. Alternatively, thaw at room temperature for about 1 hour then stir-fry in butter until just tender.

Pepper

Sweet peppers, and their near relations, red and green chillis, originally came from South America. They are now available in Britain nearly all year, but the season is at its peak in August when homegrown peppers are on the market. As well as the familiar green pepper, and its ripe red version, yellow and purple varieties are available.

Chillis look like small, slimline sweet peppers, but are much hotter and spicier in flavour. You may have to look for them in specialist and oriental stores. If freezer space is short, chillis can be dried for storage.

Both peppers and chillis are easily and successfully frozen both raw and in made-up dishes such as Prawn and Pepper Vol-au-Vent (page 79), Ratatouille Tarts (page 88). Gardener's Pizza (page 88) and Stir-Fried Summer Vegetables (page 87). If you have a green-house or very sheltered, sunny garden, it is worth growing your own pepper crop. The peppers, which need very similar growing conditions to tomatoes, can be harvested green, or left on the plants for a further 2 or 3 weeks until they ripen and turn red.

Selecting for freezing: Choose firm, shiny peppers and chillis without wrinkles or damaged areas. If peppers are to be frozen sliced or chopped, it is well worth looking out for bargains in oddly shaped fruit.

Preparation for freezing: Peppers and chillis should be frozen as soon as possible after purchase to retain their juiciness and flavour.

Peppers: Wash or wipe well. Cut in half and remove the stalk, fleshy base, seeds and membranes, then dice or cut into strips. Alternatively, remove the stalk and core and cut peppers into rings.

Chillis: Wearing rubber gloves, cut the chillis in half and remove the stalks, seeds and membranes. Avoid touching your mouth, nose or eyes during preparation.

To freeze: *Peppers:* These are one of the few vegetables that can be frozen without blanching, and in fact retain a better colour unblanched, but do not keep so long this way. Immediately after preparation, open freeze on trays until solid, then pack in polythene bags. Seal, label and return to the freezer for up to 6 months. To store in the freezer for up to 12 months, blanch in boiling water for 3 minutes, drain, cool quickly in iced water then pat dry with kitchen paper. Open freeze and pack as for unblanched peppers.

Chillis: Open freeze on trays until solid, then pack in polythene bags. Seal well and double wrap to prevent cross-flavouring, then label and return to the freezer for up to 12 months.

To thaw and serve: *Peppers:* Thaw in wrappings at room temperature for 1 to 2 hours. Use unblanched peppers in salads; add blanched ones to stuffings, rice dishes and vegetable stews. Blanched and unblanched peppers can also be added from frozen to soups, stews, casseroles and quiches, etc.

Chillis: Use from frozen in curries and other spicy dishes, or thaw in wrappings at room temperature for 1 to 2 hours, then mince or chop finely and add in cautious amounts to sauces and dips.

LEFT: Freezing peas and mangetout
RIGHT: Freezing peppers and chillis

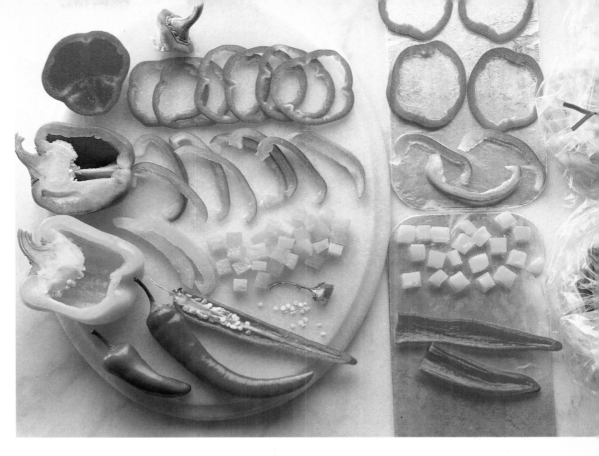

Potato

Potatoes are the edible tubers of a plant closely related to the tomato. Grown by the Peruvian Incas for thousands of years, they were introduced to Europe in the 14th century. It was not until the 18th century that the potato became a staple part of our diet.

Because potatoes keep well and are so plentiful all the year round, they are not worth a great deal of freezer space. They are not successful frozen raw, but boiled new potatoes, chips, croquettes and duchesse potatoes freeze well. See also French-style Potatoes (page 88). Good new potato varieties to grow for freezing are Epicure and Craig's Royal, which crop in June and July; while for chips, croquettes and duchesse potatoes, choose a main crop all-purpose potato such as Desiree or Majestic.

Selecting for freezing: Choose undamaged tubers with no signs of disease or decay.

New potatoes: The best new potatoes to choose for freezing are the small, even-sized ones with skins which are easily removed. Do not leave the crop in the ground too long before harvesting, or the potatoes may be too large and past their best. If buying new potatoes for freezing, avoid the first, most expensive ones on the market, and end of season ones.

Chips: Choose firm, even-sized and well-shaped potatoes which will cut into neat, even and regular-sized chips. Harvest or buy the potatoes in August or September when the crop is at its peak.

Croquette and duchesse potatoes: Select good quality potatoes which will cook evenly and mash smoothly.

Preparation for freezing: *New potatoes:* Immediately after digging, scrub or scrape or, if the skins are hard to remove, plunge the potatoes into boiling water, then drain and rub off the skins.

Chips: Peel the potatoes and cut into chips. Dry in a clean tea-towel before frying.

Croquette and duchesse potatoes: Peel and cut into even-sized pieces.

To freeze: *New potatoes:* Cook in boiling water until only just tender. Drain, cool quickly in iced water, then drain again. Pack in usable quantities in polythene bags, seal, label and freeze for up to 12 months.

Chips: Deep-fry in hot vegetable oil for 2 to 3 minutes, but do not allow to brown. Drain and cool, then open freeze on trays until solid. Pack in polythene bags, seal, label and return to the freezer for up to 3 months.

Croquette and duchesse potatoes: Cook potatoes in boiling salted water, then drain and mash to a smooth purée with butter and egg if wished. For croquettes, shape and coat in egg and breadcrumbs, then deep-fry for 4 to 5 minutes. Cool, open freeze on trays until solid, then pack in polythene bags. Seal, label and return to the freezer for up to 3 months. For duchesse potatoes, pipe rosettes of potato purée onto trays, open freeze, then pack in rigid containers, separating the layers with interleaving sheets or foil. Seal, label and return to the freezer for up to 3 months.

To thaw and serve: *New potatoes:* Always cook from frozen. Either steam them or cook in a covered pan with butter and a few tablespoons of water, turning frequently. Serve with plenty of butter and chopped mint or other herbs, or use for a potato salad.

Chips: Deep-fry chips from frozen in hot oil for 3 to 4 minutes until golden. Drain and serve immediately.

Croquette and duchesse potatoes: Reheat croquettes from frozen in a moderately hot oven (200°C/400°F/Gas Mark 6) for 20 minutes. Bake duchesse potatoes from frozen on a greased baking sheet in a hot oven (220°C/425°F/Gas Mark 7) for 20 to 25 minutes.

Tomato

Tomatoes were first cultivated by the Peruvians and brought to Europe in the 16th century. As well as the ordinary round variety, big beefsteak and tiny cherry tomatoes are available. Although imported out of season from the Channel Islands, Spain, Morocco and the Canaries, the homegrown tomato crop which is at its peak in August is considered to have the best flavour.

Tomatoes freeze best and take up less space, in juice, purée or sauce form; but if you are short of time and there is a glut of tomatoes, it is also possible to freeze whole tomatoes raw, not for salads but for later use in cooked dishes. See also Scampi Provençal (page 77), Ratatouille Tarts (page 88), Turkish Stuffed Aubergines (page 87), Gardener's Pizza (page 88), French Bean and Tomato Casserole (page 86).

As a crop, tomatoes are well worth growing at home if you have a greenhouse, but outdoor crops can be slow or difficult to ripen in the temperamental British climate. Good varieties to cultivate or to look out for when buying for freezing are Moneymaker and Eurocross BB for the greenhouse. Best outdoor ones are The Amateur and Sleaford Abundance.

Selecting for freezing: For freezing whole raw tomatoes, choose firm, evenly ripe medium-sized or cherry tomatoes in the peak of condition. They should be under, rather than over-ripe for preference, and should have no signs of damage or disease. If the tomatoes are to be frozen as juice or purée it is worth looking out for low-price bargains, but if possible, taste a sample before you buy to check that the flavour is good. A homegrown glut of green tomatoes is best made into chutney, rather than frozen.

Preparation for freezing: _Whole tomatoes:_ Wipe the fruit and remove the stalks, but do not peel. Large fruit can be halved if you wish.

Tomato juice: Chop tomatoes roughly, work in an electric blender or food processor until smooth, then simmer over low heat for 5 to 10 minutes. Pass the juice through a sieve to remove pips and skin. Cool.

Tomato purée: Prepare as for juice above, then simmer, uncovered, until a thick purée. Cool.

Tomato sauce: Skin and chop tomatoes and cook gently for about 1 hour with onions, garlic, herbs and seasonings to taste, according to your favourite recipe (basil and marjoram go particularly well with tomatoes). Sieve or blend to a purée, if liked. Cool.

To freeze: _Whole tomatoes:_ Pack in small quantities in polythene bags, then seal, label and freeze for up to 12 months.

Halved tomatoes: Pack in a single layer in rigid containers, seal, label and freeze for up to 12 months.

Tomato juice, purée and sauce: Pour usable quantities into rigid containers, leaving 2 cm/¾ inch headspace. Seal, label and freeze for up to 12 months.

To thaw and serve: _Whole tomatoes:_ Thaw in wrappings at room temperature for 2 hours, then use in cooking in the same way as fresh tomatoes.

Tomato halves: Grill from frozen allowing a little extra cooking time.

Tomato juice: Thaw in container in the refrigerator until a usable consistency, then use in soups, sauces and casseroles, or flavour with Worcestershire sauce and seasonings and serve as a drink.

Tomato purée and sauce: Thaw as for juice above then use as for fresh tomato purée and sauce, and in Italian (particularly pasta) dishes.

Herbs

Most of the popular herbs are very easy to grow in the garden in a sunny sheltered spot. Because most of them are annuals, or herbaceous perennials which die down in winter, it is well worth freezing the crop for winter use. Herbs freeze well, and as a rule, retain their flavour better than dried ones. Herbs can, of course, be added to made-up dishes before freezing.

ANGELICA: The lemon balm is the variety most usually grown as a herbaceous perennial. The leaves can be added to wine and fruit-based drinks, and are a good complement to chicken, fish and veal.

BASIL: This is sweet basil, which goes well with tomatoes and many other savoury foods. It is best grown as an annual and needs a very sunny, well-sheltered spot in the garden or windowsill to thrive.

BAY: Use the leaves of this evergreen in bouquets garnis. Apart from this, they are better dried than frozen for use in sauces, soups, casseroles, etc.

BORAGE: Freeze the flowers and leaves of this easy-to-grow annual for use in fruit and cider cups.

CHERVIL: The celery-like leaves of chervil have a mild aniseed flavour which goes well with eggs, cheese, fish and many vegetables. It is an annual and easy to grow.

CHIVES: The long, hollow leaves of chives have a delicate flavour, and like other members of the onion family grow from underground bulbs. They are well worth freezing and have many uses in salads, omelettes, sauces, etc., and for garnishing.

CORIANDER: Use the feathery leaves of coriander sparingly to flavour both savoury and sweet dishes, including curries, chutneys, lamb, pork, veal, fruit and milk puddings. The coriander plant is best grown as an annual, and needs a sunny, well-sheltered spot.

DILL: Both the feathery, well-flavoured leaves of dill, with their hint of caraway, and the strongly-flavoured seeds, are perfect with fish, eggs, cheese, cabbage and potato dishes. Grow dill as an annual in a sunny spot.

FENNEL: Freeze the feathery dill-like leaves of fennel, and its seeds, both of which have a mild aniseed flavour. Fennel and fish are perfect partners, but this herb is also a good complement to liver, pork, veal and chicken, as well as most vegetables. Fennel seeds can be sprinkled on bread or used in biscuit-making.

MARJORAM: This herb can be grown as any of three species: sweet marjoram; wild marjoram or oregano; and the perennial pot marjoram. Of them all, sweet marjoram is worth growing, because it produces new leaves all year round. Marjoram is a versatile herb and goes well with veal, pork, poultry, fish, eggs, cheese and vegetables, particularly tomatoes.

MINT: An easy-to-grow perennial herb, the perfect complement to lamb, new potatoes, cucumbers and many other foods, mint comes in a range of species from the ordinary spearmint, to delicately flavoured apple mint. Mint does not dry well, but is first class frozen, so is well worth the space in your freezer.

PARSLEY: This most widely used of all herbs comes in two varieties — curly-leaved English parsley, and the flat-leaved 'continental' parsley. Although the seeds are notoriously difficult to germinate, parsley is easy to grow and is biennial. It freezes well, and the stems are as useful as the leaves.

ROSEMARY: The stiff leaves of the rosemary have a delicate fragrance unlike any other herb. Rosemary is an evergreen perennial, but it is not wise to pick the leaves during winter, so it is well worth freezing some for use with lamb, pork, veal and minced beef.

SAGE: The pungent flavour of sage is a perfect foil for the richness of pork or goose. Like rosemary, it is a perennial which is best not picked in winter, and is therefore worth freezing.

SAVORY: This herb has two useful species, the annual summer savory and the perennial winter savory. Both go especially well with pulses — hence savory's common name of bean plant — and can be successfully frozen. Savory also complements the flavour of pork, mushrooms, veal and tomatoes.

SORREL: French sorrel is the only variety worth growing for cooking. Sorrel is excellent in salads, makes a perfect sauce to go with fish, and is also an ideal flavouring for duck, pork and veal. If the crop is large enough it can be cooked and frozen like spinach, but for small quantities it should be frozen in the same way as other herbs.

TARRAGON: The slim, spicy leaves of tarragon are the classic ingredient of a perfect Béarnaise sauce, but are also good with chicken, fish, veal, liver, kidneys, mushrooms and a whole variety of other vegetables. Tarragon is an annual that needs plenty of nourishment for its full flavour to develop: for this reason the flower heads should be pinched out as they form to enhance the flavour of the herb.

THYME: The strong, sweet summer aroma of thyme, which can also be grown as the more subtle lemon thyme, can be easily preserved by freezing. Useful for stuffings, and for flavouring beef, pork, liver and lamb dishes, thyme also goes well with fish and root vegetables, as long as it is sparingly used.

Selecting for freezing: Herbs for freezing should be picked young, abundant and fresh. Ideally pick them early in the morning when leaves are full of flavour.

Preparation for freezing: Working in a cool kitchen, wash herbs only if absolutely necessary, then separate into sprigs. Make up into bouquets garnis as desired, or strip off the leaves and chop them finely by hand or using an electric blender or food processor for large quantities. The only herbs which are best not chopped are bay, rosemary, sage and thyme. Remove dill and fennel seeds from their cases by hanging the flower heads up in a warm place until the seeds drop out.

To freeze: _Sprigs and bouquets garnis:_ Pack in rigid containers or polythene bags, seal, label and freeze for up to 6 months. Or blanch for 1 minute in boiling water, drain and cool quickly, then pat dry with kitchen paper. Pack in rigid containers or polythene bags, seal, label and freeze for up to 6 months.

Chopped leaves: Pack into ice cube trays, open freeze until solid, then remove cubes of herbs. Pack in polythene bags, seal, label and return to the freezer for up to 6 months.

Stems: For stems of parsley and angelica, blanch and freeze as for sprigs.

Seeds: Pack into small waxed cartons or polythene bags, seal, label and freeze for up to 6 months.

To thaw and serve: _Sprigs and bouquets garnis:_ Use from frozen whole, or crumble off the leaves while still frozen and use in recipes as fresh herbs.

Chopped leaves: Use from frozen in cooked dishes or defrost at room temperature for about 1 hour, then use in uncooked dishes and for garnishing.

Stems: Use from frozen in cooked dishes.

Seeds: Use from frozen, either whole or crushed.

Freezing herbs: tarragon, fennel leaves, chives, flat-leaved parsley, lemon balm, mint, bouquets garnis, dill, sage

Apricot

Nearly all of the apricots on sale in Britain in June and July come from Mediterranean countries. As long as they are protected from frost, however, they can be successfully grown in Britain and are best fan-trained against a south-facing wall, or – better still – grown in a greenhouse. The most popular and most successful variety is Moorpark, but Hemskerke is a little hardier. The fruits appear in abundance and are sweet and juicy with an attractive smattering of brown spots on their flushed, orange-yellow skins. As well as freezing successfully on their own or in made-up dishes such as Mishmish Duck (page 80) and Apricot Sorbet (page 90), apricots also make excellent jam. The kernels inside their stones are edible, tasting rather like almonds.

Selecting for freezing: Apricots have a short season, so look for them from late May onwards. Select fruits with a little 'give', a sweet smell and a full rather than pale colour. Larger patches of brown are liable to indicate unwanted bruising. For preference, choose fruit that is a little under-ripe and ripen by keeping in a paper bag in a warm, dark place for 24 to 48 hours.

Preparation for freezing: Whichever method you use, only prepare small quantities of fruit at a time, and brush skinned and cut surfaces with lemon juice as soon as they are exposed – to prevent discoloration.

Whole apricots: Plunge firm fruit into boiling water and leave for 30 seconds. Drain and cool under cold running water, then pare or rub off the skins. Fully ripe fruit can be peeled easily if held under cold water.

Apricot halves and slices: Skin as for whole apricots, then cut each fruit in half, starting from the stalk end. Carefully twist out the stone then slice, if liked.

Stewed apricots: Only remove the skins if they are tough, then halve and stone. Poach the fruit until tender with 120 ml/4 fl oz water for every 1 kg/2 lb fruit, plus sugar to taste. To give an unusual 'almondy' flavour, open a few of the stones with nutcrackers, extract the kernels and add them to the fruit.

Apricot pulp: Skin the apricots, if necessary, then stone and cook them in the minimum amount of water until very tender. Work in an electric blender or food processor or push through a nylon sieve until smooth. The pulp may also be flavoured with the kernels, but sugar is best added at the time of using.

To freeze: *Whole apricots, apricot halves and slices:* Pack in usable quantities in rigid containers and cover with a medium sugar syrup made from 350 g/12 oz sugar to 600 ml/1 pint water with ¼ teaspoon ascorbic acid added. Leave 2 cm/¾ inch headspace, seal, label, and freeze for up to 12 months.

Stewed apricots: Pack in usable quantities in rigid containers, leaving 2 cm/¾ inch headspace. Seal, label and freeze for up to 12 months.

Apricot pulp: Pour into rigid containers in usable quantities, leaving 2 cm/¾ inch headspace. Seal, label and freeze for up to 12 months.

To thaw and serve: *Whole apricots, apricot halves and slices:* Use from frozen for hot puddings and crumbles, or poach in their syrup. Alternatively, leave in container in the refrigerator for 3 to 4 hours before adding to flans, gâteaux and fruit salads.

Stewed apricots: These can be reheated from frozen in a heavy-based pan over low heat, stirring frequently to prevent sticking and adding a little water if necessary.

Apricot pulp: Thaw in container as for whole apricots, then use as for fresh apricot pulp in mousses, whips, ice creams, fillings for cheesecakes and other sweet dishes, adding sugar according to individual recipes. Or add to savoury stuffings and sauces.

Avocado

Although usually one of the most expensive items to buy at the greengrocers, avocados reduce in price during the summer months. Because the flesh turns black in the freezer, avocados cannot be frozen whole, but they can be frozen in made-up dishes such as mousses, soups and ice creams – see also Avocado Sherbet (page 75) and Avocado and Lime Ice Cream (page 90). Alernatively, the flesh can be pulped and frozen and used in composite dishes after thawing.

Selecting for freezing: Look for low-priced imported avocados during July and August. For freezing, the fruit should be just ripe – if pressed gently with the fingertips it should yield slightly. Avoid over-ripe avocados which feel very soft and have black or patchy brown skins. Under-ripe avocados can be ripened at home by keeping in a warm place for a day or two.

Preparation for freezing: Working quickly in a cool kitchen, peel the avocado and cut in half lengthways, using a stainless steel knife to help prevent discoloration, then prise out the stone using the point of the knife. Chop the flesh roughly then, with a stainless steel fork, mash to a pulp with 1 tablespoon lemon juice for each avocado. Prepare one avocado at a time, to avoid discoloration.

One of the most successful ways of freezing pulped avocado which improves its texture, is to combine it with full-fat soft cheese, a bottled blue cheese dressing or double cream. Add seasonings after thawing.

To freeze: Pack as soon as the flesh is pulped, putting the flesh of 2 to 3 avocados in each rigid container. Seal, label and freeze for up to 2 months.

To thaw and serve: Leave to stand in covered container at room temperature for 2 hours. Stir well and use immediately or the pulp will discolour.

Cherry

The cherry season is a short one spanning June and July. This makes cherries well worth freezing, both as raw and poached fruit, and in desserts such as Black Forest Gâteau (page 98) and Cherry and Chocolate Bombe (page 93). Sweet cherries come in a variety of shades from pale, pink-yellow Napoleon cherries or 'Naps', to a red so deep it is almost black, but of these it is the red and black kinds which freeze most successfully. The only sour cherries widely grown are the Morello and Amarelle, and these are red cherries which freeze well.

Sweet cherries are worth trying to grow, particularly in southern parts. Kent, Worcestershire and Herefordshire supply most of our homegrown produce. Since the crop ripens all at once, and must be picked within the space of a week or less, it is important to be prepared for picking and freezing when the moment arrives. Three strongly recommended varieties for freezing are Early Rivers, Merton Bounty, and Merton Bigarreau. The Morello is the best sour cherry to grow.

Selecting for freezing: Look out for red and black cherries on sale from late May onwards and buy them at their best. Ideally, the fruit should be firm, with a good colour and flavour. The skin should not be split or marked with signs of disease. Avoid supplies with lots of leaves and twigs attached, or naked stones interspersed between the fruit.

Preparation for freezing: *Uncooked cherries:* Pick over the fruit and remove any unripe or over-ripe cherries. Remove the stalks, then soak the fruit in iced water for 30 minutes to plump it up. Dry well with kitchen paper, then press out the stones with a cherry stoner or halve and remove the stones.

Poached cherries: Remove the stalks and stones, then poach gently in water until tender but still whole, with sugar to taste.

To freeze: The best method of freezing depends on the type of cherry and use after thawing.

Uncooked cherries: Freeze as free-flow, dry sugar or syrup packs.

Free-flow pack: Suitable for very sweet cherries only. Open freeze on trays, then pack in polythene bags, seal, label and return to the freezer for up to 12 months.

Dry sugar pack: Best for sweet red cherries intended for pie-making. Pack in usable quantities in rigid containers, sprinkling each layer with sugar and allowing 250 g/8 oz sugar for every 1 kg/2 lb fruit, or according to taste. Seal, label and freeze for up to 12 months.

Sugar syrup pack: Suitable for sweet and sour cherries. Pack in usable quantities in rigid containers. Cover sweet cherries with a medium sugar syrup made from 350 g/12 oz sugar to 600 ml/1 pint water, sour cherries with a heavy syrup made from 500 g/1 lb sugar to 600 ml/1 pint water and add 3 tablespoons lemon juice to prevent discoloration. Leave 2 cm/¾ inch headspace, seal tightly, label and freeze for up to 12 months.

Poached cherries: Pack in usable quantities in rigid containers, leaving 2 cm/¾ inch headspace. Seal, label and freeze for up to 8 months.

To thaw and serve: *Uncooked cherries:* Leave to stand in container at room temperature for 3 hours, then use immediately to prevent discoloration. Use free-flow and dry sugar packs for pies, puddings, preserves and jam-making, and for adding to flans and fruit salads. Use cherries in syrup for crumbles, dark fruit salads (e.g. with plums, prunes and black grapes), ices, or sauces. Sour cherries are particularly good steeped in brandy or cherry liqueur, but can also be used for wine-making.

Poached cherries: Thaw in container as for uncooked cherries, then serve cold or reheat gently. The cherries can be sieved or worked in a blender to make a thin purée, useful for flavouring ice creams and mousses.

Freezing apricots and cherries

Currant: black, red and white

Blackcurrants, redcurrants and whitecurrants are all worth freezing. Native to northern Europe, they have been eaten and enjoyed in Britain since the 16th century when they were called 'beyond sea gooseberries' and mistakenly thought to be the source of raisins. Black and redcurrants are derived from a species of the *Ribes* plant, with black and red fruits; white currants are simply an albino version of redcurrants, which explains the similarity in appearance between the two. All three contain plenty of Vitamin C.

Tolerant of frost, currants thrive in all parts of the country, but are at their best and most profuse for only a few weeks in late June to late July or early August. Most supplies offered for sale at shops and market stalls come from Kent, with blackcurrants also from Norfolk and the Midlands. Expensive to harvest, so never inexpensive to buy ready picked, they are a good bargain if you are able to pick your own.

When selecting varieties to pick from fruit farms, or to grow in the garden for freezing and jam-making, look out for blackcurrants named Bokskoop Giant (an early variety), Baldwin and Wellington XXX; for redcurrants named Red Lake, Laxton's No 1 and Rondom (a late, profuse cropper); and whitecurrants by the names of White Giant and White Versailles. As long as they are protected from birds, which eat both buds and fruit, all are easy to grow. Freeze currants on their own as suggested here, or in made-up dishes such as Beef Brisket with Redcurrants (page 83), Summer Pudding (page 97), Blackcurrant Charlotte (page 98), Redcurrant Tansy (page 95), Blackcurrant Parfait (page 95) and Savarin Cassis (page 103).

Selecting for freezing: For all types of currants, choose firm, plump, perfectly ripe fruit with a low proportion of unsuitable or damaged fruit on each bunch or strig. Avoid green or dried-up, wrinkled fruit, and check that the base of the punnet or container is not deeply stained, since this could indicate that the fruit at the bottom is squashed or over-ripe.

Preparation for freezing: Before freezing, all currants must be separated from the stalks that form the strigs. The best and easiest way of doing this is by threading the strigs through the prongs of a fork, then swiftly but carefully moving the fork downwards so that the currants are forced off their stalks.

Whole currants: Pick over the strigged fruit and remove any damaged, imperfectly ripe or over-ripe samples (use over-ripe fruit for stewing). If the fruit is to be used for jam-making at a later date, blanch it in boiling water for 1 minute, drain, cool in iced water, then drain again and dry thoroughly.

Stewed currants: Best for blackcurrants. Stew in the minimum amount of water possible with sugar to taste.

Currant pulp: Stew with the minimum amount of water and with sugar to taste. Pass through a sieve or work in an electric blender or food processor, then sieve to remove the pips.

Currant juice: Suitable for blackcurrants only. Stew in enough water to cover, sieve or work in an electric blender or food processor, then strain through muslin to give a clear liquid.

To freeze: *Whole currants:* These can be frozen in free-flow, dry sugar or syrup packs.

Free-flow pack: Open freeze on trays until solid, then pack in polythene bags. Seal, label and return to the freezer for up to 12 months.

Dry sugar pack: Pack in usable quantities in rigid containers, sprinkling each layer with sugar and allowing 125 to 175 g/4 to 6 oz sugar for every 500 g/1 lb fruit, according to taste. Seal, label and freeze for up to 12 months.

Sugar syrup pack: Pack in usable quantities in rigid containers and cover with a medium sugar syrup made from 350 g/12 oz sugar to 600 ml/1 pint water. Leave 2 cm/¾ inch headspace, seal, label and freeze for up to 12 months.

Stewed currants: Pack in usable quantites in rigid containers, leaving 2 cm/¾ inch headspace. Seal, label and freeze for up to 12 months.

Currant pulp: Pour into rigid containers in usable quantities, leaving 2 cm/¾ inch headspace. Seal, label and freeze for up to 8 months.

Currant juice: Pour usable quantities into rigid containers, leaving 2 cm/¾ inch headspace. Seal, label and freeze for up to 12 months. For children, freeze the juice in lollipop moulds.

To thaw and serve: *Whole currants:* From free-flow, dry sugar and sugar syrup packs, cook from frozen in pies, puddings and other desserts, according to individual recipes. To thaw and use uncooked leave to stand in wrappings at room temperature for 45 minutes, then use in fruit salads, cheesecakes and summer puddings, etc., adding sugar if necessary. Or use blanched whole fruit for making jams and jellies – redcurrant jelly is a perfect traditional accompaniment for game, and also goes well with pork and other rich meats.

Stewed currants: Thaw in container as for whole currants, then serve as a dessert. Or reheat from frozen in a heavy-based pan over the lowest possible heat, stirring frequently to prevent sticking and adding a little water if necessary. Stewed red and white currants are particularly good with a few raspberries added.

Currant pulp: Thaw in container as for whole currants, then use for ice creams, sorbets, mousses and hot and cold dessert sauces.

Currant juice: Thaw in container as for whole currants and drink cold, or reheat from frozen in a heavy-based pan over low heat. If frozen in lollipop moulds, unmould and eat frozen.

Grape

Of all fruits, grapes are probably the most ancient. In Europe, for example, Stone Age man certainly grew them and is thought to have eaten the fruit, rather than use it to make wine. Nowadays, dessert grapes can only be successfully grown in a greenhouse or conservatory in this country, except in very sheltered spots in the south, although grapes for wine-making are grown out of doors. Virtually all of the grapes on sale in Britain are imported.

Good-quality produce is available all year round. Most of the fruit sold in the winter comes from California and South Africa; summer, autumn and early winter supplies come largely from France, Italy, Spain, Israel and North Africa. Summer grapes are the most plentiful – and least expensive – so they are the best grapes to buy for freezing.

Grapes come in two colours, purple and green, which are described respectively as black and white, although the flesh of black grapes is also green. There are very many different varieties, both with and without seeds, and in a range of sizes. The best dessert grapes for freezing are those which are really sweet in flavour: white Muscatels and Almerias, and black hothouse varieties such as Black Hamburghs. Less sweet types can be frozen in brine for use in savoury dishes. Freeze fresh grapes whole and halved as here, or in made-up dishes – see Quail Parnassian (page 80) and Veal Paupiettes with Grapes (page 84).

Selecting for freezing: Choose sweet white or black grapes of a really high quality and with an even bloom on each grape. Check that the bunches do not contain a high proportion of over-ripe or damaged grapes – look particularly for signs of damage or deterioration where the fruit is joined to the stalk. If the grapes are to be frozen unpeeled, test the skins for tenderness.

Preparation for freezing: Grapes may be frozen whole or halved according to size and type.

Whole grapes: Best for seedless grapes or a perfect bunch of larger grapes. For seedless types, remove fruit from stalks, pick over and discard any damaged or low-quality fruit. Do not wash unless absolutely necessary. For a whole bunch, no pre-preparation is necessary, but the fruit must be of the highest quality.

Halved grapes: Remove the grapes from their stalks. pick over and discard sub-standard fruit. Cut each in half, flick out the pips with the point of a sharp knife, then peel off the skin.

To freeze: *Whole grapes:* Open freeze on or off the bunch. Pack single bunches in individual polythene bags, otherwise pack in usable quantities in rigid containers. Seal, label and return to the freezer. Grapes on the bunch will keep for up to 2 months, off the bunch will keep for up to 12 months.

Halved grapes: Freeze in syrup or brine.

Sugar syrup pack: Pack in usable quantities in rigid containers and cover with a medium sugar syrup made from 350 g/12 oz sugar to 600 ml/1 pint water, with ¼ teaspoon ascorbic acid added to prevent discoloration. Leave 2 cm/¾ inch headspace. Seal, label and freeze for up to 12 months.

Brine pack: For savoury dishes pack in usable quantities in rigid containers and cover with brine made from 1 tablespoon salt to 600 ml/1 pint water. Leave 2 cm/¾ inch headspace, seal, label and freeze for up to 12 months.

To thaw and serve: *Whole grapes:* Leave to stand in wrappings or container at room temperature for 2 hours. Serve a bunch of grapes as a dinner table centrepiece or to garnish a cheeseboard. Use grapes off the bunch for fruit salads, or in savoury dishes, particularly with pigeon or other game and fish.

Halved grapes: Thaw in container as for whole grapes, then use in flans, jellies, fruit salads and other desserts, or add to savoury dishes of your choice.

Loganberry

The loganberry is a cross between a Californian wild dewberry (a fruit like a blackberry) and an American raspberry but has a deep claret colour and a sharper flavour. Unfortunately, fresh loganberries are not widely available, but supplies from Kent and Worcestershire are sometimes on sale in markets during July and August.

The best way to obtain loganberries for the freezer is to grow them in the garden or to 'pick-your-own' produce from a fruit farm. The loganberry plant is more like a blackberry than a raspberry, and it is therefore best grown trained on wires in a sheltered sunny place.

Like raspberries, loganberries freeze very well: they retain their shape and flavour even after thawing, and the frozen fruit is far superior to its popular canned counterpart. Second-class fruit is best frozen as a purée which can be used for sauces, ice creams and sorbets, etc. It can also be used to make Loganberry Mousse (page 94).

Selecting for freezing: Loganberries intended for the freezer should be in perfect condition. They should be firm but deep red in colour, with no trace of mould or damage, and they should come away from the plant easily – not have to be pulled off, nor fall off without help. If freezing whole loganberries rather than purée, pick fruit that is just approaching the peak of ripeness.

Preparation for freezing: *Whole loganberries:* If absolutely necessary, wash the fruit in iced water and dry very thoroughly. Pick over the fruit and remove any remaining 'plugs' (the thick white stalks in the centre of the fruit) and any damaged fruit.

Loganberry purée: Wash the fruit, if necessary, then cook with the minimum amount of water. Press through a sieve or work in an electric blender or food processor, then sieve to remove the pips. Sweeten with 125 g/4 oz sugar for every 600 ml/1 pint purée.

To freeze: *Whole loganberries:* These can be frozen in free-flow, sugar or syrup packs.

Free-flow pack: Open freeze on trays until solid, then pack in polythene bags. Seal, label and return to the freezer for up to 12 months.

Dry sugar pack: Pack in usable quantities in rigid containers, sprinkling each layer with sugar and allowing 125 to 175 g/4 to 6 oz sugar for every 500 g/1 lb fruit, according to taste. Seal, label and freeze for up to 12 months.

Sugar syrup pack: Pack in usable quantities in rigid containers and cover with a medium sugar syrup made from 350 g/12 oz sugar to 600 ml/1 pint water. Leave 2 cm/¾ inch headspace, seal, label and freeze for up to 12 months.

Loganberry purée: Pour into rigid containers in usable quantities, leaving 2 cm/¾ inch headspace. Seal, label and freeze for up to 8 months.

To thaw and serve: *Whole loganberries:* Leave to stand in wrappings or container at room temperature for about 2 hours before using in fruit salads, ices and flans, or a traditional Summer Pudding (page 97) instead of blackberries. Or use from frozen in cooked pies, tarts and puddings, adding 10 to 15 minutes to the cooking time to allow the fruit to thaw.

Loganberry purée: Thaw as for whole loganberries, or reheat from frozen in a heavy-based pan over the lowest possible heat, stirring frequently to prevent sticking and adding a little water if necessary. Use for hot and cold sauces, as a basis for ices and mousses and as a flavouring for cheesecakes etc.

Freezing grapes and blackcurrants

Melon

Juicy ripe melons are available virtually all year round in a whole range of shapes and sizes. The best of the melon crop is on sale from midsummer through to mid-autumn, the time when the homegrown fruit (cultivated under glass, in a cold frame or conservatory) is also ready for eating. Although melons have a high water content (which makes them low in calories), all but the water melon can be successfully frozen, and only a little of their fragrance and flavour is lost in the process. See also Melon Ice Cream (page 90).

There are five types of melon worth considering for freezing. The imported cantaloupe, with their sectioned, mottled skins and yellow flesh are on sale from spring onwards, but are at their best in July and August. Charentais are small green-skinned melons, with orange flesh and an outstanding fragrance. They are mostly imported from France, and are normally at their best from August until mid-autumn. Gallia melons have a netted surface like cantaloupes but their flesh is green. They are largely imported from Israel, and are at their best from April to June. The oval honeydew melons, with their bright yellow skin and green flesh, are the ones with the least definite flavour. They are available throughout the year, but are at their best from July to October, and are mostly imported from Europe, Israel and South Africa. Ogen melons from Israel are available from spring through to midwinter, but are at their most prolific in the summer months. They are small, with green flesh as well as skin.

Melons have been grown in temperate Europe since the times of the ancient Greeks and Romans. Because they are frost-tender, they must be suitably protected if grown at home. Charentais and ogens can be tried, and Tiger is a good variety of cantaloupe.

Selecting for freezing: To obtain the best flavour after thawing, choose melons that are perfectly ripe but not over-ripe, and which are firm and undamaged. To test for ripeness, press the melon gently at the 'point' – the end furthest from the stalk. If the fruit is ripe, it should give a little to this pressure. Any under-ripe fruit can be ripened at home by placing it on a sunny windowsill.

Preparation for freezing: Cut the melon into halves or quarters, according to size, and remove the seeds and any fibres left clinging to the flesh. Cut the flesh into cubes or slices, or scoop into balls using a melon baller.

To freeze: _Melon pieces:_ These can be frozen in two different ways.

Dry sugar pack: Pack in usable quantities in rigid containers, sprinkling each layer with sugar and allowing 125 to 175 g/4 to 6 oz sugar for every 500 g/1 lb fruit, according to taste. Seal, label and freeze for up to 12 months.

Sugar syrup pack: Pack in usable quantities in rigid containers and cover with a medium sugar syrup made from 350 g/12 oz sugar to 600 ml/1 pint water. Leave 2 cm/¾ inch headspace, seal, label and freeze for up to 12 months.

To thaw and serve: Leave to stand in container in the refrigerator for about 1 hour, then serve chilled with lemon juice and ginger, or in a fruit salad. Alternatively, thaw for 2 hours and then use for ice cream making.

Nectarine

A nectarine is a peach with a smooth, rosy-red skin. This skin is less furry and therefore more palatable than that of the peach, and the nectarine's flesh is finer in texture, with a more delicate flavour. The tree which gave rise to both the peach and the nectarine was first cultivated centuries ago in China. Most of the nectarine supplies on the market during July and August are imported from the warm climates of the Mediterranean, the Middle East and North America. Nectarines – like peaches – need careful handling to prevent them from discolouring.

For those who like to grow their own produce for freezing, the nectarine is only a practical possibility in a warm, sheltered spot not susceptible to late spring frosts which prevent the fruit from setting. A fan-trained tree on a south-facing wall is ideal, or the tree can, with care, be grown in a greenhouse. Of the varieties readily available, the most successful are Early Rivers, Lord Napier and Pitmaston Orange. Freeze nectarines raw as here, or in made-up dishes, such as Calves' Liver with Nectarines (page 84) and Nectarine Baked Alaska (page 93). In any recipe calling for peaches, you can use nectarines, if preferred.

Selecting for freezing: Nectarines perfect for freezing are firm to the touch with shiny skins. They should be deep red or reddish orange in colour; avoid fruit which is bruised, over-ripe or mushy.

Preparation for freezing: As with apricots and peaches, prepare small quantities (preferably only one) at a time to prevent discoloration. The skin can be left on, in which case it should be thoroughly washed. To remove the skin, pour boiling water over the fruit, leave for 30 seconds only (the fruit should not be allowed to start cooking); drain and cool under cold running water. The skins should then rub off, or be easy to peel away with a small sharp knife. After this, cut each fruit in half, twist the halves in opposite directions to separate the fruit, then remove the stone. The halves may then be sliced, if wished. Brush the pieces all over with lemon juice immediately after exposure to air.

To freeze: Working as quickly as possible, pack the prepared fruit in usable quantities in rigid containers, then cover with a medium sugar syrup made from 350 g/12 oz sugar to 600 ml/1 pint water, or a heavy syrup made from 500 g/1 lb sugar to the same amount of water, according to taste. In both cases, add ¼ teaspoon ascorbic acid to every 600 ml/1 pint syrup to prevent discoloration. Leave 2 cm/¾ inch headspace, seal, label and freeze for up to 12 months.

To thaw and serve: Nectarines frozen in syrup are best thawed in the refrigerator in their sealed containers to help preserve their colour. Allow 3 to 4 hours for thawing, then use the fruit at once in fruit salads, flans and gâteaux. They are also good with ham, cheese and cold savoury dishes. If being used for decoration, add at the last possible minute to prevent unsightly discoloration. Thawed nectarines in syrup can be poached and puréed, then used for ices, mousses and whipped desserts in a similar way to peaches.

Peach

The peach was first cultivated by the Chinese as long ago as 3,000 BC. Its excellent flavour and succulence was not appreciated in Europe until the 1st century AD when it was introduced – probably by the Romans and it has remained popular ever since.

Over the centuries, more than 2,000 different varieties of peach have been cultivated, and the peach is also the parent of the nectarine. Only a handful of varieties are, however, suitable for growing outdoors in Britain, and even so are dependent for success on a warm, sheltered position and luck with the weather. Peregrine and Rochester are the two best varieties to try outdoors. For growing peaches in a greenhouse, use Duke of York or Hale's Early. Because the British climate does not suit the peach ideally, most of the fruit on sale in June, July and August is imported from warmer European countries and the USA.

Peaches, with their furry, pink-flushed skins, are divided into two groups: the cling peaches in which the flesh adheres closely to the stone, and the freestone varieties where the stone is easily separated from the flesh. Of the two, freestone peaches are generally best for freezing, since they are easier to prepare, but cling

peaches can be used for making peach purée. Peaches can be frozen raw as halves, slices or pulp, or in ready-made desserts such as Vacherin aux Pêches (page 97), Peach Charlotte (page 96), Pêches Carmen (page 96) and Peach Gâteau (page 100).

Selecting for freezing: When buying peaches for freezing it is advisable not to buy the first fruit to appear on the market. Later in the season it is usually possible to obtain better flavoured fruit at a lower price. Choose firm, undamaged produce with a sweet, fragrant smell, and check with the supplier that the fruit is of the freestone type. To test for ripeness, examine the stalk end of the fruit: if it is perfectly ripe it will have no trace of green.

Preparation for freezing: As with apricots and nectarines, peaches should be prepared quickly and in small quantities (one at a time) because of the problem of discoloration.

Peach halves and slices: First skin the fruit. Pour boiling water over the fruit, leave for 30 seconds only, then drain and cool under cold running water. Rub or peel off the skin, then halve and remove the stone. Cut into slices, if wished, then immediately brush all cut surfaces with lemon juice.

Peach pulp: Peel and stone the fruit, as for halves and slices. Chop roughly, then mash with a wooden or silver fork, adding 125 g/4 oz sugar and 1 tablespoon lemon juice to every 500 g/1 lb fruit.

To freeze: *Peach halves and slices:* Pack in usable quantities in rigid containers and cover with a medium sugar syrup made from 350 g/12 oz sugar to 600 ml/1 pint water, or a heavy syrup made from 500 g/1 lb sugar to the same quantity of water, according to taste. Add ¼ teaspoon ascorbic acid to every 600 ml/1 pint syrup to prevent discoloration. Leave 2 cm/¾ inch headspace, seal, label and freeze for up to 12 months. *Peach pulp:* Pack in usable quantities in rigid containers, leaving 2 cm/¾ inch headspace. Seal, label and freeze for up to 12 months.

To thaw and serve: *Peach halves and slices:* Leave to stand in covered container in the refrigerator for 3 to 4 hours, then use at once in flans, fruit salads, gâteaux, crumbles and for Peach Melba. If using for decoration, add at the last possible moment to prevent unsightly discoloration. These peaches can also be served with brandy or made into jam, or drained, soaked in spiced vinegar and served as an accompaniment to hot and cold savoury dishes.

Peach pulp: Thaw as for peach halves and slices. Peach pulp is prone to discolour quickly, so is best not used for dishes in which a perfect 'peach' colour is important. Use immediately for ice creams, mousses and sweet sauces, also in savoury stuffings and sauces.

ABOVE: *Freezing peaches and nectarines*
OPPOSITE: *Freezing gallia and canteloupe melons*

Persimmon

The persimmon, also known as the kaki fruit or 'apple of the Orient', is a strange, heavy fruit that looks rather like a large, orange tomato. Beneath its rather leathery skin is a firm, sweet but astringent-tasting orange flesh scattered with a few stony seeds. Persimmons come in two varieties, American and Japanese, and it is the latter that are most usually sold in Britain. Supplies do not, however, come from the East, but stem chiefly from Italy, Europe's largest fruit producer. Look for persimmons in July and August.

Selecting for freezing: Choose firm but ripe fruit with no signs of bruising or other damage.

Preparation for freezing: _Whole persimmons:_ Peel off the skin.

Sliced persimmons: Peel off the skin, then cut the flesh into slices (or chunks), flicking out any seeds with the point of a sharp knife.

To freeze: _Whole persimmons:_ Wrap individually in foil, seal, label and freeze for up to 2 months.

Sliced persimmons: Pack in usable quantities in rigid containers and cover with a heavy syrup made from 500 g/1 lb sugar to 600 ml/1 pint water with 2 teaspoons lemon juice added to prevent the flesh from discolouring. Leave 2 cm/¾ inch headspace, seal, label and freeze for up to 12 months.

To thaw and serve: _Whole persimmons:_ Leave to stand in wrappings at room temperature for 3 hours, then serve alone, with cream or ice cream, or as part of a tropical flan or fruit salad.

Sliced persimmons: Thaw as for whole persimmons, then serve alone, with cream or ice cream, or add to a fruit salad or other fruit dessert.

Raspberry

Raspberries were prized by the Ancient Greeks, but today grow wild on cool, damp hillsides throughout northern Europe. They have been popular in Britain since the 17th century.

Raspberries freeze exceptionally well; their sharp, yet full flavour is excellent and they have a succulent texture. They are also rich in Vitamin C.

The raspberry crop reaches its peak in July. Two thirds of all the fruit bought in Britain comes from Scotland, the remainder largely from Kent and Norfolk. Autumn-cropping canes are being increasingly grown, and it is well worth buying both summer and autumn raspberries for freezing from pick-your-own fruit farms, or from farm shops.

In the garden, raspberries are rewarding and easy to grow, but need protection from birds. If space allows, plant several varieties which fruit at different times to spread the crop as much as possible. For freezing, the best earlies are Glen Cova and Malling Promise. For midseason, choose Lloyd George, Malling Jewel and Norfolk Giant; for autumn, Heritage and September.

Freeze raspberries whole or puréed, or in desserts such as Summer Pudding (page 97), Raspberry Cheesecake (page 98), Raspberry Sorbet (page 90), Pêches Carmen (page 96), Meringue Glacé (page 92), Raspberry and Hazelnut Roll (page 100).

Selecting for freezing: When picking raspberries, always do so when the fruit is completely dry; wet fruit will only freeze successfully as a purée. Pick berries just coming up to their peak of ripeness, which bear no trace of mould, squashiness or uneven ripening. When buying raspberries ready packed in punnets, avoid any that look damp or over-ripe, or have juice leaking from the bottoms of the punnets indicating that the fruit has been squashed and damaged.

Preparation for freezing: Pick over the fruit and discard any mouldy specimens. Remove any plugs from the centres of the fruit, then grade into those suitable for freezing whole and those for puréeing.

Whole raspberries: Need no further preparation.

Raspberry purée: Work through a nylon sieve, or work in an electric blender or food processor, then sieve to remove the pips. If liked, sweeten with 125 g/4 oz sugar to every 500 g/1 lb fruit. Alternatively, cook in the minimum amount of water before puréeing.

To freeze: _Whole raspberries:_ These can be frozen in free-flow or dry sugar packs.

Free-flow pack: Open freeze on trays until solid, then pack in polythene bags. Seal, label and return to the freezer for up to 12 months.

Dry sugar pack: Pack in usable quantities in rigid containers, sprinkling each layer with sugar and allowing 125 to 175 g/4 to 6 oz sugar for every 500 g/1 lb fruit, according to taste. Seal, label and freeze for up to 12 months.

Raspberry purée: Pour usable quantities into rigid containers, leaving 2 cm/¾ inch headspace. Seal, label and freeze for up to 7 months.

To thaw and serve: _Whole raspberries:_ Leave to stand in wrappings at room temperature for 2 hours, then serve still very slightly iced (_frappé_), with added sugar if liked. Whole thawed fruit can also be used in mixed fruit salads, flans, cheesecakes and gâteaux, and for all kinds of decoration. Or it can be cooked from frozen in hot pies and puddings, and used in jam-making. Surprisingly, raspberries also make excellent vinegar.

Raspberry purée: Thaw as for whole raspberries, then use for cold sauces, mousses, ice creams and sorbets. To serve hot, cook from frozen in a heavy-based pan over the lowest possible heat, stirring frequently to prevent sticking and adding a little water if necessary.

Freezing strawberries and raspberries

Strawberry

Strawberries and cream are traditional fare, inseparable from thoughts of high summer. Strawberries with small but flavoursome fruits have grown wild in Europe for many millennia, but the types cultivated today have a much shorter history, dating back from the 18th century when cross-breeding in Holland began a line of large-fruited varieties.

Since these times, strawberries have gradually improved and expanded worldwide: varieties have been developed to spread the length of the season, and perpetual and small, sweet alpine types are also becoming widely grown. In England the main strawberry crop comes largely from Kent and Norfolk and is on sale from May to July. It is also worth looking out for autumn crops in September, particulary if the weather is good. As well as the homegrown crops, supplies are also imported from other European countries, from the USA, North and South Africa and from Israel and Cyprus. Out of season, strawberries grown under glass are, in fact, available all year, but are not worth buying for the freezer since they are expensive and often lacking in flavour.

Strawberries are high in vitamin C and minerals and low in calories. They keep their rich fragrance and sharp, unmistakable flavour well when frozen, but, because of their high water content, they tend to lose some of their texture when thawed. For this reason, many freezer owners prefer to freeze strawberries lightly crushed as a pulp or in ready-made desserts and gâteaux such as Strawberry Soufflé (page 94) and Strawberry Cream Sponge (page 100).

If it is possible to find out the names of strawberry varieties when buying from shops, supermarkets, farm shops or 'pick-your-own' farms (or when choosing for growing at home) remember that Cambridge Vigour,

Cambridge Favourite and Royal Sovereign are the best for freezing. Alpine types, which are firmer than the standard varieties and so freeze rather better, include Fraise des Bois, Baron Solemacher and Alexandria.

Selecting for freezing: For freezing whole, select firm, perfectly ripe fruit with no trace of mould, squashiness or uneven ripening. For freezing mashed or as a pulp, inexpensive lower quality fruit is perfectly acceptable as long as it bears no trace of mould. As with raspberries, strawberries for freezing should always be picked absolutely dry, unless they are to be pulped or crushed. When buying strawberries in punnets, check that there are no signs of leakage from the punnet bases which could be a tell-tale sign of squashed fruit.

Preparation for freezing: Grade the fruit into high and lower quality groups, discarding any that is mouldy. Leave any unripened fruit in a sunny place to redden. Remove any leaves still attached to the base of the fruit and pull out and discard the hulls. Only wipe or rinse the fruit if it is in the lower grade and very dirty. Then prepare the fruit as follows.

Whole strawberries: Need no further preparation.

Strawberry slices: Cut large fruit into 3 to 4 slices.

Crushed Strawberries: Mash fruit lightly with a fork and sweeten with sugar to taste.

Strawberry pulp: Work the fruit in an electric blender or food processor, or pass through a nylon sieve. Sweeten to taste, if liked, and add a little lemon juice or 1/4 teaspoon ascorbic acid to keep fruit a good colour.

To freeze: *Whole strawberries:* These can be frozen in free-flow or dry sugar packs.

Free-flow pack: Open freeze on trays until solid, then pack in polythene bags. Seal, label and return to the freezer for up to 12 months.

Dry sugar pack: Pack in usable quantities in rigid containers, sprinkling each layer with sugar and allow-

ing 125 to 175 g/4 to 6 oz sugar for every 500 g/1 lb fruit according to taste. Seal, label and freeze for up to 12 months.

Strawberry slices: Pack in usable quantities in rigid containers and cover with a medium sugar syrup made from 350 g/12 oz sugar to 600 ml/1 pint water. Leave 2 cm/3/4 inch headspace, seal, label and freeze for up to 12 months.

Crushed strawberries: Pack in usable quantities in rigid containers, seal, label and freeze for up to 12 months.

Strawberry pulp: Pour usable quantities into rigid containers, leaving 2 cm/3/4 inch headspace. Seal, label and freeze for up to 6 months.

To thaw and serve: *Whole strawberries:* Leave to stand in wrappings or container at room temperature for about 1 1/2 hours and serve still slightly chilled (frappé) to prevent mushiness and give the best texture. Serve simply with sugar and cream or ice cream, or use in flans and fruit salads, or as a decoration for desserts and gâteaux. They can also be poached in sugar syrup from frozen, or used to make jam.

Strawberry slices: Thaw as for whole strawberries, then serve simply with cream or ice cream, add to fruit salads, or drain if necessary and add to flans, tarts and pies. Strawberry slices can also be lightly poached from frozen, or used for jam-making.

Crushed strawberries: Thaw as for whole strawberries, then use for ices, sorbets, mousses and desserts set with gelatine. Or mix with cream and use to fill gâteaux and flans, etc.

Strawberry pulp: Thaw as for whole strawberries, then sweeten to taste or according to specific recipe, and use for ice creams, mousses, sorbets and sauces. For hot sauces, heat from frozen in a heavy-based pan over the lowest possible heat, stirring frequently to prevent sticking and adding a little water if necessary.

TOMATO AND ROSEMARY SOUP

This is a delicious soup to make when there is a glut of tomatoes from the garden or market, and when fresh rosemary is at its most prolific. It is equally good made from frozen whole tomatoes, in which case the soup should be boiled for an extra 10 minutes to reduce any excess liquid.

25 g/1 oz butter
2 onions, peeled and chopped
1–2 garlic cloves, peeled and crushed
25 g/1 oz plain flour
1 kg/2 lb ripe tomatoes, quartered
150 ml/¼ pint dry white wine
2 large sprigs fresh rosemary, tied in muslin
salt and freshly ground black pepper
2 tablespoons tomato purée
dash of Worcestershire sauce
juice of ½ lemon
TO SERVE
2 tomatoes, skinned, seeded and chopped

Melt the butter in a pan, add the onions and garlic and fry gently for 5 minutes without browning. Add the flour and cook for a further 2 minutes, stirring.

Add the tomatoes and any juices. Bring to the boil, stirring occasionally, then add the wine, rosemary and salt and pepper to taste. Lower the heat, cover and simmer for 20 minutes until the tomatoes are soft.

Remove lid, increase the heat and boil rapidly for 10 minutes. Stir in the tomato purée. Worcestershire sauce and lemon juice. Leave to cool slightly, then work to a purée in an electric blender or food processor, or pass through a nylon sieve. Cool completely.

To freeze: Pour the soup into a rigid container, leaving 2 cm/¾ inch headspace, then seal, label and freeze for up to 6 months.

To thaw and serve: Leave to stand in container at room temperature for 3 to 4 hours, then transfer to a pan and bring to the boil, stirring frequently. Taste and adjust the seasoning, then pour into a soup tureen or individual bowls. Garnish with the chopped tomato and serve hot.

Serves 6

ICED COURGETTE SOUP

This soup has a delicate summery flavour, which is even better if the courgettes are freshly picked. Do not peel the courgettes as the skin gives a good flavour and colour.

1 tablespoon vegetable oil
2 large onions, peeled and chopped
1 kg/2 lb courgettes, trimmed and chopped
750 ml/1¼ pints homemade chicken stock
150 ml/¼ pint dry white wine
salt and freshly ground white pepper
1 bouquet garni
TO SERVE
150 ml/¼ pint single or double cream
snipped chives

Heat the oil in a pan, add the onions and fry gently for 5 minutes without browning. Stir in the courgettes, then the stock and wine. Bring to the boil, add salt and pepper to taste and the bouquet garni.

Lower the heat, cover the pan and simmer for 30 minutes until the courgettes are soft. Leave to cool slightly, discard the bouquet garni, then work the soup to a purée in an electric blender or food processor, or pass through a nylon sieve. Leave to cool completely.

To freeze: Pour the soup into a rigid container, leaving 2 cm/¾ inch headspace, then seal, label and freeze for up to 4 months.

To thaw and serve: Thaw in container in the refrigerator overnight. Stir vigorously, then taste and adjust the seasoning. Pour into a soup tureen or individual bowls, swirl in the cream and garnish with snipped chives. Serve chilled.

Serves 6

VARIATION

To make iced cucumber soup, replace the courgettes with 2 peeled and diced cucumbers and 1 diced potato. Prepare as above, adding the potato with the cucumber; simmer the soup for 20 minutes only.

For a slightly sharper flavour, swirl soured cream on top of the chilled soup and garnish with mint sprigs just before serving.

OPPOSITE: Avocado Sherbet; Cucumber and Mint Sorbet with Cheese Straws
BELOW: Tomato and Rosemary Soup; Iced Courgette Soup

CUCUMBER AND MINT SORBET WITH CHEESE STRAWS

An unusual, refreshing starter for a warm summer's day or evening, which is inexpensive to make. Do not peel the cucumber as the skin gives the sorbet a good colour.

1 × 425 g/15 oz can consommé
1 large handful of fresh mint leaves
150 ml/¼ pint dry white wine
1 cucumber, grated
juice of ½ lemon
2 egg whites
CHEESE STRAWS
250 g/8 oz plain flour
pinch of salt
pinch of cayenne pepper
125 g/4 oz butter
125 g/4 oz Parmesan cheese, grated
beaten egg, to bind

Put the consommé, mint and wine in a pan and bring to the boil. Lower the heat and simmer for 10 minutes. Remove from the heat and leave to cool. Strain through a nylon sieve, then stir in the cucumber and lemon juice. Transfer to a rigid container and freeze for 2 to 3 hours, stirring occasionally until the mixture is mushy. (Meanwhile, make the cheese straws). Whisk the egg whites until very stiff, then carefully fold into the half-frozen sorbet mixture. Return to the container.

To make the cheese straws: Sift the flour, salt and cayenne into a bowl. Rub in the butter until the mixture resembles fine breadcrumbs. Stir in the cheese and enough egg to mix to a stiff dough. Turn the dough onto a floured surface and knead lightly until smooth. Wrap in cling film, then chill in the refrigerator for 30 minutes.

Roll out the dough on a floured surface until 5 mm/¼ inch thick, then cut into about 40 fingers, 13 cm/5 inches long and 1 cm/½ inch wide. Twist each one several times, place on a baking sheet and bake in a preheated moderately hot oven (200°C/400°F/Gas Mark 6) for 8 to 10 minutes until golden brown. Cool on wire rack.

To freeze: Open freeze the cheese straws until solid, then pack carefully in rigid containers, separating the layers with interleaving sheets or foil. Cover the sorbet container. Seal, label and return both containers to the freezer for up to 4 months.

To thaw and serve: Place the cheese straws on a baking sheet and reheat from frozen in a preheated moderate oven (180°C/350°F/Gas Mark 4) for 10 to 12 minutes until crisp and golden brown. Transfer to a wire rack and leave to cool. Leave the sorbet to stand in container at room temperature for 15 to 20 minutes to soften slightly. Scoop into chilled individual serving dishes. Serve immediately, accompanied by the cheese straws.

Serves 6

AVOCADO SHERBET

A cross between a sorbet and an ice cream, this sherbet has a refreshing, delicate flavour.

2 large ripe avocado pears
juice of ½ lemon
2 spring onions, trimmed and roughly chopped
73 g/3 oz full-fat soft cheese
2 tablespoons natural yogurt
dash of Tabasco sauce
dash of Worcestershire sauce
salt and freshly ground black pepper
2 egg whites
TO SERVE
2 tablespoons homemade mayonnaise
1 garlic clove, peeled and crushed
1 tablespoon chopped parsley

Peel and stone the avocados and chop the flesh roughly. Put the avocado flesh in an electric blender or food processor with the lemon juice, spring onions, cheese and yogurt and work until very smooth and creamy. Mix in the Tabasco and Worcestershire sauces and salt and pepper to taste.

Transfer the mixture to a rigid container and freeze for 2 to 3 hours, stirring occasionally until the mixture is mushy.

Whisk the egg whites until very stiff, then carefully fold into the half-frozen avocado mixture until evenly incorporated.

To freeze: Cover the container, then seal, label and return to the freezer for up to 3 months.

To serve: Leave to stand in container at room temperature for 15 to 20 minutes. Scoop or spoon into individual dishes. Mix the mayonnaise, garlic and parsley together. Serve the sorbet immediately, with the sauce handed separately.

Serves 6

TROUT AND LEMON MOUSSE

Individual smoked trout mousses, made and frozen in scooped-out lemon shells, are very pretty and make a delicious light starter for a dinner party. They can be made at any time of year, but ideally prepare them when there are plenty of juicy lemons around. Serve with Melba toast (see opposite).

6 even-sized large lemons
2 smoked trout, skinned, boned and flaked
50 g/2 oz unsalted butter, softened
4 tablespoons double cream
1 tablespoon snipped chives
1 tablespoon chopped parsley
pinch of cayenne pepper
salt and freshly ground white pepper
TO SERVE
1 tablespoon crushed or finely chopped herbs (e.g. mint, lemon balm, parsley)
few sprigs of fresh herbs (e.g. mint, lemon balm, parsley)

Cut the tops off the lemons. Squeeze and strain the juice from the lemons and measure 2 tablespoons. Carefully scoop out the membranes from the lemon shells and cut away the excess pith, taking care not to cut through the skin. Cut the base of each lemon so that it stands upright.

Put the trout flesh in an electric blender or food processor with the butter. Work until smooth, then add 1 tablespoon lemon juice. Whip the cream until it will just stand in soft peaks, then fold into the trout mixture. Add the herbs, cayenne, and salt and pepper to taste. Add more lemon juice to taste, if wished.

Spoon the mixture into the lemon shells and shape the tops into domes.

To freeze: Open freeze until the mousse is solid, then wrap each lemon individually in cling film. Overwrap in polythene bags, then seal, label and return to the freezer for up to 4 months.

To thaw and serve: Unwrap the lemons and leave to stand at room temperature for 3 hours. Stand the lemons in individual dishes and top with crushed herbs. Surround with crushed ice and garnish with sprigs of fresh herbs. Serve immediately.

Serves 6

VARIATION

For a stronger flavoured mousse, use smoked mackerel instead of smoked trout.

If you do not wish to serve the mousse in lemon shells, freeze it in a rigid container. Thaw in container, then spoon into individual dishes to serve. Alternatively, the mousse can be spread on to thin triangles of toasted brown bread, garnished with sliced olives and served as canapés, with drinks.

Trout and Lemon Mousse; Seafood Puffs; Scampi Provençal

SEAFOOD PUFFS

Take advantage of the abundance of shellfish in late summer to make these Seafood Puffs. As the choux puffs are frozen separately from the seafood filling, they can be used with other fillings, and the seafood filling can be used to stuff crêpes or pancakes.

CHOUX PASTRY
50 g/2 oz butter
150 ml/¼ pint water
65 g/2½ oz plain flour
2 eggs, lightly beaten
2 tablespoons grated Parmesan cheese
FILLING
24 fresh mussels, soaked and cleaned
50 g/2 oz butter
1 small onion, peeled and finely chopped
1 garlic clove, peeled and crushed
25 g/1 oz plain flour
150 ml/¼ pint dry white wine or vermouth
150 ml/¼ pint double cream
125 g/4 oz peeled prawns
50 g/2 oz Gruyère cheese, grated
2 tablespoons snipped chives
½ teaspoon French mustard
salt and freshly ground black pepper
TO SERVE
lemon or lime slices

Make the choux pastry: Put the butter and water in a pan and bring to the boil. Remove from the heat and immediately beat in the flour all at once. Beat well until the mixture leaves the sides of the pan clean. Cool slightly, then add the eggs a little at a time, beating well between each addition. Spoon the dough into a piping bag fitted with a 1 cm/½ inch plain nozzle and pipe small mounds approximately 5 cm/2 inches diameter on 2 dampened baking sheets, spacing them well apart.

Sprinkle the Parmesan evenly over the puffs and bake in a preheated moderately hot oven (200°C/400°F/Gas Mark 6) for about 25 minutes until well risen and golden brown. Slit each puff open with the point of a sharp knife, then cool on a wire rack.

To make the filling: Discard any mussels that are open, then cook the remainder in boiling salted water for 5 minutes until the shells open; discard any that do not. Drain, remove from their shells and chop roughly.

Melt the butter in a pan, add the onion and garlic and fry gently for 5 minutes without browning. Add the flour and cook for a further 2 minutes, stirring constantly. Gradually stir in the wine and cream. Bring to the boil and simmer, stirring, for 2 minutes. Add the mussels and the remaining filling ingredients with salt and pepper to taste and cook for 2 minutes.

To freeze: Open freeze the choux puffs until solid, then pack into rigid containers, separating the layers with interleaving sheets or foil. Seal, label and return to the freezer for up to 2 months. Spoon the filling into a rigid container, cool quickly, then seal, label and freeze for up to 2 months.

To thaw and serve: Leave the filling to stand in container at room temperature for 3 hours. Place the choux puffs on a baking sheet and reheat from frozen in a preheated moderate oven (180°C/350°F/Gas Mark 4) for 10 to 12 minutes. Transfer the filling to a pan and bring slowly to the boil. Simmer, stirring occasionally, for 10 minutes, then taste and adjust the seasoning.

Spoon the filling into the puffs. Serve immediately, garnished with lemon or lime slices.
Serves 6

SCAMPI PROVENÇAL

This delicious starter can quickly be assembled from ingredients in the freezer if it is to be served immediately. Frozen, thawed scampi or prawns can be used, and the sauce can be made from frozen whole or chopped tomatoes, in which case the cooking time should be increased by 20 minutes. For a light lunch or supper dish for 4 people, serve with boiled rice.

1 tablespoon vegetable oil
2 onions, peeled and chopped
1 garlic clove, peeled and crushed
500 g/1 lb ripe tomatoes, roughly chopped
3 tablespoons dry white wine
1 tablespoon chopped parsley
1 tablespoon chopped oregano
1 tablespoon chopped basil
dash of Tabasco sauce
1 teaspoon Worcestershire sauce
salt and freshly ground black pepper
1 tablespoon tomato purée
350 g/12 oz cooked shelled scampi or prawns
TO SERVE
few whole prawns
basil leaves

Heat the oil in a pan, add the onions and garlic and fry gently for 5 minutes without browning. Add the tomatoes and wine and bring to the boil, then lower the heat and add the herbs, Tabasco and Worcestershire sauces. Season with salt and pepper to taste. Simmer uncovered for 20 minutes, until reduced and thickened.

Increase the heat and boil rapidly for a further 5 minutes until the sauce has reduced and thickened. Lower the heat and stir in the tomato purée and scampi or prawns. Simmer gently for 5 minutes.

To freeze: Pour the mixture into a rigid container, leaving 2 cm/¾ inch headspace. Cool quickly, then seal, label and freeze for up to 3 months.

To thaw and serve: Leave to stand in container at room temperature for 3 to 4 hours, then transfer to a pan and bring slowly to the boil, stirring occasionally. Simmer for 5 minutes until thoroughly heated through, then taste and adjust the seasoning. Transfer to a warmed serving dish and garnish with whole prawns and basil leaves. Serve immediately.
Serves 4 to 6

AUBERGINES WITH CAPERS

It is recommended that aubergines should be salted to remove the excess water content along with the bitter taste which is often associated with this vegetable. It also reduces the amount of oil needed for frying. Serve this dish chilled with Melba toast for an unusual summer starter. Alternatively reheat gently from frozen in a heavy-based pan and serve hot as a vegetable accompaniment to roast and grilled meats or poultry.

2 aubergines
salt
3 tablespoons olive oil
1 onion, peeled and chopped
1 garlic clove, peeled and thinly sliced
3 celery sticks, chopped
1 × 396 g/14 oz can tomatoes
1 teaspoon dried mixed herbs
3–4 tablespoons dry white wine
salt and freshly ground black pepper
1 tablespoon tomato purée
2–3 tablespoons capers
12 black olives, stoned
TO SERVE
chopped parsley

Dice the aubergines, then put them in a colander and sprinkle each layer lightly with salt. Cover with a plate, put heavy weights on top and leave to stand for 30 minutes.

Rinse the aubergines under cold running water, then drain and dry thoroughly on kitchen paper.

Heat the oil in a large frying pan, add the aubergines and fry over moderate heat for 10 minutes until lightly browned. Remove from the pan with a slotted spoon and drain on kitchen paper. Add the onion and garlic to the pan and fry gently for 7 minutes until lightly browned. Return the aubergines to the pan. Add the celery and tomatoes with their juice, the wine and salt and pepper to taste. Bring to the boil, then lower the heat and simmer, uncovered, for 15 minutes. Stir in the tomato purée, capers and olives.

To freeze: Pour the mixture into a rigid container, leaving 2 cm/¾ inch headspace. Cool quickly, then seal, label and freeze for up to 6 months.

To thaw and serve: Thaw in container in the refrigerator overnight, then stir well to mix. Spoon into individual dishes and sprinkle with chopped parsley. Serve chilled.
Serves 4 to 6

MELBA TOAST

To make Melba toast, remove the crusts from six 5 mm/¼ inch thick slices of white bread and toast lightly on both sides. Using a very sharp knife, split each one horizontally into two very thin slices. Place under the grill, untoasted surfaces upwards, until they are golden brown and the edges have curled up. Take care that the edges do not burn.

WHITSUN HAKE

Enjoy hake at its summer best, cooked from frozen with bacon and cheese to enhance its splendid flavour.

To serve immediately, bake for only 25 minutes before removing the foil and 10 minutes afterwards.

500 g/1 lb middle cut of hake, cleaned and scaled
4 rashers streaky bacon, rinds removed
50 g/2 oz Gruyère cheese, cut into 4 thin slices
2 tomatoes, skinned, seeded and chopped
1 onion, peeled and chopped
salt and freshly ground black pepper

Put the hake in an ovenproof dish lined with a large sheet of greased foil. Make 4 large slashes in the fish, down to the bone. Wrap a bacon rasher around each slice of cheese and put inside each slash. Surround with the tomatoes and onion. Sprinkle with salt and pepper.

To freeze: Open freeze the hake until solid, then remove from the dish in the foil and fold over the foil to make a tight parcel. Seal, label and return to the freezer for up to 2 months.

To thaw and serve: Unwrap and return to the original dish. Cover with the foil, place in an unheated oven and bake from frozen at moderately hot (190°C/375°F/Gas Mark 5) for 1 hour. Remove the foil and bake for a further 30 minutes. Serve hot.

Serves 4

SALMON TROUT MOUSSE

Celebrate midsummer eve with this epicurean steamed fish mousse, thawed on the day. Cool and refreshing, it has an accompanying sauce made of cream, walnuts and horseradish.

250 g/8 oz smoked salmon, cut into thin strips
500 g/1 lb salmon trout fillets
125 g/4 oz coley fillets, skinned and boned
1 egg white
juice of ½ lemon
salt and freshly ground white pepper
FILLING
150 ml/¼ pint double cream
25 g/1 oz shelled walnuts, chopped
1 tablespoon strong hot horseradish
TO SERVE
2 tablespoons mayonnaise
few fennel or dill fronds (optional)

Lightly oil a 600 ml/1 pint ring mould, line with strips of foil, then oil the foil. Line the mould with the strips of smoked salmon, overlapping them slightly.

Work the salmon trout and coley to a purée in an electric blender or food processor. While the machine is still running, add the egg white, then the lemon juice and salt and pepper to taste. Pack the fish purée carefully but firmly into the lined mould. Lightly butter

a piece of foil, make a pleat in it, then place over the mould, buttered side down. Twist the foil firmly at the edge to secure it under the rim.

Put the mould into a large pan, pour in enough boiling water to come half way up the mould, then cover and simmer for 25 minutes. Cool slightly. Line the inside of the lid of a shallow tin into which the mousse will fit with cling film. Turn the mousse out onto the cling film, remove the foil strips and leave to cool completely.

To make the filling: Whip the cream until stiff, then gently fold in the chopped walnuts and horseradish. Press a square of oiled foil into the centre of the mousse, put in the filling and fold the foil over the top to enclose the filling.

To freeze: Invert the tin base onto the lid, seal and label. Place the tin upside down in the freezer (i.e. with the mousse still standing on the lid) and freeze for up to 2 months.

To thaw and serve: Remove the base from the tin and take out the foil parcel from the centre of the mousse. Place the mousse on a serving plate and leave to thaw at room temperature for 6 hours. Stir the mayonnaise into the filling and spoon into the centre of the mousse. Garnish with fennel or dill fronds, if wished. Serve cold, accompanied by a crisp green salad.

Serves 4

OPPOSITE: Prawn and Pepper Vol-au-Vent
BELOW: Whitsun Hake; Poacher's Salmon

PRAWN AND PEPPER VOL-AU-VENT

This cooked vol-au-vent case and its filling are frozen separately, then combined after thawing to make an elegant luncheon dish, with a freshly cooked appearance.

350 g/12 oz puff pastry (total weight)
1 egg, beaten, to glaze
40 g/1½ oz butter
1 red pepper, cored, seeded and diced
3 tablespoons plain flour
300 ml/½ pint milk
1 tablespoon dry sherry
pinch of cayenne pepper
salt
TO SERVE
350 g/12 oz peeled cooked prawns
few parsley sprigs
few unpeeled cooked prawns (optional)

Roll the pastry on a lightly floured surface to a 39 × 19 cm/15 × 7½ inch rectangle. Cut into two 19 cm/7½ inch circles (using a plate as a guide). Put 1 circle on a dampened baking sheet. Using a very sharp knife, lightly mark a criss-cross pattern over the other circle, then cut a 13 cm/5 inch circle from the centre of it. Brush the first circle with beaten egg and fit the pastry ring onto it. Brush the ring with the beaten egg. Put the smaller circle on a separate dampened baking sheet and brush with egg. Bake both circles in a preheated very hot oven (230°C/450°F/Gas Mark 8) for 15 minutes. Cool on a wire rack.

To make the sauce: Melt the butter in a pan, add the diced red pepper and fry gently for 2 to 3 minutes without browning. Add the flour and cook for a further 2 minutes, stirring all the time. Remove from the heat and gradually add the milk, beating vigorously after each addition. Return to the heat and bring to the boil, stirring constantly. Lower the heat and simmer for 2 minutes, then add the sherry, cayenne and salt to taste. Pour into a rigid container, leaving 2 cm/¾ inch headspace, cover the surface of the sauce closely with cling film or lightly buttered greaseproof paper to prevent a skin forming and leave to cool.

To freeze: Put the pastry circles in a rigid container, separating them with an interleaving sheet or piece of foil to avoid breakage. Seal, label and freeze for up to 1 month. Remove the cling film from the sauce, seal, label and freeze for up to 1 month.

To thaw and serve: Leave pastry and sauce to stand in containers at room temperature for 1 hour. Put the vol-au-vent case and lid on baking sheets and reheat in a preheated hot oven (220°C/425°F/Gas Mark 7) for 10 minutes. Meanwhile, transfer the sauce to a pan and bring to the boil, stirring frequently. Add the prawns and simmer until hot. Spoon the filling into the vol-au-vent case and put the lid on top. Garnish with parsley and prawns if wished. Serve immediately.

Serves 4

POACHER'S SALMON

Salmon, king of the summer fish, needs little more than cucumber and a little dill to become a veritable feast. Ask the fishmonger to skin and bone the salmon, to give 2 fillets.
To serve immediately, without freezing, bake as below for about 25 minutes.

750 g/1½ lb tail cut of salmon, skinned and boned
25 g/1 oz butter
125 g/4 oz cucumber, skinned and diced
1 teaspoon chopped dill
salt and freshly ground white pepper
TO SERVE
few lemon slices, halved
cucumber shreds

Put 1 salmon fillet, skinned side down, in an ovenproof dish lined with a large sheet of foil. Melt the butter in a pan, add the cucumber and fry very gently without browning. Pour all the cucumber and some of its butter over the salmon, then sprinkle with the dill and salt and pepper to taste. Top with the second salmon fillet, skinned side up, and pour over the remaining butter. Leave for a few minutes until the butter cools and hardens.

To freeze: Open freeze the salmon until solid, then remove from the dish in the foil and fold over the foil to make a tight parcel. Seal, label and return to the freezer for up to 2 months.

To thaw and serve: Unwrap and return to the original dish. Cover with the foil, place in an unheated oven and reheat from frozen at moderately hot (190°C/375°F/Gas Mark 5) for 1 hour. Garnish with the lemon and cucumber and serve immediately.

Serves 4

SPATCHCOCKED GUINEA FOWL ST. HUBERT

This is a traditional method for cooking guinea fowl – St. Hubert came to be regarded as the patron saint of hunters and trappers in Ardenne – hence the name. Ask your supplier to remove the backbone from the guinea fowl, cut off the wing tips, then press down upon the breastbone until the bird lies flat. Prepared in this way, the bird is ideal to store in the freezer and simple to cook, given extra flavour by its marinade. Serve with game chips.

1 oven-ready guinea fowl, about 1.25 kg/2½ lb
MARINADE
2 tablespoons vegetable oil
juice of 1 lemon
2 shallots, peeled and chopped
2 teaspoons chopped marjoram
salt and freshly ground black pepper
TO SERVE
few watercress sprigs

Insert 2 skewers crossways in the guinea fowl to keep it flat. Put the bird in an ovenproof dish lined with a large sheet of foil. Mix all the marinade ingredients together with salt and pepper to taste, pour over the bird, then turn to coat the other side. Cover and leave to marinate for 1 hour, turning occasionally.

Roast uncovered in a preheated moderately hot oven (200°C/400°F/Gas Mark 6) for 1 hour, turning after 20 minutes. Cool quickly, then remove skewers.
To freeze: Fold the foil over the guinea fowl to make a tight parcel. Seal, label and freeze for up to 3 months.
To thaw and serve: Thaw in wrappings at room temperature for 4 hours, then place the parcel on a baking sheet and loosen the foil. Reheat in a preheated moderately hot oven (200°C/400°F/Gas Mark 6) for 45 minutes, turning after 20 minutes. Garnish with watercress and serve hot. Alternatively, thaw at room temperature overnight and serve cold.
Serves 4

CHICKEN-IN-A-BAG

Plump young summer chicken, frozen in a roasting bag with its own marinade, then thawed and baked in the same bag, is easy to prepare – and a delight to eat.

1 oven-ready chicken, about 1.25 kg/2½ lb
juice of 1 large lemon
2 tablespoons olive oil
2 garlic cloves, peeled and crushed
1 tablespoon chopped rosemary
salt and freshly ground black pepper
TO SERVE
2 tablespoons chopped parsley
few rosemary sprigs (optional)

Cut the chicken into quarters and cover any sharp bones with a thick wad of foil. Put the chicken pieces in a single layer in a roasting bag and put on a flat foil tray. Mix the remaining ingredients together with salt and pepper to taste and pour into the bag.
To freeze: Twist tie to seal the bag tightly, excluding all air. Label and freeze for up to 6 months.
To thaw and serve: Leave to stand in roasting bag at room temperature for 6 hours or until thawed completely, then open the bag and remove the foil from the chicken bones. Cut a few small holes in the top of the bag, then loosely seal the open end. Put into a roasting tin and roast in a preheated moderately hot oven (200°C/400°F/Gas Mark 6) for 45 minutes, then cut the bag and open completely. Baste the chicken well and roast for a further 15 minutes. Transfer the chicken to a warmed serving dish, pour over the cooking juices and sprinkle with the parsley. Serve immediately, garnished with rosemary if preferred.
Serves 4

MISHMISH DUCK

Apricots – *mishmish* in Arabic – are summer's golden bounty. Combined with vinegar and spice, they give a Middle Eastern flavour to this duckling, which is frozen whole, ready to cook.

1 oven-ready duck, about 1.5 kg/3–3½ lb
1 tablespoon vegetable oil
3 tablespoons cider vinegar
2 tablespoons dark soft brown sugar
1 teaspoon ground cumin
500 g/1 lb whole fresh apricots
salt and freshly ground black pepper
TO SERVE
1 bunch watercress

Wipe the duck, dry thoroughly, then place in an ovenproof dish lined with a large sheet of foil.

Put the oil, vinegar, sugar and cumin into a pan and heat gently, stirring until the sugar has dissolved. Add the apricots and simmer for 4 to 5 minutes until the fruit softens. Cool quickly, then spoon around the duck and sprinkle with salt and pepper.
To freeze: Open freeze the duck and apricots until solid, then remove from the dish in the foil and fold over the foil to make a tight parcel. Seal, label and return to the freezer for up to 3 months.
To thaw and serve: Thaw in wrappings in the refrigerator overnight, then return to the original dish and loosen the foil. Cook in a preheated moderately hot oven (200°C/400°F/Gas Mark 6) for 1 hour, then open the foil, baste well and pour off excess juices; cool these quickly. Cook the duck for a further 1 hour.

Place the duck and apricots on a warmed serving dish. Remove the excess fat from the cooled juices, then reheat and pour over the duck. Surround with the watercress and serve immediately.
Serves 4 to 6

QUAIL PARNASSIAN

Reheating the quail in a bain marie ensures that their delicate flesh is not toughened and spoilt by too high a heat.

4 oven-ready quail
1 tablespoon potato flour (fécule)
salt and freshly ground black pepper
25 g/1 oz butter
25 g/1 oz (2 slices) Parma ham
4 fresh vine leaves, blanched
300 ml/½ pint dry white wine
25 g/1 oz sultanas
¼ teaspoon ground cinnamon
125 g/4 oz seeded black grapes
TO SERVE
fresh vine leaves (optional)

Coat the quail in the potato flour seasoned with salt and pepper. Melt the butter in a large pan, add the quail and fry until browned on all sides. Drain. Cut 1 slice of ham into 4 pieces and shred the other piece. Put the vine leaves into an ovenproof dish, sprinkle with the shredded ham, then put each bird on a vine leaf, breast side down. Cover each bird with a piece of ham. Pour the wine into the pan, scraping up the sediment to deglaze, then add the sultanas and cinnamon. Pour over the birds.

Cover the dish with a lid or foil and bake in a preheated moderate oven (180°C/350°F/Gas Mark 4) for 45 minutes. Transfer the birds and vine leaves to a foil container. Pour the cooking liquid into a pan, add the grapes and boil for 1 minute, then pour over the quail. Cool quickly.
To freeze: Seal the container, label and freeze for up to 2 months.
To thaw and serve: Leave to stand in container at room temperature for 2 hours, then put the container into a large pan and pour in enough boiling water to come one third up the sides of the container. Remove the foil lid, cover the pan and simmer for 30 minutes. Transfer the quail and sauce to a warmed serving dish, garnish with fresh vine leaves, if available, and serve immediately.
Serves 2 or 4

VARIATION

When quail are not available, this is a delicious way of serving poussins or chicken portions. The sultanas can be omitted if preferred, and the dish garnished with seeded green grapes, if liked.

Mishmish Duck; Chicken-in-a-Bag; Quail Parnassian

DOUBLE LAMB CHOPS SOUBISE

English summer lamb cut as double chops (also called butterfly or whisker chops) yields a generous portion for each person; and the creamy-crunchy topping cooks perfectly as the chops heat from frozen in their open foil parcel.
To serve immediately, without freezing, cook uncovered in an ovenproof dish in a preheated moderate oven (180°C/350°F/Gas Mark 4) for about 35 minutes until the lamb is tender.

4 double lamb chops
2 tablespoons, plus 2 teaspoons potato flour (fécule)
4 tablespoons vegetable oil
2 thick slices white bread, crusts removed, diced
2 onions, peeled and sliced
300 ml/½ pint milk
2 tablespoons chopped parsley
salt and freshly ground black pepper
TO SERVE
few parsley sprigs (optional)

Coat the chops with 2 tablespoons of the potato flour. Heat 2 tablespoons oil in a frying pan, add the chops and fry over brisk heat until browned on both sides. Remove the lamb chops with a slotted spoon and put them into an ovenproof dish lined with a large sheet of foil.

Add the bread cubes to the pan and fry gently, stirring, until evenly browned on all sides. Remove with a slotted spoon and drain on kitchen paper. Heat the remaining oil in the pan, add the sliced onions and fry gently for 5 minutes until they are softened but not brown.

Mix the remaining 2 teaspoons potato flour to a smooth paste with a little of the milk, then add the remaining milk. Pour into the pan and bring to the boil, stirring constantly. Lower the heat and simmer for 2 to 3 minutes until the sauce is thickened. Remove from the heat, stir in the parsley and salt and pepper to taste, then pour over the chops and top with the bread cubes. Cool quickly.

To freeze: Open freeze the chops and sauce until solid, then remove from the dish in the foil and fold over the foil to make a tight parcel. Seal, label and return to the freezer for up to 3 months.

To thaw and serve: Return to the original dish and completely open up the foil. Cook from frozen in a preheated moderate oven (180°C/350°F/Gas Mark 4) for 1 hour. Transfer the chops to a warmed serving dish and spoon over the sauce and bread cubes. Garnish with parsley sprigs, if wished, and serve immediately, accompanied by courgettes, or French beans, and new potatoes.

Serves 4

ALGERIAN LAMB

Succulent lamb shoulder is first braised with aubergine, then sliced into a freezer container which can be placed conveniently in the oven to reheat. Yogurt and mint are added at serving time to give the finished dish extra flavour.

1.25 kg/2½ lb piece shoulder of lamb, boned and
*   trimmed of excess fat, then rolled and tied*
1 large aubergine, quartered and thickly sliced
1 garlic clove, peeled and chopped
a little olive oil (if necessary)
2 tablespoons French mustard
2 tablespoons tomato purée
2 tablespoons wine or cider vinegar
TO SERVE
150ml/¼ pint natural yogurt
few fresh mint sprigs

Put the lamb into a dry, non-stick pan and fry until evenly browned on all sides, turning constantly. Stir in the aubergine and garlic and fry for a few minutes, adding a little oil if necessary.

Mix the mustard, tomato purée and vinegar together and make up to 150 ml/¼ pint with water. Add to the pan, cover and simmer for 1 hour or until the lamb is tender. Cool quickly.

Remove the lamb from the sauce and slice thickly, discarding the string. Overlap the slices in a 23 cm/9 inch square foil container and spoon over the sauce.

To freeze: Seal, label and freeze for up to 2 months.

To thaw and serve: Leave to stand in container at room temperature for 4 to 5 hours. Loosen but do not remove the foil lid, then reheat in a preheated moderate oven (170°C/325°F/Gas Mark 3) for 50 minutes or until very hot, turning the meat slices over carefully halfway through the cooking time. Transfer to a warmed serving dish, swirl the yogurt over the top and garnish with the mint.

Serves 4

LEFT: Double Lamb Chops Soubise; Algerian Lamb
RIGHT: Beef Brisket with Redcurrants; Topside Glenfiddich

TOPSIDE GLENFIDDICH

Quick to make and serve, this stir-fried beef is flamed in whisky, which gives savour to its creamy sauce. Serve with rice or buttered noodles and a crisp green salad.

750 g/1½ lb piece beef topside, cut 1 cm/½ inch thick
2 tablespoons vegetable oil
25 g/1 oz butter
2 green peppers, cored, seeded and very thinly sliced
3 garlic cloves, peeled and chopped
2 tablespoons whisky
2 chillies, seeded and finely chopped
150 ml/¼ pint soured cream
TO SERVE
salt and freshly ground black pepper
½ small green pepper, cored, seeded and sliced into rings (optional)

Slice the topside very thinly across the grain. Heat the oil and butter in a large frying pan until very hot, add the beef and stir over brisk heat for about 1 minute, until the meat is browned. Add the green peppers and garlic and stir for a further 1 minute.

Warm the whisky in a small pan or ladle, set alight, then pour over the beef off the heat. Toss the pan gently until all the ingredients are well mixed, then stir in the chillies and soured cream. Cool quickly.

To freeze: Transfer the beef mixture to a rigid container, seal, label and freeze for up to 3 months.

To thaw and serve: Leave to stand in container at room temperature for 2 hours, then transfer to a pan and reheat gently. Increase the heat and cook for a further 2 to 3 minutes, until the meat is very hot. Add salt and pepper to taste, transfer to a warmed serving dish and garnish with green pepper rings, if liked. Serve immediately.

Serves 4

BEEF BRISKET WITH REDCURRANTS

Perfect for a cold lunch or picnic, this salted beef is fully cooked, sliced and covered with a fruit sauce to keep it moist and tasty during thawing.

1.5 kg/3–3½ lb piece rolled salted brisket
450 ml/¾ pint water
150 ml/¼ pint sweet vermouth
300 ml/½ pint sweet white wine
1 bunch fresh herbs, tied together with string
250 g/8 oz baby carrots, scraped
250 g/8 oz redcurrants, stalks removed
4 tablespoons redcurrant jelly
1 tablespoon Worcestershire sauce
TO SERVE
few sprigs of fresh herbs (optional)

Put the meat into a pan with the water, vermouth, wine, herbs, baby carrots and half of the redcurrants. Bring to the boil, then lower the heat, cover and simmer for 3 hours, or until the meat is very tender. Cool quickly.

Remove the beef from the cooking liquid and slice thinly, discarding the string. Overlap the slices in a 23 cm/9 inch square foil container and add the carrots.

Put the redcurrant jelly and Worcestershire sauce in a small pan and heat gently, stirring until the jelly has melted. Strain the cooking liquid from the beef and measure 300 ml/½ pint. Stir into the sauce in the pan, then pour over the meat. Add the remaining redcurrants. Leave until the sauce is cold.

To freeze: Seal the container, label and freeze for up to 2 months.

To thaw and serve: Thaw in container at room temperature for 8 hours or overnight. Transfer the beef and redcurrants to a serving platter and pour over enough sauce to cover the meat. Garnish with the herbs and serve cold.

Serves 6

ROSY BACON WITH OKRA

Give bacon steaks an interesting summery taste by cooking them with okra and tomatoes in a rosé wine sauce.

4 thick bacon steaks, each about 1 cm/½ inch thick
1 tablespoon vegetable oil
2 tomatoes, skinned, quartered and seeded
2 teaspoons tomato purée
150 ml/¼ pint rosé wine
125 g/4 oz okra, stalk ends trimmed
salt and freshly ground black pepper
TO SERVE
few watercress sprigs (optional)

Wipe the bacon steaks dry with kitchen paper. Heat the oil in a large frying pan, add the steaks and fry over moderate heat until well browned on both sides. Remove the steaks from the pan with a slotted spoon and place overlapping in an ovenproof dish lined with a large sheet of foil.

Add the remaining ingredients to the pan with salt and pepper to taste and cook for 8 minutes, stirring occasionally until the okra is just tender. Pour over the bacon. Cool quickly.

To freeze: Open freeze the bacon mixture until solid, then remove from the dish in the foil and fold over the foil to make a tight parcel. Seal, label and return to the freezer for up to 3 months.

To thaw and serve: Unwrap and return to the original dish. Cover with the foil, place in an unheated oven and reheat from frozen at moderately hot (200°C/400°F/Gas Mark 6) for 45 minutes. Serve hot, garnished with watercress if preferred.
Serves 4

PORK OLIVIER

Olivier is the French word for an olive grower; in this recipe, prime loin of pork is stuffed with green olives and kidney, then rolled and roasted to be frozen whole. Anchovy-stuffed green olives are available in jars from good delicatessens and supermarkets; if you find them difficult to obtain, use ordinary stoned green olives, or the ones stuffed with pimiento. Alternatively, make them yourself by stuffing the centre of stoned green olives with a little chopped canned anchovy. Serve Pork Olivier cold, with a bowl of cold apple sauce handed separately if liked.

1.5 kg/3–3½ lb piece loin of pork with kidney
    attached, rind removed and boned
salt and freshly ground black pepper
18 anchovy-stuffed green olives
½ teaspoon celery salt
TO SERVE
1 bunch watercress

Open out the pork as flat as possible by cutting the fleshiest part diagonally. Sprinkle liberally with salt and pepper. Skin, core and finely chop the kidney. Insert the kidney into one fold of the meat, the olives into the other. Roll up the meat and tie securely at regular intervals with thread or fine string, then rub all over with celery salt. Weigh the pork and calculate the cooking time at 30 minutes per 500 g/1 lb.

Put the pork in a small roasting tin lined with a large sheet of foil and roast in a preheated moderately hot over (200°C/400°F/Gas Mark 6) for the calculated cooking time. Cool quickly.

To freeze: Remove the pork from the tin in the foil and fold over the foil to make a tight parcel. Seal, label and freeze for up to 2 months.

To thaw and serve: Thaw in wrappings at room temperature for 8 hours or overnight. Cut into thin slices, removing the thread or string, then arrange the slices on a bed of watercress. Serve cold, with apple sauce if preferred.
Serves 6

CALVES' LIVER WITH NECTARINES

The creamy texture of calves' liver is not impaired in this recipe because it is cooked, frozen, then steamed in its foil container after partial thawing. Nectarines add a fresh seasonal touch.

625 g/1¼ lb calves' liver, thinly sliced
2 tablespoons olive oil
25 g/1 oz butter
salt and freshly ground black pepper
3 tablespoons dry red wine
1 tablespoon red wine vinegar
4 small nectarines, stoned and sliced
pinch of ground mace
TO SERVE
few parsley sprigs

Wipe the liver dry with kitchen paper. Heat the olive oil and butter in a large frying pan, add the liver slices and fry over moderate heat for about 30 seconds on each side. Remove from the pan with a slotted spoon, sprinkle with salt and pepper, then place overlapping in a foil container. Add the wine and vinegar to the pan and scrape up the sediment to deglaze, then add the nectarines and mace. Cook for 2 to 3 minutes, stirring carefully until the fruit is just tender. Pour over the liver and cool quickly.

To freeze: Seal the container, label and freeze for up to 2 months.

To thaw and serve: Leave to stand in container at room temperature for 2 hours, then put the container into a pan and pour in enough boiling water to come one third up the sides of the container. Remove the foil lid, cover the pan and simmer for 30 minutes. Transfer to a warmed serving dish and garnish with parsley. Serve immediately.
Serves 4

VEAL PAUPIETTES WITH GRAPES

A deliciously light dish to tempt jaded summer appetites. Totally cooked in advance, there is no need for the cook to waste precious summer hours in the kitchen.

2 large veal escalopes, each about 250 g/8 oz, halved
    crossways
salt and freshly ground black pepper
350 g/12 oz minced veal
2 tablespoons chopped parsley
2 tablespoons chopped tarragon
2 tablespoons snipped chives
2 tablespoons plain flour
2 tablespoons olive oil
300 ml/½ pint light stock
350 g/12 oz seedless green grapes
TO SERVE
a little chopped tarragon (optional)

Beat the 4 pieces of veal between 2 sheets of cling film until very thin. Sprinkle with salt and pepper. Mix together the minced veal and herbs with salt and pepper to taste, then place a cork-shaped portion of the veal mixture on each piece of veal. Roll up and tie securely at regular intervals with thread or fine string. Season the flour with salt and pepper and roll the paupiettes in it to coat thoroughly.

Heat the oil in a large frying pan, add the paupiettes and fry over moderate heat until well browned on all sides. Remove from the pan with a slotted spoon and drain on kitchen paper.

Sprinkle any remaining seasoned flour into the juices in the pan and stir well, scraping up the sediment on the bottom, then gradually stir in the stock and bring to the boil. Lower the heat, return the paupiettes to the pan, cover and simmer for 30 minutes. Add the grapes and simmer for a further 15 minutes. Cool quickly.

To freeze: Transfer the veal paupiettes, grapes and sauce to a rigid container, seal, label and freeze for up to 2 months.

To thaw and serve: Leave to stand in container at room temperature for 2 hours, then put the container into a pan and pour in enough boiling water to come one third up the sides of the container. Remove the foil lid, cover the pan and simmer for 30 minutes. Remove the paupiettes from the sauce and cut off and discard the thread or string. Slice the paupiettes neatly and arrange on a warmed serving platter. Pour over the sauce and garnish with tarragon, if liked. Serve immediately.
Serves 4

Rosy Bacon with Okra; Pork Olivier; Veal Paupiettes with Grapes

FRENCH-STYLE MANGETOUTS

This is a variation of the traditional *petits pois à la française*. If you cannot buy mangetouts, use freshly shelled peas.

40 g/1 ½ oz butter
1 bunch (about 8) spring onions, trimmed and cut into 5 cm/2 inch lengths
500 g/1 lb mangetouts, topped and tailed
300 ml/½ pint well-flavoured chicken stock
1 bouquet garni
salt
1 tablespoon cornflour, blended with 2 tablespoons water
1 firm lettuce, cut into 8 wedges
4 tablespoons double cream
1 tablespoon green peppercorns, drained

Melt the butter in a pan, add the spring onions and cook for 2 minutes without browning. Add the mangetouts, stock, bouquet garni and salt to taste. Bring to the boil, then lower the heat and simmer for 10 to 12 minutes until the vegetables are just tender.

Discard the bouquet garni, stir in the blended cornflour and bring to the boil, stirring constantly. Lower the heat and simmer for 2 minutes, then add the lettuce and cream. Heat through gently for 1 to 2 minutes, then add the peppercorns.

To freeze: Transfer to a rigid container, cool quickly, then seal, label and freeze for up to 3 months.

To thaw and serve: Leave to stand in the container at room temperature for 3 to 4 hours, then transfer to a pan and reheat gently, stirring occasionally. Taste and adjust seasoning. Serve at once.

Serves 4 to 6

French-Style Mangetouts: French Bean and Tomato Casserole

PURÉE CLAMART

This pea purée with fresh herbs makes a good accompaniment to grilled and roast meats.

500 g/1 lb shelled fresh peas
1 bunch spring onions, trimmed and chopped
25 g/1 oz butter
4 tablespoons well-flavoured chicken stock
salt and freshly ground black pepper
1 tablespoon chopped parsley
1 tablespoon chopped basil
1 tablespoon chopped thyme
TO SERVE
few mint or chervil sprigs

Put the peas, spring onions and butter in a pan, add the stock and salt and pepper to taste and bring to the boil. Lower the heat, cover and simmer for 25 to 30 minutes, until the peas are very tender and the liquid has been absorbed.

Leave to cool slightly, then purée in an electric blender or food processor until smooth. Return the purée to the rinsed-out pan, stir in the herbs and salt and pepper to taste and heat through very gently for 5 to 7 minutes.

To freeze: Transfer the purée to a rigid container, leaving 2 cm/¾ inch headspace. Cool quickly, then seal, label and freeze for up to 4 months.

To thaw and serve: Leave to stand in container at room temperature for 3 hours, then transfer to a pan and reheat gently for 10 to 15 minutes, stirring frequently. Serve hot, garnished with mint or chervil sprigs.

Serves 4 to 6

FRENCH BEAN AND TOMATO CASSEROLE

A filling summer vegetable casserole which can be served as a supper dish on its own.

750 g/1 ½ lb French beans, topped and tailed
250 g/8 oz courgettes, trimmed and sliced
25 g/1 oz butter
2 onions, peeled and sliced
1–2 garlic cloves, peeled and sliced
500 g/1 lb tomatoes, skinned, seeded and chopped
2 spring onions, trimmed and chopped
salt and freshly ground black pepper
250 g/8 oz Danish or Scottish Mozzarella cheese, thinly sliced
TO SERVE
2 tablespoons sesame seeds, toasted
few sprigs of fresh herbs (optional)

Blanch the beans and courgettes in boiling salted water for 3 minutes. Drain. Melt the butter in a pan, add the onions and garlic and fry gently for 5 minutes without browning. Stir in the tomatoes, bring to the boil and cook, uncovered, for 15 minutes until thickened. Stir in the spring onions and salt and pepper to taste, then add the drained beans and courgettes.

Spoon a layer of bean and tomato mixture in the bottom of a lightly greased ovenproof dish or foil container. Cover with a layer of cheese, then another layer of bean and tomato mixture. Continue with these layers until all the ingredients are used up, finishing with a layer of cheese. Leave to cool.

To freeze: Open freeze the mixture until solid, then turn out of the dish or container and wrap in foil. Seal, label and return to the freezer for up to 4 months.

To thaw and serve: Unwrap and return to the original dish or container. Leave to stand at room temperature for 3 to 4 hours, then bake in a preheated moderate oven (180°C/350°F/Gas Mark 4) for 30 to 35 minutes. Sprinkle over the sesame seeds, return to the oven and bake for a further 5 minutes. Serve hot, garnished with sprigs of fresh herbs if liked.

Serves 4 to 6

STIR-FRIED SUMMER VEGETABLES

Any selection of fresh summer vegetables can be used for this crunchy vegetable concoction. Salt is not used in this recipe because of the saltiness of the soy sauce.

2 tablespoons vegetable oil
4 spring onions, trimmed and cut into 5 cm/2 inch
  lengths
2 garlic cloves, peeled and thinly sliced
1 cm/½ inch slice root ginger, peeled and shredded
125 g/4 oz French beans, topped, tailed and halved
½ small cauliflower, broken into florets
125 g/4 oz mangetouts, topped and tailed
3 celery sticks, sliced diagonally
50 g/2 oz courgettes, trimmed and sliced diagonally
1 red pepper, cored, seeded and thinly sliced
1 green pepper, cored, seeded and thinly sliced
1 yellow pepper, cored, seeded and thinly sliced
freshly ground black pepper
TO SERVE
2 tablespoons soy sauce
1 teaspoon sesame seed oil

Heat the oil in a wok or large frying pan, add the spring onions and garlic and stir-fry for 30 seconds without browning. Add all the remaining ingredients with pepper to taste, and toss well. Stir-fry for 2 minutes.

To freeze: Transfer the mixture to a rigid container, cool rapidly, then seal, label and freeze for up to 3 months.

To thaw and serve: Leave to stand in container at room temperature for 3 to 4 hours, then turn into a wok or large frying pan. Pour over the soy sauce and sesame seed oil and stir-fry over brisk heat for 3 to 4 minutes until the vegetables are hot but still crisp. Serve immediately.

Serves 6

TURKISH STUFFED AUBERGINES

Serve hot as a first course or vegetable accompaniment.

4 medium aubergines
salt
2 tablespoons vegetable oil
2 large onions, peeled and chopped
2 garlic cloves, peeled and sliced
1 cm/½ inch piece root ginger, peeled and shredded
1 teaspoon chilli powder
½ teaspoon ground turmeric
1 small chilli pepper, seeded and chopped
500 g/1 lb tomatoes, skinned, seeded and chopped
freshly ground black pepper
TO SERVE
few thyme sprigs (optional)

Cut the aubergines in half lengthways. Carefully scoop out the flesh, taking care not to cut the skin. Chop the flesh roughly. Sprinkle the aubergine shells and flesh with salt and leave to stand for 30 minutes. Rinse under cold running water, drain and dry on kitchen paper.

Heat the oil in a pan, add the onions and garlic and fry gently for 5 minutes without browning. Remove from the pan with a slotted spoon and set aside. Add the aubergine shells to the pan, skin side down, and fry gently for 3 to 4 minutes. Remove from the pan and drain on kitchen paper.

Return the onions and garlic to the pan. Add the ginger, spices and chilli, then the tomatoes, chopped aubergine flesh and salt and pepper to taste. Cook uncovered for 20 minutes, until thickened.

Stand the aubergine shells in a single layer in an ovenproof dish or foil container, then spoon in the filling mixture. Cover with foil and bake in a preheated moderate oven (160°C/325°F/Gas Mark 3) for 35 to 40 minutes. Remove the foil and leave to cool.

To freeze: Cover the dish or container, then seal, label and freeze for up to 4 months.

To thaw and serve: Reheat from frozen covered with foil in a preheated moderate oven (160°C/325°F/Gas Mark 3) for 1 to 1¼ hours. Serve hot, garnished with thyme if available.

Serves 4

Stir-Fried Summer Vegetables; Turkish Stuffed Aubergines

RATATOUILLE TARTS

These tarts are filled with a concoction of summer vegetables cooked together with lots of fresh herbs.

The usual ingredients are onions, tomatoes, courgettes, peppers and aubergines but, according to availability, the balance of vegetables can be changed.

CHEESE PASTRY
175 g/6 oz plain flour
salt
75 g/3 oz butter
2 tablespoons grated Parmesan cheese
50 g/2 oz mature Cheddar cheese, grated
½ teaspoon dried mixed herbs
I egg yolk
a little iced water
FILLING
I aubergine, diced
I tablespoon vegetable oil
I onion, peeled and sliced
I–2 garlic cloves, peeled and crushed
I small green pepper, cored, seeded and thinly sliced
I yellow or red pepper, cored, seeded and thinly sliced
2 courgettes, trimmed and sliced
250 g/8 oz tomatoes, skinned, seeded and chopped
I tablespoon chopped thyme
I tablespoon chopped basil
I tablespoon chopped oregano
freshly ground black pepper
2 eggs
150 ml/¼ pint single cream
TO SERVE
few sprigs of fresh herbs (optional)

To make the pastry: Sift the flour and a pinch of salt into a bowl. Rub in the butter until the mixture resembles fine breadcrumbs. Stir in the cheeses, herbs and egg yolk and enough water to mix to a fairly stiff dough. Turn the dough onto a floured surface and knead lightly until smooth. Wrap in cling film and chill in the refrigerator for 30 minutes.

For the filling: Put the diced aubergine in a colander, sprinkling each layer with salt. Cover with a plate, put weights on top and leave to stand for 30 minutes.

Meanwhile roll out the dough on a floured surface and use to line eight 7.5 cm/3 inch tartlet tins. Prick the base and sides of the dough and chill for 20 minutes.

Rinse the aubergine under cold running water, drain and dry thoroughly on kitchen paper. Heat the oil in a pan, add the onion and garlic and fry gently for 5 minutes without browning. Add the aubergine and remaining vegetables, the herbs and salt and pepper to taste and bring to the boil. Lower the heat, cover and simmer for 20 minutes. Leave to cool.

Line the pastry cases with foil and baking beans. Bake 'blind' in a preheated moderate oven (180°C/350°F/Gas Mark 4) for 7 minutes. Remove the foil and beans. Spoon the cool filling into the pastry cases. Beat the eggs and cream together, season with salt and pepper, then spoon over the filling. Return to the oven for a further 15 minutes until the egg mixture is set. Remove from the oven and leave in the tins for 10 minutes, then place on a wire rack to cool completely.

To freeze: Open freeze the tarts until solid, then pack in a rigid container, separating the layers with interleaving sheets or foil. Seal, label and return to the freezer for up to 4 months.

To thaw and serve: Remove the tarts from the container and place on a wire rack; leave to stand at room temperature for 2 hours until thawed completely. Serve cold, or reheat in a preheated moderate oven (180°C/350°F/Gas Mark 4) for 7 to 8 minutes and serve warm, garnished with herbs.
Makes 8

GARDENER'S PIZZA

Pizzas are very useful to keep in the freezer for quick snacks, lunches and suppers. Any seasonal homegrown or shop vegetables can be used for the topping. If the soft Italian Mozzarella cheese is difficult to obtain, use the harder-textured Danish or Scottish Mozzarella.

15 g/½ oz fresh yeast
150 ml/¼ pint tepid water
200 g/7 oz strong plain flour
salt
25 g/1 oz butter, melted and cooled
TOMATO SAUCE
I tablespoon vegetable oil
I large onion, peeled and finely chopped
I–2 garlic cloves, peeled and crushed
500 g/1 lb tomatoes, skinned, seeded and roughly chopped
I tablespoon chopped oregano
I tablespoon chopped basil
4 tablespoons dry white wine
I tablespoon tomato purée
freshly ground black pepper
TOPPING
I red pepper, cored, seeded and thinly sliced
I green pepper, cored, seeded and thinly sliced
I small chilli, seeded and thinly sliced
12 black olives
125 g/4 oz Mozzarella cheese, thinly sliced
50 g/2 oz Gruyère cheese, grated

Dissolve the yeast in the water. Sift the flour and I teaspoon salt into a large bowl, make a well in the centre, then pour in the yeast and melted butter. Mix thoroughly to a firm, elastic dough. Cover with a piece of greased polythene and leave to rise in a warm place for about I hour, until doubled in size.

Meanwhile, heat the oil in a pan, add the onion and garlic and fry gently for 5 minutes without browning. Add the tomatoes, herbs and wine, bring to the boil and cook for 25 minutes until thickened. Remove from the heat, add salt and pepper to taste and cool.

Turn the dough onto a floured surface, divide in half, then knead each piece lightly. Use to line two 20 to 25 cm/8 to 10 inch lightly greased pizza trays. Spread the tomato sauce over the dough, arrange the peppers, chilli and cheeses on top. Finish each pizza with 6 olives.

To freeze: Open freeze until solid, then wrap in foil, seal, label and return to the freezer for up to 4 months.

To thaw and serve: Unwrap and place on a lightly greased baking sheet. Bake from frozen in a preheated moderately hot oven (200°C/400°F/Gas Mark 6) for 30 to 35 minutes until golden brown. Serve hot.
Makes 2 pizzas, each serving 4 to 6

FRENCH-STYLE POTATOES

This potato casserole makes a substantial snack or supper as well as an accompaniment. For a lighter dish, omit the ham, in which case the dish can be stored in the freezer for up to 4 months.

I kg/2 lb potatoes, peeled
2 tablespoons vegetable oil
4 onions, peeled and sliced
3 garlic cloves, peeled and thinly sliced
75 g/3 oz mature Cheddar cheese, grated
175 g/6 oz cooked ham, diced
300 ml/½ pint single cream
salt and freshly ground black pepper
TO SERVE
I × 50 g/2 oz can anchovy fillets, drained and soaked in milk for 15 minutes, rinsed and dried
50 g/2 oz butter
3 tablespoons fresh breadcrumbs

Cook the potatoes in boiling salted water for 12 minutes until just tender, drain, then slice into 1 cm/½ inch rings.

Heat the oil in a pan, add the onions and garlic and fry gently for 5 minutes without browning. Arrange a layer of potatoes and onions in the base of a lightly greased ovenproof dish, then sprinkle over a little cheese and ham and pour over some of the cream. Sprinkle with salt and pepper to taste. Continue with these layers until all the ingredients are used up, finishing with a layer of potato.

Cover the dish with foil and bake in a preheated moderate oven (180°C/350°F/Gas Mark 4) for 30 minutes. Remove the foil and leave to cool.

To freeze: Cover with clean foil, then wrap in a polythene bag. Seal, label and freeze for up to 2 months.

To thaw and serve: Unwrap and thaw at room temperature for 2 to 3 hours. Arrange a lattice of anchovies over the potatoes. Melt the butter in a pan, add the breadcrumbs and stir to coat them in the butter. Sprinkle over the anchovies. Reheat in a preheated moderately hot oven (200°C/400°F/Gas Mark 6) for 30 minutes until the topping is golden brown. Serve hot.
Serves 4 to 6

COURGETTE CHEESECAKE

This savoury cheesecake has a light summery taste. The courgettes can be replaced by aubergines, which should first be salted in a colander for 30 minutes, then well rinsed, drained and dried before use (see page 59). It is essential to use *freshly* grated Parmesan cheese for this recipe.

75 g/3 oz butter
1 × 150 g/5.29 oz packet Cheddar cheese biscuits, finely crushed
1 tablespoon grated Parmesan cheese
FILLING
1 tablespoon olive oil
1 garlic clove, peeled and sliced
4 courgettes, trimmed and sliced
3 × 80 g/2¾ oz packets garlic and herb soft cheese
3 eggs, separated
25 g/1 oz plain flour
50 g/2 oz grated Parmesan cheese
2 teaspoons French mustard
1 teaspoon dried mixed herbs
salt and freshly ground black pepper
TO SERVE
few sprigs of fresh herbs

Melt the butter in a pan. Remove from the heat and stir in the crushed biscuits and Parmesan cheese. Press the mixture onto the base and 2.5 cm/1 inch up the sides of a lightly greased 20 cm/8 inch loose-bottomed cake tin. Chill in the refrigerator for 30 minutes.

To make the filling: Heat the oil in a pan, add the garlic and fry quickly until lightly browned. Remove the garlic with a slotted spoon and discard, then add the courgettes and cook for 2 minutes until just tender. Remove with a slotted spoon and drain on kitchen paper.

Beat the soft cheese until creamy, then add the egg yolks, flour, Parmesan cheese, mustard, herbs and salt and pepper to taste. Beat well to mix. In a separate bowl, whisk the egg whites until stiff. Stir 2 tablespoons of the egg whites into the cheese mixture to lighten it, then fold in the remainder with the courgettes.

Spoon the mixture into the prepared tin. Bake in a preheated moderate oven (170°C/325°F/Gas Mark 3) for 1 hour until the filling is set and golden brown. Remove from the oven and leave to cool.

To freeze: Carefully remove the tin, leaving the cheesecake on the base, then open freeze until solid. Remove the base of the tin and wrap the cheesecake in foil. Seal, label and return to the freezer for up to 4 months.

To thaw and serve: Unwrap and place on a serving plate. Leave to stand at room temperature for 3 to 4 hours. Serve cold, garnished with fresh herbs.
Serves 6

Ratatouille Tarts; Courgette Cheesecake; Gardener's Pizza

MELON ICE CREAM

The subtle, delicate flavour of this ice depends on the type of melon used. Gallia, Ogen or Charentais give a more pronounced flavour, but honeydew melon can also be used. It makes a very refreshing dessert after a rich main course. If you are going to serve the ice the day after making, serve in the reserved melon shells.

1 kg/2 lb melon
125 g/4 oz icing sugar, sifted
juice of 1 lime
300 ml/½ pint double cream

Cut the melon in half and discard the seeds. Scoop out the flesh with a spoon and place in an electric blender or food processor with the icing sugar and lime juice. Work to a purée, then pour into a rigid container, cover and freeze for 2 to 3 hours until the mixture is half-frozen.

Remove from the freezer and turn into a bowl, then whisk to break up the ice crystals. Whip the cream until it will stand in soft peaks, then whisk in the melon purée.

To freeze: Return the ice cream to the container, seal, label and return to the freezer for up to 3 months.

To thaw and serve: Transfer to the refrigerator 30 minutes before serving to soften. Scoop into chilled glasses and serve immediately.

Serves 4 to 6

AVOCADO AND LIME ICE CREAM

Avocados are not only delicious in savoury dishes – they also make many excellent desserts. Their silky texture makes a very smooth, creamy ice; this one is flavoured with lime, but orange also blends very well with avocado.

2 ripe avocado pears, peeled, halved and stoned
150 ml/¼ pint single cream
125 g/4 oz icing sugar, sifted
300 ml/½ pint double cream
juice of 1 lime
TO SERVE
few mint sprigs

Work the avocado flesh, single cream and icing sugar in an electric blender or food processor until smooth.

Whip the double cream until it will stand in soft peaks. Fold in the avocado mixture, then the lime juice. Pour into a rigid container, cover and freeze for 2 to 3 hours until half-frozen. Remove from the freezer and stir well.

To freeze: Seal the container, label and return to the freezer for up to 3 months.

To thaw and serve: Transfer to the refrigerator 45 minutes before serving to soften. Scoop into chilled glasses, decorate with mint and serve immediately.

Serves 4

COFFEE GRANITA

Perfectly refreshing on a hot summer's day – this coffee-flavoured water ice has a delicious flavour and a granular texture.

150 g/5 oz finely ground fresh coffee
75 g/3 oz caster sugar
1 litre/1¾ pints boiling water
TO SERVE
120 ml/4 fl oz whipping cream, whipped

Place the coffee and sugar in a warmed coffee jug and pour in the boiling water. Stir, then cover and leave to infuse for 20 to 30 minutes.

When cold, strain through a filter paper into another jug. Pour into a rigid container, cover and freeze for 2 to 3 hours until half-frozen. Remove from the freezer, turn into a bowl and whisk to break up the ice crystals.

Transfer to the container and freeze for a further 2 to 3 hours. Remove from the freezer, turn into a bowl and whisk again.

To freeze: Return the water ice to the container, seal, label and return to the freezer for up to 2 months.

To thaw and serve: Transfer to the refrigerator 10 minutes before serving to soften, then stir until crumbly. Spoon into tall glasses and top each serving with a swirl of whipped cream.

Serves 4 to 6

RASPBERRY SORBET

Make this sorbet for the freezer in summer with fresh raspberries, or out of season with frozen raspberry purée. For a special occasion, pour a little liqueur, such as Cointreau, over each serving.

500 g/1 lb raspberries
300 ml/½ pint water
125 g/4 oz granulated sugar
1 egg white

Work the raspberries in an electric blender or food processor until smooth, then work through a nylon sieve to remove the pips.

Heat the water and sugar gently in a pan, stirring until the sugar has dissolved. Boil rapidly for 5 minutes, stir into the raspberry purée and leave to cool. Pour the mixture into a rigid container, cover and freeze for 2 to 3 hours until half-frozen.

Remove from the freezer and turn into a bowl. Whisk the egg white until stiff, then whisk into the half-frozen raspberry mixture.

To freeze: Return the sorbet to the container, seal, label and return to the freezer for up to 2 months.

To thaw and serve: Transfer to the refrigerator 10 minutes before serving to soften. Scoop into chilled glasses and serve immediately.

Serves 4 to 6

APRICOT SORBET

Little macaroons make an ideal accompaniment to this delicious refreshing ice.

500 g/1 lb fresh apricots, stoned
450 ml/¾ pint water
juice of ½ lemon
175 g/6 oz granulated sugar
1 egg white
2 tablespoons kirsch

Place the apricots in a pan with 150 ml/¼ pint of the water. Cover and simmer gently for 15 minutes until tender. Cool slightly, then put the apricots in an electric blender or food processor with the lemon juice and work until smooth.

Heat the remaining water and the sugar gently in a pan, stirring, until the sugar has dissolved. Boil rapidly for 5 minutes, then sitr into the apricot purée and leave to cool completely.

Add the kirsch and pour the mixture into a rigid container, cover and freeze for 2 to 3 hours until half-frozen. Remove from the freezer and turn into a bowl. Whisk the egg white until stiff, then whisk into the half-frozen apricot mixture.

To freeze: Return the sorbet to the container, seal, label and return to the freezer for up to 2 months.

To thaw and serve: Transfer to the refrigerator 10 minutes before serving to soften. Scoop into chilled glasses and serve immediately.

Serves 6 to 8

BLACKCURRANT SORBET

500 g/1 lb blackcurrants
150 ml/¼ pint + 2 tablespoons water
125 g/4 oz sugar
juice of ½ lemon
1 egg white

Place the blackcurrants in a pan with 2 tablespoons of the water. Cover and simmer until soft, then purée in an electric blender or food processor until smooth.

Place the sugar and remaining water in a pan and heat gently, stirring, until dissolved. Bring to the boil, simmer for 5 minutes, then cool. Add to the black-currant purée with the lemon juice. Turn into a rigid container and freeze for 2 to 3 hours or until half-frozen. Whip the egg white lightly and fold into the half-frozen mixture.

To freeze: Return the sorbet to the container, seal, label and freeze for up to 2 months.

To thaw and serve: Transfer to the refrigerator 10 minutes before serving to soften. Scoop into chilled glasses and serve immediately.

Serves 4

Apricot Sorbet; Melon Ice Cream; Avocado and Lime Ice Cream; Raspberry Sorbet

MERINGUE GLACÉ

This special occasion dessert takes a long time to prepare but it can be made well ahead. The crunchy meringue makes the perfect contrast to the soft, creamy ice.

RASPBERRY ICE CREAM
350 g/12 oz raspberries
2 egg whites
75 g/3 oz caster sugar
300 ml/½ pint double cream
MERINGUES
3 egg whites
175 g/6 oz caster sugar
FILLING
250 ml/8 fl oz double cream
1 tablespoon icing sugar, sifted
175 g/6 oz raspberries
TO SERVE
3 tablespoons double cream, whipped
8 raspberries

Line 3 baking sheets with non-stick silicone paper. With a pencil, draw three 15 cm/6 inch circles on the paper.

To make the ice cream: Work the raspberries in an electric blender or food processor until smooth, then work through a nylon sieve to remove the pips.

Whisk the egg whites until stiff, then whisk in the sugar 1 tablespoon at a time. Continue whisking until the meringue is very stiff and holds its shape. Whip the cream until it will stand in soft peaks, then whisk in the raspberry pureé. Fold the raspberry cream into the meringue mixture. Pour into a rigid container, cover and freeze for 2 to 3 hours until half-frozen. Stir well, then return to the freezer until almost solid.

To make the meringues: Whisk the egg whites until stiff, then whisk in 3 tablespoons of the sugar. Carefully fold in the remaining sugar with a metal spoon. Spoon into a piping bag fitted with a 1 cm/½ inch plain nozzle and pipe into the circles marked on the paper. Bake in a preheated very cool oven (120°C/250°F/Gas Mark ½) for 2 hours or until crisp. Carefully peel the paper off the meringues, then place on a wire rack to cool.

To make the filling: Whip the cream with the icing sugar until it will stand in soft peaks, then fold in the raspberries.

Line a 20 cm/8 inch cake tin with a layer of raspberry ice cream. Place a meringue round on top and cover with half the raspberry filling. Repeat these layers and top with the third meringue round, filling any space at the sides with ice cream.

To freeze: Cover the tin with foil, wrap in a polythene bag, then seal, label and freeze for up to 3 months.

To thaw and serve: Unwrap the tin and invert onto a serving plate. Rub with a cloth wrung out in very hot water until the cake drops out. Decorate with piped cream and raspberries, then transfer to the refrigerator 1 hour before serving to soften. Serve chilled.
Serves 8

HAZELNUT BOMBE

This bombe has a delicious richness which, combined with a nutty wholesome flavour, makes it irresistible!

75 g/3 oz hazelnuts, ground
75 g/3 oz wholemeal breadcrumbs
50 g/2 oz demerara sugar
3 egg whites
125 g/4 oz soft brown sugar
300 ml/½ pint whipping cream
TO SERVE
6 tablespoons double cream, whipped
8 toasted hazelnuts

Mix the ground hazelnuts, breadcrumbs and demerara sugar together on a baking sheet. Place under a preheated hot grill for about 2 minutes, stirring occasionally until golden brown. Leave to cool.

Whisk the egg whites until stiff, then whisk in the brown sugar 1 tablespoon at a time. Continue whisking until the meringue is very stiff and holds its shape. Whip the cream until it forms soft peaks, then fold into the meringue with the hazelnut mixture. Pour into a 1.2 litre/2 pint bombe mould or freezerproof basin.

To freeze: Cover the bombe mould with its lid or cover the basin with foil, then wrap in a polythene bag. Seal, label and freeze for up to 3 months.

To thaw and serve: Unwrap the mould and invert onto a serving plate. Rub with a cloth wrung out in very hot water until the bombe drops out. Decorate with piped whipped cream and hazelnuts, then transfer to the refrigerator 30 minutes before serving to soften. Serve chilled.

Serves 6 to 8

CHERRY AND CHOCOLATE BOMBE

A bombe makes a very impressive dinner-party dessert. Although quite time-consuming to make, it can be prepared well in advance and stored in the freezer until required. It can be decorated several hours before serving and returned to the freezer, but remember to soften in the refrigerator for about 30 minutes before serving.

CHOCOLATE ICE CREAM
3 egg yolks
50 g/2 oz caster sugar
125 g/4 oz plain chocolate, broken into small pieces
300 ml/½ pint single cream
150 ml/¼ pint double cream
FILLING
250 g/8 oz black cherries, stoned and quartered
2 tablespoons kirsch
1 tablespoon caster sugar
250 ml/8 fl oz double cream
TO SERVE
4 tablespoons double cream, whipped

Beat the egg yolks and sugar in a heatproof bowl until blended. Put the chocolate and single cream in a small heavy-based pan and heat gently until the chocolate has melted. Pour onto the egg yolk mixture, stirring vigorously. Transfer to the top of a double boiler or a heatproof bowl over a pan of simmering water, and cook gently, stirring constantly, until the custard is thick enough to coat the back of a spoon. Strain into a bowl and leave to cool, stirring occasionally to prevent a skin forming.

Whip the double cream until it will stand in soft peaks, then fold in the custard. Turn into a rigid container, cover and freeze for 2 to 3 hours until half-frozen. Stir well, then return to the freezer for 3 hours or until firm but still soft enough to mould.

To make the filling: Put the cherries in a bowl with the kirsch and sugar; leave to macerate for 1 hour. Whip the cream until it will stand in stiff peaks, then fold in the cherries and kirsch.

Line a chilled 1.5 litre/2½ pint bombe mould or freezerproof basin thickly with chocolate ice cream. Fill the centre with the cherry filling.

To freeze: Cover the bombe mould with its lid or cover the basin with foil, then wrap in a polythene bag. Seal, label and freeze for up to 3 months.

To thaw and serve: Unwrap the mould and invert onto a serving plate. Rub with a cloth wrung out in very hot water until the bombe drops out. Decorate with the cream and transfer to the refrigerator 30 minutes before serving to soften. Serve chilled.
Serves 6 to 8

LEFT: Cherry and Chocolate Bombe; Meringue Glacé
RIGHT: Nectarine Baked Alaska

NECTARINE BAKED ALASKA

A spectacular dessert that normally needs to be prepared at the last minute, but can be frozen fully prepared and baked just a few minutes before serving. It is best not to keep it in the freezer for more than 1 to 2 days.

2 eggs
75 g/3 oz caster sugar
50 g/2 oz plain flour, sifted
4 tablespoons sweet sherry
2–3 nectarines
juice of ½ small lemon
MERINGUE
4 egg whites
250 g/8 oz caster sugar
600 ml/1 pint vanilla ice cream

Grease a 20 cm/8 inch sandwich tin, line the base with greaseproof paper, then grease the paper. Dust the inside of the tin lightly with flour.

Put the eggs and sugar in a bowl and whisk with an electric beater until thick and mousse-like. Carefully fold in the flour. Turn the mixture into the prepared tin and level the surface. Bake in a preheated moderately hot oven (190°C/375°F/Gas Mark 5) for 15 to 20 minutes until the cake springs back when lightly pressed in the centre. Turn out onto a wire rack, peel off the lining paper, turn the cake the right way up and leave to cool.

Place the sponge on a heatproof serving dish and sprinkle over the sherry. Stone and finely slice the nectarines; sprinkle with the lemon juice. Arrange the nectarines over the sponge.

For the meringue: Whisk the egg whites until stiff, then gradually whisk in the sugar and set aside.

Soften the ice cream slightly, then shape it into a dome over the nectarines, leaving a 2.5 cm/1 inch margin all around. Quickly spoon the meringue over the ice cream and sponge to cover them completely.

To freeze: Open freeze the alaska until solid, then pack in a rigid container. Seal, label and return to the freezer for up to 2 days.

To thaw and serve: Bake from frozen in a preheated hot oven (220°C/425°F/Gas Mark 7) for 8 to 10 minutes until the meringue has browned lightly. Serve the baked alaska immediately.
Serves 6 to 8

LOGANBERRY MOUSSE

Make this mousse with fresh loganberries in summer,
or use 450 ml/¾ pint frozen loganberry purée at
other times of year. Raspberries or blackberries can
be used instead, but they may need less sugar,
according to taste.

500 g/1 lb loganberries
2 eggs
1 egg yolk
175 g/6 oz caster sugar
300 ml/½ pint whipping cream
15 g/½ oz (1 envelope) powdered gelatine, dissolved
 in 3 tablespoons water
TO SERVE
4 tablespoons double cream, whipped
125 g/4 oz loganberries (optional)

Work the loganberries in an electric blender or food
processor until smooth, then work through a nylon
sieve to remove the pips.

Put the eggs, egg yolk and sugar in a bowl and whisk
with an electric beater until thick and mousse-like.
Whip the cream until it will stand in soft peaks. Add
the gelatine to the fruit purée, then fold into the cream.

Carefully fold the loganberry mixture into the egg
mixture and turn into a greased 1.5 litre/2½ pint
decorative mould. Chill in the refrigerator for about
1 hour or until set.

To freeze: Cover the mould with foil, wrap in a
polythene bag, then seal, label and freeze for up to 3
months.

To thaw and serve: Leave to stand in wrappings at
room temperature for 4 to 5 hours, then unwrap and
dip the base of the mould in hot water for a few
seconds. Invert and turn out onto a serving plate.
Decorate with piped whipped cream and loganberries
if available. Chill in the refrigerator until required.
Serves 8

STRAWBERRY SOUFFLÉ

This soufflé can be made with fresh strawberries as
here, or with strawberry purée from the freezer.

500 g/1 lb strawberries, hulled
4 eggs, separated
125 g/4 oz caster sugar
15 g/½ oz (1 envelope) powdered gelatine,
juice of 1 orange
300 ml/½ pint whipping cream
TO SERVE
15 g/½ oz ratafias, crushed
4 tablespoons double cream, whipped
few strawberry slices (optional)

Tie a band of foil tightly around the outside of a 1 litre/
1¾ pint soufflé dish to stand 5 cm/2 inches above rim.

Work the strawberries in an electric blender or
food processor until smooth, then work through a
nylon sieve to remove the pips.

Put the egg yolks and sugar in a bowl and whisk with
an electric beater until thick and mousse-like. Soak the
gelatine in the orange juice, then heat gently until
dissolved. Stir into the egg mixture.

Whip the cream until it will stand in soft peaks, then
lightly fold in the strawberry purée. Carefully fold in
the egg mousse mixture. Leave in a cool place until just
beginning to set.

Whisk the egg whites until stiff; stir 1 tablespoon into
the soufflé mixture to lighten it, then fold in the
remainder. Spoon into the prepared soufflé dish and

level the surface. Chill in the refrigerator for about
1 hour or until set.

To freeze: Open freeze the soufflé until solid, then
wrap in a polythene bag. Seal, label and return to the
freezer for up to 3 months.

To thaw and serve: Unwrap and leave to stand in the
refrigerator overnight. Remove the foil carefully and
press the crushed ratafias around the side. Decorate
with the whipped cream and strawberry halves if
available. Serve chilled.
Serves 6 to 8

Strawberry Soufflé; Loganberry Mousse

BLACKCURRANT PARFAIT

This parfait is made from a half-frozen fruit pureé combined with a meringue mixture and whipped cream. It should be the consistency of a very thick fool and served immediately before it melts. Sweet crisp biscuits make the perfect accompaniment.

500 g/1 lb blackcurrants, stalks removed
4 tablespoons water
2 teaspoons lemon juice
50 g/2 oz granulated sugar
TO SERVE
2 egg whites
75 g/3 oz caster sugar
300 ml/½ pint double cream

Put the blackcurrants in a pan with the water, lemon juice and sugar. Simmer gently for 8 to 10 minutes until the blackcurrants are softened. Leave to cool.

Work the cooled blackcurrant mixture in an electric blender or food processor until smooth, then work through a nylon sieve to remove the pips. Pour the pureé into a rigid container, cover and freeze for 2 to 3 hours until half-frozen. Remove from the freezer and transfer to a bowl. Whisk thoroughly to break up the ice crystals.

To freeze: Return the blackcurrant parfait to the rigid container. Seal, label and return to the freezer for up to 2 months.

To thaw and serve: Transfer to the refrigerator and leave to soften until half-frozen, then whisk to break up the ice crystals.

Whisk the egg whites until stiff, then whisk in the sugar 1 tablespoon at a time. Continue whisking until the meringue is very stiff and holds its shape. Whip the cream until it will stand in soft peaks, then fold into the meringue with the half-frozen blackcurrant mixture. Spoon into chilled glasses and serve immediately, with crisp biscuits if preferred.
Serves 4 to 6

REDCURRANT TANSY

Tansies take their name from the pungent herb which, in by-gone days, was used to flavour them. In this recipe, the fruit purée is frozen with a thick egg custard, then whipped cream is folded in after thawing to give a marbled effect. Serve with crisp biscuits.

500 g/1 lb redcurrants, stalks removed
125 g/4 oz granulated sugar
3 egg yolks
1 tablespoon caster sugar
2 teaspoons cornflour
300 ml/½ pint milk
TO SERVE
150 ml/¼ pint double cream, whipped

Put the redcurrants in a pan with the sugar and simmer gently for 8 to 10 minutes until softened. Leave to cool, then work in an electric blender or food processor until smooth, or work through a nylon sieve.

Put the egg yolks, caster sugar and cornflour in a bowl and beat until thoroughly blended. Bring the milk to the boil in a pan, then stir into the egg mixture. Strain into the top of a double boiler or a heatproof bowl over a pan of simmering water and cook gently, stirring constantly, until the custard is thick enough to coat the back of a spoon. Remove from the heat and fold in the redcurrant purée. Leave to cool, stirring occasionally to prevent a skin forming.

To freeze: Pour the tansy into a rigid container, seal, label and freeze for up to 3 months.

To thaw and serve: Leave to stand in the container at room temperature for 4 to 5 hours. Whisk the redcurrant mixture, then carefully fold in the whipped cream with a metal spoon to create a marbled effect. Spoon the tansy into individual glasses and chill in the refrigerator until required. Serve chilled, with crisp biscuits.
Serves 6

Blackcurrant Parfait; Redcurrant Tansy

PÊCHES CARMEN

This is a quick, refreshing dessert, suitable to serve at a dinner party after a rich main course. Serve with a bowl of whipped cream handed separately.

500 g/1 lb raspberries
75 g/3 oz icing sugar, sifted
2 tablespoons kirsch
TO SERVE
6 ripe peaches, halved and stoned, or 12 frozen peach
*   halves, thawed*

Work the raspberries and icing sugar in an electric blender or food processor until smooth, then work through a nylon sieve to remove pips. Stir in the kirsch.
To freeze: Pour the mixture into a rigid container, seal, label and freeze for up to 12 months.
To thaw and serve: Leave to stand in container at room temperature for 4 hours. Put the peaches in a serving bowl and pour over the raspberry sauce. Chill in the refrigerator until serving time.
Serves 6

PEACH CHARLOTTE

This charlotte has a delicious moulded custard filling flavoured with peaches. It must be poured into the mould when on the point of setting.

20 sponge fingers
4 ripe peaches, peeled, halved and stoned
juice of ½ lemon
3 egg yolks
25 g/1 oz caster sugar
350 ml/12 fl oz milk
15 g/½ oz (1 envelope) powdered gelatine, dissolved
*   in 3 tablespoons water*
2 tablespoons kirsch
150 ml/¼ pint whipping cream
TO SERVE
2 peaches, stoned and sliced
2 teaspoons lemon juice

Arrange the sponge fingers to fit closely around the inside of a lightly oiled 1.5 litre/2½ pint charlotte mould, trimming to fit where necessary.

Put 3 peaches and the lemon juice in an electric blender or food processor and work until smooth.

Put the egg yolks and sugar in a bowl and beat until thoroughly blended. Bring the milk to the boil in a pan, then stir into the egg mixture. Strain into the top of a double boiler or a heatproof bowl over a pan of simmering water and cook gently, stirring constantly, until it is thick enough to coat the back of a spoon.

Pour the custard into a bowl and stir in the dissolved gelatine. Leave to cool, stirring occasionally to prevent a skin forming. Stir the peach pureé and kirsch into the cooled custard and continue stirring over a bowl of iced water until the mixture starts to thicken. Whip the cream until it forms soft peaks. Slice the remaining peach and fold into the peach custard, with the whipped cream. Pour into the prepared mould. Chill in the refrigerator for about 1 hour or until set completely.
To freeze: Cover with foil, wrap in a polythene bag, then seal, label and freeze for up to 3 months.
To thaw and serve: Leave to stand in the mould in the refrigerator overnight, then unwrap and turn out onto a serving plate. Dip the peach slices into the lemon juice and arrange them on top. Serve chilled.
Serves 6

VACHERIN AUX PÊCHES

Meringue with cream is always a popular dessert, and a vacherin looks most impressive for a dinner party. The fruit can be varied according to what is in season.

MERINGUES
4 egg whites
250 g/8 oz caster sugar
FILLING
300 ml/½ pint double cream
4 ripe peaches, peeled, stoned and sliced
TO SERVE
a little icing sugar
4 tablespoons double cream, whipped
1 peach, stoned and sliced (optional)

Line 2 baking sheets with non-stick silicone paper. With a pencil, draw on two 23 cm/9 inch circles.
To make the meringues: Whisk the egg whites until stiff, then whisk in 3 tablespoons of the sugar. Carefully fold in the remaining sugar with a metal spoon. Spoon into a piping bag fitted with a 1 cm/½ inch plain nozzle and pipe into the circles marked on the paper. Bake in a preheated very cool oven (110°C/225°F/Gas Mark ¼) for 2 hours until crisp. Peel the paper carefully off the meringues, then place on a wire rack to cool.

To make the filling: Whip the cream until it will stand in soft peaks, then fold in the peach slices. Use to sandwich the meringue rounds together.
To freeze: Open freeze the vacherin until solid, then pack carefully in a rigid container. Seal, label and return to the freezer for up to 3 months.
To thaw and serve: Remove from the container, place on a serving plate and leave to stand at room temperature for 3 to 4 hours. Sift icing sugar lightly over the top of the vacherin, then pipe rosettes of whipped cream around the edge and decorate with the peach slices if using. Serve as soon as possible.
Serves 8

SUMMER PUDDING

The ideal dessert to make when soft fruits are in season. If making later in the summer, use fresh blackberries mixed with fruits from the freezer.

500 g/1 lb mixed blackcurrants and redcurrants, stalks removed
125 g/4 oz caster sugar
250 g/8 oz raspberries
8 slices white bread, crusts removed

Put the currants in a heavy pan with the sugar. Cook gently, stirring occasionally, for 10 to 15 minutes until tender. Remove from the heat, stir in the raspberries and leave to cool. Strain the fruit, reserving the juice.

Cut 3 circles of bread in graduating sizes to fit the bottom, centre and top of a 900 ml/1½ pint freezer-proof basin. Shape the remaining bread to fit around the sides of the basin. Dip all the bread in the reserved fruit juice.

Line the bottom of the basin with the smallest circle of bread, then arrange the shaped bread around the sides. Spoon in half the fruit and place the second largest circle of bread on top. Cover with the remaining fruit, then top with the largest circle of bread.

Cover with a saucer small enough to fit inside the basin and put a 500 g/1 lb weight on top. Leave in the refrigerator overnight.
To freeze: Remove the weight and saucer from the basin and cover with cling film. Wrap in a polythene bag, seal, label and freeze for up to 6 months.
To thaw and serve: Unwrap and leave to stand at room temperature for 6 to 8 hours. Turn out onto a serving dish. Serve immediately, with whipped cream.
Serves 8

ABOVE: Summer Pudding; Vacherin aux Pêches
OPPOSITE: Peach Charlotte; Pêches Carmen

BLACK FOREST GÂTEAU

This deliciously rich gâteau is from the Black Forest in Germany, where it is called Schwartzwaldertorte. Traditionally made with fresh black cherries, it can also be made with canned black cherries although, of course, these do not need to be simmered in the orange juice. For a quick alternative topping, combine a can of black cherry pie filling with a can of black cherries – drained and stoned.

3 large eggs
125 g/4 oz caster sugar
50 g/2 oz plain flour
25 g/1 oz cocoa powder
1 tablespoon vegetable oil
FILLING
500 g/1 lb black cherries, stoned
50 g/2 oz caster sugar
juice of 1 orange
1 tablespoon arrowroot
4 tablespoons kirsch
300 ml/½ pint double cream
chocolate curls

Grease a deep 20 cm/8 inch round cake tin, line the base with greaseproof paper, then grease the paper.

Put the eggs and sugar in a bowl and whisk with an electric beater until thick and mousse-like. Sift the flour with the cocoa powder and lightly fold into the egg mixture with a metal spoon. Carefully fold in the oil.

Turn the mixture into the prepared tin and level the surface. Bake in a preheated moderately hot oven (190°C/375°F/Gas Mark 5) for 30 to 35 minutes until the cake springs back when lightly pressed in the centre. Turn out onto a wire rack, carefully peel off the lining paper, turn the cake the right way up and leave to cool.

To make the filling: Put the cherries, sugar and orange juice in a pan, cover and bring slowly to the boil. Stir gently and simmer for 4 to 5 minutes. Drain and reserve the cherries; return the juice to the pan. Blend the arrowroot with a little water, then stir into the juice in the pan. Bring to the boil, stirring, then lower the heat and simmer for 1 minute, until clear. Remove from the heat and leave to cool slightly, then add the reserved cherries and half the kirsch. Leave to cool completely.

Slice the cake in half horizontally and sprinkle both layers with the remaining kirsch. Whip the cream until it will stand in soft peaks. Place one cake layer on a plate and spread with half the cream. Spread half the cherry mixture over the cream, then top with the second cake layer. Spread a thin layer of cream around the sides of the gâteau and press the chocolate curls into it. Pipe a decorative border around the top of the gâteau and fill the centre with the remaining cherry mixture, spreading it smoothly to meet the cream.

To freeze: Open freeze the gâteau until solid, then pack carefully in a rigid container. Seal, label and return to the freezer for up to 3 months.

To thaw and serve: Remove from the container, place on a serving plate and leave to stand in the refrigerator overnight. Serve chilled.

Serves 6 to 8

BLACKCURRANT CHARLOTTE

This is an easy method of making a charlotte – the biscuits are arranged around the moulded cream filling after it has been turned out.

350 g/12 oz blackcurrants, stalks removed
2 tablespoons water
1 tablespoon granulated sugar
2 eggs
1 egg yolk
75 g/3 oz caster sugar
15 g/½ oz (1 envelope) powdered gelatine, dissolved in 3 tablespoons water
300 ml/½ pint double cream
TO SERVE
150 ml/¼ pint double cream, whipped
30 langues de chat biscuits
frosted blackcurrant clusters (see below)
blackcurrant leaves

Put the blackcurrants in a pan with the water and granulated sugar and simmer gently for 8 to 10 minutes until softened. Leave to cool, then work in an electric blender or food processor until smooth. Work through a nylon sieve to remove the pips.

Put the eggs, egg yolk and caster sugar in a bowl and whisk with an electric beater until thick and mousse-like. Whip the cream until it will stand in soft peaks. Fold the dissolved gelatine into the blackcurrant purée, then fold into the cream.

Carefully fold the blackcurrant mixture into the egg mixture and turn into a greased 18 cm/7 inch freezer-proof soufflé dish. Chill in the refrigerator for about 1 hour or until set completely.

To freeze: Open freeze the charlotte until solid, then invert and rub the dish with a cloth wrung out in very hot water until the charlotte drops out. Wrap in a polythene bag, seal, label and freeze for up to 3 months.

To thaw and serve: Unwrap the charlotte, turn out onto a serving plate, then leave in the refrigerator overnight. Spread a little of the whipped cream around the sides of the charlotte, then press the biscuits onto the cream, overlapping them slightly. Pipe the remaining cream in a border around the top. Decorate with frosted blackcurrant clusters, and leaves if available.

Serves 8

FROSTED FRUIT

Select small clusters of fresh fruit or ones which have been open-frozen. Using a fine paintbrush, lightly coat the fruit with lightly whisked egg white. Brush off any excess. Dip the fruit in caster sugar to coat evenly. Place on greaseproof paper to dry for 1 to 2 hours.

RASPBERRY CHEESECAKE

This is a very light cheesecake, which makes a good finale for a dinner party. If fresh raspberries are not available for the decoration, use frozen ones, thawing them before applying to the cheesecake. Any soft fruit – fresh or frozen – may be used to cover the top.

50 g/2 oz butter or margarine
125 g/4 oz digestive biscuits, crushed
350 g/12 oz curd cheese
50 g/2 oz caster sugar
3 eggs, separated
300 ml/½ pint double cream
15 g/½ oz (1 envelope) powdered gelatine, dissolved in 3 tablespoons orange juice
TO SERVE
4 tablespoons double cream, whipped
250 g/8 oz raspberries

Melt the butter or margarine in a small pan, then remove from the heat and mix in the biscuit crumbs. Press the mixture over the base of a lightly oiled 20 cm/8 inch springform cake tin; chill in the refrigerator for about 15 minutes until firm.

Put the cheese in a bowl and beat in the sugar and egg yolks. Whip the cream until it will stand in soft peaks. Stir the dissolved gelatine into the cheese mixture, then fold in the cream.

Whisk the egg whites until stiff, then fold 2 tablespoons into the cheese mixture to lighten it. Fold in the remaining egg whites, then spoon the mixture over the biscuit base and level the surface. Chill the cheesecake in the refrigerator for 1 to 1½ hours or until the filling is set.

To freeze: Open freeze the cheeecake until solid, then remove from the tin and place on a cake board. Wrap in a polythene bag, seal, label and return to the freezer for up to 1 month.

To thaw and serve: Unwrap, place on a serving plate and leave to stand in the refrigerator overnight. Pipe a whipped cream border around the edge of the cheesecake and arrange the raspberries over the top. Serve chilled.

Serves 6 to 8

VARIATION

For a sharper citrus flavour, use lemon juice instead of orange juice, and add the grated rind of 1 lemon to the curd cheese, with the sugar and egg yolks.

Raspberry Cheesecake; Blackcurrant Charlotte; Black Forest Gâteau

PEACH GÂTEAU

This gâteau is best made with fresh peaches, but when out of season, canned sliced peaches may be used.

3 eggs, separated
125 g/4 oz caster sugar
finely grated rind and juice of ½ lemon
50 g/2 oz semolina
25 g/1 oz ground almonds
TO SERVE
4 ripe peaches, stoned and thinly sliced
300 ml/½ pint double cream, whipped
4 tablespoons apricot jam
2 teaspoons lemon juice
50 g/2 oz ground hazelnuts, toasted

Grease a deep 20 cm/8 inch cake tin, line the base with greaseproof paper, then grease the paper. Dust the inside of the tin lightly with flour.

Put the egg yolks, sugar, lemon rind and juice in a bowl and whisk with an electric beater until thick and mousse-like. Stir in the semolina and ground almonds. Whisk the egg whites until stiff, then fold in.

Turn the mixture into the prepared tin and level the surface. Bake in a preheated moderate oven (180°C/350°F/Gas Mark 4) for 35 to 40 minutes until the cake springs back when lightly pressed in the centre. Turn out onto a wire rack, peel off the lining paper, turn the cake the right way up and leave to cool.

To freeze: Wrap the cake in a polythene bag, seal, label and freeze for up to 10 months.

To thaw and serve: Unwrap and leave to stand at room temperature for 2 to 3 hours, then cut into 2 layers. Fold half of the peach slices into three quarters of the cream and use to sandwich the layers together.

Put the apricot jam and lemon juice in a small pan and heat gently, stirring, until the jam has melted. Sieve and reheat. Arrange the remaining peach slices overlapping in a circle on top of the cake. Brush the peaches and the sides of the cake with the warm glaze. Press the hazelnuts around the sides, then pipe the remaining cream around the top. Serve chilled.

Serves 8

STRAWBERRY CREAM SPONGE

This light and fruity sponge can be served at tea-time, or as a dessert. It is best eaten on the day it is assembled.

3 eggs
150 g/5 oz caster sugar
75 g/3 oz plain flour, sifted
1 tablespoon vegetable oil
TO SERVE
150 ml/¼ pint double cream, whipped
250 g/8 oz strawberries, hulled and sliced
a little icing sugar, to taste

Grease a deep 20 cm/8 inch cake tin, line the base with greaseproof paper, then grease the paper. Dust the inside of the tin lightly with flour.

Put the eggs and sugar in a bowl and whisk with an electric beater until thick and mousse-like. Carefully fold in the flour and oil.

Turn the mixture into the prepared tin and level the surface. Bake in a preheated moderately hot oven (190°C/375°F/Gas Mark 5) for 20 to 25 minutes until the cake springs back when lightly pressed in the centre. Turn out onto a wire rack, peel off the paper, turn the cake the right way up and leave to cool.

To freeze: Pack in a polythene bag, seal, label and freeze for up to 10 months.

To thaw and serve: Unwrap and leave to stand at room temperature for 2 to 3 hours. Cut the cake into 2 layers, put the bottom half on a serving plate and spread with the cream. Cover with the strawberries. Apply the top layer and sift over icing sugar to serve.

Serves 8

RASPBERRY AND HAZELNUT ROLL

This light sponge roll is delicious served with coffee, but it can also be served as a dessert.

3 eggs
125 g/4 oz caster sugar
50 g/2 oz plain flour, sifted
50 g/2 oz ground hazelnuts, toasted
1 tablespoon vegetable oil
caster sugar, for dredging
FILLING
250 ml/8 fl oz double cream
250 g/8 oz raspberries
1 tablespoon icing sugar, sifted
TO SERVE
6 tablespoons double cream, whipped
8 raspberries (optional)

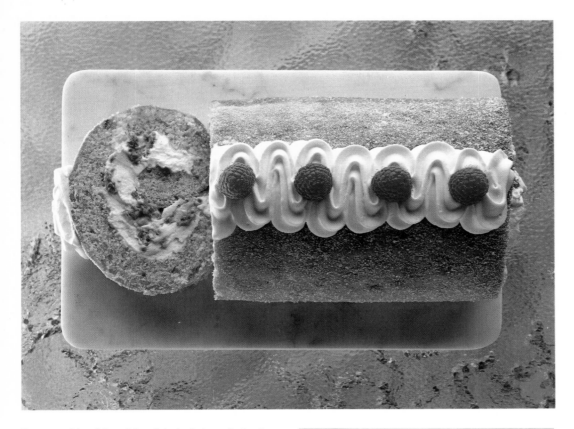

Turn the dough onto a floured surface, then roll out and use to line a 23 cm/9 inch fluted flan ring on a baking sheet. Chill in the refrigerator for 15 minutes.

To make the filling: Put the eggs and sugar in a bowl and whisk together, using an electric beater until thick and creamy. Stir in the cream, ground almonds and vanilla flavouring.

Turn the filling into the flan case and level the surface. Bake in a preheated moderately hot oven (200°C/400°F/Gas Mark 6) for 20 minutes, then reduce the temperature to 190°C/375°F/Gas Mark 5 and bake for a further 10 to 15 minutes until firm to the touch. Leave to cool on a wire rack.

To freeze: Open freeze until solid, then remove carefully from the flan ring and wrap in foil. Seal, label and return to the freezer for up to 4 months.

To thaw and serve: Unwrap and place on a wire rack. Leave to stand at room temperature for 2 to 3 hours. Arrange the cherries over of the almond filling. Put the redcurrant jelly and water in a small pan and heat gently, stirring until dissolved. Brush the redcurrant glaze over the cherries and leave until cool and set. Serve the cherry tart as soon as possible.

Serves 8

SCONES

Scones freeze very well; they are also extremely useful because they can be reheated from frozen and on the table within 5 to 7 minutes! They are delicious served with clotted cream and strawberries in the summer.

250 g/8 oz plain flour
1 teaspoon cream of tartar
½ teaspoon bicarbonate of soda
½ teaspoon salt
50 g/2 oz butter or margarine
25 g/1 oz caster sugar
120 ml/4 fl oz milk
a little extra milk, to glaze

Sift the flour, cream of tartar, soda and salt into a bowl. Rub in the butter or margarine until the mixture resembles fine breadcrumbs. Stir in the sugar, then the milk and mix to a soft dough.

Turn the dough onto a floured surface, knead lightly until smooth, then roll out until 2 cm/¾ inch thick. Cut into about twelve 5 cm/2 inch rounds with a fluted biscuit cutter. Place on a floured baking sheet and brush with milk to glaze.

Bake in a preheated hot oven (220°C/425°F/Gas Mark 7) for 12 to 15 minutes. Cool on a wire rack.

To freeze: Pack the scones in a polythene bag, seal, label and freeze for up to 4 months.

To thaw and serve: Unwrap and place on a baking sheet. Reheat from frozen in a preheated moderate oven (180°C/350°F/Gas Mark 4) for 5 to 7 minutes until hot. Slice in half, leave to cool slightly, then spread with butter and serve as soon as possible.

Makes about 12

Grease a 30 × 20 cm/12 × 8 inch Swiss roll tin, line with greaseproof paper, then grease the paper.

Put the eggs and sugar in a bowl and whisk with an electric beater until thick and mousse-like. Carefully fold in the flour and hazelnuts with the oil.

Turn the mixture into the prepared tin and level the surface. Bake in a preheated moderately hot oven (200°C/400°F/Gas Mark 6) for 8 to 10 minutes until the cake springs back when lightly pressed in the centre.

Wring out a clean tea-towel in hot water. Lay it on a work surface, place a sheet of greaseproof paper on top and dredge lightly with caster sugar.

Turn the sponge upside down onto the paper. Carefully peel off the lining paper and trim off the crisp edges all around the cake. Turn the bottom edge in neatly for the first roll, then continue to roll with the paper inside. Place on a wire rack with the join underneath and leave to cool.

To make the filling: Whip the cream until it will stand in soft peaks. Crush the raspberries with a fork, then fold into the cream with the icing sugar. Unroll the sponge and remove the paper. Spread with the filling, then roll up again carefully.

To freeze: Open freeze the roll until solid, then wrap in cling film and pack in a polythene bag. Seal, label and return to the freezer for up to 3 months.

To thaw and serve: Unwrap, place on a serving plate, then leave to stand at room temperature for 2 to 3 hours. Decorate with piped cream and raspberries if available.

Serves 8 to 10

LEFT: Strawberry Cream Sponge; Peach Gâteau
ABOVE: Raspberry and Hazelnut Roll

TARTE AUX CERISES

This delicious tart, with its moist almond filling and cherry topping, is perfect served with thick, fresh cream. Use fresh or frozen cherries for the topping; when neither of these are available, use canned black cherries instead.

PÂTE SUCRÉE
175 g/6 oz plain flour
75 g/3 oz butter, softened
75 g/3 oz caster sugar
3 egg yolks
few drops of vanilla flavouring
ALMOND FILLING
2 eggs
75 g/3 oz caster sugar
150 ml/¼ pint double cream
125 g/4 oz ground almonds
2 drops almond flavouring
TO SERVE
500 g/1 lb black cherries, stoned
4 tablespoons redcurrant jelly
2 teaspoons water

Sift the flour onto a marble slab or cool work surface. Make a well in the centre, then put in the butter, sugar, egg yolks and vanilla flavouring. Using the fingertips of one hand, work these ingredients together, then draw in the flour and work to a paste. Knead lightly until smooth, then wrap in cling film or foil and chill in the refrigerator for 1 hour.

SAVARIN CASSIS

This blackcurrant savarin (sweet yeast cake) can be served either at teatime, or as a dinner party dessert with whipped cream. Fresh or frozen blackcurrants can be used for the filling.

SAVARIN
15 g/½ oz fresh yeast
4 tablespoons warm milk
250 g/8 oz plain flour
pinch of salt
4 eggs, beaten
50 g/2 oz butter, softened
TO SERVE
300 ml/½ pint water
250 g/8 oz granulated sugar
4 tablespoons kirsch
350 g/12 oz blackcurrants
4 tablespoons water
75 g/3 oz caster sugar
2 teaspoons arrowroot
2 tablespoons orange juice

Cream the yeast with the milk and leave in a warm place for 10 minutes until frothy. Sift the flour and salt into a bowl and make a well in the centre. Pour in the yeast mixture and the eggs and mix to a thick batter. Beat with the hands for 5 minutes until smooth. Scrape down the batter from the sides of the bowl and cover with a damp cloth. Leave to rise in a warm place for 1 to 1½ hours until doubled in bulk.

Add the softened butter to the dough, beating with the hands until thoroughly mixed. Turn the dough into an oiled 23 cm/9 inch savarin mould and leave in a warm place until the dough has risen almost to the top of the mould.

Bake in a preheated moderately hot oven (200°C/400°F/Gas Mark 6) for 20 to 25 minutes until golden brown. Turn onto a wire rack and leave to cool.
To freeze: Wrap the savarin in foil, then pack in a polythene bag. Seal, label and freeze for up to 4 months.
To thaw and serve: Remove the polythene bag and leave to stand at room temperature for 2 hours. Place the foil-wrapped savarin on a baking sheet and reheat in a preheated moderately hot oven (200°C/400°F/Gas Mark 6) for about 15 minutes until warmed through. Unwrap and place on a wire rack.

Put the water and granulated sugar in a pan and heat gently, stirring, until the sugar has dissolved. Increase the heat and boil steadily for 5 minutes. Remove from the heat and stir in the kirsch.

Place a plate underneath the wire rack and spoon the syrup over the savarin while it is still warm. Continue spooning over any syrup that has run off onto the plate, until most of it has been absorbed. Return the remaining syrup to the pan and boil steadily until reduced to a thick syrup; brush over the savarin.

Put the blackcurrants in a pan with the water and caster sugar and simmer gently for 6 to 8 minutes until softened. Remove the blackcurrants from the pan with a slotted spoon and set aside in a bowl. Blend the arrowroot with the orange juice, then stir into the blackcurrant juice in the pan. Bring to the boil, stirring, then lower the heat and simmer for 1 minute until clear. Mix with the blackcurrants and leave to cool.

Place the savarin on a serving plate and spoon the currants into the centre. Serve as soon as possible.
Serves 8

PICNIC PLAITS

Bread freezes beautifully, and can be taken out of the freezer when needed so that you can always have fresh bread. This granary plait is ideal to take on a picnic with a meat or fish pâté. If you have time, thaw the bread for 2 to 3 hours before eating (it will easily thaw out during the journey to the picnic), but if time is short the bread can be thawed quickly by reheating from frozen in a preheated moderately hot oven (200°C/400°F/Gas Mark 6) for 30 minutes.

20 g/¾ oz fresh yeast
600 ml/1 pint lukewarm water
500 g/1 lb granary flour
500 g/1 lb wholemeal flour
2 teaspoons salt
1 tablespoon vegetable oil
sesame seeds, for sprinkling

Cream the yeast with a little of the water and leave in a warm place for 10 minutes until frothy. Mix the flours and salt together in a warm bowl, make a well in the centre, then pour in the yeast mixture with the remaining water and the oil. Mix to a soft dough.

Turn the dough onto a floured surface and knead until smooth and elastic. Place in a clean bowl, cover with a damp cloth and leave to rise in a warm place for about 1½ hours until doubled in bulk.

Turn the dough onto a floured surface and knead again for 2 to 3 minutes. Divide in half, cut one half into 3 equal pieces and shape into long thin sausages. Join the ends together by dampening with water, then plait the sausages and dampen the ends to join. Repeat with the other half. Place the 2 plaits on greased baking sheets, brush with water and sprinkle with sesame seeds. Cover loosely with foil and leave to prove in a warm place for about 30 minutes until almost doubled in size.

Bake in a preheated hot oven (220°C/425°F/Gas Mark 7) for 20 to 25 minutes or until the plaits sound hollow when tapped underneath. Transfer to a wire rack and leave to cool.
To freeze: Wrap the plaits individually in foil, then pack in polythene bags. Seal, label and freeze for up to 6 months.
To thaw and serve: Remove the polythene bags and leave the picnic plaits to stand in foil wrappings at room temperature for 2 to 3 hours.
Makes 2 granary plaits

POPPY SEED ROLLS

These little rolls can be taken from the freezer and used within 20 minutes, and because they are refreshed in the oven, they are as good as when freshly baked. They are ideal to take on a summer picnic with cheese and tomatoes.

50 g/2 oz margarine
300 ml/½ pint milk
15 g/½ oz fresh yeast
500 g/1 lb plain flour
1 teaspoon salt
2 small eggs
poppy seeds

Put the margarine in a pan with the milk and heat gently until lukewarm. Cream the yeast with a little of the warm milk and leave in a warm place for 10 minutes until frothy. Sift the flour and salt into a warm bowl, make a well in the centre, then pour in the yeast mixture, 1 beaten egg and enough of the remaining milk to mix to a soft dough.

Turn the dough onto a floured surface and knead until smooth and elastic. Place in a clean bowl, cover with a damp cloth and leave to rise in a warm place for about 30 minutes until doubled in bulk.

Turn the dough onto a floured surface and knead again for 2 to 3 minutes. Cut into 14 pieces, shape into rolls, then place, well apart, on greased baking sheets. Cover and leave to prove in a warm place for about 10 to 15 minutes until doubled in size.

Beat the remaining egg, brush over the rolls to glaze, then sprinkle with poppy seeds. Bake in a preheated hot oven (220°C/425°F/Gas Mark 7) for 15 minutes. Transfer to a wire rack and leave to cool.
To freeze: Wrap in a single layer in foil, then pack in a polythene bag. Seal, label and freeze for up to 3 months.
To thaw and serve: Remove the polythene bag and place the foil package on a baking sheet. Reheat in a preheated moderate oven (180°C/350°F/Gas Mark 4) for 10 to 12 minutes. Serve while still warm, or as soon as possible after reheating.
Makes 14

VARIATIONS
These rolls can be shaped in various ways; you can roll the dough into balls, ovals or elongated cigar shapes. You can even make knot-shaped rolls by rolling each piece of dough into a long sausage shape, then crossing the ends of the sausage and bringing one end through the loop, to make a loose knot.

You can sprinkle over sesame seeds instead of poppy seeds, or simply brush the rolls with the beaten egg, to give them a shiny glazed surface.

Savarin Cassis; Picnic Plaits; Poppy Seed Rolls

Summer Picnics

Outdoor meals seem more of a treat in this country than anywhere else, mainly because the weather is seldom good enough for long, so picnics and barbecues tend to be rare events. To catch the good weather while it lasts, spontaneity is therefore a must. This summer, pack away a picnic or two in the freezer and be prepared for when the sun comes out.

Breads, rolls, cakes and biscuits can all be stored in the freezer for picnic fare, to be taken out at a moment's notice – by the time you arrive at your destination they will have thawed of their own accord. Choose these from the recipes in this book, together with pâtés, pizzas and quiches, which are perfect picnic fare. The individual quiches on this page are ideal in that you can take out as few or as many as you need, and they're just the right size to pick up and eat with your fingers. The veal croquettes are equally convenient to eat: little bite-sized nuggets of savoury minced veal and herbs in a crumbly coating, which can be popped straight into your mouth, or speared on cocktail sticks and dipped into a blue cheese dressing, or a simple tomato ketchup or chilli relish. And for those who like a 'fishy' flavour, make a pot or two of smoked mackerel pâté. It keeps wonderfully well in the freezer and thaws out in next to no time. Spread liberally on bread or crackers, it tastes even better with a glass of chilled white wine – so don't forget to take the cool box on your picnics.

Smoked Mackerel Pâté

Smoked trout can be used instead of mackerel, but the flavour of the pâté will be less strong.

500 g/1 lb smoked mackerel fillets, skinned, boned and
  flaked
1 large garlic clove, peeled and crushed
juice of 1 lemon
125 g/4 oz unsalted butter, softened
175 g/6 oz full-fat soft cheese
about 1 tablespoon grated horseradish
freshly ground black pepper

Put the flaked fish in a bowl with the garlic and lemon juice. Mash well with a fork until the mackerel is finely broken up.

Work in the softened butter a little at a time, then the cheese. When the mixture is smooth and well blended, add horseradish and pepper to taste.

To freeze: Turn the pâté into a rigid container and smooth the surface. Seal, label and freeze for up to 1 month.

To thaw and serve: Leave the pâté to stand in the container at room temperature for about 4 hours. Beat thoroughly before serving.

Serves 6

Individual Prawn Quiches

If you prefer a crisper pastry, the quiches can be baked blind before filling: Line each pastry case with foil and baking beans and bake in the oven for 7 minutes. Remove the foil and beans, then add the filling and bake for 25 minutes.

PASTRY
275 g/9 oz plain flour
salt
125 g/4 oz butter
1 egg, beaten
about 1 tablespoon iced water
FILLING
25 g/1 oz butter
1 small onion, peeled and finely chopped
1 garlic clove, peeled and crushed
3 tomatoes, skinned, seeded and chopped
175 g/6 oz shelled prawns
1 tablespoon chopped basil or 1 ½ teaspoons dried
  basil
freshly ground black pepper
1 egg
150 ml/¼ pint double cream

Make the pastry: Sift the flour and a pinch of salt into a bowl. Rub in the butter until the mixture resembles fine breadcrumbs. Stir in the egg and enough water to mix to a fairly stiff dough.

Turn the dough onto a floured surface, knead lightly until smooth, then roll out and use to line six 11 cm/4½ inch individual tartlet tins or fluted flan rings placed on baking sheets. Chill in the refrigerator for 30 minutes.

Make the filling: Melt the butter in a pan, add the onion and garlic and fry gently for 5 minutes without browning. Stir in the tomatoes and prawns, then remove from the heat and stir in the basil and salt and pepper to taste. Divide equally between the pastry cases.

Beat the egg and cream together with a little salt and pepper, then pour over the prawn mixture. Bake in a preheated moderately hot oven (200°C/400°F/Gas Mark 6) for 30 minutes until set. Transfer to a wire rack and leave until completely cold.

To freeze: Open freeze the quiches in the flan rings until solid, then remove from the rings and wrap individually in cling film or foil. Overwrap in polythene bags, then seal, label and return to the freezer for up to 3 months.

To thaw and serve: Remove polythene bags and leave to stand in cling film or foil wrappings for about 4 hours. To refresh, remove wrappings, place quiches on a baking sheet and reheat in a preheated moderately hot oven (200°C/400°F/Gas Mark 6) for 10 minutes. Serve warm or cold, with salad if liked.

If taking the quiches on a picnic, transfer them to shallow rigid containers and pack carefully in single layers to avoid crushing.

Makes 6

Dutch Veal Croquettes

If minced veal is difficult to obtain, buy pie veal and mince it yourself at home. Minced pork, or a mixture of minced pork and veal, can be used instead, if preferred.

500 g/1 lb minced veal
1 tablespoon grated onion
finely grated rind of 1 lemon
1 teaspoon dried mixed herbs
pinch of freshly grated nutmeg
salt and freshly ground black pepper
40 g/1½ oz butter
40 g/1½ oz plain flour
300 ml/½ pint veal or chicken stock
1 teaspoon powdered gelatine, dissolved in
  1 tablespoon water
1 egg yolk
8–10 tablespoons breadcrumbs
2 egg whites, beaten
TO SERVE
vegetable oil, for deep-frying

Put the veal in a bowl with the onion, lemon rind, herbs, nutmeg and salt and pepper to taste. Mix with your hands until well combined. Set aside.

Melt the butter in a pan, add the flour and cook for 2 minutes, stirring. Gradually stir in the stock, bring to the boil, then lower the heat and simmer, stirring, for 2 minutes.

Remove the sauce from the heat, then beat in the dissolved gelatine. Leave to cool slightly, then beat in the egg yolk. Add to the veal mixture and mix well together. Chill in the refrigerator for about 30 minutes or until firm.

Divide the mixture into about 24 pieces and form into balls with your hands. Roll in breadcrumbs, then in the beaten egg whites. Roll again in the breadcrumbs until evenly coated.

To freeze: Open freeze the croquettes until solid, then pack in a rigid container. Seal, label and return to the freezer for up to 3 months.

To thaw and serve: Spread the croquettes out in a single layer on a board or plate and leave to stand in the refrigerator for 2 hours. Heat the oil in a deep fat fryer to 180°C/350°F, then deep-fry the croquettes in batches for about 7 minutes until golden brown and crisp. Leave to drain and cool on kitchen paper. Serve the croquettes warm or cold, with crisp salad vegetables.

If taking on a picnic, pack in rigid containers, lined with kitchen paper.

Makes about 24

Individual Prawn Quiches; Dutch Veal Croquettes; Smoked Mackerel Pâté.

AUTUMN

Autumn is harvest time for the freezer: time to reap the benefits of the previous months, to gather in the crops before winter's harmful frosts. But don't just freeze your fruit and vegetables raw, make the most of freezer space by freezing the made-up dishes suggested in this section — with the nights drawing in you'll find a little more time to 'feed' your freezer as well as your family. And keep an eye out for end-of-season bargains, autumn's a time when there's often a glut of garden produce, especially if it's been an Indian summer. Nothing should be wasted: if you have a freezer and stock it wisely, even windfalls can be turned to good use.

VEGETABLES IN SEASON

Aubergine	Lettuce
Bean, runner	Marrow*
Beetroot	Mushroom*
Broccoli,	Onion*
sprouting	Parsnip*
Brussels sprout	Pepper
Cabbage	Potato
Carrot	Pumpkin*
Cauliflower	Radish
Celery	Spinach
Courgette	Swede*
Cucumber	Sweetcorn*
Kohlrabi*	Tomato
Leek	Turnip*

FRUIT IN SEASON

Apple*	Lemon
Avocado	Mango
Banana	Melon
Blackberry*	Orange
Chestnut*	Papaya
Damson*	Passionfruit
Date	Pear*
Elderberry*	Persimmon
Fig*	Pineapple
Grape	Plum*
Grapefruit	Pomegranate*
Greengage*	Quince*
Guava	Strawberry
Kiwi fruit*	

*Freezing instructions given in this section

Kohlrabi

This oddly titled member of the cabbage family derives its name from the German word meaning 'cabbage turnip'. It first became popular in Germany in the 16th century, but it is only in recent years that it has become more widely appreciated in this country.

Both the leaves and the swollen underground stem of the kohlrabi are edible, but the plant is usually grown for the stem which may be green, white or purple, and has a delicate flavour much more subtle than that of a turnip. When small and young, these stems can be thinly sliced and eaten raw, but otherwise are best steamed or lightly boiled. As long as they are young, kohlrabi stems can be successfully frozen. They are available in the shops from October onwards, but are very easy to grow. For a purple variety choose Purple Vienna, for a pale green one select White Vienna. Both can be grown from seeds planted from April to September to be ready 8 weeks later.

Selecting for freezing: Choose small, well-shaped firm stems – avoid any larger than a tennis ball as they will be tough and woody.

Preparation for freezing: Cut off any remaining leaves near their bases, then wash, if necessary, and peel off the skin as thinly as possible. Leave small kohlrabi whole, but dice larger ones or slice them thickly.

To freeze: Blanch whole kohlrabi for 3 minutes, sliced or diced ones for 2 minutes. Drain, cool quickly in iced water, then drain again and pat dry with kitchen paper. Pack in usable quantities in polythene bags, seal, label and freeze for up to 12 months. Alternatively, sliced and diced kohlrabi can be frozen in free-flow packs. Open freeze until solid, pack into polythene bags, seal, label and return to the freezer for up to 12 months.

To thaw and serve: Cook from frozen in boiling water for 10 to 12 minutes, or steam for 15 to 20 minutes until tender. Serve in a cream or mild cheese sauce, or simply toss in butter and sprinkle with parsley or dill. Diced and sliced kohlrabi can also be stir-fried from frozen in butter, with a little water added if necessary to prevent sticking. If thawed in wrappings at room temperature, kohlrabi can be used in salads without further cooking, or coated in batter and deep-fried.

Marrow

The huge prize marrow, with its glossy skin, is a larger relation of the courgette. It has only been cultivated in Britain in any quantity since the 18th century.

If marrows are to thrive and produce their vegetable fruits in autumn, they must have a well-drained soil, a sunny well-protected site and plenty of water. Plants are available in two types, the traditional trailing type and the newer bush varieties. Fruit may be green all over or striped and flecked in yellow. Good trailing varieties are Golden Delicious and Long Green Trailing; good bush varieties are Early Gem and Smallpack.

Marrows are at their best in September, when they are also available in the shops. Because of their high water content, marrows do not freeze outstandingly well, so they are really only worth freezing if you have a glut in the garden. Freeze them cut into rings and stuffed with minced meat or breadcrumb-based stuffings, in dishes such as Swede and Marrow Provençal (page 133), or in chunks as described here.

Selecting for freezing: Marrows contain least water and have the best flavour when they are young, so it is important to choose fruit of small to medium size for freezing – prize marrows may look impressive, but rarely have a taste to match! Harvest firm undamaged fruit, with no slug holes or soft downy patches.

Preparation for freezing: Young tender marrows can be frozen with their skins on if liked, in which case they should be wiped thoroughly. Alternatively, peel off the skin with a sharp knife or a potato peeler. Cut each marrow in half lengthways, scoop out pips and fibres from the centre, then cut flesh into 2.5 cm/1 inch dice.

To freeze: Blanch in boiling water for 2 minutes, drain, cool quickly in iced water, then drain to remove as much water as possible. Dry thoroughly with kitchen paper. Open freeze until solid, then pack in polythene bags and return to the freezer for up to 6 months.

To thaw and serve: Always cook marrow from frozen. Steam for 1 to 2 minutes, or plunge into boiling salted water for 3 to 5 minutes. Drain and serve with a cheese, tomato or parsley sauce, or toss in butter with dill or paprika. Diced marrow can be used as a substitute for courgettes in ratatouille.

Mushroom

Field mushrooms were first cultivated in France in the 17th century. Cultivated mushrooms are on sale here all the year round, and can therefore be frozen at any time. They freeze well alone and in made-up dishes, such as Stuffed Mushrooms (page 121), Chicken Suprêmes Alisonia (Page 124), Woodland Grouse (page 124), Mushrooms in Cream Sauce (page 132). In the autumn, however, you may have the chance of picking (and sometimes buying) wild mushrooms, and these can be frozen successfully. Among the many edible mushrooms suitable for freezing are the field mushroom, the cèpe (*Boletus edulis*), the chanterelle, the puffball and the morel. It is essential to be *absolutely* sure that you identify these mushrooms correctly; use an authoritative illustrated guide, such as Mushrooms by Roger Phillips (Pan Books, 1981). With this proviso, autumn mushroom hunting is great fun, and with a freezer you can benefit all year round. If this is not possible, try growing your own mushrooms in a dark cupboard or garage with purchased spawn sold buried in bags or boxes of compost.

Selecting for freezing: Choose firm, undamaged mushrooms, with no trace of damp. Select unopened button mushrooms, half-opened cups or large flats according to personal preference.

Preparation for freezing: Wipe (do not wash) and trim stalks if necessary. Leave raw, or sauté in butter (allow 65 g/2½ oz butter to 500 g/1 lb mushrooms).

To freeze: *Whole uncooked mushrooms:* Open freeze until solid, then pack in polythene bags, seal, label and return to the freezer for up to 1 month.
Sautéed mushrooms: Cool quickly, pack in usable quantities in rigid containers, then seal, label and freeze for up to 3 months.

To thaw and serve: *Whole uncooked mushrooms:* These may be grilled or sautéed in butter direct from frozen, then used in a recipe or served as a vegetable accompaniment. They can also be used from frozen in soups and casseroles. Alternatively, leave mushrooms to stand in wrappings in refrigerator for 1 to 2 hours until beginning to soften, then use in quiches, pies, etc.
Sautéed mushrooms: Leave to stand in wrappings in the refrigerator for 1 to 2 hours until beginning to soften, then heat through gently. Alternatively, use from frozen in soups and casseroles, adding them about 5 minutes before the end of cooking time.

Onion

Onions are thought to have originated in Asia, although they were first grown in quantity in the Middle East. They are widely on sale here all year and are imported from many parts of the world, but the best of the homegrown crop appears in the shops in autumn. Many varieties are available, from the green-topped spring onions popular in salads, through small button onions and purple-skinned shallots to the large bulb Spanish and Egyptian types.

Because of their wide availability, onions are not worth a great deal of freezer space. They also need careful packing to avoid the spread of their aroma. The best ones to freeze are shallots and button onions which are sometimes hard to obtain; spring onions cannot be frozen successfully. It is worth freezing sliced onions if you do not have ideal dry conditions for storing a garden crop. See also Crispy Onion Rings (page 130), Honey Glazed Onions (page 130).

Onions can be grown from seed and from tiny bulbs or 'sets'. Good varieties to grow from seed include Yellow Globe, Express Yellow, Ailsa Craig and Wijbo. Best names in sets are Sturton and Stuttgarter Giant, while for shallots select Dutch Red.

Selecting for freezing: Whatever their size, onions for freezing should always feel firm to the touch, and the outermost layer of skin should be crisp and papery thin. The skin should never bear signs of mould or softness, or have dark patches on it. Never buy onions that are sprouting at the top.

Preparation for freezing: All types of onions must be trimmed at top and tail and peeled. Peeling onions under cold running water helps prevent eyes watering. Shallots and small onions are easier to peel if first plunged in boiling water for 1 minute. After peeling, grade for size; large onions can be sliced or chopped.

To freeze: *Whole button onions and shallots:* Blanch in boiling water for 2 to 4 minutes, according to size. Drain, cool quickly in iced water, drain again, then pat dry with kitchen paper. Pack in usable quantities in polythene bags, seal, then overwrap and seal again. Label and freeze for up to 6 months.
Sliced and chopped onions: Blanch in boiling water, allowing 1 minute for chopped onions, 2 minutes for sliced. Drain, cool quickly in iced water, drain again and pat dry with kitchen paper. Pack in usable quantities in polythene bags or rigid containers, seal, overwrap and seal again. Label and freeze for up to 6 months. If preferred, onion slices can be blanched in hot oil for 1 minute, drained, packed and stored as above.

To thaw and serve: _Whole button onions and shallots:_ Add from frozen to casseroles, sautéed dishes, or thick, ready-prepared white or parsley sauces (the onions will dilute the sauce as they thaw during cooking). Alternatively, leave to stand in wrappings at room temperature for about 2 hours, then use in recipes as for fresh onions.

Sliced and chopped onions: Use from frozen in soups, sauces and casseroles, or leave to stand in wrappings for about 1 hour and use as for fresh onions.

Parsnip

One of the few vegetables native to Britain, parsnips were only 'discovered' to be good for eating by the Romans. The sugar content of these edible underground roots renders them useful for both sweet and savoury dishes. They are a perfect accompaniment to roast beef, but are also used for making jam. Parsnips are available throughout the autumn and winter, so it is only worth freezing them if there is a glut on the market, or in your garden. See also Parsnip and Tomato Bake (page 130). Parsnip Croquettes (page 131).

Growing your own parsnips is not difficult, as long as the soil is well-drained. The seeds should be planted in spring and the crops harvested in autumn. Many gardeners recommend that the roots should be left in the ground over the winter, but if you have a freezer it is worth lifting small roots before they have a chance to become hard and woody. Try long-rooted varieties Tender and True, Offenham or Leda, or shorter-rooted types White Gen and Avonresister.

Selecting for freezing: Choose young, firm parsnips which have no brown blemishes. For ease of preparation, avoid roots with too many offshoots or 'fangs'.

Preparation for freezing: Prepare parsnips in small batches, since they have a tendency to discolour when their cut surfaces are exposed to air. Trim the roots and wash them thoroughly, scrubbing them with a brush if necessary. Peel thinly, remove any woody cores and dice, slice into rings or cut into strips. Plunge immediately into cold water containing lemon juice.

To freeze: Drain parsnips and blanch by plunging into boiling water. Allow 2 minutes for strips, 4 minutes for diced or sliced roots. Drain, cool quickly in iced water, then drain again and pat dry with kitchen paper. Pack in usable quantities in polythene bags, seal, label and freeze for up to 12 months.

To thaw and serve: Parsnips are usually best cooked from frozen. Plunge into boiling salted water and simmer for 10 to 15 minutes until tender, or add from frozen to soups, stews and casseroles, but use with caution since they have a very pronounced flavour. Alternatively, leave to stand in wrappings at room temperature for 3 to 4 hours, pat dry and roast around a joint or in hot oil. Boiled parsnips are delicious served with plenty of butter and black pepper. They may be mashed if preferred.

Freezing mushrooms (cèpes, pied de mouton, little chanterelles, parasols, morels, flat and button mushrooms) and onions (bulb, red-skinned and button onions)

Swede

Swedes came to Britain from Scandinavia in the 18th century as 'Swedish turnips' – hence their name. Also called rutabagas, these roots are popular winter vegetables hardy enough to withstand the worst of the winter weather. They are available from autumn all through the winter.

Widely available at low prices all winter, swedes are really only worth freezing if there is a glut on the market or if you have excess produce in the garden. One of the most convenient ways to freeze them is by mixing them with other root vegetables to make 'stewpacks' – handy for use throughout the winter – or soups. See Autumn Vegetable Soup (page 118), also Swede and Marrow Provençal (page 133).

For growing your own swedes in the garden, remember that they need nutrient-rich soil, which is both light and well-drained. Three good varieties are Bronze Top, Chignecto and Purple Top.

Selecting for freezing: The most important aspect of choosing swedes for freezing is to buy or lift small roots which have no chance of being woody. The bigger the roots, the more likely they are to suffer from this problem. Choose firm roots without excessive worm damage, and without large areas of brusiing or blemishing.

Preparation for freezing: Wash well, top and tail, then peel thinly. Cut into 2 cm/¾ inch dice.

Diced swedes: Need no further preparation.

Swede purée: Cook diced swede in boiling salted water for about 15 minutes until tender. Drain and cool slightly, then purée in an electric blender or food processor, or work through a vegetable mill or mash with a potato masher. Cool completely.

To freeze: *Diced swedes:* Blanch by plunging into boiling water for 2 minutes. Drain, cool quickly in iced water, then drain again and pat dry with kitchen paper. Pack in usable quantities in polythene bags, seal, label and freeze for up to 12 months.

Swede purée: Pack in usable quantities in rigid containers, leaving 2 cm/¾ inch headspace. Seal, label and freeze for up to 12 months.

To thaw and serve: *Diced swedes:* Cook from frozen in boiling salted water for 8 to 10 minutes, or add from frozen to soups and casseroles. Boiled swedes are traditionally served mashed with butter, black pepper and nutmeg. A little cream adds extra interest.

Swede purée: Reheat from frozen in a double boiler with butter and salt to taste. Add nutmeg or other spices to taste and serve as a vegetable accompaniment to meat dishes, or use as a topping in place of potato in dishes such as Shepherd's pie.

Pumpkin

The pumpkin is a large, round, orange relation of the marrow. Native to the Americas, it was first discovered by the Spanish and was brought to Britain before the 16th century.

Pumpkins harvested in autumn store well over the winter, so they are only worth freezing in pulp form, for convenience. Freezing is also good for storing flesh left over after part of a pumpkin has been used. If

grown in the garden, pumpkins need plenty of warmth and water. Two good varieties are Hundredweight and Mammoth.

Selecting for freezing: Choose firm fruit without too many blemishes – although some small marks are inevitable. If visible, the flesh should be clean and well-coloured. If harvesting at home, cut the pumpkins off the plant as they are ready. Do not leave them on too long or they will rot.

Preparation for freezing: Peel the pumpkin and remove the seeds. Cut into chunks, then cook in boiling water or steam until soft. Drain and mash with a fork, then leave to cool.

To freeze: Pack in usable quantities in rigid containers, leaving 2 cm/¾ inch headspace. Seal, label and freeze for up to 12 months.

To thaw and serve: Steam pumpkin from frozen, then serve as a vegetable accompaniment as an alternative to potatoes and swedes, seasoned liberally with freshly ground black pepper or other spices such as paprika or nutmeg. Alternatively, leave to stand in wrappings at room temperature for about 2 hours, then use in sweet and savoury pies.

Sweetcorn

Native to the Americas, sweetcorn (or corn-on-the-cob) has only recently become popular in this country. It can be grown here for harvesting in September and October, but needs plenty of sun to ripen successfully. For this reason the bulk of the fresh produce on sale is imported, largely from Israel and Spain. Varieties worth trying to grow yourself are Earli King, Northern Belle and North Star. Sweetcorn freezes well, and it is worth looking for produce at pick-your-own farms. See also Corn-on-the-Cob Savoury Butters (page 121), Sweetcorn and Prawn Chowder (page 118).

Selecting for freezing: When buying or picking sweetcorn for freezing, it is vital to look at the kernels, and this may mean pulling back the green sheath of leaves, and its underlying tassel of threads, which surround the cob. Corn for freezing is best just ripe, with plump, pale-coloured kernels, which are even in size and distribution, and show no signs of brownness or wrinkling. If pierced with a fingernail they should exude a milky juice with little difficulty. When picking or buying corn, remember that it is best if frozen within 1 hour of picking.

Preparation for freezing: Pull away the leaves and all the silks clinging to the corn, then trim the stems level with the base of cobs. Work as quickly as you can, grading the cobs for size if necessary.

To freeze: Blanch the cobs in boiling water for 2 to 6 minutes according to size, drain, cool quickly in iced water, then drain again and pat dry with kitchen paper. The corn can then be treated as follows:

Corn-on-the-cob: Wrap the cobs individually in foil or cling film. Open freeze on trays until solid, then pack in polythene bags, seal, label and return to the freezer for up to 12 months.

Corn-off-the-cob: After blanching, remove the kernels from the cob. Stand each cob upright, pointed end uppermost, then cut off the kernels with a sharp knife, pressing the knife blade as close to the cob as possible. Pack in usable quantities in polythene bags, seal, label and freeze for up to 12 months.

To thaw and serve: *Corn-on-the-cob:* Cook from frozen in plenty of boiling water with a little sugar added; allowing 4 to 8 minutes, depending on size, but be sure not to overcook. Do not add salt or the corn will toughen. Alternatively, leave to stand in wrappings at room temperature for up to 2 hours before cooking. Serve with plenty of melted butter, salt and freshly ground black pepper as a starter.

Corn-off-the-cob: Cook from frozen in boiling water for about 4 minutes, then serve as a vegetable accompaniment, either alone or mixed with other vegetables such as beans, peas and peppers. Or add to soups and casseroles a few minutes before the end of cooking time. For use as an ingredient in pies and other composite savoury dishes, leave to stand in wrappings at room temperature for about 2 hours.

Turnip

The turnip is one of the many members of the cabbage family, and both its leaves and its swollen, globe-shaped underground roots are edible. Turnips were first brought to Britain by the Romans. They have always been popular for soups and hot pots.

Turnips are on the market from spring onwards, the first ones of the season being a special variety which are sold in bunches like young carrots. The main crop, from which produce should be chosen for freezing, appears from late August onwards. To grow turnips in your garden you need light, well-drained soil. Sow seeds in June or July, choosing varieties such as Golden Ball and Manchester Market for cropping in autumn and right through the winter.

Both turnip tops and roots are nutritionally valuable, but only the roots are worth freezing, and then only if you have plenty of freezer space. Like swedes they are useful if frozen as part of a 'stew pack', or in Autumn Vegetable Soup (page 118).

Selecting for freezing: Choose small- to medium-sized maincrop turnips lifted as soon as they are mature – if left in the ground they become woody. The roots should be firm and undamaged, the leaves bright green and not wilted.

Preparation for freezing: Wash the turnips if necessary, top and tail, then peel thinly. Leave small turnips whole, cut large ones into 1 to 2 cm/½ to ¾ inch dice.

Whole and diced turnips: Need no further preparation.

Turnip purée: Cook diced turnips in boiling salted water for about 10 minutes until tender. Drain, then mash or work in an electric blender or food processor. Cool.

To freeze: *Whole and diced turnips:* Blanch before freezing by plunging into boiling water for 2 to 3 minutes. Drain, cool quickly in iced water, then drain again and pat dry with kitchen paper. Open freeze until solid, then pack in polythene bags, seal, label and return to the freezer for up to 12 months.

Turnip purée: Pack in usable quantities in rigid containers, leaving 2 cm/¾ inch headspace. Seal label and freeze for up to 12 months.

To thaw and serve: *Whole and diced turnips:* Cook from frozen in boiling salted water for 5 to 10 minutes, according to size. Or add from frozen to soups and casseroles.

Turnip purée: Reheat from frozen in a double boiler, then serve with butter and seasonings as a vegetable accompaniment. Turnip purée can be used in place of mashed potato in recipes such as Shepherd's pie, but remember that it has rather a strong flavour.

OPPOSITE: Freezing sweetcorn
BELOW: Freezing swede and turnip

Apple

Archaeological finds in Italy and Switzerland have discovered that apple trees have been cultivated since as long ago as 10,000 BC. Although Britain had her own native 'wilding' apple, cultivated varieties were brought here by both Roman and Norman invaders. Apples have always been regarded as a healthy food; they are also an aid to slimmers because if eaten before a meal, they help fill the stomach with cellulose which reduces appetite.

Apples of some kind are on sale all the year round, at reasonable prices both home-grown and imported. For this reason, apples are not worth a great deal of freezer space, although it is always a good idea to have some sliced apples and apple purée on hand for making quick desserts, and it is certainly worth freezing them in times of glut in made-up dishes such as Apple and Cinnamon Pie (page 136), Flan Normande (page 138), Mincemeat and Apple Flan (page 138), Walnut Galette (page 140), Apple Shortcake (page 139), Wholemeal Apple Cake (page 143) and Ginger Applecake (page 148).

There are so many different varieties of apples to choose from that choice is bound to be a personal one, but for cooking, the Bramley Seedling is a traditional and excellent choice. Amongst the dessert apples, Cox's Orange Pippin, Laxton's Superb, Discovery, Grenadier, Worcester Permain and Egremont Russet are all good for freezing. Look out for the best apple bargains in September and October, and never turn down the chance of a bag of windfalls from a friend or neighbour!

Selecting for freezing: For apples to be frozen diced or sliced, choose firm, ripe fruit of even shape. Avoid apples with bruises, blemishes or other signs of damage or decay. If picking your own fruit, take it off the tree carefully to avoid damage. For freezing apple purée, all but the most badly damaged or decaying fruits are suitable.

Preparation for freezing: Both dessert and cooking apples can be prepared in several different ways, but it is always important to work quickly, if necessary preparing the fruit in very small batches to prevent discoloration.

Diced apple, apple rings and slices: Peel and core, then dice, slice, or cut them into rings. Rings and slices should be about 5 mm/¼ inch thick. Peel and core only 1 apple at a time, then cut it straight into a bowl full of iced water with plenty of lemon juice added to prevent discoloration. Alternatively slice into a syrup (see To Freeze), also containing lemon juice. Rings and slices are best for cooking apples, dice and slices for dessert apples.

Apple purée: Working in small batches, peel, core and slice the apples, discarding any bruised, decayed or insect-infected areas, then toss slices in lemon juice. Cook gently in the minimum amount of water until soft. Sweeten, if liked, after cooking, but remember that this does limit uses. The mixture can either be left rather lumpy or puréed in an electric blender or food processor until smooth, or passed through a nylon sieve before freezing.

To Freeze: _Diced apple, apple rings and slices:_ For cooking apples, blanch in boiling water for 1 minute, drain and cool quickly in iced water, then drain again and pat dry with kitchen paper. Dessert apples do not need blanching.

Dry sugar pack: Pack in usable quantities in rigid containers, sprinkling each layer with sugar and allowing 125 to 175 g/4 to 6 oz sugar to 500 g/1 lb fruit, according to taste. Seal, label and freeze for up to 12 months.

Sugar syrup pack: Pack in usable quantities in rigid containers and cover with a medium sugar syrup made from 350 g/12 oz sugar to 600 ml/1 pint water. Leave 2 cm/¾ inch headspace, seal, label and freeze for up to 12 months.

Apple purée: Pour into rigid containers in usable quantities, leaving 2 cm/¾ inch headspace. Seal, label and freeze for up to 8 months.

To thaw and serve: _Diced apple, apple rings and slices:_ Leave to stand in container at room temperature for 1 to 2 hours, then use in all kinds of hot and cold desserts, including fruit salads, pies, puddings, tarts and crumbles. Apples frozen in dry sugar packs can also be fried successfully if well dried beforehand, and go well with many savoury dishes, especially those containing pork or chicken.

Apple purée: Thaw as for diced apple, and use cold for jellies, mousses, or any other cooked or uncooked dessert calling for apple purée. Alternatively, serve hot as an accompaniment to pork and other savoury recipes, particularly those high in fat, such as duck and goose dishes. If using apple purée hot, heat directly from frozen in a heavy-based pan over the lowest possible heat, stirring frequently and adding a little water if necessary, to prevent sticking.

Blackberry

Native to Europe, the fruits of the bramble (_Rubus fruticosus_) have been appreciated in Britain since at least the 1st century AD. They were variously known in the past as lawyers, brumble-berries and brumble-kites. Blackberries are an excellent source of vitamin C.

The popularity of the wild blackberry has led, in recent years, to the breeding of varieties with bigger, juicier (though arguably less well-flavoured) fruit earlier in the season. Varieties such as Bedford Giant, Himalaya Giant, Oregon Thornless and Smoothstem will grow well in almost any garden, and need little care and attention. As well as conventional blackberries, gardeners can also try new hybrids with other soft fruits such as the Tayberry and Boysenberry, which more closely resemble the loganberry.

Both cultivated blackberries, available at markets and pick-your-own farms from late July to mid-September, and wild blackberries, which ripen from early August onwards, freeze well and are perfect for desserts all year. See also Blackberry and Pear Crumble (page 136), Tarte Française (page 140) and Bramble Fool (page 135).

Selecting for freezing: Choose ripe berries with a rich black colour and no traces of red, avoiding any that are very soft and overripe. Reject any fruit with signs of mould or damage. If the fruit is packed in punnets, reject any with bad signs of leakage at the base – this could mean squashed fruit. When picking blackberries yourself, choose a dry day so that the fruit will be in the best possible condition. Avoid any dirty fruit and, if possible, do not pick blackberries from the sides of a busy road, since medical evidence suggests that these may be tainted with lead.

Preparation for freezing: Blackberries can be frozen whole or as a purée, depending on their quality and intended use:

Whole blackberries: Pick over the fruit and discard any mouldy or underripe berries. Remove any damaged, wet or overripe fruit and reserve for purée. Wash the selected fruit only if necessary and remove any green stalks.

Blackberry purée: Cook the fruit in the minimum amount of water with sugar to taste until just tender. Pass through a sieve, or work in an electric blender or food processor, then sieve to remove the pips.

To freeze: _Whole blackberries:_ These can be frozen using any of the following methods.

Free-flow pack: Open freeze on trays until solid, then pack in polythene bags. Seal, label and return to the freezer for up to 12 months.

Dry sugar pack: Pack in usable quantities in rigid containers, sprinkling each layer with sugar and allowing 125 to 175 g/4 to 6 oz sugar to 500 g/1 lb fruit, according to taste. Seal, label and freeze for up to 12 months.

Sugar syrup pack: Pack in usable quantities in rigid containers and cover with a medium sugar syrup made from 350 g/12 oz sugar to 600 ml/1 pint water. Leave 2 cm/¾ inch headspace, seal, label and freeze for up to 12 months.

Blackberry purée: Pour into rigid containers in usable quantities, leaving 2 cm/¾ inch headspace. Seal, label and freeze for up to 8 months.

To thaw and serve: _Whole blackberries:_ Leave to stand in wrappings at room temperature for 2 to 3 hours, or tip into a bowl to thaw in less time. Blackberries frozen in syrup can be heated from frozen in a heavy-based pan, but need frequent stirring. Use whole blackberries for fruit salads, especially with other dark-coloured fruit, for pies and crumbles (they go particularly well with apples) and in summer puddings. They can also be used for making jams, jellies and chutneys.

Blackberry purée: Thaw as for whole blackberries. Use in ice creams, sorbets and mousses, or serve as a hot or cold sauce to accompany desserts. Blackberry purée is a good substitute for raspberry purée in many dessert recipes.

Freezing dessert and cooking apples

Chestnut

Sweet or Spanish chestnuts, roasted over the fire, are traditional autumn and winter fare. These large, brown-skinned nuts, which form inside prickly green cases, are native to the Mediterranean region. Unlike other nuts, they have a floury texture and contain a low proportion of fat, so can be used in cooking as both a fruit and vegetable.

Although they can be grown in Britain, and occur naturally in woods all over the country, sweet chestnuts give the best yield of fruit when grown in warmer climates. The ones on sale at greengrocers and market stalls are largely imported from Italy. In a good year, however, it may be possible to gather large nuts from woods and gardens which will be worth freezing.

Sweet chestnuts are best frozen skinned and whole, or as unsweetened purée, or in made-up dishes, such as Braised Red Cabbage with Chestnuts (page 175).

Selecting for freezing: Choose large, plump chestnuts with shiny skins that bear no traces of splitting or of damage or disease.

Preparation for freezing: Wash the nuts and make a slit just through the skin of each one. Put them into a pan, cover with boiling water and bring to the boil. Remove the nuts with a slotted spoon a few at a time and skin them with a small, sharp knife as quickly as possible. Do not let them cool or the skins will 'cook' on the flesh and be impossible to remove.

Whole chestnuts: Need no further preparation.

Chestnut purée: Work the nuts to a purée in an electric blender or food processor.

To freeze: *Whole nuts:* Pack in usable quantities in rigid containers or polythene bags, then seal, label and freeze for up to 6 months.

Chestnut purée: Pack in usable quantities in rigid containers, leaving 2 cm/¾ inch headspace. Seal, label and freeze for up to 6 months.

To thaw and serve: *Whole chestnuts:* Leave to stand in container at room temperature until they can be separated. Steam or boil and serve as a vegetable (e.g. with sprouts), or cook in casseroles and soups. Alternatively purée whole chestnuts and use as below.

Chestnut purée: Leave to stand in container until it can be whipped up with a fork. Use for savoury stuffings, or sweeten with sugar and/or chocolate and use in desserts such as gâteaux, pancakes and meringues. Chestnut purée is delicious served simply sweetened, mixed with melted chocolate and rum, then chilled and topped with whipped cream.

Damson

The damson is an ancient relation of the plum – dark in colour and tart in flavour. Many varieties of damson are available and they are easier to grow than plums. When choosing a tree, or selecting fruit from a pick-your-own farm or farm shop, look out for Farleigh Damson, Shropshire and Merryweather. The damson season is from late August to the end of September.

Selecting for freezing: Select firm, ripe fruit with no sign of splitting skin, although any slightly damaged fruit can be frozen as a purée. Buy or pick the fruit on the same day that it is to be frozen.

Preparation for freezing: Damsons can be frozen in several ways, but the skins tend to toughen when frozen and the stones, if left in the fruit, will impart a strong, rather bitter almond-like flavour. For this reason, damson purée is the most successful method.

Damson halves: Wipe the damsons well or wash if necessary. Halve lengthways and remove the stones.

Damson purée: Wipe or wash the fruit, halve and remove the stones, then cook in the minimum amount of water, with sugar to taste, until tender. Pass the damsons through a nylon sieve, or work in an electric blender or food processor, then sieve.

To freeze: *Damson halves:* These can be frozen dry or in a syrup.

Dry sugar pack: Pack in usable quantities in rigid containers, sprinkling each layer generously with sugar and allowing about 250 g/8 oz sugar to 500 g/1 lb prepared fruit, according to taste. Seal, label and freeze for up to 12 months.

Sugar syrup pack: Pack in rigid containers and cover with a medium sugar syrup made from 275 g/9 oz sugar and 600 ml/1 pint water. Leave 2 cm/¾ inch headspace, seal, label and freeze for up to 12 months.

Damson purée: Pour into rigid containers in usable quantities, leaving 2 cm/¾ inch headspace. Seal, label and freeze for up to 12 months.

To thaw and serve: *Damson halves:* Leave to stand in containers at room temperature for 2 hours, then use cold as a tart addition to fruit salads, or with ice creams, mousses or creamed rice. Heated through, damsons are delicious served simply with cream or custard, or they can be cooked in pies and crumbles. The halves can also be used for jam- and jelly-making or for a traditional damson cheese.

Damson purée: Thaw as for damson halves, then use in fools, ice creams and mousses, or as a tart sauce for sweet desserts or cold meats such as pork and game. Or reheat from frozen in a heavy-based pan over the lowest possible heat, stirring frequently and adding a little water, if necessary, to prevent sticking. Use as a hot sauce with sweet and savoury dishes.

Elderberry

In early September, clusters of purple-black berries ripen in profusion on the elderberry shrub, native to Europe. Long appreciated for wine making, elderberries are also excellent used in cooking.

Although large-berried varieties, such as Kent, Nova and York, have been bred specifically for garden cultivation, the most usual source of elderberries is country lanes, woods and hedgerows. The berries are well worth freezing.

Selecting for freezing: When ripe and ready for freezing, elderberries are dark in colour with a whitish bloom like grapes, and no traces of red. Always choose a dry day and pick the berries in bunches.

Preparation for freezing: Separate the berries from their stalks by running a fork through the bunch. Pick over the berries, removing any that are under- or overripe. Do not wash them unless they are very dirty and are to be made into a sauce before freezing.

Elderberry sauce: Cook in the minimum amount of water with sugar to taste until tender. Rub through a sieve, or work in an electric blender or food processor, then sieve.

To freeze: *Whole elderberries:* These can be frozen either in free-flow or dry sugar packs.

Free-flow pack: Open freeze on trays until solid, then pack in polythene bags or rigid containers. Seal, label and return to the freezer for up to 12 months.

Dry sugar pack: Pack in usable quantities in rigid containers, sprinkling each layer with sugar and allowing 125 to 175 g/ 4 to 6 oz sugar to 500 g/1 lb fruit. Seal, label and freeze for up to 12 months.

Elderberry sauce: Pour in usable quantities into rigid containers, leaving 2 cm/¾ inch headspace. Seal, label and freeze for up to 12 months.

To thaw and serve: *Whole elderberries:* Leave to stand in wrappings at room temperature for 2 to 3 hours. Add the raw berries to fruit salads or summer puddings, or cook them in pies and crumbles, etc.

Elderberry sauce: Thaw as for whole elderberries, or reheat from frozen in a heavy-based pan on the lowest possible heat, stirring frequently and adding a little water, if necessary, to prevent sticking. Use like cranberry sauce as an accompaniment to savoury dishes, or in making ice creams, sorbets, mousses, etc.

Fig

Figs are one of the oldest – and most delicious – of fruits. A native of western Asia, figs are now grown all round the Mediterranean and most fruit on sale here in the autumn comes from this area, although figs can be grown in a greenhouse in this country. There are green and purple-skinned varieties, while the seeded flesh can be white, purple or red. Figs freeze well, and are well worth freezer space because their season is so short.

Selecting for freezing: Look for plump fruits which are soft and ripe. Skins may be slightly wrinkled as long as they are not split or bruised.

Preparation for freezing: Wipe carefully with a damp cloth or wash quickly in iced water, then dry gently with kitchen paper. Snip off stems. Figs can be frozen peeled or unpeeled. Peel figs with a sharp knife, taking great care not to bruise them as they are fragile. Peel one fig at a time, and drop the fruit into sugar syrup (see below).

To freeze: *Unpeeled figs:* Open freeze until solid, then pack in polythene bags, seal, label and return to the freezer for up to 12 months.

LEFT: Freezing chestnuts
RIGHT: Freezing figs and elderberries

Peeled figs: Freeze as soon as possible after peeling. Pack in rigid containers in a light sugar syrup made from 125 g/4 oz sugar to 600 ml/1 pint water. Seal, label and freeze for up to 12 months.

To thaw and serve: *Unpeeled figs:* Leave to stand in wrappings at room temperature for 1½ hours, then serve as for fresh figs.

Peeled figs: Thaw as for unpeeled figs, then serve cold as a dessert with fresh pouring cream, or heat gently in a heavy-based pan and serve hot. Figs in sugar syrup make an excellent addition to a winter fruit salad.

Greengage

Greengages are a green-fruited form of a particular type of plum known as a gage. They can be grown successfully in Britain as long as they are protected from late frosts and have plenty of sun. However most of the greengages on sale in late summer and early autumn are imported from France and Italy. If growing a greengage, or picking your own fruit from a farm, the varieties to look out for are Cambridge Gage, Old Green Gage, Jefferson and Denniston's Superb.

Greengages freeze well, but should always have their stones removed to prevent their flavour becoming tainted. If frozen dry there is a chance that the skins may become unacceptably tough.

Selecting for freezing: Choose firm, ripe or slightly underripe fruit that has a slight 'give'. Avoid fruit that looks wet, bruised or mouldy, or has split skin. Pick greengages as they are ready, with the stalks on.

Preparation for freezing: Remove stalks and wipe clean; do not wash unless the fruit is to be stewed or puréed. Dry, cut in half and remove the stones.

Greengage halves: Need no further preparation.

Stewed greengages: Cook until just tender in a sugar syrup of 350 g/12 oz sugar to every 600 ml/1 pint water, with ¼ teaspoon ascorbic acid added.

Greengage purée: Cook in minimum amount of water with sugar to taste. Pass through a sieve, or work in an electric blender or food processor, then sieve.

To freeze: *Greengage halves:* These can be frozen in free-flow or sugar syrup packs, as for plums (page 116).

Stewed greengages: Freeze as for Stewed plums.

Greengage purée: Freeze as for Plum purée.

To thaw and serve: *Greengage halves and stewed greengages:* Thaw as for plums (see page 117). Use halves and stewed fruit for fruit salads and compotes, pies, tarts and crumbles; jam- and chutney-making.

Greengage purée: Thaw as for Plum purée. Use for ices, mousses and fools, or as hot or cold sauce for sweet and savoury dishes – the tart greengage flavour goes particularly well with duck, goose and pork.

Kiwi Fruit

Commonly known as kiwi fruit because most fruit first available in Britain was grown in New Zealand, this fruit is also called Chinese gooseberry after its native land. It is rapidly increasing in popularity. Surprisingly, perhaps, kiwi fruit can be cultivated in Britain as long as it has plenty of warmth in summer and is protected from frost and long periods of cold in winter.

A kiwi fruit is about the size and shape of an egg, with a furry brown skin and a bright green flesh. The seeds are arranged in a circle near the centre of the fruit. The delicate flavour of kiwi fruit is best appreciated after they have been stored inside for 4 to 6 weeks after picking. They are most plentiful and least expensive in October, but available nearly all the year. Because of their high water content, they are not ideal for freezing, but worthwhile if there is a glut. See also Kiwi Lamb Chops (page 128).

Selecting for freezing: Choose firm fruit which 'gives' when squeezed gently. Avoid fruit with damaged skins.

Preparation for freezing: Peel off the skin with a small, sharp knife, taking care not to damage the flesh.

To freeze: Open freeze on trays until solid, then pack in polythene bags, seal, label and return to the freezer for up to 6 months.

To thaw and serve: Leave to stand in wrappings at room temperature until partially thawed, then slice and serve on their own as a starter or dessert, accompanied respectively by vinaigrette dressing or whipped cream. Or use as a topping for ice creams and other desserts. If used for decorating desserts and gâteaux, apply just before serving as they may cause discoloration. Thawed fruit can also be puréed and used in making ice creams, sorbets and mousses, etc.

Pear

Although pears were brought to Britain by the Romans, it was not until the 12th century that pear cultivation began here in earnest. Today's pear crop comes from both home and abroad, with supplies available for most of the year. The domestic crop reaches its height in autumn with Williams and other dessert pears such as Fertility, Beurre Hardy and Dr Jules Guyot ripening early in September, Conference later in the month and Comice in October.

Whatever their source, pears are notoriously difficult to shop for – it seems almost impossible to choose them in a perfect state of ripeness, and to keep them without their turning 'sleepy' or overripe. This, combined with the fact that their texture deteriorates in the freezer, means that pears are not worth buying specifically for freezing, but if you have a pear tree in the garden, it is worth freezing excess supplies. Freeze them in a sugar syrup as here, or in dishes such as Blackberry and Pear Crumble (page 136), Pears in Red Wine (page 136) and Veal Tournedos Epicure (page 126).

Selecting for freezing: Best dessert pears for freezing are those just coming up to their peak of ripeness. If necessary, leave them to ripen in an airing cupboard. If pears are to be cooked before being frozen, which is the best method, it does not matter if they are still hard – in fact this can be an advantage. In all cases, avoid pears that are bruised or damaged, and always handle them very carefully.

Preparation for freezing: Apart from hard cooking pears, fruit should be frozen as soon as possible after picking. Work in small batches to prevent discoloration. Ripe dessert and hard cooking pears need slightly different treatments.

Dessert pears: Peel and cut into halves or quarters, then remove cores. Cover immediately with a medium sugar syrup (see below). If the pears are a little hard, cook them in this syrup for about 1½ minutes, with cloves, cinnamon and/or grated lemon rind added if wished, then leave until cold.

Cooking pears: For hard pears, peel the fruit, then leave whole and core, or cut into halves or quarters, then core. Place immediately in a pan, just cover with water, sweeten with sugar to taste and add flavourings as for dessert pears, if liked. Simmer until just tender, then drain well and leave until cold.

To freeze: *Dessert pears:* Pack ripe fruit in usable quantities in rigid containers, then cover with a medium sugar syrup made from 350 g/12 oz sugar to 600 ml/1 pint water. Pack hard fruit in the syrup in which it was cooked. Leave 2 cm/¾ inch headspace, seal, label and freeze for up to 12 months.

Cooking pears: Pack as for ripe dessert pears, covering them with a fresh medium sugar syrup (see above).

To thaw and serve: Leave both dessert and cooking pears to stand in containers at room temperature for about 3 hours. Dessert pears can be used in fruit salads, or puréed for ices and mousses, or served hot or cold with ice cream, cream and/or chocolate sauce. Cooking and dessert pears can be used in pies, tarts and crumbles, or in combination with sponge mixtures; they can also be used for dishes such as pears in red wine or Madeira.

Plum

The plum tree has its origins in the Middle East, where it is thought to have arisen as a natural hybrid between the sloe and the cherry plum. It was probably brought here by the Romans. Most of today's homegrown plum crop, which starts in early August and goes on to late September or early October, comes from Worcestershire, East Anglia and Kent, where conditions of warmth and rainfall are perfect for it to thrive. Imported plums are also available, and out of season supplies come from Spain, South Africa and the USA.

When growing plum varieties for freezing, consider both the timing of the crop and its intended use. Good all-purpose plums are Prolific (formerly called Early Rivers) which crops in early August, and Victoria which bears its fruit later in that month and on into September. Good varieties of cooking plums include Czar, which is an 'early', and the later-cropping Monarch and Marjorie's Seedling. For dessert plums, choose Early Laxton or Kirke's.

Plums freeze well and are worth both growing and buying for this purpose. In September, there is often a glut which brings prices down, so wait a while after the first fruit appears on the market before you buy. See also Victorian Haunch of Venison (page 125), Plums in Port Wine (page 136) and Plum Layer Pudding (page 136).

Selecting for freezing: Choose firm, fully or just underripe plums. Avoid soft, overripe fruit or any with split skins, traces of brown or any mould. If possible, pick or buy the fruit dry, unless it is to be frozen stewed or puréed. Pick plums as they ripen, in batches.

Preparation for freezing: Remove any stalks and wipe the fruit (only wash if absolutely necessary). Pat dry, halve and remove the stones, then prepare as follows.

Plum halves: Need no further preparation.

Stewed plums: Cook until just tender in a sugar syrup made from 350 g/12 oz sugar to 600 ml/1 pint water with ¼ teaspoon ascorbic acid added.

Plum purée: Cook in the minimum amount of water with sugar to taste, then pass through a sieve or work in an electric blender or food processor, then sieve.

To freeze: *Plum halves:* These can be frozen in free-flow or sugar syrup packs.

Free-flow pack: Open freeze until solid, then pack in polythene bags, seal, label and return to the freezer for up to 12 months. This method may toughen skins.

Sugar syrup pack: Pack in usable quantities in rigid containers, then cover with a medium sugar syrup made from 350 g/12 oz sugar to 600 ml/1 pint water. Leave 2 cm/¾ inch headspace, seal, label and freeze for up to 6 months.

Stewed plums: Pack in usable quantities in rigid containers, leaving 2 cm/¾ inch headspace. Seal, label and freeze for up to 6 months.

Plum purée: Pour usable quantities into rigid containers, leaving 2 cm/¾ inch headspace. Seal, label and freeze for up to 6 months.

To thaw and serve: Leave all frozen plums to stand in wrappings at room temperature for 2 hours, then use at once before the fruit discolours. Use plum halves and stewed plums in fruit salads, pies, tarts and crumbles, or serve, either hot or cold, with ice creams or whipped cream. They can also be used for making jams, jellies and chutneys. Plum purée can be used in ice creams, sorbets, jellies and mousses, or as a hot or cold sauce which goes well with desserts, but also with savoury dishes, especially those with rich meats.

To use hot, reheat plums in syrup, stewed plums and plum purée from frozen in a heavy-based pan over the lowest possible heat, stirring frequently and adding a little water, if necessary, to prevent sticking.

Pomegranate

One of the most ancient of all cultivated fruits, the pomegranate is a native of the Middle East. It is imported to Britain from the tropics and sub-tropics, and is only on sale in late autumn and early winter. Inside the yellow-pink skin the fruit is packed with a mass of seeds or pips, each cloaked in a succulent pink flesh. Pomegranates can be frozen if properly treated, and provide a refreshing change when fresh fruit is lacking in variety. Look out for a glut of inexpensive pomegranates for freezing in October and November.

Selecting for freezing: Choose firm fruit which is perfectly ripe inside. It does not matter if the skin is marked with a few pale brown patches.

Preparation for freezing: Cut the fruit in half and carefully scoop out the seeds. Take care to separate and discard all fibrous membranes within the fruit.

To freeze: Pomegranate seeds are best frozen in a sugar syrup. Pack in usable quantities in rigid containers, then cover with a medium sugar syrup made from 350 g/12 oz sugar to 600 ml/1 pint water. Leave 2 cm/¾ inch headspace, seal, label and freeze for up to 12 months.

To thaw and serve: Leave to stand in container at room temperature for about 3 hours, then add to fruit salads or serve with ice cream or as a substitute for passion fruit pulp in meringue dishes, such as pavlova.

Quince

The true quince was originally cultivated in South-East Asia and later became cherished by the Greeks. Today, quinces grow wild in southern Europe and are cultivated to some extent all over the Continent, but they have become rather neglected in Britain. A quince tree deserves a place in the garden, since the fruit is often hard to come by commercially, and it freezes very well. It needs a moist soil and protection from prolonged, heavy frosts, but is otherwise easy to look after. Of the varieties on the market, Champion, Lusitanica, Maliformis and Vranja are recommended.

Look for homegrown produce – available from September to November. Quinces are shaped like pears or apples and have golden downy skins, enclosing aromatic flesh and rows of dark-coloured, rather large pips. False or oriental quinces are the fruits of the japonica. Smaller than true quinces, their greenish-red fruits are rather lacking in flavour, but they can be frozen and used in the same way as true quinces.

Selecting for freezing: For their full flavour and aroma to develop, quinces need to be left on the tree for as long as possible, but not so long that they risk being damaged by frost. October is the best month for harvesting the crop. For freezing, select large, undamaged fruit with no scabs or soft brown patches.

Preparation for freezing: Wash quinces well, peel, core and quarter or cut into slices. Put the flesh, plus all the peel, into a medium sugar syrup made from 350 g/12 oz sugar to 600 ml/1 pint water with lemon and/or orange juice added to taste, if liked. Simmer until just tender. Discard the peel and leave until cold.

To freeze: Pack in usable quantities in rigid containers, leaving 2 cm/¾ inch headspace. Seal in a double layer of wrapping to prevent the aroma tainting other foods, then label and freeze for up to 12 months.

To thaw and serve: Leave to stand in container at room temperature for about 3 hours. Use for making jam or jelly, or serve hot or cold as a dessert on their own or in a fruit salad or compote. In small quantities they enhance the flavour of apple and pear dishes.

Freezing pears and plums

HERBY TOMATO AND POTATO SOUP

This nourishing soup can be served as a lunch or supper, with French bread.

50 g/2 oz butter
2 large onions, peeled and finely chopped
1 garlic clove, peeled and crushed
2 celery sticks, chopped
500 g/1 lb potatoes, peeled and diced
1.2 litres/2 pints homemade chicken stock
2 teaspoons dried mixed herbs
salt and freshly ground black pepper
250 g/8 oz tomatoes, skinned, seeded and diced
TO SERVE
150 ml/1/4 pint double cream
2 tablespoons chopped parsley

Melt the butter in a pan, add the onions and garlic and fry gently for 5 minutes without browning. Add the celery and potatoes and cook for a further 2 minutes. Pour in the stock and bring to the boil, then add the herbs and salt and pepper to taste. Lower the heat, cover and simmer for 20 minutes.

Remove the soup from the heat, stir in the diced tomatoes, then cool quickly.

To freeze: Pour into a rigid container, leaving 2 cm/3/4 inch headspace. Seal, label and freeze for up to 3 months.

To thaw and serve: Reheat gently from frozen in a heavy-based pan. Bring to the boil, then lower the heat and simmer for 2 minutes. Taste and adjust the seasoning, then stir in the cream and parsley. Serve immediately.

Serves 6

SWEETCORN AND PRAWN CHOWDER

Fresh corn kernels provide the distinctive flavour in this version of an American seafood chowder.

3 whole corn on the cob
500 g/1 lb potatoes, peeled and diced
salt
50 g/2 oz streaky bacon, rinds removed, diced
2 onions, peeled and finely chopped
1 tablespoon plain flour
450 ml/3/4 pint homemade chicken stock
300 ml/1/2 pint milk
1 small green pepper, cored, seeded and diced
175 g/6 oz peeled prawns, roughly chopped
1 teaspoon paprika
freshly ground black pepper
TO SERVE
150 ml/1/4 pint double cream
2 tablespoons snipped chives

Cook the corn on the cob in boiling water for 4 to 5 minutes until tender, then drain and scrape off the kernels with a sharp knife.

Cook the potatoes in boiling salted water for 5 minutes, drain thoroughly.

Cook the bacon in a frying pan, without additional fat, until lightly browned. Add the onions and fry for 3 to 4 minutes, until the onions are soft and transparent. Add the flour and cook for a further 2 minutes, stirring all the time. Gradually stir in the stock, then the milk. Bring to the boil, stirring. Add the potatoes, lower the heat and simmer for 7 minutes, or until the potatoes are tender. Stir in the sweetcorn kernels and the remaining ingredients, adding pepper to taste. Bring to the boil, lower the heat and simmer for a further 2 minutes. Remove from the heat and cool the soup quickly.

To freeze: Pour the soup into a rigid container, leaving 2 cm/3/4 inch headspace. Seal, label and freeze for up to 3 months.

To thaw and serve: Reheat gently from frozen in a heavy-based pan. Bring to the boil, then lower the heat and simmer for 2 minutes. Taste and adjust the seasoning, then stir in the cream and chives. Serve immediately.

Serves 6

AUTUMN VEGETABLE SOUP

Any selection of seasonal vegetables may be used, as long as there is a good variety.

2 large onions, peeled and chopped
1 leek, trimmed and chopped
2 celery sticks, chopped
1 small swede, peeled and diced
2 small turnips, peeled and diced
1.2 litres/2 pints homemade chicken stock
10 cm/4 inch piece marrow, peeled, seeded and chopped
few cauliflower florets, broken up
1/4 small green cabbage, shredded
1 tablespoon tomato purée
1 bay leaf
1 bouquet garni
salt and freshly ground black pepper
GARLIC BUTTER BALLS TO SERVE
50 g/2 oz butter, softened
1 tablespoon chopped parsley
2 teaspoons chopped thyme
2 garlic cloves, peeled and crushed

Put the onions, leek, celery, swede and turnips into a large pan. Pour in the stock and bring to the boil, then lower the heat, cover and simmer for 15 minutes.

Add the remaining vegetables to the pan with the tomato purée, herbs and salt and pepper to taste. Stir well, then bring back to the boil, cover and simmer for 15 to 20 minutes, until the vegetables are tender. Discard the bay leaf and bouquet garni. Leave to cool.

To freeze: Pour the soup into a rigid container, leaving 2 cm/¾ inch headspace, then seal, label and freeze for up to 3 months.

To thaw and serve: Put all the ingredients for the garlic butter balls in a bowl and beat well to mix. Form into tiny balls, then freeze for 5 minutes until firm. Meanwhile gently reheat the soup from frozen in a heavy-based pan. Bring to the boil, lower the heat and simmer for 2 minutes. Taste and adjust the seasoning.

Pour the soup into a tureen or individual bowls, then float the butter balls on top. Serve immediately.

Serves 6

MACKEREL AND PEPPERCORN PÂTÉ

This pâté is equally good made with smoked trout, in which case the lemon juice should be reduced by half because trout has a more delicate flavour than mackerel. Serve with thinly sliced hot buttered toast.

350 g/12 oz smoked mackerel
50 g/2 oz butter, softened
150 ml/¼ pint double cream
1 tablespoon lemon juice
dash of Worcestershire sauce
dash of Tabasco sauce
salt
1 tablespoon finely chopped parsley
1 tablespoon green peppercorns, drained and lightly crushed
TO SERVE
fresh dill leaves or snipped chives
3 tablespoons clarified butter, melted

Flake the mackerel flesh into a bowl, discarding all skin and bones. Gradually beat in the butter, then transfer to an electric blender or food processor and work until smooth. Return to the bowl.

Whip the cream until it will just hold its shape, then fold into the fish with the lemon juice, Worcestershire and Tabasco sauces. Taste and add a little salt, if necessary. Stir in the parsley and peppercorns. Spoon into 6 ramekins and level the surface.

To freeze: Cover with cling film; overwrap in a polythene bag. Seal, label and freeze for up to 2 months.

To thaw and serve: Leave to stand in wrappings in the refrigerator overnight. Unwrap, arrange the dill or chives attractively on the pâté, then slowly pour over the clarified butter. Chill in the refrigerator for at least 30 minutes until the butter has solidified. Serve chilled.

Serves 6

PHEASANT PÂTÉ

Grouse or partridge may be used instead of pheasant, whichever is the most reasonably priced. Serve with French bread or Melba toast.

1 large oven-ready pheasant
750 g/1½ lb loin of pork, trimmed of skin and fat, diced
150 ml/¼ pint dry red wine
2 tablespoons brandy
250 g/8 oz streaky bacon rashers, rinds removed
8 large chicken livers
250 g/8 oz pork fat
2 garlic cloves, peeled
1 egg, beaten
2 tablespoons chopped parsley
1 teaspoon dried thyme
1 teaspoon ground ginger
pinch of ground allspice
pinch of grated nutmeg
salt and freshly ground black pepper
TO SERVE
rosemary sprigs
lime or lemon wedges

Cut all the meat from the pheasant, discarding the skin. Cut all but the leg meat into 1 cm/½ inch cubes, then place in a bowl with the pork. Pour over the wine and brandy, cover and leave to marinate over night.

The next day, stretch the bacon rashers with the flat of a knife blade, then use to line the base and sides of a 1.2 litre/2 pint ovenproof dish. Mince the chicken livers together with the pork fat, reserved leg meat from the pheasant, the garlic and any leftover bacon. Add the egg, herbs, spices and salt and pepper to taste and mix well. Stir in the meat and marinade.

Spoon the pâté mixture into the dish and level the top, then fold over the ends of the bacon rashers. Cover with a lid or foil, then stand in a bain-marie (roasting tin half filled with hot water).

Bake in a preheated moderate oven (180°C/350°F/Gas Mark 4) for 1½ hours, until the pâté is cooked through and the juices run clear. Remove the lid or foil and return to the oven for a further 20 minutes, until the top of the pâté is golden brown. Remove from the bain-marie and leave until completely cold, then place heavy weights on top of the pâté and chill in the refrigerator until firm.

To freeze: Cover the dish with cling film, then overwrap in foil or a polythene bag. Seal, label and freeze for up to 3 months.

To thaw and serve: Leave to stand in wrappings in the refrigerator overnight. Unwrap and cut into slices. Serve garnished with rosemary and lime or lemon wedges.

Serves 6 to 8

ABOVE: Pheasant Pâté; Smoked Mackerel Pâté
OPPOSITE: Sweetcorn and Prawn Chowder; Autumn Vegetable Soup

MEDITERRANEAN VEGETABLE APPETIZER

This is a variation of the French vegetable dish ratatouille. It has a rich flavour, with lots of herbs. Red peppers may be used instead of the green ones suggested here, but they will not give such a good contrast in colour. Serve this delicious starter with garlic bread.

4 tablespoons olive oil
1 clove garlic, crushed
3 large onions, peeled and sliced
3 large green peppers, cored, seeded and sliced
1 × 396 g/14 oz can tomatoes
3 tablespoons chopped parsley or chervil
2 tablespoons chopped basil
2 tablespoons chopped thyme
salt and freshly ground black pepper
TO SERVE
1–2 tablespoons capers
10–12 black olives, stoned

Heat the oil in a pan, add the garlic and onions and fry very gently for 10 minutes, stirring occasionally. Add the green peppers and cook gently, stirring, for 1 minute. Add the tomatoes and their juice, the herbs and salt and pepper to taste. Bring to the boil, then lower the heat, cover and simmer for 30 minutes, stirring occasionally until the vegetables are very soft. Remove from the heat and cool quickly.

To freeze: Spoon the mixture into a rigid container, seal, label and freeze for up to 4 months.

To thaw and serve: Leave to stand in container in the refrigerator overnight. Stir in the capers and black olives, then taste and adjust the seasoning. Spoon the appetizer into individual serving dishes and serve chilled.

Serves 4

VARIATION

Replace the green peppers with 3 sliced courgettes and 125 g (4 oz) button mushrooms. Cook the vegetables for 15 to 20 minutes only. Sprinkle with chopped parsley and the black olives to serve.

Corn on the Cob with Savoury Butters (lemon and paprika butter, herb butter); Stuffed Mushrooms; Mediterranean Vegetable Appetizer

PISSALADIÈRE

This is the French version of the Italian pizza. A few mushrooms, prawns or green olives may be added for a change.

15 g/½ oz fresh yeast
about 2 tablespoons tepid water
150 g/5 oz plain flour
salt
40 g/1½ oz butter
1 egg, beaten
FILLING
4 tablespoons olive oil
750 g/1½ lb onions, peeled and thinly sliced
6 tomatoes, skinned and roughly chopped
1 garlic clove, peeled and crushed
1 teaspoon dried mixed herbs
freshly ground black pepper
1 × 50 g/2 oz can anchovy fillets, drained and soaked in
    milk for 15 minutes, rinsed and dried
12 black olives, stoned

Blend the yeast and the 2 tablespoons water together in a bowl, then leave in a warm place for 10 minutes until frothy. Sift the flour and a pinch of salt into a bowl. Rub in the butter until the mixture resembles fine breadcrumbs, then make a well in the centre. Add the egg and yeast liquid and mix well to a firm but pliable dough, adding a little more tepid water if necessary. Knead well. Place in a clean bowl, cover with a damp cloth and leave to rise in a warm place for 1 to 1½ hours, until doubled in bulk.

To make the filling: Heat 3 tablespoons oil in a pan, add the onions and fry over low heat until pale golden. Stir in the tomatoes, garlic and herbs and cook, uncovered, for 15 minutes, until the sauce is thick. Add salt and pepper to taste.

Turn the dough onto a floured surface and knead lightly. Form into a ball and place in the centre of a lightly greased 20–25 cm/8–10 inch round baking sheet. Using your knuckles, press the dough outwards until it is spread evenly over the base and sides of the tin. Spread the filling over the dough, then arrange the anchovy fillets in a lattice design over the top and stud with the olives.

Bake in a preheated moderately hot oven (200°C/400°F/Gas Mark 6) for 20 minutes, then reduce the temperature to moderate (180°C/350°F/Gas Mark 4) and bake for a further 10 to 15 minutes, until well risen and golden brown. Slide the pissaladière onto a wire rack and leave until cold.

To freeze: Open freeze the pissaladière until solid, then wrap carefully in foil and overwrap in a polythene bag. Seal, label and return to the freezer for up to 4 months.

To thaw and serve: Unwrap and place on a baking sheet. Reheat from frozen in a preheated moderate oven (180°C/350°F/Gas Mark 4) for 15 to 20 minutes. Serve hot, cut into slices.
Serves 4 to 6

CORN ON THE COB SAVOURY BUTTERS

A selection of savoury butters such as these is useful in the freezer for serving with corn on the cob as a quick starter. Make four different flavours as suggested here or make a large quantity of just one or two. Serve with fresh or frozen corn on the cob, remembering that it is important not to overcook it, as this toughens the kernels (both fresh and frozen corn on the cob take only 4 to 8 minutes to cook in boiling water). Cooking in salted water also tends to make them hard, so seasoning should always be added aftwerwards.

GARLIC BUTTER
75 g/3 oz butter, softened
2 garlic cloves, peeled
salt and freshly ground black pepper
CURRY BUTTER
75 g/3 oz butter, softened
1½ teaspoons curry powder
pinch of ground turmeric
1 teaspoon lemon juice
salt and freshly ground black pepper
HERB BUTTER
75 g/3 oz butter, softened
1 teaspoon chopped parsley
1 teaspoon chopped tarragon
1 teaspoon chopped chervil
1 teaspoon snipped chives
1 teaspoon chopped marjoram
salt and freshly ground black pepper
2 teaspoons grated onion
LEMON AND PAPRIKA BUTTER
75 g/3 oz butter, softened
2 teaspoons finely grated lemon rind
2 teaspoons lemon juice
1 teaspoon paprika
salt

To make the garlic butter: Cook the garlic in a little boiling water for 2 minutes, then drain, cool and crush. Beat into the softened butter with salt and pepper to taste.

Make the curry, herb, and lemon and paprika butters by beating the flavouring ingredients into the softened butter as for garlic butter.
To freeze: Form each flavoured butter into a sausage shape about 2.5 cm/1 inch in diameter. Alternatively, spread butter evenly over a sheet of foil until about 1 cm/½ inch thick. Wrap in foil, seal, label and freeze for up to 2 months.
To thaw and serve: Leave butters to stand in their wrappings, in the refrigerator for 3 hours, until thawed but still very firm.

Cut the sausage-shaped butters into 1 cm/½ inch discs and the flattened butter into pretty shapes, using small pastry or petit fours cutters. Place on a plate and refrigerate while cooking the corn on the cob.
Makes 350 g/12 oz savoury butter, sufficient for 6 corn on the cob

STUFFED MUSHROOMS

As an alternative to this crab filling, use 350 g/12 oz chopped peeled prawns or diced ham.
To make the tomato garnish, pare the skin from a tomato in one piece, using a sharp knife, then curl to form a flower head shape.

16 large flat mushrooms, total weight 500–750 g/
    1–1½ lb
75 g/3 oz butter
3 tablespoons dry white wine
25 g/1 oz plain flour
250 ml/8 fl oz creamy milk
1 garlic clove, peeled and crushed
salt and freshly ground black pepper
50 g/2 oz walnuts, roughly chopped
350 g/12 oz crabmeat, flaked
juice of 1 lemon
2 tablespoons dried breadcrumbs
1 tablespoon finely chopped parsley
1 tablespoon snipped chives
TO SERVE
tomato flowers
stuffed olive slices

Remove the stalks from the mushrooms and chop them. Melt 50 g/2 oz butter in a pan, add the mushroom caps and fry gently for 2 minutes. Pour in the wine, cook for a further 2 minutes, then remove the mushroom caps from the pan with a slotted spoon and arrange in a lightly greased shallow ovenproof dish or foil container. Reserve the cooking liquid.

Melt the remaining butter in a clean pan, add the flour and cook for 2 minutes, stirring all the time. Remove from the heat and gradually add the milk, beating vigorously after each addition. Return to the heat and bring to the boil, stirring constantly. Lower the heat, add the garlic and salt and pepper to taste and simmer for 2 minutes.

Remove the sauce from the heat and stir in the walnuts, chopped mushroom stalks, crabmeat and lemon juice until evenly mixed. Spoon a little mixture into each mushroom cap. Mix the breadcrumbs and herbs together and sprinkle over the top. Bake in a preheated moderate oven (180°C/350°F/Gas Mark 4) for 10 to 12 minutes, basting occasionally with the reserved cooking liquid from the mushrooms. Cool quickly.
To freeze: Cover the dish with foil, then overwrap in a polythene bag. Seal, label and freeze for up to 2 months.
To thaw and serve: Unwrap and leave to stand at room temperature for 3 to 4 hours. Reheat, uncovered, in a preheated hot oven (220°C/425°F/Gas Mark 7) for 10 minutes, until golden brown. Serve hot, garnished with tomato flowers and stuffed olive slices.
Serves 6 to 8

HALIBUT AURORA WITH SPINACH CROÛTES

A fish recipe with outstanding flavour. The decorative and tasty addition of the spinach-topped croûtes makes it a dish to grace any party table, with absolutely no last-minute attention. Buy prawns in the shell for maximum flavour.

625 g/1¼ lb tail piece halibut, boned, skinned and
    divided into 4 fillets
300 ml/½ pint dry white wine
1 shallot, peeled and chopped
salt and freshly ground black pepper
½ teaspoon anchovy relish
½ teaspoon tomato purée
125 g/4 oz cooked prawns, shelled
4 tablespoons double cream
SPINACH CROÛTES
4 thin slices white bread
25 g/1 oz butter
1 tablespoon vegetable oil
4 large spinach or Swiss chard leaves, blanched and
    chopped
½ teaspoon anchovy paste or gentleman's relish

Put the fish fillets in a large pan, add the wine, shallot and salt and pepper to taste and poach over low heat for 5 minutes. Using a fish slice, lift the fish carefully into an ovenproof dish lined with a large sheet of foil.

Add the anchovy relish, tomato purée, and prawns to the liquid in the pan and boil until reduced by half. Stir in the cream, heat until thickened, then pour around the fish. Cool quickly.

To make the spinach croûtes: Cut four 7.5 cm/3 inch circles from the bread slices, using a fluted biscuit or pastry cutter. Heat half the butter and the oil in a frying pan, add the bread circles and fry over moderate heat until evenly browned on both sides. Drain and cool on kitchen paper. Mix the remaining butter with the spinach or chard leaves, anchovy paste or relish, and pepper to taste. Spread over the bread.

To freeze: Open freeze the fish and croûtes separately until solid. Wrap the croûtes together in foil. Remove the fish from the dish in the foil and fold over the foil to make a tight parcel, tucking the croûtes into the parcel. Seal, label and return to the freezer for up to 1 month.

To thaw and serve: Unwrap the fish and return to the original dish. Cover with foil and leave to stand at room temperature for 2 hours. Leave the croûtes to stand in their foil wrapping at the same time. Reheat in a preheated moderately hot oven (200°C/400°F/Gas Mark 6) for about 20 minutes, placing the spinach croûtes in the lower part of the oven, with the foil open. Serve immediately.
Serves 4

RIGHT: Halibut Aurora with Spinach Croûtes
OPPOSITE: Perranporth Mussels; Stir-Fried Prawn Supper

PERRANPORTH MUSSELS

Mussels gathered in early autumn to be savoured later – baked from frozen with bacon, onions and cheese for a tasty luncheon or supper dish. The tomato sauce may be spooned over the mussels or served separately.

1.5 kg/3 lb fresh mussels, scrubbed clean and beards
    removed
4 tablespoons dry cider
2 tablespoons olive oil
500 g/1 lb unsmoked streaky bacon, rinds removed,
    cut into strips
2 medium onions, peeled and chopped
6 tablespoons chopped parsley
6 tablespoons grated Parmesan cheese
TOMATO SAUCE
2 tablespoons olive oil
2 garlic cloves, peeled and crushed
2 small onions, peeled and finely chopped
4 large tomatoes, skinned and chopped
2 bay leaves
salt and freshly ground black pepper

Put the mussels into a wide-based pan with the cider, discarding any that are already open. Cover and cook until the shells open. Discard the top shells and any whole mussels that have not opened. Put the mussels in their shells in a single layer in a shallow ovenproof dish lined with a large sheet of foil.

Heat the oil in a pan, add the bacon and onions and fry gently without browning. Remove from the heat, stir in the parsley and Parmesan, then spoon over the mussels. Cool quickly.

To make the tomato sauce: Heat the oil in a pan, add the remaining ingredients, cover and simmer for about 15 minutes until very soft. Discard the bay leaves. Pour the sauce into a small rigid container and cool quickly.

To freeze: Open freeze the mussels until solid, then remove from the dish in the foil and fold over the foil to make a tight parcel. Seal, label and freeze for up to 1 month. Cover the container of sauce with the lid. Seal, label and freeze for up to 3 months.

To thaw and serve: Unwrap the mussels and return to the original dish. Cover with the foil and reheat from frozen in a preheated moderately hot oven (200°C/400°F/Gas Mark 6) for 25 minutes. Reheat the sauce from frozen in a separate dish on a lower shelf of the oven, then taste and adjust the seasoning. Serve hot.
Serves 4

STIR-FRIED PRAWN SUPPER

Use a mixture of ordinary prawns and the luxuriously large Dublin Bay prawns for this rosy-glazed stir-fry, according to your pocket! Buy them in the shell – they have far more flavour than the ready-peeled variety.

4 tablespoons vegetable oil
15 g/½ oz fresh root ginger, peeled and finely sliced
2 garlic cloves, peeled and chopped
8 spring onions, trimmed and sliced diagonally
1 medium carrot, peeled and cut into matchstick strips
8 celery sticks, sliced diagonally
350 g/12 oz cauliflower, separated into tiny florets
2 red peppers, cored, seeded and sliced into thin rings
1 green pepper, cored, seeded and thinly shredded
1 kg/2 lb cooked prawns in shells, peeled
GLAZE
2 teaspoons cornflour
6 tablespoons water
2 tablespoons white wine vinegar
2 teaspoons soy sauce
2 teaspoons tomato purée
salt and freshly ground black pepper
TO SERVE
celery leaves

Heat the oil in a wok or deep frying pan, add the ginger and garlic and stir-fry over moderate heat for 30 seconds. Add the onions, carrot and celery. Stir-fry for 1 minute, then add the cauliflower and stir-fry for 30 seconds. Add the peppers and stir-fry for a further 30 seconds. Add the prawns and heat through.

Mix together the ingredients for the glaze, pour into the pan and stir over brisk heat until all the prawns and vegetables are coated. Cool quickly.

To freeze: Pour the prawns and vegetables into a rigid container, seal, label and freeze for up to 1 month.

To thaw and serve: Reheat gently from frozen in a heavy-based pan for 20 to 25 minutes, stirring as necessary. Taste and adjust the seasoning and serve hot, garnished with celery leaves.

Serves 4

CHEVRON CODLING

A simple recipe for freshly caught codling, or a tail cod portion. The clearly visible flakes of the skinned fish form the design which gives the dish its name.

1 tablespoon vegetable oil
1.2 kg/2¼ lb codling (or tail piece of cod)
1 red pepper, cored, seeded and sliced into thin rings
1 green pepper, cored, seeded and sliced into thin rings
2 large tomatoes, skinned and roughly chopped
50 g/2 oz black olives
2 tablespoons tomato purée
3 tablespoons water
salt and freshly ground black pepper

Pour the oil into an ovenproof dish lined with a large sheet of foil. Turn the fish in the oil until evenly coated, then remove from the dish and set aside.

Put the peppers, tomatoes and olives in the dish with the tomato purée, water and salt and pepper to taste. Mix well, then replace the fish in the dish and fold over the foil loosely.

Bake in a preheated moderate oven (180°C/350°F/Gas Mark 4) for 20 minutes. Uncover and carefully remove the top skin from the fish. Cool fish quickly.

To freeze: Open freeze until solid, then remove from the dish in the foil and fold over the foil to make a tight parcel. Seal, label and return to the freezer for up to 1 month.

To thaw and serve: Unwrap and return to the original dish. Cover with foil and leave to stand at room temperature for 2 hours. Reheat in a preheated moderately hot oven (190°C/375°F/Gas Mark 5) for 30 to 40 minutes. Serve very hot.

Serves 4 to 6

Maudie's Capon

Succulent farmhouse capon, poached in cider with bacon and parsley, recalls recipes of bygone days.

---

1 oven-ready capon, weighing 1.75 kg/4 lb, giblets reserved
4 rashers streaky bacon, rinds removed, halved
1 garlic clove, peeled and chopped
1 onion, peeled and chopped
300 ml/½ pint dry cider
2 parsley sprigs
salt and freshly ground black pepper
TO SERVE
chopped parsley

Put the capon and giblets in a large pan. Roll up the bacon rashers and secure with wooden cocktail sticks. Add to the pan with the remaining ingredients, bring to the boil, then lower the heat, cover and simmer for 1 hour or until the capon is tender. Cool quickly, then discard the parsley and giblets.

To freeze: Transfer to a rigid container, seal, label and freeze for up to 2 months.

To thaw and serve: Leave to stand in container at room temperature for 8 hours or overnight, then reheat gently on top of the stove for 45 to 55 minutes until very hot. Transfer the capon to a warmed serving dish and sprinkle with chopped parsley. Remove the onion and bacon rolls with a slotted spoon, discard the cocktail sticks and arrange around the capon. Serve immediately, accompanied by the cooking liquid.

Serves 4 to 6

Chicken Suprêmes Alisonia

Remove the breast fillets from autumn chickens to make this excellent recipe – you will need 2 chickens for 4 breast fillets or suprêmes. Use the remaining carcasses for casseroles and stock. To serve immediately, without freezing, fry the coated fillets in the butter and oil until tender, turning once.

---

4 chicken breasts, each weighing 75 g/3 oz, skinned
2 eggs
6 tablespoons grated Parmesan cheese
6 tablespoons dried breadcrumbs
salt and freshly ground black pepper
75 g/3 oz butter
2 tablespoons vegetable oil
MUSHROOM GARNISH
2 tablespoons vegetable oil
250 g/8 oz flat mushrooms, quartered
2 tablespoons lemon juice
1 teaspoon chopped thyme

Beat out the chicken breasts until they are flat and thin. Beat the eggs in a shallow dish. Mix the cheese and breadcrumbs with salt and pepper and spread out on a flat plate. Dip the chicken fillets first into the beaten egg, then into the breadcrumb mixture. Press firmly so that the coating adheres well. Place the chicken breasts in a single layer in an ovenproof dish lined with a large sheet of foil. Heat the butter and oil together in a small pan, then pour evenly over the fillets.

To make the mushroom garnish: Heat the oil in a frying pan, add the mushrooms, lemon juice, thyme and salt and pepper to taste and cook until the mushrooms are soft and the juices run. Pour into a small rigid container. Cool quickly.

To freeze: Open freeze the chicken until solid, then remove from the dish in the foil and fold over the foil to make a tight parcel. Seal, label and return to the freezer for up to 4 months. Cover the mushroom container. Seal, label and freeze for up to 4 months.

To thaw and serve: Unwrap the chicken and return to the original dish. Leave to stand at room temperature for 2 hours. Leave the mushrooms to thaw in their container at the same time.

Bake the chicken in a preheated hot oven (220°C/425°F/Gas Mark 7) for 15 to 20 minutes. Reheat the mushroom garnish in a covered dish in the lower part of the oven for the last 10 minutes. Serve the chicken hot, topped with the garnish.

Serves 4

Woodland Grouse

One of autumn's treats, these halved grouse are very simply cooked with mushrooms, wine and fruit jelly.

---

2 oven-ready grouse, each weighing 350 g/12 oz
salt and freshly ground black pepper
15 g/½ oz butter, softened
2 shallots, peeled and chopped
125 g/4 oz button mushrooms, sliced
300 ml/½ pint red wine
2 tablespoons redcurrant jelly
TO SERVE
chopped parsley

Sprinkle the grouse with salt and pepper to taste, then spread with the butter. Put into a roasting tin and roast in a preheated moderate oven (180°C/350°F/Gas Mark 4) for 25 minutes.

Cut the birds in half lengthways, then put in a casserole lined with a large sheet of foil. Mix together the shallots, mushrooms, wine and redcurrant jelly with the juices from the roasting tin. Pour over the grouse, cover and return to the oven for a further 35 minutes. Cool quickly.

To freeze: Open freeze the grouse until solid, then remove from the casserole in the foil and fold over the foil to make a tight parcel. Seal, label and return to the freezer for up to 2 months.

To thaw and serve: Unwrap and return to the original casserole. Cover with foil and leave to stand at room temperature for 2 hours. Reheat in a preheated moderate oven (180°C/350°F/Gas Mark 4) for 20 to 30 minutes. Sprinkle with parsley and serve hot.

Serves 4

VICTORIAN HAUNCH OF VENISON

Prime cut of venison is marinated and cooked for the shortest possible time – to maximize its gamey flavour and pink centre. Ask your butcher for a large sheet of barding fat or pork back fat long enough to wrap around the meat to keep it moist during cooking; it should be very thin so that it is pliable. Serve the venison with watercress and sauté potatoes, and accompany with a really first-class Burgundy!

750 g/1 ½ lb piece haunch of venison, boned, rolled
   and tied
250 g/8 oz dark red plums, halved and stoned
1 small onion, peeled and sliced
3 tablespoons olive oil
3 tablespoons port
4 allspice berries, slightly crushed
freshly ground black pepper
thin sheet of pork barding fat
TO SERVE
watercress sprigs

Wipe the venison and dry thoroughly. Mix together the plums, onion, 2 tablespoons oil, the port, allspice berries and pepper to taste. Put into a polythene bag with the venison, close the bag with a tie fastener and leave to marinate in the refrigerator for 12 to 48 hours, turning the bag occasionally.

Remove the venison from the marinade and pat dry with kitchen paper. Heat the remaining oil in a flameproof casserole, add the venison and brown quickly on all sides. Remove from the pan and wrap in the barding fat. Return the venison to the casserole and pour in the plum marinade. Cover and cook over low heat for 35 minutes.

Put the venison and plums in a deep foil container. Strain the cooking liquid, leave to cool, then remove the solidified fat from the surface. Pour the liquid over the meat in the foil container. Leave until the meat is completely cold.

To freeze: Cover the container with the lid, seal, label and freeze for up to 2 months.

To thaw and serve: Leave to stand in container at room temperature for 8 hours, then put the container into a large pan and pour in enough boiling water to come one-third up the container. Remove the foil lid, cover the pan and simmer for 20 to 25 minutes, turning the venison once during this time. Remove the barding fat and string. Carve the meat into thin slices and serve immediately, garnished with watercress.
Serves 4

Victorian Haunch of Venison; Woodland Grouse; Chicken
Suprêmes Alisonia

VEAL TOURNEDOS EPICURE

These tiny 'bites' of veal with their fruity sauce are light and delicate.

8 veal tournedos, each weighing 50 g/2 oz
salt and freshly ground black pepper
25 g/1 oz butter
2 tablespoons olive oil
8 pears, peeled, quartered and cored
300 ml/½ pint rosé vermouth
1 teaspoon potato flour (fécule)
2 tablespoons water

Sprinkle each tournedo with salt and pepper. Heat the butter and oil in a large frying pan, add the tournedos and fry over moderate heat for about 3 minutes until browned on both sides. Add the pears and fry for 1 minute.

Pour in the vermouth and simmer for 5 minutes, turning the meat over halfway through this time. Mix the potato flour to a smooth paste with the water, stir into the pan and cook for 2 minutes, stirring until the sauce thickens. Cool quickly.

To freeze: Transfer the veal and sauce to a rigid container, seal, label and freeze for up to 3 months.

To thaw and serve: Leave to stand in container at room temperature for 2 hours, then put the container into a large pan and pour in enough boiling water to come one-third up the container. Remove the foil lid, cover the pan and simmer for about 20 minutes until heated through. Remove the string from the tournedos. Serve immediately.

Serves 4

SIRLOIN SALLY MAY

Home-produced beef is 'seasoned' with a combination of sliced leeks and smoked mussels for an unusual contrast in flavours. Cooked and frozen whole it is served thinly sliced, hot or cold.

1.25 kg/2¾ lb piece boned and rolled sirloin
105 g/4 oz can smoked mussels in oil, drained, with oil
    reserved
1 small leek (green and white parts), finely sliced
salt and freshly ground black pepper

Stuff the sirloin with the mussels and leek, pressing them into the seams formed within the rolled meat. Place the meat in a roasting tin, sprinkle with salt and pepper and pour over the reserved oil from the mussels. Roast in a preheated moderately hot oven (200°C/400°F/Gas Mark 6) for 55 minutes. Lift the meat onto a large sheet of foil and cool quickly. Pour the juices from the pan into a small rigid container, leave to cool, then remove the fat.

To freeze: Wrap the meat in the foil to make a tight parcel. Seal, label and freeze for up to 3 months.

Cover the container containing the meat juices with the lid. Seal, label and freeze for up to 3 months.

To thaw and serve: Leave both meat and juices to stand at room temperature for 8 hours. Slice the beef, if serving cold, and hand the juices separately. To serve hot, place the beef in a roasting tin, pour over the juices and reheat in a preheated moderately hot oven (200°C/400°F/Gas Mark 6) for 30 minutes.

Serves 6 to 8

POCKETED RUMP

This stuffed rump steak with its rosy pink centre and creamy sauce can be sliced thinly or thickly according to preference.

850 g/1¾ lb piece rump steak, 5 cm/2 inches thick
100 g/4 oz packet Westphalian or other sliced raw
    smoked ham
15 g/½ oz butter
75 g/3 oz button mushrooms, quartered
1 tablespoon chopped parsley
freshly ground black pepper
1 tablespoon vegetable oil
salt
1 tablespoon soured cream
4 tablespoons red wine
½ teaspoon paprika
TO SERVE
watercress sprigs

Cut through the flesh of the steak to form a pocket. Overlap half the ham slices in the bottom of the pocket. Melt the butter in a frying pan, add 50 g/2 oz mushrooms and fry gently for a few minutes. Remove from the heat and stir in the parsley and pepper to taste, then spread over the ham. Cover with the remaining slices of ham.

Close the pocket and secure with wooden cocktail sticks. Heat the oil in the pan, add the meat and fry over brisk heat for 3 minutes on each side. Remove the meat from the pan, sprinkle with salt and pepper, then pad the ends of the cocktail sticks with foil. Place in an ovenproof dish lined with a large sheet of foil.

Add the cream and wine to the pan and stir to dissolve the sediment. Add the paprika and the remaining mushrooms, cook for 2 minutes, then pour over the steak. Cool quickly.

To freeze: Open freeze the steak until solid, then remove from the dish in the foil and fold over the foil to make a tight parcel. Seal, label and return to the freezer for up to 2 months.

To thaw and serve: Unwrap and return to the original dish. Cover with foil and leave to stand at room temperature overnight. Reheat in a preheated moderately hot oven (200°C/400°F/Gas Mark 6) for 20 to 25 minutes. Remove the cocktail sticks and slice the meat into moderate or thick slanting slices. Garnish with watercress and serve immediately.

Serves 6

TERRINE DE GIROUDET

Mashed partially-cooked chicken livers and cream give a rich, distinctive French-farmhouse texture and taste to this terrine. Individual wrapping of the slices speeds up the thawing time considerably, and one-person portions are easy and convenient. Serve with hot toast or crusty French bread.

10 rashers streaky bacon, rinds removed
15 g/½ oz butter
1 tablespoon vegetable oil
500 g/1 lb chicken livers
1 garlic clove, peeled and crushed
350 g/12 oz minced veal
350 g/12 oz minced pork
4 tablespoons soured cream
2 tablespoons red wine
¾ teaspoon chopped thyme
salt and freshly ground black pepper
24 pistachio nuts, shelled

Stretch the bacon rashers with the flat of a knife blade, then use to line the base and sides of a lightly oiled 1.2 litre/2 pint terrine or ovenproof dish.

Heat the butter and oil in a frying pan, add the chicken livers and fry briefly until browned on the outside. Remove from the pan with a slotted spoon and put half on one side, choosing the best-shaped pieces. Mash the remaining livers roughly with a fork.

Add the garlic to the pan, fry for 1 minute, then add to the mashed livers with the veal, pork, cream, wine, thyme and salt and pepper to taste. Carefully put half of this mixture into the prepared terrine and level the surface. Place the reserved livers in a line down the centre, overlapping them slightly, then place the nuts on either side. Cover with the remaining meat mixture, putting it round the edges first and then in the centre, to avoid disturbing the chicken livers. Pack the mixture in firmly.

Cover the terrine with a lid or greased foil, then stand in a bain-marie (roasting tin half full of hot water). Bake in a preheated moderate oven (160°C/325°F/Gas Mark 3) for 1 hour. Leave to cool for 30 minutes, then cover with greased foil and place heavy weights on top. Leave until completely cold.

To freeze: Turn the terrine out of the dish, then wrap in cling film and overwrap in a polythene bag. Alternatively, cut the terrine into 8 slices and wrap each individually, or re-assemble with oiled grease-proof paper between the slices. Seal, label and freeze for up to 2 months.

To thaw and serve: Leave to stand in wrappings at room temperature for 2 to 3 hours for individual slices, overnight for whole or re-assembled terrine.

Serves 8

Veal Tournedos Epicure; Sirloin Sally May; Pocketed Rump

DAUBE OF MUTTON

If your butcher supplies mutton it is by far the best meat to use for this recipe. Cooked in a rich, red wine sauce it tastes very similar to the more usual *daube de boeuf*. If mutton is not available, lamb may be used instead, but the flavour of the finished dish will not be quite so rich.

1 kg/2 lb piece fillet end leg of mutton, bone removed and reserved
3 tablespoons vegetable oil
4 medium carrots, peeled and halved lengthways
1 onion, peeled and cut into 8 wedges
1 large aubergine, quartered lengthways and thickly sliced
300 ml/½ pint red wine
2 teaspoons tomato purée
1 bouquet garni
salt and freshly ground black pepper
8 walnuts, shelled and halved

Cut the meat into 3.5 cm/1½ inch cubes. Heat the oil in a flameproof casserole, add the meat and fry over brisk heat until browned on all sides. Remove with a slotted spoon and drain on kitchen paper.

Add the vegetables to the pan and fry over gentle heat, stirring occasionally, until lightly coloured. Return the meat to the pan with its bone, then add the wine, tomato purée, bouquet garni and salt and pepper to taste.

Bring to the boil, then lower the heat, cover and simmer for 1½ hours or until the meat is very tender. Remove the bouquet garni and add the walnuts. Cool quickly.

To freeze: Transfer the meat and vegetables to a rigid container, seal, label and freeze for up to 3 months.

To thaw and serve: Leave to stand in container at room temperature overnight, then reheat gently on top of the stove for 10 to 15 minutes or until heated through. Serve immediately.

Serves 4

KIWI LAMB CHOPS

Chunky lamb chops are tenderized and their flavour is enhanced by the addition of kiwi fruit to the marinade and sauce.

2 kiwi fruit (1 very ripe)
1 tablespoon lemon juice
freshly ground black pepper
4 lamb chump chops, total weight about 750 g/1½ lb
1 tablespoon olive oil
150 ml/¼ pint dry cider
salt

Peel and mash the very ripe kiwi fruit and mix with the lemon juice and pepper to taste. Spread this mixture over both sides of the chops, then put in a single layer in a dish and leave to marinate in a cool place for 2 to 4 hours.

Heat the oil in a flameproof casserole, add the chops and fry quickly until browned on both sides. Remove the chops with a slotted spoon and put them in a foil container. Add any remaining marinade to the pan with the cider and stir to dissolve the meat juices and sediment in the bottom of the pan. Add salt to taste.

Slice the remaining kiwi fruit into 8 pieces, add to the liquid in the pan and cook for 1 minute only. Put 2 slices kiwi fruit on each chop and pour the liquid over. Cool quickly.

To freeze: Cover the container with the lid, seal, label and freeze for up to 3 months.

To thaw and serve: Leave to stand in container at room temperature for 2 hours, then transfer the chops and sauce to the original casserole, arranging the chops in a single layer. Reheat gently on top of the stove for 20 to 25 minutes, until heated through, basting occasionally. Taste and adjust the seasoning of the sauce and serve hot.

Serves 4

ABOVE: Daube of Mutton; Kiwi Lamb Chops
RIGHT: West Coast Pork Fillets; Sweetbread Triangles

WEST COAST PORK FILLETS

Cooking, freezing and reheating tender pork fillets in the piece' prevents dryness and preserves flavour.

2 pork (tenderloin) fillets, total weight about 850 g/
*   1¾ lb*
salt and freshly ground black pepper
1 tablespoon olive oil
25 g/1 oz butter
2 shallots, peeled and sliced
finely grated rind and juice of 2 oranges
about 150 ml/¼ pint cider or white wine
350 g/12 oz cauliflower, separated into small florets
TO SERVE
orange slices

Cut the pork fillets in half crossways and dry well with kitchen paper. Insert a skewer along the centre of each to prevent curling. Sprinkle liberally with salt and pepper.

Heat the oil and butter in a flameproof casserole, add the meat and fry over moderate heat for 1 minute on each side or until golden brown. Remove from the pan with a slotted spoon and drain on kitchen paper.

Add the shallots to the pan and fry for 1 minute. Make the orange juice up to 300 ml/½ pint with cider or wine, stir into the pan and bring to the boil. Return the meat to the pan, lower the heat, cover and simmer for 8 minutes, turning the meat after 5 minutes and adding the cauliflower.

Remove the meat from the sauce and take out the skewers. Put the meat in a rigid container. Stir the orange rind into the sauce, then pour over the meat. Cool quickly.

To freeze: Seal the container, label and freeze for up to 3 months.

To thaw and serve: Leave to stand in container at room temperature for 8 hours or overnight. Transfer to an ovenproof serving dish and reheat in a preheated moderately hot oven (190°C/375°F/Gas Mark 5) for 20 minutes, turning the meat halfway through this time.

Slice and serve immediately, garnished with orange.
Serves 4

SWEETBREAD TRIANGLES

Crisp pastry parcels with a delicate filling are baked from frozen in 20 minutes, making them ideal for last-minute meals. Filo or strudel pastry leaves can be bought fresh or frozen from Greek and Middle Eastern stores and some good delicatessens.
To serve immediately without freezing, bake as below but for 5 minutes each side only.

750 g/1½ lb lamb's sweetbreads
600 ml/1 pint cold water
1 teaspoon lemon juice
1 thyme sprig
150 g/5 oz butter
1 shallot, peeled and chopped
50 g/2 oz button mushrooms, sliced
3 tablespoons plain flour
300 ml/½ pint (less 2 tablespoons) creamy milk
2 tablespoons medium sherry
50 g/2 oz cooked or canned sweetcorn kernels,
*   drained*
2 tablespoons chopped parsley
salt and freshly ground black pepper
8 leaves or sheets filo pastry
TO SERVE
50 g/2 oz butter, melted
150 ml/¼ pint soured cream
2 tablespoons chopped mint

Put the sweetbreads in a pan with the water, lemon juice and thyme. Bring to the boil, simmer for 2 minutes, then drain and cut each one in half.

Melt 25 g/1 oz butter in a pan, add the shallot and mushrooms and fry gently until soft. Add the flour and cook, stirring, for 2 minutes. Remove from the heat and gradually stir in the milk and sherry. Return to the heat and bring to the boil, stirring. Lower the heat and simmer for 2 minutes, then add the sweetbreads, corn, parsley and salt and pepper to taste. Remove from the heat and leave to cool. Divide into 12 portions.

Melt the remaining butter. Put 2 filo leaves on top of each other and brush with melted butter. Cut lengthways into 3 strips. Put a portion of filling towards one corner of a strip and fold over the pastry to make a triangle. Continue folding to the end of the strip, keeping the triangular shape and folding the last edges inside to make a neat triangle. Brush all sides liberally with melted butter. Make 11 more triangles in this way with the remaining ingredients.

To freeze: Pack the triangles into a rigid container, separating the layers with interleaving sheets or foil. Seal, label and freeze for up to 2 months.

To thaw and serve: Brush both sides of each triangle with the melted butter, then place on a baking sheet. Bake from frozen in a preheated very hot oven (230°C/450°F/Gas Mark 8) for 10 minutes, then turn the triangles over and bake for a further 10 minutes. Combine the soured cream and mint in a serving bowl. Serve the triangles hot or warm, with the sauce.
Makes 12

CRISPY ONION RINGS

This is a good recipe to make when onions are cheap and plentiful: they store well in the freezer and are an excellent accompaniment to grilled and roast meats.

4 large onions, peeled and sliced into 5 mm/¼ inch
  rings
2 tablespoons plain flour
salt and freshly ground black pepper
vegetable oil, for deep-frying
BATTER
125 g/4 oz plain flour
1 teaspoon salt
2 tablespoons corn oil
150 ml/¼ pint milk
1 teaspoon dried mixed herbs
pinch of cayenne pepper
1 egg white

To make the batter: Sift the flour and salt into a bowl. Make a well in the centre, gradually mix in the oil and milk and beat until smooth. Stir in the herbs and cayenne. Whisk the egg white until very stiff, then fold into the batter.

Separate the onions into rings and toss in the flour seasoned with salt and pepper. Using a fork, dip the rings into the batter, then shake lightly to remove any excess.

Heat the oil in a deep-fat fryer to 180°C/350°F and deep-fry the onion rings a few at a time for 20 seconds or until golden brown. Leave to cool on kitchen paper while frying the remainder.

To freeze: Open freeze the onion rings until solid, then pack in a polythene bag. Seal, label and return to the freezer for up to 3 months.

To thaw and serve: Spread the frozen onion rings out on a baking sheet and reheat in a preheated moderately hot oven (200°C/400°F/Gas Mark 6) for 12 to 15 minutes, until heated through and crisp. Serve at once.
Serves 6

PARSNIP AND TOMATO BAKE

This is an unusual accompaniment to serve with roast pork or lamb. It can also be served on its own as a light lunch or supper dish, maybe with bacon or sausages.

2 tablespoons vegetable oil
1 kg/2 lb parsnips, peeled and sliced
500 g/1 lb tomatoes, skinned and sliced
salt and freshly ground black pepper
300 ml/½ pint double cream
175 g/6 oz Gruyère cheese, grated
2 tablespoons chopped parsley
2 garlic cloves, peeled and thinly sliced
4 tablespoons fresh breadcrumbs
50 g/2 oz butter

Heat the oil in a large frying pan, add the parsnips and fry over moderate heat for 4 minutes until lightly browned. Drain on kitchen paper.

Arrange a layer of parsnips in the base of a lightly greased 1.2 litre/2 pint ovenproof dish or foil container. Top with a layer of tomatoes, season well with salt and pepper, then spoon over a little cream and sprinkle with some grated cheese, parsley and garlic. Continue layering the ingredients in the dish in this way until all the ingredients are used up, finishing with a layer of cheese.

Cover the cheese with the breadcrumbs and dot with the butter. Bake in a preheated moderate oven (180°C/350°F/Gas Mark 4) for 45 minutes. Cool quickly.

To freeze: Cover with foil, then overwrap in a polythene bag. Seal, label and freeze for up to 3 months.

To thaw and serve: Unwrap and leave to stand at room temperature for 3 to 4 hours. Reheat in a preheated moderately hot oven (200°C/400°F/Gas Mark 6) for 30 to 35 minutes until bubbling. Serve hot.
Serves 6

HONEY GLAZED ONIONS

These slightly sweet, spicy onions are a delicious but inexpensive vegetable accompaniment. They go particularly well with roast meats and gammon.

500 g/1 lb small button onions, peeled, but left whole
25 g/1 oz butter
1 tablespoon clear honey
1 tablespoon sugar
juice of ½ lemon
1 teaspoon Worcestershire sauce
1 teaspoon wine vinegar
salt and freshly ground black pepper
TO SERVE
thyme or parsley sprigs

Put the button onions in a pan, pour over enough cold water to cover and bring to the boil. Simmer for 5 minutes, then drain thoroughly.

Melt the butter in a clean pan, stir in the honey, sugar, lemon juice, Worcestershire sauce and vinegar, and season to taste with salt and pepper. Stir over low heat, add the onions and stir well until coated in the glaze. Cover and cook very gently for 15 to 20 minutes until the onions are tender, stirring occasionally. Remove the lid and cook for a further 5 minutes. Cool quickly.

To freeze: Transfer the glazed onions and any remaining cooking liquor to a rigid container, seal, label and freeze for up to 3 months.

To thaw and serve: Reheat the onions gently from frozen in a heavy-based pan. Serve hot, garnished with thyme or parsley sprigs.

Serves 4 to 6

CREAMED RUNNER BEANS

Runner beans which have been frozen may lose a little of their crispness and flavour, but they can be combined with other ingredients to delicious effect. The combination of beans and cream sauce makes an excellent accompaniment for plain grilled or roast meats. Frozen French beans (*haricots verts*) can be used instead of runner beans.

---

350 g/12 oz frozen runner beans
TO SERVE
25 g/1 oz butter
1 small onion, peeled and finely chopped
1–2 garlic cloves, peeled and crushed
125 g/4 oz button mushrooms, thinly sliced
150 ml/¼ pint soured cream or double cream
1 teaspoon dried mixed herbs
salt and freshly ground black pepper
1 tablespoon chopped parsley or snipped chives, to garnish

Melt the butter in a pan, add the onion and garlic and fry gently for 5 minutes without browning. Add the mushrooms and fry gently for 5 minutes.

Plunge the beans into a separate pan of boiling salted water, bring back to the boil and simmer for 3 minutes. Drain the beans and add to the mushrooms with the cream. Fold gently to mix, add the herbs and salt and pepper to taste, then cook gently for 3 to 4 minutes until the beans are tender. (Do not let the mixture boil or the cream may separate.)

Spoon the mixture into a warmed serving dish, sprinkle with the chopped parsley or chives and serve immediately.

Serves 4

PARSNIP CROQUETTES

These make a welcome change from potatoes, and are quickly reheated from frozen.

---

1 kg/2 lb parsnips, peeled and sliced
salt
50 g/2 oz butter, softened
2 teaspoons dried mixed herbs
1 teaspoon grated nutmeg
freshly ground black pepper
plain flour, for coating
1 egg, beaten
fresh breadcrumbs
vegetable oil, for deep frying

Cook the parsnips in boiling salted water for 15 to 20 minutes until tender. Drain thoroughly, then mash or pass through a sieve until very smooth. Beat in the butter, then the herbs, nutmeg and pepper to taste.

Leave the mixture to cool slightly, then shape into croquettes 6 cm/2½ inches long and 2.5 cm/1 inch wide. Roll the croquettes in flour, then coat in the egg and breadcrumbs. Chill in the refrigerator for 1 hour.

Heat the oil in a deep-fat fryer to 180°C/350°F and deep fry the croquettes for 3 to 4 minutes, until golden brown. Leave to cool on kitchen paper.

To freeze: Open freeze the croquettes until solid, then pack in a rigid container, separating the layers with interleaving sheets or foil. Seal, label and return to the freezer for up to 3 months.

To thaw and serve: Place the frozen croquettes under a preheated hot grill for 10 to 12 minutes until crisp and golden brown, or reheat from frozen on a baking sheet in a preheated moderately hot oven (200°C/400°F/Gas Mark 6) for 15 to 20 minutes.

Serves 6

LEFT: Honey Glazed Onions, Crispy Onion Rings
RIGHT: Parsnip Croquettes; Creamed Runner Beans

MUSHROOMS IN CREAM SAUCE

This is a very versatile vegetable recipe: it can be used as an accompaniment to fish and chicken, or as a filling for omelettes, pancakes and vol-au-vents for a quick supper or lunch dish.

3 tablespoons olive oil
1 onion, peeled and finely chopped
1 garlic clove, peeled and crushed (optional)
500 g/1 lb small button mushrooms, trimmed
1 teaspoon dried mixed herbs
4 tablespoons Madeira or Marsala
salt and freshly ground black pepper
TO SERVE
300 ml/½ pint double cream or soured cream
thyme sprigs (optional)

Heat the oil in a pan, add the onion and garlic if using, and fry gently for 5 minutes without browning. Add the mushrooms and fry for a further 2 minutes. Stir in the herbs and Madeira or Marsala, then season to taste with salt and plenty of pepper. Bring to the boil, then lower the heat, cover and simmer for 5 to 7 minutes. Cool quickly.

To freeze: Transfer the mushrooms to a rigid container, seal, label and freeze for up to 2 months.

To thaw and serve: Leave to stand in container at room temperature for 3 hours, then transfer to a pan. Stir in the cream and heat through for 5 minutes, until the sauce has thickened. Taste and adjust the seasoning, then spoon the mushrooms and sauce into a warmed serving dish and garnish with thyme, if available. Serve immediately.

Serves 4 to 6

LEEK RISOTTO

Leeks are available through autumn and winter. The young, early leeks are particularly suitable for this substantial vegetable dish.

2 tablespoons olive oil
25 g/1 oz butter
1 onion, peeled and finely chopped
2 garlic cloves, peeled and thinly sliced (optional)
350 g/12 oz Italian rice
300 ml/½ pint dry white wine
about 900 ml/1½ pints homemade chicken consommé
* or stock*
6 saffron strands, soaked in 3 tablespoons boiling
* water for 20 minutes*
salt and freshly ground black pepper
6 small leeks, trimmed and thinly sliced
TO SERVE
50 g/2 oz butter
4 tablespoons freshly grated Parmesan cheese
2 tablespoons chopped parsley

Heat the olive oil and butter in a pan, add the onion and garlic (if using) and fry gently for 5 minutes without browning. Stir in the rice and fry for 1 minute. Pour in the wine and half the stock and bring to the boil. Strain the liquid from the saffron into the pan. Season with salt and pepper to taste, then lower the heat and simmer for 7 minutes.

Add the leeks with a little more stock and continue cooking for a further 10 minutes until the rice is tender, stirring in more stock as required. Cool quickly.

To freeze: Transfer the risotto to a rigid container, seal, label and freeze for up to 4 months.

To thaw and serve: Leave to stand in container at room temperature for 3 to 4 hours. Melt the butter in a pan, add the risotto, stir in the Parmesan cheese and heat through. Taste and adjust the seasoning, then pile into a warmed serving dish. Sprinkle over the chopped parsley and serve immediately.

Serves 4 to 6

INDIAN CAULIFLOWER

An exciting way to pep up frozen cauliflower florets, which often lack flavour and texture is to cook them in stock with a mixture of other vegetables and spices.

500 g/1 lb frozen cauliflower florets
TO SERVE
2 tablespoons vegetable oil
1 garlic clove, peeled and thinly sliced
1 cm/½ inch piece fresh root ginger, peeled and
* shredded*
2 teaspoons ground coriander
1 teaspoon chilli powder
1 teaspoon ground turmeric
1 teaspoon whole coriander seeds
1 onion, peeled and finely chopped
2 celery sticks, sliced
2 carrots, peeled and thinly sliced
1 green pepper, cored, seeded and diced
150 ml/¼ pint homemade chicken stock
salt
150 ml/¼ pint natural yogurt
1 tablespoon chopped coriander or parsley

Heat the oil in a large frying pan, add the garlic and ginger and fry gently for 2 minutes. Add the spices, stir over low heat for 2 minutes, then add the onion, celery, carrots and green pepper and fry for a further 5 minutes. Increase the heat, add the frozen cauliflower florets, stock and salt to taste. Bring to the boil, lower the heat, cover and simmer gently for 7 minutes.

Stir in the yogurt, heat through gently for 1 minute, stirring, then spoon into a warmed serving dish and sprinkle with the chopped coriander or parsley. Serve immediately, with plain boiled rice and traditional curry accompaniments if desired.

Serves 6

SWEDE AND MARROW PROVENÇAL

This unusual vegetable accompaniment can be served
cold with autumn salads.
For a change, use large courgettes instead of marrow.
If a hot vegetable accompaniment is required – for
grilled or roasted meat or poultry – reheat gently after
thawing.

1 tablespoon vegetable oil
2 small onions, peeled and finely chopped
2 garlic cloves, peeled and crushed
350 g/12 oz young swede, peeled and roughly
  chopped
500 g/1 lb tomatoes, skinned and chopped
1 tablespoon chopped parsley
1 tablespoon chopped thyme
1 tablespoon chopped rosemary
salt and freshly ground black pepper
juice of ½ lemon
500 g/1 lb small marrow, peeled, seeded and cubed
2 teaspoons tomato purée
TO SERVE
250 g/8 oz black olives, stoned
2 tablespoons chopped parsley

Heat the oil in a pan, add the onions and garlic and fry
gently for 5 minutes without browning. Add the swede
and fry for 1 minute, then add the tomatoes, herbs and
salt and pepper to taste. Bring to the boil, then lower
the heat, cover and simmer for 10 minutes.

Stir in the lemon juice and marrow and simmer,
uncovered, for a further 15 minutes, until all the
vegetables are tender. Stir in the tomato purée. Cool
quickly.

To freeze: Pour the vegetables into a rigid container,
seal, label and freeze for up to 4 months.

To thaw and serve: Leave to stand in container at
room temperature for 3 hours, then taste and adjust
the seasoning and stir in the black olives. Turn the
vegetable mixture into a serving dish and sprinkle with
the parsley. Serve cold.

Serves 6

Swede and Marrow Provençal; Mushrooms in Cream Sauce;
Indian Cauliflower

CALEDONIAN ICE CREAM

For this quick ice cream brown breadcrumbs may be used in place of oatmeal. Serve with Lacy Almond Wafers (page 146) or other crisp biscuits.

75 g/3 oz medium oatmeal
50 g/2 oz blanched almonds, finely chopped
450 ml/¾ pint double cream
2 tablespoons clear honey
3 tablespoons whisky
2 egg whites
125 g/4 oz caster sugar

Combine the oatmeal and almonds on a baking sheet and bake in a preheated moderately hot oven (190°C/375°F/Gas Mark 5) until pale golden brown. Leave to cool.

Whip the cream with the honey and whisky until it will stand in soft peaks. Whisk the egg whites until stiff, then gradually whisk in the caster sugar until very thick. Fold in the cream and oatmeal mixture until evenly blended.

To freeze: Turn the ice cream into a rigid container, seal, label and freeze for up to 3 months.

To thaw and serve: Transfer to the refrigerator 30 minutes before serving to soften. Scoop into chilled glasses and serve immediately.

Serves 6 to 8

MOCHA ICE CREAM CAKE

Chocolate rose leaves give this dinner party dessert a sophisticated finish. To make these, coat the underside of clean rose leaves with melted chocolate, using a fine paint brush. Allow to set, then lift the tip of each rose leaf and peel away from the chocolate.

CHOCOLATE SPONGE
3 eggs
150 g/5 oz caster sugar
75 g/3 oz plain flour
2 tablespoons cocoa powder
3 tablespoons Tia Maria or other coffee liqueur
FILLING
1 tablespoon instant coffee powder
1 tablespoon boiling water
1 egg white
50 g/2 oz caster sugar
300 ml/½ pint double cream
TO SERVE
150 ml/¼ pint double cream, whipped
chocolate rose leaves (optional)

For the sponge: Line and grease a 30 × 20 cm/12 × 8 inch Swiss roll tin and a 1.75 litre/3 pint charlotte mould.

Put the eggs and sugar in a bowl and whisk with an electric beater until thick and mousse-like. Sift the flour and cocoa powder together, then carefully fold into the egg mixture.

Turn the mixture into the prepared Swiss roll tin and level the surface. Bake in a preheated moderately hot oven (200°C/400°F/Gas Mark 6) for 10 to 15 minutes until the cake springs back when lightly pressed in the centre. Turn out onto a wire rack, carefully peel off the lining paper, turn the cake the right way up and leave to cool.

Carefully cut the sponge cake into 2 layers. Cut a circle of sponge to fit the base of the prepared charlotte mould and place in the bottom. Cut strips the depth of the charlotte mould and shape them so that they fit closely around the sides of the mould. Cut another circle of sponge to fit the top of the mould and reserve. Sprinkle the cake in the mould with 1 tablespoon of the coffee liqueur.

To make the filling: Dissolve the coffee in the boiling water, then leave to cool. Whisk the egg white until stiff, then gradually whisk in the sugar. Whip the cream with the dissolved coffee and remaining liqueur until it will stand in soft peaks. Fold into the meringue mixture, then spoon into the lined charlotte mould. Cover with the reserved circle of sponge.

To freeze: Freeze the cake until solid, then turn out of the mould and pack in a rigid container. Seal, label and return to the freezer for up to 3 months.

To thaw and serve: Remove from the container and place on a serving plate. Pipe the cream around the base and the top of the cake, then transfer to the refrigerator 45 minutes before serving to soften. Decorate with chocolate leaves if using, and serve.

Serves 6 to 8

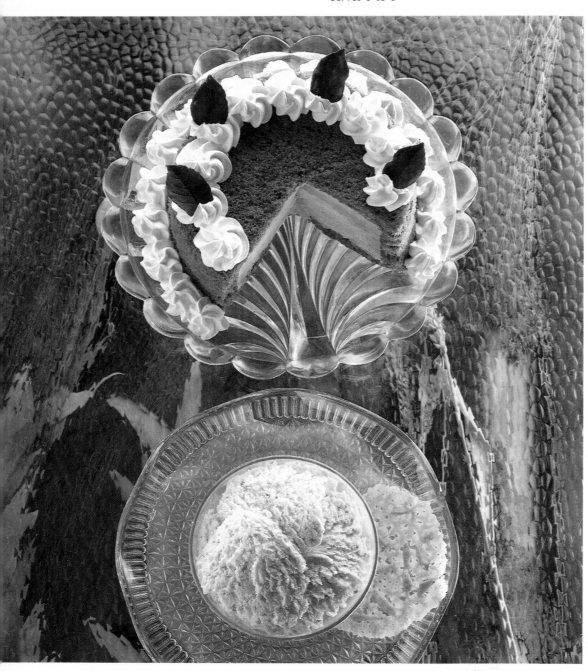

ICED CHOCOLATE MOUSSES

Frozen individual mousses are useful to have in the freezer as you can take them out one at a time whenever you need an individual serving.

4 eggs, separated
125 g/4 oz caster sugar
125 g/4 oz plain chocolate, broken into small pieces
3 tablespoons water
300 ml/½ pint double cream
TO SERVE
8 tablespoons double cream, whipped

Put the egg yolks and sugar in a bowl and whisk with an electric beater until thick and mousse-like.

Melt the chocolate with the water in a heatproof bowl over a pan of hot water. Remove from the heat and cool slightly, then whisk into the egg mixture. Whip the cream until it will stand in soft peaks, then carefully fold into the chocolate mixture. Whisk the egg whites until stiff, carefully fold 1 tablespoon into the mousse, then fold in the remainder. Pour into 8 individual freezerproof dishes.

To freeze: Cover the dishes with cling film, wrap in polythene bags, then seal, label and freeze for up to 3 months.

To thaw and serve: Unwrap and pipe a rosette of cream on top of each mousse. Place in the refrigerator for 10 minutes before serving to soften.
Makes 8

BRAMBLE FOOL

As a less expensive alternative to double cream, make an egg custard with 2 egg yolks, 1 teaspoon cornflour and 300 ml/½ pint single cream; when it has cooled, fold in the blackberry purée. Serve with Golden Curls (page 146).

350 g/12 oz blackberries
50 g/2 oz caster sugar
2 teaspoons lemon juice
300 ml/½ pint double cream

Put the blackberries in a pan with the sugar and simmer gently for 5 to 8 minutes until softened. Leave to cool, then strain off any excess liquid. Work the blackberries in an electric blender or food processor until smooth, then work through a nylon sieve to remove the pips. Stir in the lemon juice.

Whip the cream until it will stand in soft peaks and fold in the blackberry purée. Spoon into 6 individual freezerproof serving dishes.

To freeze: Cover with cling film, wrap in polythene bags, then seal, label and freeze for up to 3 months.

To thaw and serve: Leave to stand in wrappings in the refrigerator for 4 hours. Unwrap and serve chilled.
Serves 6

CHOCOLATE MOUSSE CARAQUE

This is a very rich chocolate mousse with a contrasting topping of light, frothy cream. Chocolate caraque gives a very professional finish, but grated chocolate can be used instead.

300 ml/½ pint single cream
250 g/8 oz plain chocolate, finely chopped
4 egg yolks
3 tablespoons brandy
TO SERVE
1 egg white
150 ml/¼ pint double cream, whipped
CHOCOLATE CARAQUE
50 g/2 oz plain chocolate, broken into small pieces

Place the cream in a pan and bring to simmering point. Pour into an electric blender or food processor, add the chocolate and egg yolks and blend for 30 seconds. Add the brandy and blend for a further 10 seconds. Pour into a freezerproof serving bowl and chill in the refrigerator until set.

To freeze: Cover the bowl with foil, overwrap in a polythene bag, seal, label and freeze for up to 3 months.

To thaw and serve: Unwrap and leave to stand in the refrigerator overnight. Whisk the egg white until stiff and carefully fold into the whipped cream. Pile on top of the chocolate mousse.

To make the caraque: Melt the chocolate in a heatproof bowl over a pan of hot water. Spread a thin layer of melted chocolate on a cold work surface with a palette knife. Leave until firm, not hard. With a sharp knife at a slight angle, push the knife across the chocolate with a slight sawing movement, scraping off a thin layer each time to form a long scroll.

Place the chocolate caraque on top of the mousse. Serve chilled.
Serves 8

ABOVE: Iced Chocolate Mousses; Bramble Fool, served with Lacy Almond Wafers (Page 146)
OPPOSITE: Mocha Ice Cream Cake; Caledonian Ice Cream, served with Lacy Almond Wafers (page 146)

BLACKBERRY AND PEAR CRUMBLE

A refreshing change from the more usual autumn combination of blackberry and apple, this crumble is delicious served with custard or whipped cream. To serve immediately, rather than freeze, bake in a preheated moderately hot oven (200°C/400°F/Gas Mark 6) for 15 minutes, then reduce the temperature to (190°C/375°F/Gas Mark 5) and bake for a further 20 to 25 minutes.

175 g/6 oz plain flour
75 g/3 oz butter or margarine
75 g/3 oz demerara sugar
500 g/1 lb cooking pears
250 g/8 oz blackberries
50 g/2 oz granulated sugar
25 g/1 oz blanched almonds, chopped

Sift the flour into a bowl. Rub in the butter or margarine until the mixture resembles fine breadcrumbs, then stir in the demerara sugar.

Peel and slice the pears and mix with the blackberries. Arrange in a 900 ml/1 ½ pint pie dish, layering the fruit with the sugar. Sprinkle the crumble mixture over the fruit to cover it completely, then sprinkle over the almonds and press down lightly.

To freeze: Cover the pie dish with foil, then wrap in a polythene bag. Seal label and freeze for up to 6 months.

To thaw and serve: Unwrap and bake from frozen in a preheated hot oven (220°C/425°F/Gas Mark 7) for 20 minutes, then reduce the temperature to moderately hot (190°C/375°F/Gas Mark 5) and bake for a further 40 to 45 minutes. Serve hot.
Serves 4 to 6

PEARS IN RED WINE

Pears cooked in this way freeze well; they also look most attractive when served. Do not use over-ripe pears for this dessert or they may disintegrate and spoil the look of the finished dish.

150 g/5 oz sugar
150 ml/¼ pint water
6 dessert pears
about 150 ml/¼ pint red wine
strip of orange peel
TO SERVE
150 ml/¼ pint double cream
1–2 tablespoons kirsch

Put the sugar and water in a saucepan just large enough to hold the pears standing side by side. Heat gently until the sugar has dissolved, then boil for 3 minutes.

Peel the pears, but do not remove their stalks. Put the pears into the pan containing the syrup. Pour over enough red wine just to cover the pears, add the orange peel and poach very gently until the pears are just soft. (The poaching time will vary from 15 to 45 minutes according to ripeness and size.)

Lift the pears out with a slotted spoon and transfer to a small bowl. Bring the liquid in the pan to the boil, then boil rapidly to reduce by about half. Strain over the pears and leave them to cool in the syrup, turning them from time to time so that they become evenly coloured. Discard the orange peel.

To freeze: Transfer the pears and syrup to a rigid container. Seal, label and freeze for up to 6 months.
To thaw and serve: Leave in container for 5 to 6 hours at room temperature. Transfer the pears and syrup to a serving dish. Whip the cream with the kirsch until it will form soft peaks. Serve with the pears.
Serves 6

APPLE AND CINNAMON PIE

This pie is best frozen unbaked for the freshest, crispiest results. It can be baked before freezing if you prefer, in which case it should be baked at the specified temperature for 30 to 40 minutes and then stored in the freezer in its pie dish, as frozen cooked pastry is very fragile. Serve with custard or whipped cream.

PASTRY
300 g/10 oz plain flour
150 g/5 oz butter or margarine
3–4 tablespoons iced water
FILLING
750 g/1 ½ lb cooking apples, peeled, cored and thinly sliced
75 g/3 oz soft brown sugar
1 teaspoon ground cinnamon
4 cloves
TO SERVE
caster sugar, for sprinkling

To make the pastry: Sift the flour into a bowl. Rub in the butter or margarine until the mixture resembles fine breadcrumbs. Stir in enough water to mix to a fairly stiff dough.

Turn the dough onto a floured surface, knead lightly until smooth, then divide in half. Roll out 1 piece thinly and use to line a 20 cm/8 inch shallow pie dish. Layer the apples with the sugar and spices in the dish, then brush the edge of the pastry with cold water.

Roll out the remaining pastry and use to cover the pie. Seal the edges well. Trim off any surplus pastry with a sharp knife, then knock up and flute the edges. Make a hole in the centre of the pie.

To freeze: Open freeze until solid, then remove from the pie dish and wrap in a polythene bag. Seal, label and return to the freezer for up to 3 months.

To thaw and serve: Unwrap and return to the original pie dish. Brush lightly with water, sprinkle with sugar and bake from frozen in a preheated moderately hot oven (200°C/400°F/Gas Mark 6) for 55 to 60 minutes. Serve warm or cold.
Serves 6

PLUMS IN PORT WINE

This is an excellent, simple way of freezing delicious autumn plums.

750 g/1 ½ lb Victoria plums
3 tablespoons soft brown sugar
5 tablespoons port wine
TO SERVE
150 ml/¼ pint double cream, lightly whipped

Make a slit in each plum following the natural division of the fruit. Place the fruit in a deep ovenproof baking dish and sprinkle over the sugar. Pour over the wine and bake, uncovered, in a preheated cool oven (150°C/300°F/Gas Mark 2) for 45 minutes. Cool.

To freeze: Transfer the plums and juice to a rigid freezerproof container, seal, label and freeze for up to 12 months.

To thaw and serve: Leave to stand in container at room temperature for 4 hours and serve cold, Alternatively, transfer to original dish and reheat from frozen in a preheated moderate oven (160°C/325°F/Gas Mark 3) for 50 minutes and serve hot. Hand whipped cream separately.
Serves 4

PLUM LAYER PUDDING

The slightly tart flavour of plums contrasts with a sweet, crunchy crumble layer in this tempting dessert.

As an alternative, substitute layers of cooked and sweetened apples or blackberries for the plums. Serve with pouring cream.

1 kg/2 lb plums, stoned
25 g/1 oz granulated sugar
300 ml/½ pint water
175 g/6 oz wholemeal breadcrumbs
50 g/2 oz demerara sugar
50 g/2 oz butter

Put the plums, granulated sugar and water in a saucepan; bring gently to the boil and simmer until just soft. Allow to cool.

Combine the breadcrumbs and demerara sugar. Melt the butter in a pan, add the crumb mixture and fry until crisp. Cool.

Layer the plums and crumb mixture in a 1.2 litre/2 pint pie dish, finishing with a layer of crumbs.

To freeze: Cover the dish with foil, then wrap in a polythene bag. Seal, label and freeze for up to 2 months.

To thaw and serve: Unwrap and reheat from frozen in a preheated moderately hot oven (190°C/375°F/Gas Mark 5) for 30 minutes. Serve hot, with cream.
Serves 6

Blackberry and Pear Crumble; Plums in Port Wine; Apple and Cinnamon Pie

To thaw and serve: Place the flan on a baking sheet in its foil wrapping. Reheat from frozen in a preheated moderately hot oven (200°C/400°F/Gas Mark 6) for 15 minutes, then remove the foil and bake for a further 5 to 10 minutes. Meanwhile, heat the jam with the lemon juice, stirring until the jam has melted. Sieve, reheat and brush over the apples to glaze. Serve the flan warm or cold.

Serves 8

FLAN NORMANDE

This scrumptious flan comes from Normandy in north-western France, a region where apples and cream are used prolifically in cooking.

PÂTE SUCRÉE
175 g/6 oz plain flour
75 g/3 oz butter, softened
75 g/3 oz caster sugar
3 egg yolks
few drops of vanilla essence
FILLING
750 g/1½ lb sharp dessert apples (e.g. Cox's Orange Pippins)
300 ml/½ pint single cream
2 egg yolks
50 g/2 oz caster sugar

To make the pâte sucrée: Sift the flour onto a marble slab or cool work surface. Make a well in the centre, then put in the butter, sugar, egg yolks and vanilla essence. Using the fingertips of one hand, work these ingredients together, then draw in the flour and work to a paste. Knead lightly until smooth, then wrap in cling film or foil and chill in the refrigerator for about 1 hour.

Turn the dough onto a floured surface, then roll out and use to line a 23 cm/9 inch fluted flan ring placed on a baking sheet. Chill in the refrigerator for a further 15 minutes.

To make the filling: Peel, core and slice the apples, then arrange them in the flan case, finishing with an overlapping layer of apples on top. Mix together the cream, eggs and sugar and pour over the apples. Bake in a preheated moderately hot oven (190°C/375°F/Gas Mark 5) for 45 minutes until golden, then cover loosely with foil and cook a further 10 to 15 minutes until the apples are tender. Remove the flan carefully from the flan ring and cool on a wire rack.

To freeze: Open freeze the flan until solid, then wrap in foil. Seal, label and return to the freezer for up to 2 months.

To thaw and serve: Place the flan on a baking sheet in its foil wrapping. Reheat from frozen in a preheated moderate oven (180°C/350°F/Gas Mark 4) for 35 to 40 minutes and serve hot. Alternatively, unwrap the flan and leave at room temperature for about 4 hours, then serve cold.

Serves 8

MINCEMEAT AND APPLE FLAN

The apples give the mincemeat a sharpness so the flan is not too sweet. Serve with whipped cream.

RICH SHORTCRUST PASTRY
250 g/8 oz plain flour
150 g/5 oz butter or margarine
1 tablespoon caster sugar
1 egg yolk
1–2 tablespoons iced water
FILLING
350 g/12 oz cooking apples
500 g/1 lb mincemeat (see page 194)
1 tablespoon sherry
2–3 dessert apples
TO SERVE
4 tablespoons apricot jam
2 teaspoons lemon juice

To make the pastry: Sift the flour into a bowl. Rub in the butter or margarine until the mixture resembles fine breadcrumbs. Stir in the sugar, the egg yolk and enough water to mix to a fairly stiff dough. Turn the dough onto a floured surface, knead lightly until smooth, then roll out thinly and use to line a 23 cm/9 inch fluted flan ring placed on a baking sheet. Chill in the refrigerator for 30 minutes.

To make the filling: Peel, core and chop the cooking apples and mix with the mincemeat and sherry. Turn into the flan ring and spread evenly to the edges. Quarter, core and thinly slice the dessert apples and arrange them overlapping in a circle on top of the mincemeat mixture.

Bake in a preheated moderately hot oven (190°C/375°F/Gas Mark 5) for 35 to 40 minutes. Remove the flan carefully from the flan ring and leave to cool on a wire rack.

To freeze: Open freeze the flan on the baking sheet until solid, then wrap in foil. Seal, label and return to the freezer for up to 3 months.

APPLE SHORTCAKE

Cinnamon shortbread combines beautifully with the flavour of apples. Serve as a dessert with cream, or at tea-time on its own.

125 g/4 oz butter or margarine
50 g/2 oz plus 1 tablespoon caster sugar
175 g/6 oz plain flour
1 teaspoon ground cinnamon
2 dessert apples, quartered, cored and thinly sliced
TO SERVE
3 tablespoons apricot jam
2 teaspoons lemon juice

Cream the butter or margarine and 50 g/2 oz sugar together until light and fluffy. Sift the flour and cinnamon together and add to the creamed mixture. Stir until the shortcake mixture binds together.

Turn the dough onto a lightly floured surface and knead until smooth. Roll out to a 20 cm/8 inch round and place on a baking sheet. Pinch the edges with your fingers and prick well with a fork.

Bake in a preheated moderate oven (160°C/325°F/Gas Mark 3) for 20 minutes. Remove from the oven and increase the temperature to moderately hot (190°C/375°F/Gas Mark 5). Arrange the apples in overlapping circles on top of the shortbread, sprinkle with remaining 1 tablespoon sugar and return to the oven for a further 20 minutes. Remove from the oven, transfer carefully to a wire rack and leave to cool.

To freeze: Place the shortcake on a cake board, wrap in a polythene bag, then seal, label and freeze for up to 3 months.

To thaw and serve: Unwrap, place on a serving plate and leave to stand at room temperature for 3 to 4 hours. Heat the apricot jam with the lemon juice, stirring until the jam has melted. Sieve, reheat and brush over the apples. Leave the apple shortcake to cool before serving.
Serves 6

OPPOSITE: *Mincemeat and Apple Flan*
BELOW: *Flan Normande; Apple Shortcake*

TARTE FRANÇAISE

This attractive puff pastry flan case is a very useful standby to keep in the freezer because it can be filled with a mixture of any fruits in season to make a quick dessert. If you haven't a flan case or any puff pastry in the freezer, use a 400 g/14 oz packet puff pastry.

PUFF PASTRY
200 g/7 oz plain flour
½ teaspoon salt
1 teaspoon lemon juice
120–150 ml/4–5 fl oz water
200 g/7 oz butter
FILLING
125 g/4 oz blackberries
125 g/4 oz green grapes, seeded
2 oranges, peeled and cut into segments
TO SERVE
1 egg yolk, mixed with 1 teaspoon water
4 tablespoons apricot jam
1 tablespoon lemon juice

To make the puff pastry: Sift the flour and salt into a bowl. Add the lemon juice and enough water to mix to a soft dough. Roll out the dough on a lightly floured surface to a 30 × 20 cm/12 × 8 inch rectangle. Shape the butter into an oblong and place in the centre of the dough. Fold the ends of the dough to the centre, enclosing the butter, like a parcel. Press the edges together to seal. Give the dough a quarter turn and roll out to a rectangle again. Fold the bottom third up and the top third down; seal the edges. Wrap in a polythene bag and chill in the refrigerator for 10 to 15 minutes. Repeat the rolling, folding and chilling 6 times, giving the dough a quarter turn between each rolling. Chill for 1 hour.

Roll out the pastry on a floured surface to a 30 × 20 cm/12 × 8 inch rectangle. Sprinkle lightly with flour and fold in half lengthways. Cut out a rectangle from the folded edge, leaving a 3.5 cm/1½ inch wide band on the remaining 3 sides.

Open out the rectangle and roll out until 30 × 20 cm/12 × 8 inches. Place on a dampened baking sheet or on a piece of stiff cardboard. Prick all over with a fork and brush the edges with water.

Open out the band of pastry and place on the rectangle to make a border. Knock up the edges and make a criss-cross pattern on the border with a knife.
To freeze: Cover the pastry case and its base with foil, seal the edges, label and freeze for up to 3 months.
To thaw and serve: Unwrap carefully and place on a baking sheet. Brush the border with the egg yolk and water and bake from frozen in a preheated hot oven (220°C/425°F/Gas Mark 7) for 20 to 25 minutes until golden brown. Transfer to a wire rack and leave to cool. Heat the apricot jam with the lemon juice, stirring until melted. Sieve, reheat and brush a little over the base of the pastry case. Arrange the fruit in the tart and brush with remaining glaze. Cool before serving.
Serves 6

WALNUT GALETTE

Crisp walnut shortcake rounds sandwich a spiced apple and whipped cream filling. Ground hazelnuts can be used in place of the walnuts if preferred.

WALNUT PASTRY
75 g/3 oz shelled walnuts
75 g/3 oz butter or margarine
50 g/2 oz soft brown sugar
125 g/4 oz plain flour
FILLING
500 g/1 lb dessert apples
2 tablespoons apple juice
50 g/2 oz sultanas
½ teaspoon ground mixed spice
TO SERVE
150 ml/¼ pint double cream, whipped
icing sugar, for sprinkling

To make the walnut pastry: Grind the walnuts to a coarse powder using an electric blender or food processor. Cream the butter or margarine and sugar together until fluffy. Sift in the flour and walnuts and mix to a firm dough using one hand.

Turn the dough onto a lightly floured surface and knead until smooth. Divide the mixture in half and roll each piece into a 20 cm/8 inch round. Place on baking sheets.

Bake in a preheated moderately hot oven (190°C/375°F/Gas Mark 5) for 15 to 20 minutes until golden. Cut 1 round into 8 sections while still warm. Transfer both rounds to a wire rack and leave to cool.
To make the filling: Peel, core and slice the apples, then put into a pan with the apple juice. Cover and cook gently for 15 minutes, stirring occasionally. Remove from the heat, add the sultanas and mixed spice and leave to cool.
To freeze: Open freeze the shortcake until solid, then pack carefully in a shallow rigid container, separating the layers with an interleaving sheet or foil. Spoon the apple mixture into a rigid container. Seal, label and freeze for up to 3 months.
To thaw and serve: Remove the shortcake from its container and place the uncut round on a serving plate; leave the apple mixture to stand in its container. Thaw both at room temperature for about 3 hours.

Spread a layer of cream over the shortcake round. Cover with the apple mixture, then the remaining cream. Arrange the shortcake wedges on top, at an angle, and sprinkle with icing sugar. Serve chilled.
Serves 8

VARIATION

Before baking the shortcake rounds, brush one of them with a little beaten egg white, and then sprinkle on 1 tablespoon of finely chopped walnuts (or hazelnuts). Bake the rounds as above and cut the nut-covered one into 8 sections while still warm. Freeze, thaw and assemble the galette as above, placing the nut-covered wedges on top.

ICED HAZELNUT GÂTEAU

Autumn hazelnuts add a crunchiness to this delicious iced gâteau.

75 g/3 oz shelled hazelnuts
75 g/3 oz caster sugar
150 ml/¼ pint double cream
150 ml/¼ pint cold strong black coffee
1 tablespoon soft brown sugar
3 tablespoons brandy
16 sponge fingers
TO SERVE
150 ml/¼ pint double cream
2 tablespoons cold strong black coffee
1 teaspoon soft brown sugar
25 g/1 oz plain chocolate, melted and cooled

Grease a 500 g/1 lb loaf tin, line the base with greaseproof paper, then grease the paper.

Put the nuts and caster sugar in a pan and heat gently until the sugar has melted. Cook slowly until the sugar caramelizes and the nuts begin to pop, shaking the pan occasionally. Turn onto an oiled baking sheet, leave until hard, then break into pieces and grind to a praline (powder) using an electric blender, food processor or rolling pin.

Whip the cream with 4 tablespoons of the coffee and the brown sugar until it will stand in stiff peaks. Fold in the hazelnut praline.

Mix the remaining coffee with the brandy and quickly dip the sponge fingers into it. Arrange half of the sponge fingers in the bottom of the prepared tin and spread the coffee cream on top. Arrange the remaining sponge fingers over the coffee cream, covering it completely.
To freeze: Cover the tin with foil, wrap in a polythene bag, then seal, label and freeze for up to 3 months.
To thaw and serve: Unwrap and turn out onto a serving plate. Whip the cream with the coffee and sugar until it will stand in soft peaks. Spread over the top and sides of the gâteau and smooth evenly with a palette knife. Put the cool melted chocolate in a greaseproof piping bag, snip off the tip, then drizzle the chocolate across the top of the gâteau. Transfer to the refrigerator 45 minutes before serving to soften.
Serves 6

VARIATION

The hazelnut praline mixture makes a delicious rich ice cream by itself. Make the praline as above; whip the cream with the coffee and brown sugar and fold in the praline. Turn the mixture into a rigid freezerproof container, seal, label and freeze for up to 3 months. Soften the ice cream in the refrigerator for 30 minutes before serving in scoops, decorated, if liked, with whole hazelnuts.

Tarte Française; Walnut Galette; Iced Hazelnut Gâteau

PEAR TART FRANGIPANE

This tart is delicious served cold at tea-time, but it can also be served warm with cream as a dessert.

RICH SHORTCRUST PASTRY
250 g/8 oz plain flour
150 g/5 oz butter or margarine
1 tablespoon caster sugar
1 egg yolk
1–2 tablespoons cold water
FRANGIPANE FILLING
75 g/3 oz butter or margarine
75 g/3 oz caster sugar
1 egg, beaten
75 g/3 oz ground almonds
25 g/1 oz plain flour, sifted
TOPPING
3 small pears
1–2 teaspoons icing sugar
TO SERVE
icing sugar, for sifting

To make the pastry: Sift the flour into a bowl. Rub in the butter or margarine until the mixture resembles fine breadcrumbs. Stir in the sugar and the egg yolk and enough water to mix to a fairly stiff dough. Turn the dough onto a floured surface, knead lightly until smooth, then roll out thinly and use to line a 20 cm/ 8 inch flan ring placed on a baking sheet. Chill in the refrigerator for 30 minutes.

To make the filling: Cream the butter or margarine and sugar together until light and fluffy, then beat in the egg thoroughly. Fold in the ground almonds and flour. Spoon the filling into the flan case and smooth the surface with a palette knife.

For the topping: Peel, halve and core the pears and cut each half across into thin slices. Slide a palette knife under the sliced pear halves and lay them on top of the filling, sliding the slices slightly apart, and arranging them so they radiate from the centre. Press the slices down slightly into the filling. Sift icing sugar lightly over the top.

Bake in a preheated moderately hot oven (200°C/ 400°F/Gas Mark 6) for 20 minutes, then reduce the temperature to 190°C/375°F/Gas Mark 5 and bake for a further 15 to 20 minutes until golden brown and firm in the centre. Carefully remove the flan ring and leave to cool on a wire rack.

To freeze: Open freeze the tart until solid, then wrap in foil. Seal, label and return to the freezer for up to 3 months.

To thaw and serve: Unwrap, place on a serving plate and leave to stand at room temperature for 2 to 3 hours. Sift icing sugar over the pear tart just before serving.

Serves 6

Lemon Cream Sponge; Wholemeal Apple Cake; Pear Tart Frangipane

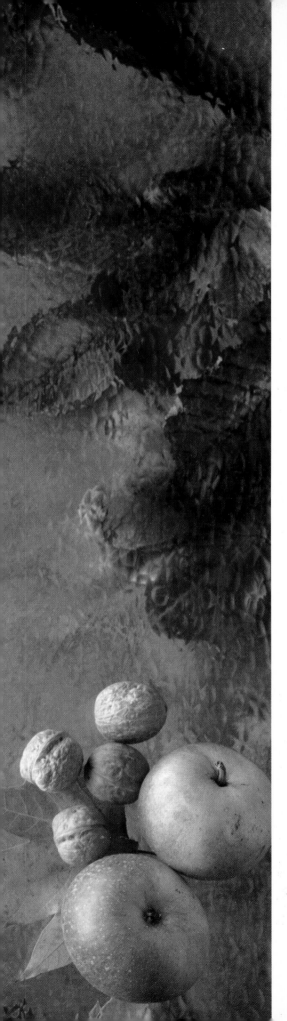

DATE AND WALNUT CAKE

125 g/4 oz shelled walnuts
250 g/8 oz plain flour
2 teaspoons baking powder
1 teaspoon ground mixed spice
150 g/5 oz butter or margarine
150 g/5 oz soft brown sugar
2 eggs, beaten
175 g/6 oz dates, stoned and chopped
3 tablespoons cold tea

Grease a deep 18 cm/7 inch round cake tin, line the base and sides with a double layer of greaseproof paper, then grease the paper. Roughly chop half of the walnuts.

Sift the flour, baking powder and spice together. Cream the butter or margarine and sugar together in a bowl until light and fluffy. Beat in the eggs, a little at a time, adding 1 tablespoon flour after each addition. Fold in the remaining flour with the dates, chopped walnuts and the tea until evenly incorporated.

Turn into the prepared tin, level the surface and arrange the walnut halves over the top. Bake in a preheated moderate oven (160°C/325°F/Gas Mark 3) for 1½ to 1¾ hours, or until a skewer inserted in the centre comes out clean. Leave to cool in the tin for 1 minute, then turn out onto a wire rack and carefully peel off the lining paper. Turn the cake the right way up and leave to cool completely.

To freeze: Wrap the cake in a polythene bag, seal, label and freeze for up to 4 months.

To thaw and serve: Unwrap, place on a serving plate and leave to stand at room temperature for 4 hours.
Serves 6 to 8

WHOLEMEAL APPLE CAKE

The combination of apples and dates makes this a beautiful moist cake that will keep well for over a week once removed from the freezer.

300 g/10 oz wholemeal flour
1 tablespoon baking powder
2 teaspoons ground cinnamon
125 g/4 oz soft brown sugar
4 tablespoons clear honey
250 g/8 oz dates, stoned and chopped
175 ml/6 fl oz apple juice
120 ml/4 fl oz vegetable oil
2 eggs, beaten
250 g/8 oz apples, peeled, cored and chopped
50 g/2 oz shelled walnuts, chopped

Grease a deep 20 cm/8 inch square cake tin, line with greaseproof paper, then grease the paper.

Mix the flour, baking powder and cinnamon together in a bowl. Put the sugar, honey, dates, and apple juice in a pan and heat gently until the sugar has dissolved. Remove from the heat and leave to cool slightly, then add to the flour with the oil. Beat until smooth. Add the eggs and apples and mix thoroughly.

Turn the mixture into the prepared tin, then sprinkle with the walnuts. Bake in a preheated moderate oven (180°C/350°F/Gas Mark 4) for 1 to 1¼ hours until the cake springs back when lightly pressed in the centre. Turn out onto a wire rack, peel off the paper, turn cake the right way up and leave to cool.

To freeze: Wrap the cake in a polythene bag, seal, label and freeze for up to 4 months.

To thaw and serve: Unwrap, place on a serving plate and leave to stand at room temperature for 4 hours.
Serves 12

LEMON CREAM SPONGE

Suitable to serve at tea-time or as a dessert, this sponge has a delicious soft cheese filling and topping, similar to an uncooked cheesecake.

3 eggs
150 g/5 oz caster sugar
finely grated rind of 1 lemon
75 g/3 oz plain flour, sifted
LEMON CREAM
175 g/6 oz full-fat soft cheese
2 tablespoons icing sugar
finely grated rind and juice of 1 lemon
250 ml/8 fl oz double cream, whipped
TO SERVE
lemon shreds

Grease a deep 20 cm/8 inch cake tin, line the base with greaseproof paper, then grease the paper. Dust the inside of the tin lightly with flour.

Put the eggs, sugar and lemon rind in a bowl and whisk with an electric beater until thick and mousse-like. Carefully fold in the flour.

Turn the mixture into the prepared tin and level the surface. Bake in a preheated moderately hot oven (190°C/375°F/Gas Mark 5) for 20 to 25 minutes until the cake springs back when lightly pressed in the centre. Turn out onto a wire rack, carefully peel off the paper, turn cake the right way up and leave to cool.

To make the lemon cream: Put the cheese in a bowl and beat in the sugar, lemon rind and juice. Carefully fold in the cream. Slice the cake in half horizontally and sandwich together with half the cheese mixture. Spread half the remaining cheese mixture over the top of the cake and mark into swirls. Spoon the remaining cheese mixture into a piping bag fitted with a large fluted nozzle and pipe around the edge of the cake.

To freeze: Open freeze the cake until solid, then carefully pack in a rigid container. Seal, label and return to the freezer for up to 3 months.

To thaw and serve: Unwrap, place on a serving plate and leave to stand at room temperature for 2 to 3 hours. Decorate with lemon shreds and serve.
Serves 6 to 8

WALNUT AND CHERRY TEABREAD

This quick and easy teabread is a very useful standby to keep in the freezer. It is ideal to serve at tea-time, or with coffee, cut into slices and spread generously with butter.

350 g/12 oz self-raising flour
1 teaspoon ground mixed spice
1 teaspoon ground cinnamon
125 g/4 oz dates, stoned and chopped
50 g/2 oz shelled walnuts, chopped
175 ml/6 fl oz milk
4 tablespoons golden syrup
125 g/4 oz butter or margarine
75 g/3 oz glacé cherries, halved
6 walnut halves

Grease a 1 kg/2 lb loaf tin, line the base and sides with greaseproof paper, then grease the paper.

Sift the flour and spices into a bowl and stir in the dates and walnuts. Put the milk, syrup and butter or margarine in a pan and heat gently until just melted. Remove from the heat and leave to cool slightly, then mix into the dry ingredients.

Turn into the prepared tin, level the surface and arrange the cherries and walnuts on top. Bake in a pre-heated moderate oven (180°C/350°F/Gas Mark 4) for 1 to 1¼ hours or until a skewer inserted in the centre comes out clean. Leave in the tin for 1 minute, then turn out onto a wire rack. Carefully peel off the lining paper, turn the cake the right way up and leave to cool.

To freeze: Wrap the teabread in a polythene bag, seal, label and freeze for up to 4 months.

To thaw and serve: Unwrap and leave to stand at room temperature for about 4 hours. Serve sliced, as soon as possible.

Serves 6 to 8

CHOCOLATE ÉCLAIRS

These éclairs can be varied by adding a little coffee-flavoured liqueur to the cream, and covering them with a coffee glacé icing.

CHOUX PASTRY
50 g/2 oz butter
150 ml/¼ pint water
65 g/2½ oz plain flour, sifted
2 eggs, beaten
TO SERVE
125 g/4 oz plain chocolate
175 ml/6 fl oz double cream, whipped

To make the choux pastry: Put the butter and water in a pan and bring to the boil. Remove from the heat and immediately beat in the flour all at once. Beat well until the mixture leaves the sides of the pan clean. Cool slightly, then add the eggs a little at a time, beating well between each addition.

Spoon the dough into a piping bag fitted with a 1 cm/½ inch plain nozzle and pipe ten to twelve 7.5 cm/3 inch lengths onto a dampened baking sheet, spacing them well apart. Bake in a preheated moder-ately hot oven (200°C/400°F/Gas Mark 6) for about 25 minutes until well risen and golden brown. Make a slit in the side of each éclair with the point of a sharp knife, then leave to cool on a wire rack.

To freeze: Open freeze the éclairs until solid, then pack in rigid containers, separating the layers with interleaving sheets or foil. Seal, label and return to the freezer for up to 3 months.

To thaw and serve: Place the éclairs on a baking sheet and reheat from frozen in a preheated moderate oven (180°C/350°F/Gas Mark 4) for 10 to 12 minutes. Leave to cool.

Melt the chocolate with 2 tablespoons of the cream in a small pan over a very low heat and mix well. Whip the remaining cream until it will stand in soft peaks. Spoon it into a piping bag fitted with a 5 mm/¼ inch plain nozzle and pipe a little into each éclair. Dip the top of each éclair into the chocolate to coat evenly. Leave until the chocolate has set before serving the éclairs.

Makes 10 to 12

VARIATION

Instead of piping the choux pastry into finger-shaped éclairs, spoon the mixture into 10 mounds and bake as above for 30 to 35 minutes. Cool, freeze and reheat as above.

Cool, then split the choux buns and fill with whipped cream. Top with melted chocolate as above.

LEFT: Chocolate Éclairs
RIGHT: Hazelnut and Chocolate Fingers; Walnut and Cherry Teabread; Nutty Shortbread Circle

HAZELNUT AND CHOCOLATE FINGERS

These quickly made uncooked biscuits will be so popular, that the safest place to keep them is in the freezer! They are an excellent standby and can be removed from the freezer a few at a time as required.

50 g/2 oz butter or margarine
175 g/6 oz plain chocolate
2 tablespoons clear honey
250 g/8 oz digestive biscuits, crushed
50 g/2 oz shelled hazelnuts, chopped and toasted

Grease a shallow 18 cm/7 inch square cake tin, line the base with greaseproof paper, then grease the paper.

Put the butter or margarine, chocolate and honey in a pan and heat gently until melted. Stir in the biscuits and hazelnuts until thoroughly mixed, turn into the prepared tin and smooth the top with a palette knife. Leave until set, then cut into fingers.

To freeze: Pack the fingers into a rigid container, separating the layers with interleaving sheets or foil. Seal, label and freeze for up to 6 months.

To thaw and serve: Leave to stand in container at room temperature for about 2 hours.

Makes 12

NUTTY SHORTBREAD CIRCLE

A change from the traditional Scottish shortbread. Almonds can be used in place of the hazelnuts.

125 g/4 oz butter or margarine
50 g/2 oz caster sugar
125 g/4 oz plain flour, sifted
50 g/2 oz ground rice
50 g/2 oz shelled hazelnuts, finely chopped

Cream the butter or margarine and sugar together until light and fluffy, then stir in the flour, rice and two thirds of the nuts until the mixture binds together.

Turn the dough onto a floured surface, knead lightly until smooth, then roll out to a 23 cm/9 inch round on a baking sheet. Pinch the edges between thumb and forefinger. Prick well with a fork and mark into 8 portions. Sprinkle over the remaining hazelnuts and lightly press them into the shortbread.

Bake in a preheated moderate oven (160°C/325°F/Gas Mark 3) for 40 to 45 minutes until pale golden. Leave to cool on the baking sheet for 2 minutes, then transfer to a wire rack and leave to cool completely.

To freeze: Place the shortbread on a cake board or piece of stiff cardboard. Wrap in a polythene bag, then seal, label and freeze for up to 6 months.

To thaw and serve: Place on a serving plate and leave to stand at room temperature for 2 to 3 hours. Serve as soon as possible.

Makes 8 portions

GOLDEN CURLS

These crisp little wafers are ideal to serve with ice cream. They may be left flat instead of curling over a rolling pin, if you prefer.

125 g/4 oz butter
125 g/4 oz demerara sugar
125 g/4 oz golden syrup
125 g/4 oz plain flour, sifted

Put the butter, sugar and syrup into a pan and heat gently until the butter has melted and the sugar has dissolved. Remove from the heat and leave to cool slightly, then beat in the flour until smooth.

Place teaspoonsful of the mixture on baking sheets, spacing them at least 10 cm/4 inches apart. Bake them in batches in a preheated moderate oven (180°C/350°F/Gas Mark 4) for 10 to 12 minutes until golden.

Leave to cool for 30 seconds, then scrape off with a palette knife and place on a rolling pin to curl. Leave until set in a curl, then slide off very carefully.

To freeze: Pack the curls in rigid containers, separating the layers with interleaving sheets or foil and carefully fitting one into another. Seal, label and freeze for up to 6 months.

To thaw and serve: Leave to stand in container at room temperature for 30 minutes, then serve as soon as possible.

Makes 35

LACY ALMOND WAFERS

For serving with coffee, ice creams and fruit fools.

75 g/3 oz split blanched almonds
75 g/3 oz butter or margarine
75 g/3 oz caster sugar
50 g/2 oz plain flour, sifted

Soak the almonds in boiling water for 2 to 3 minutes, then drain and dry. Cut each almond into about 4 shreds and set aside.

Cream the butter or margarine and sugar together until light and fluffy, then stir in the flour and almonds. Place teaspoonfuls of the mixture well apart on greased baking sheets and flatten them with a damp fork.

Bake in a preheated moderately hot oven (190°C/375°F/Gas Mark 5) for 6 to 8 minutes until pale golden. Leave on the baking sheets for 30 seconds, then transfer to a wire rack with a palette knife or lay on rolling pins to curl. Leave to cool.

To freeze: Pack the wafers in rigid containers, separating the layers with interleaving sheets or foil. Seal, label and freeze for up to 6 months.

To thaw and serve: Place on a serving plate and leave to stand at room temperature for 30 minutes. Serve as soon as possible.

Makes 25

WHOLEMEAL ROLLS

The malt extract helps to keep these bread rolls moist, improves the volume of the dough and also the flavour.

15 g/½ oz fresh yeast
450 ml/¾ pint warm water
750 g/1½ lb wholemeal flour
2 teaspoons salt
1 tablespoon malt extract
1 tablespoon vegetable oil
1 tablespoon cracked wheat

Cream the yeast with a little of the water and leave in a warm place for 10 minutes until frothy. Put the flour and salt into a bowl, make a well in the centre, then pour in the yeast mixture and the remaining water. Add the malt extract and oil and mix quickly to a soft dough.

Turn the dough onto a floured surface and knead until smooth and elastic. Place in a clean bowl, cover with a damp cloth and leave to rise in a warm place for 1½ to 2 hours until doubled in bulk.

Turn the dough onto a floured surface and knead again for 2 to 3 minutes. Cut into 18 pieces, shape into rolls, then place on greased baking sheets, brush with water and sprinkle with cracked wheat. Cover and leave to prove in a warm place for about 20 minutes until almost doubled in size.

Bake in a preheated hot oven (220°C/425°F/Gas Mark 7) for 15 to 20 minutes. Transfer to a wire rack and leave to cool.

To freeze: Wrap in batches in single layers of foil, then pack in polythene bags. Seal, label and freeze for up to 6 months.

To thaw and serve: Remove packages from the polythene bags as required and place on a baking sheet. Reheat in a preheated moderate oven (180°C/350°F/Gas Mark 4) for 10 to 12 minutes. Remove foil and serve while still warm, or as soon as possible after reheating.

Makes 16 to 18

IRISH WHOLEMEAL SODA BREAD

Soda bread is best eaten on the day you remove it from the freezer. If you have no buttermilk add 2 teaspoons lemon juice to 300 ml/½ pint fresh milk and use instead.

250 g/8 oz plain flour
2 teaspoons salt
1 teaspoon bicarbonate of soda
350 g/12 oz wholemeal flour
300 ml/½ pint buttermilk
4 tablespoons water
plain flour, for sprinkling

Sift the plain flour, salt and soda into a bowl. Mix in the wholemeal flour, then add the buttermilk and water and mix quickly to a soft dough.

Turn the dough onto a floured surface, knead lightly until smooth, then shape into a large round, 4 cm/1½ inches thick. Place on a floured baking sheet, cut a deep cross on the top and sprinkle with flour. Bake in a preheated hot oven (220°C/425°F/Gas Mark 7) for 25 to 30 minutes. Transfer to a wire rack to cool.

To freeze: Wrap the loaf in foil, then pack in a polythene bag. Seal, label and freeze for up to 6 months.

To thaw and serve: Remove the polythene bag and place the foil package on a baking sheet. Reheat from frozen in a preheated moderately hot oven (200°C/400°F/Gas Mark 6) for 25 to 30 minutes. Serve while still warm, with butter.

Serves 10 to 12

RYE STICKS

Delicious served with cheese and pickles for a snack lunch, rye sticks also make an unusual base for open sandwiches. The caraway seeds impart an aniseed flavour, but they can be omitted.

15 g/½ oz fresh yeast
450–600 ml/¾–1 pint warm water
350 g/12 oz rye flour
500 g/1 lb wholemeal flour
2 teaspoons salt
2 tablespoons black treacle
2 tablespoons vegetable oil
2 teaspoons caraway seeds (optional)
1 egg yolk mixed with 1 teaspoon water, to glaze

Cream the yeast with a little of the water and leave in a warm place for 10 minutes until frothy. Mix the flours and salt together in a bowl, make a well in the centre, then pour in the yeast mixture and the remaining water. Add the black treacle, oil and the caraway seeds if using, reserving a few for decoration. Mix to a soft dough.

Turn the dough onto a floured surface and knead until smooth and elastic. Place in a clean bowl, cover with a damp cloth and leave to rise in a warm place for 1½ to 2 hours until doubled in bulk.

Turn the dough onto a floured surface and knead again for 3 minutes. Shape into 2 long sticks and place each on a greased baking sheet. Prick with a fork and leave to prove in a warm place for 40 to 50 minutes until almost doubled in size.

Brush the sticks with the glaze, then sprinkle with the reserved caraway seeds if using. Bake in a preheated hot oven (220°C/425°F/Gas Mark 7) for 10 minutes, then reduce the temperature to moderately hot (190°C/375°F/Gas Mark 5) and bake for a further 15 minutes until the sticks sound hollow when tapped underneath. Transfer to a wire rack and leave to cool.

To freeze: Wrap the sticks individually in foil, then pack in polythene bags. Seal, label and freeze for up to 6 months.

To thaw and serve: Remove the polythene bags and leave to stand in foil wrappings at room temperature for 2 to 3 hours. Alternatively, reheat quickly from frozen in a preheated moderately hot oven (200°C/400°F/Gas Mark 6) for 30 minutes.

Makes 2 rye sticks

Wholemeal Rolls; Rye Sticks; Irish Wholemeal Soda Bread

BONFIRE PARTY

On a cold November's evening there's nothing better to cheer the spirit than to invite a handful of friends and neighbours round to share in Bonfire Night celebrations. Gingerbread, parkin and bonfire toffee are the traditional fare, especially in the north of England, but the important thing is that the food should be warming, nourishing and easy to eat while standing around the fire with cold hands and feet!

As on any other party occasion, if you can get most of the food in the freezer beforehand, it will leave you free to do the other things the party involves. The goulash soup is really a meal-in-itself, although the children will probably still want jacket-baked potatoes cooked in the fire. Simply carry the casserole dish outside, provide a ladle and the guests can help themselves to as much soup as they like. Serve plenty of thick slices of hot French bread for mopping up the juices.

Ginger applecake is scrumptious, and at this time of year it hardly costs anything at all to make when apples are so inexpensive in the shops. Nutty Brownies are moist, munchy and certainly more-ish, so its worth making up a few batches to be sure you don't run out. They keep fresh in an airtight tin for a few days after thawing so any that aren't eaten on Bonfire Night needn't be wasted – serve them the American way for dessert with vanilla ice cream.

GOULASH SOUP

This hearty soup only needs to be warmed up quickly, and is therefore ideal for a trouble-free party menu.

2 tablespoons vegetable oil
1 onion, peeled and chopped
1 red pepper, cored, seeded and chopped
1 green pepper, cored, seeded and chopped
1 garlic clove, peeled and crushed
500 g/1 lb pie veal, cut into small cubes
2 tablespoons plain flour
1 tablespoon sweet paprika
½ teaspoon caraway seeds (optional)
500 g/1 lb tomatoes, skinned, seeded and roughly
  chopped
1.5 litres/2½ pints chicken stock
salt and freshly ground black pepper
1 kg/2 lb potatoes, peeled and cut into small chunks
TO SERVE
about 150 ml/¼ pint soured cream

Heat the oil in a large pan, add the onion, peppers and garlic and fry gently for 5 minutes without browning. Add the veal, increase the heat and fry briskly, stirring constantly for 5 minutes until sealed and evenly browned on all sides.

Lower the heat, sprinkle in the flour, paprika and caraway seeds, if using, and fry for a further 1 minute, stirring. Add the chopped tomatoes, gradually stir in the stock, then bring to the boil. Lower the heat, add salt and pepper to taste, cover and simmer gently for 1 hour.

Add the potatoes and simmer for 40 minutes or until the veal and potatoes are just tender. Remove from the heat and cool quickly.

To freeze: Transfer the soup to rigid containers, leaving 2 cm/¾ inch headspace. Seal, label and freeze for up to 3 months.

To thaw and serve: Leave to stand in container at room temperature for 4 hours. Turn into a flameproof casserole and bring slowly to the boil. Simmer gently for 10 minutes until the veal is heated through, then taste and adjust seasoning. Serve hot in warmed individual soup bowls topped with soured cream.

Serves 8

NUTTY BROWNIES

Do not worry if the cake mixture seems soft at the end of the cooking time. It firms up as it cools, resulting in the moist 'chewy' texture of authentic American brownies.

75 g/3 oz plain flour
¼ teaspoon salt
25 g/1 oz cocoa powder
250 g/8 oz caster sugar
125 g/4 oz unsalted butter, softened
2 eggs, beaten
1 teaspoon vanilla essence
75 g/3 oz mixed chopped nuts
TO SERVE
icing sugar, for sprinkling (optional)

Grease a 20 cm/8 inch square cake tin, line the base with greaseproof paper and grease the paper.

Sift the flour, salt and cocoa powder into a bowl. Stir in the caster sugar. Add the butter, eggs and vanilla essence and beat thoroughly. Fold in the nuts until evenly distributed.

Turn the mixture into the prepared tin and level the surface. Bake in a preheated moderate oven (180°C/ 350°F/Gas Mark 4) for 25 minutes or until the top is just firm to the touch in the centre. Leave the cake to cool in the tin, then turn out, peel off the lining paper and cut into sixteen 5 cm/2 inch squares.

To freeze: Pack the brownies in a rigid container, separating the layers with interleaving sheets or foil. Seal, label and freeze for up to 3 months.

To thaw and serve: Transfer brownies to a plate, cover loosely, then leave to stand at room temperature for about 4 hours. Serve sprinkled with icing sugar, if preferred.

Makes 16

GINGER APPLECAKE

For Bonfire Night you will want to serve this applecake warm, but at other times of year it can be served cold as a cake. It is also delicious served as a pudding – with custard or cream poured over.

175 g/6 oz self-raising flour
1 teaspoon ground ginger
1 teaspoon baking powder
pinch of salt
75 g/3 oz caster sugar
1 egg, lightly beaten
6–8 tablespoons milk
25 g/1 oz unsalted butter, melted and cooled
TOPPING
500 g/1 lb cooking apples
juice of 1 lemon
75 g/3 oz demerara sugar
1 teaspoon ground ginger
50 g/2 oz unsalted butter, melted and cooled

Sift the flour into a bowl with the ginger, baking powder and salt. Stir in the caster sugar. Add the egg, 6 tablespoons milk and the melted butter and beat to a soft dropping consistency, adding more milk if the mixture is too stiff. Set aside.

Make the topping: Peel, core and slice the apples into thin wedges. Put the apple wedges in a bowl with the lemon juice, demerara sugar and ginger. Fold gently to mix.

Spoon the cake mixture into a well greased 35 × 20 cm/12 × 8 inch Swiss roll tin and level the surface. Arrange the apple wedges over the top, overlapping them in rows. Pour over any liquid remaining in the bowl, then drizzle over the melted butter.

Bake in a preheated moderately hot oven (200°C/ 400°F/Gas Mark 6) for 35 minutes until the apples are golden brown on top. Remove from the oven and leave to cool.

To freeze: Open freeze the applecake until solid, then remove from tin and peel off the lining paper. Wrap in cling film, then overwrap in foil. Seal, label and freeze for up to 4 months.

To thaw and serve: Unwrap, return to greased Swiss roll tin, cover loosely with foil and leave to stand at room temperature for about 4 hours. Refresh in a preheated moderately hot oven (200°C/400°F/Gas Mark 6) for 10 minutes. Cut the applecake into wedges to serve.

Makes 16 wedges

Ginger Applecake; Nutty Brownies; Goulash Soup

WINTER

Warm up in winter by cooking and freezing hearty, nourishing soups and stews — just the right thing when you come in from the cold; take them straight from the freezer and quickly heat through. And although you can't compare winter with the other seasons for garden produce, you'll find there's still a good number of fresh fruit and vegetables to choose from. Exotic mangoes and lychees, colourful citrus fruit, even the ubiquitous Brussels sprout — all these can be successfully frozen, and many more. Don't forget that winter's the time for game, so pack a pheasant or two away to extend their short season. And with Christmas to look forward to, remember to reserve a space for the turkey in your freezer, thus avoiding last-minute panics and rising prices.

VEGETABLES IN SEASON

Artichoke, Jerusalem*
Beetroot
Brussels sprout*
Cabbage, red and white*
Carrot
Cauliflower, winter*
Celeriac*
Celery*
Chicory*
Fennel*
Kale*
Leek*
Mushroom
Onion
Parsnip
Potato
Radish, winter*
Salsify and scorzonera*
Swede
Turnip

FRUIT IN SEASON

Apple
Avocado
Banana
Clementine*
Coconut*
Cranberry*
Date*
Fig
Grape
Grapefruit*
Guava
Kiwi fruit
Kumquat*
Lemon*
Lime*
Lychee*
Mandarin*
Mango*
Melon
Orange*
Papaya
Passionfruit
Pear
Persimmon
Pineapple*
Pomegranate
Rhubarb
Satsuma*
Tangerine*
Ugli fruit*

*Freezing instructions given in this section

Artichoke, Jerusalem

These knobbly, tuberous vegetables which are native to the Americas are not true artichokes, despite their name, nor do they have any documented link with the city of Jerusalem. It is most likely that they were dubbed artichokes because of their delicate flavour, which resembles that of the globe artichoke. The 'Jerusalem' possibly arose as a natural evolution of the spoken name of the Dutch town Ter Heusen, from where they were imported into Britain in the 17th century.

In season from late October right through to spring, Jerusalem artichokes make good vegetable accompaniments and are excellent for soups and casseroles. They keep well in the soil as long as they are protected from frost, but are more conveniently stored in the freezer if you have the space, either on their own as below or in made-up dishes such as Curried Artichoke Soup (page 162). Artichokes with either white or reddish-purple skins are available. Like potatoes, they are best planted in the garden in tuber form in spring; look out for the white variety Fuseau which has very few knobbles.

Selecting for freezing: Choose firm tubers with as few knobbles as possible for ease of preparation. Avoid any damaged tubers and any that have holes indicating damage by worms or slugs. If lifting tubers from the garden, do so when the ground is not too wet.

Preparation for freezing: Jerusalem artichokes should be prepared in smallish batches, both because the preparation is time-consuming and because the tubers have a tendency to discolour. Scrub the tubers thoroughly, removing the smallest knobbles, then proceed as follows:

Artichoke cubes and slices: Peel the artichokes thinly, cut into cubes or slice thickly, then place in iced water with a little lemon juice or vinegar added to prevent discoloration.

Artichoke purée: Cook the artichokes in boiling water for about 15 minutes until tender, drain and leave until cool enough to handle, then pull or rub off the skins. Work to a purée in an electric blender or food processor, or a vegetable mill.

To freeze: *Artichoke cubes and slices:* Blanch in boiling water for 2 minutes, drain, cool rapidly in iced water, drain again and pat dry with kitchen paper. Pack in usable quantities in polythene bags, seal, label and freeze for up to 3 months.

Artichoke purée: Pack in usable quantities in rigid containers, leaving 2 cm/¾ inch headspace. Seal, label and freeze for up to 3 months.

To thaw and serve: *Artichoke cubes and slices:* Cook from frozen in boiling salted water for about 3 minutes until just tender, then serve as a vegetable accompaniment covered with a cheese, tomato or parsley sauce. Or leave to cool, then toss while still just warm in an oil, vinegar and mustard dressing, or serve in a parsley, mayonnaise or tartare sauce. Frozen cubes and slices can also be added to casseroles or stews about 10 minutes before the end of cooking.

Artichoke purée: Leave to stand in container at room temperature for about 2 hours, then use for soups.

Brussels Sprout

Brussels sprouts, named after the city near which they most probably originated as long ago as the 13th century, look like miniature cabbages. In fact they are a variety of cabbage with 'sprouts' growing up their stems.

Excellent for the freezer, sprouts are easy to grow in the garden and are increasingly available from pick-your-own farms, which guarantees their freshness for freezing. The best varieties to look out for are the F₁ hybrids Citadel, King Arthur and Peer Gynt. Plant out seedings or small plants in early summer and sprouts will be ready for picking from autumn right through until early spring.

Selecting for freezing: Choose small, very firm tight sprouts (large or 'blown' ones are too watery to freeze well whole, but they can be frozen as purée). Select those with no traces of yellowing or blackness, and make sure that the outside leaves are not dirty or loose, nor showing any signs that they have been attacked by birds or insects.

Always pick sprouts from the bottom of the plant stem to give the ones at the top a chance to mature, and be sure to set aside time for freezing as soon as possible after picking or purchase. Ideally, sprouts should make the transfer from plant to freezer within 1 to 2 hours.

Preparation for freezing: Working quickly in a cool kitchen, wash the sprouts well, trim the base and remove any damaged outside leaves. Grade them for size, but do not cut a cross in the base.

Whole sprouts: Need no further preparation.

Sprout purée: Cook any very large or 'blown' sprouts in boiling salted water until just tender, then drain and work to a purée in an electric blender or food processor, or vegetable mill.

To freeze: *Whole sprouts:* Blanch in boiling water, allowing 1½ to 3 minutes according to size. Drain, cool rapidly in iced water, then drain again and pat dry with kitchen paper. Open freeze until solid, then pack into polythene bags, seal, label and return to the freezer for up to 12 months.

Sprout purée: Pack in usable quantities in rigid containers, leaving 2 cm/¾ inch headspace. Seal, label and freeze for up to 12 months.

To thaw and serve: *Whole sprouts:* Cook from frozen in boiling salted water for 5 to 7 minutes according to size, then toss in butter, freshly grated nutmeg and seasonings to taste and serve as a vegetable accompaniment. For variety, add pieces of crisply grilled bacon or some boiled chestnuts. Sprouts can also be cooked from frozen in a tomato sauce for an interesting change, or coated with a white or cheese sauce and breadcrumbs and cooked *au gratin*.

Sprout purée: Reheat gently from frozen in a heavy-based pan over very low heat, stirring constantly and adding a little water if necessary to prevent sticking, then beat in some butter and a little cream with freshly grated nutmeg and seasonings to taste. Or use the purée from frozen for soup, either alone or in combination with other vegetables such as watercress, potatoes, leeks or onions.

Cabbage, Hard Red and White

Of the many varieties of cabbage that are ready for eating during the winter months, the best two for freezing are the hard red and white varieties. Red cabbage is on the market from autumn onwards, and is well worth buying or harvesting for freezing before the worst of the winter weather, since it can be damaged by severe frost. Good varieties such as Blood Red and Ruby Ball can be grown from seed sown in spring. White or Dutch cabbages are also grown from spring sowings of seed, and Christmas Drumhead is one of the best varieties.

Cabbages are readily available all year, so they are not worth a great deal of freezer space, but are convenient in made-up dishes such as a red cabbage casserole cooked with onions, apples and cider or stock; see also Pork and Cabbage Potée (page 172), Winter Cabbage and Apples (page 175), Braised Red Cabbage with Chestnuts (page 175).

Selecting for freezing: Cut or buy red and white cabbages as near as possible to the time they are to be frozen, and never more than 24 hours ahead — the sooner they are frozen, the better their flavour and food value. Select firm cabbages of the sort you prefer. Red ones should have a bluish bloom on their outer leaves, while the heart leaves should be a shiny purple. White cabbage will probably have its outermost leaves removed if it is bought from a market stall, and the remaining leaves should form a firm, white casing for the cabbage. Avoid any cabbages that feel at all soft to the touch or have badly damaged outer leaves. For preference, choose cabbages that feel rather heavy for their size.

Preparation for freezing: Remove the outer leaves and discard them, then cut the cabbage into quarters, remove the woody triangle of stem from the base and shred the leaves finely.

To freeze: Blanch in boiling water for 1 minute, drain, cool rapidly in iced water, then drain again and pat dry with kitchen paper. Pack in usable quantities in polythene bags, seal, label and freeze for up to 12 months.

To thaw and serve: Cook both red and white cabbage from frozen in boiling salted water for about 5 minutes until just tender (adding a little red wine vinegar to the water for red cabbage to help preserve its colour); or cook in a little water with a generous knob of butter added. Alternatively, both sorts of cabbage can be thawed in their wrappings at room temperature, then braised in the oven. Braise white cabbage with onions and caraway seeds, red cabbage with apples, onions and red wine.

Freezing Jerusalem artichokes and Brussels sprouts

Cauliflower, Winter

Cauliflowers are a variety of cabbage with a head of white, immature flowers called 'curds'. They originated in the Mediterranean, and although they were grown in Britain before the 17th century, they did not become popular until the Victorian era when they were considered a luxury. Cauliflowers are now an everyday vegetable, and are available nearly all the year round. The winter cauliflower, which is also known in some parts of the country as 'heading broccoli', is well worth growing – and freezing is the best method of storing since damage from winter frosts is always a problem with cauliflower. Good varieties for growing from seed planted in spring are Late Enterprise, Snowball and Thanet.

Selecting for freezing: Cauliflowers should be frozen when really fresh. If freezing homegrown produce, arrange to freeze it immediately after it has been cut. If buying cauliflowers, or picking your own from a farm, plan to freeze them as soon as they are brought home. Choose really white, firm cauliflowers with no signs of 'blowing' or 'feathering' of the curds. The leaves surrounding the head of curds should be bright green and show no signs of limpness. Avoid buying cauliflowers that have had the leaves cut off, or have leaves that show any signs of yellowing – they may not be really fresh. As a guide to good quality, select heads that feel heavy for their size.

Preparation for freezing: Cut off the base of the cauliflower and carefully remove the leaves (these can be used for soup or cooked as a vegetable). Break or cut the curds into sprigs of florets, each about 5 cm/ 2 inches in diameter. Wash well, then grade according to size.

To freeze: Blanch in boiling water with 1 tablespoon lemon juice added to every 600 ml/1 pint – this helps to keep the cauliflower a good colour. Allow 2 to 3 minutes blanching, depending on size. Drain, cool rapidly in iced water, then drain again and pat dry with kitchen paper. Open freeze until solid, then pack in polythene bags, seal, label and return to the freezer for up to 6 months.

To thaw and serve: Cook from frozen in boiling salted water for 4 to 6 minutes until just tender. Serve with butter, herbs and seasoning, or with a béchamel sauce. For cauliflower cheese, coat with a cheese sauce, sprinkle with grated cheese and brown under the grill before serving. Cauliflower can also be cooked from frozen in soups, or can be stir-fried from frozen, either alone or with other frozen vegetables such as peas and carrots. See also Indian Cauliflower (page 132).

Celeriac

This globe-shaped root vegetable, brought to Britain from southern Europe in the 18th century, looks rather like a large, knobbly turnip – and is sometimes given the name 'turnip-rooted celery'.

Celeriac is easy to grow from seedlings reared indoors and planted out in early summer. Good varieties which crop from October to March include Alabaster, Globus and Marble Ball.

Celeriac freezes well and, if you like its mild celery-like flavour, it is well worth freezer space since it will not keep well in the ground unless completely protected from frost. Freeze cubed, sliced or grated, or in made-up dishes such as Farmhouse Pheasant (page 169), Carrot Purée (page 175), Winter Vegetable Casserole (page 176).

Selecting for freezing: Choose firm, small roots – really large heads of celeriac are likely to be woody or hollow inside. Avoid specimens that are very knobbly – they are time-consuming and wasteful to prepare. Discard any with signs of rotting or damage by pests or diseases.

Preparation for freezing: Peel and wash, then cut into cubes or thick slices, or grate.

Freezing celery and celeriac

To freeze: *Celeriac cubes and slices:* Blanch in boiling water for 1 to 2 minutes, depending on size or thickness. Drain, cool rapidly in iced water, drain again and pat dry with kitchen paper. Open freeze until solid, then pack in polythene bags, seal, label and return to the freezer for up to 12 months.

Grated celeriac: Blanch in boiling water for 1 minute, then drain, cool and dry as for cubes and slices above. Pack in usable quantities in rigid containers or polythene bags, seal, label and freeze for up to 12 months.

To thaw and serve: *Celeriac cubes and slices:* Cook from frozen in boiling salted water for about 5 minutes until tender, then serve as a vegetable accompaniment, either tossed in butter, herbs and seasonings, or with a béchamel, Hollandaise or parsley sauce. Celeriac can also be served *au gratin.* Alternatively, leave to stand in wrappings at room temperature for about 2 hours, then use in stir-fried dishes with other vegetables. Frozen celeriac can be added to casseroles.

Grated celeriac: Use from frozen in soups and casseroles, or cook from frozen in boiling salted water for about 3 minutes, then work to a purée in an electric blender or food processor with butter, cream, herbs and seasonings to taste.

Celery

Renowned since Greek and Roman times as a medicinal plant, celery is a vegetable which only became popular in Britain – its native land – in the 18th century. Although imported from countries such as Israel and America to increase its availability, celery is really at its best in winter when homegrown produce comes on to the market. It is available in both white and green-stemmed varieties.

Celery is not hard to grow, and is now available in varieties which do not have to be laboriously tied and earthed up to whiten or blanch the stems. These varieties include Golden Self Blanching and American Green. Varieties recommended for growing in trenches include Giant White and Prizetaker. Grow celery from seed in spring for harvesting in winter.

Although celery cannot be eaten raw after freezing, it is well worth storing in the freezer in made-up dishes such as Braised Celery with Sherry (page 174), Winter Vegetable Casserole (page 176) and on its own as described here, for serving as a cooked vegetable and for use in soups and casseroles.

Selecting for freezing: Select large, firm heads with no sign of brown on the outer stalks. The stalks should have wide, fat bases, while the leaves should be fresh and green, never yellow or limp. Avoid buying celery that has been 'topped' – it is probably not at its freshest. Pre-washed celery saves preparation time, but does not always have the best flavour.

Preparation for freezing: Prepare celery for freezing as soon as possible after it is bought or lifted. Cut off the base with a sharp knife and separate the stalks. Discard any that are tough or discoloured. Trim off the

leaves (use them in salads, stocks and soups, with fish dishes and as an attractive savoury garnish), then wash the stalks very thoroughly. Scrub or scrape with a small sharp knife if necessary, to remove every trace of dirt and stringiness. Cut the stalks into 5 cm/2 inch lengths.

To freeze: Blanch cut lengths of celery in boiling water for 3 minutes, drain, cool rapidly in iced water, then drain again and pat dry with kitchen paper. Pack in usable quantities in polythene bags, seal, label and freeze for up to 9 months.

To thaw and serve: Cook celery from frozen in boiling salted water for about 10 minutes until tender, then serve alone as a vegetable accompaniment or coated with a béchamel, tomato or cheese sauce (finished *au gratin* if liked). Celery can also be used from frozen in soups, casseroles and stews, or it can be thawed in its wrappings at room temperature for about 2 hours, then stir-fried (either alone or with a mixture of other vegetables). Thawed celery can also be used in baked dishes, for example with cheese.

Chicory

Confusingly known in many other countries as 'endive', chicory is a vegetable grown both for its roots, which are used to flavour coffee, and for its edible leaves. Allowed to develop in conditions of complete darkness, the tightly packed heads of leaves are white tipped with pale green, and they taste slightly bitter. Nearly all of the chicory grown and sold in Britain is of the Witloof variety, first bred in Belgium from the wild plant succory.

Fresh chicory can be used both raw and cooked, but due to its high water content its texture changes after freezing, which makes it unsuitable for eating raw. Homegrown chicory is well worth freezing if you have a glut, or can find bargains in shops and markets during the winter (especially at the end of the day's trading), because it can be served as a cooked vegetable accompaniment.

Selecting for freezing: Choose conical, tightly packed heads, with no traces of brown on the outside leaves. The leaves themselves should be firm and cool to the touch, and should snap crisply when broken.

Preparation for freezing: Prepare chicory for the freezer as soon as possible after it has been bought or harvested. Working in a cool kitchen, trim the base with a stainless steel knife (to avoid discoloration of white leaves), then wipe clean, removing any substandard outside leaves.

To freeze: Blanch whole heads in boiling water for 4 minutes, drain, cool rapidly in iced water, then drain again and pat dry with kitchen paper. Pack in usable quantities in rigid containers or polythene bags, seal, label and freeze for up to 5 months.

To thaw and serve: Cook chicory heads from frozen in boiling salted water for about 8 minutes until tender, then drain thoroughly and serve in a béchamel or cheese sauce. Or braise from frozen in a well-flavoured stock which can then be thickened to make a sauce. Or thaw the chicory in its wrappings at room temperature for about 2 hours, then squeeze carefully to remove excess water and cook as above.

Fennel

Native to the Mediterranean region, fennel has always been a popular vegetable in Italy, and its name is often linked with the Italian city of Florence. It is available as tightly packed heads consisting of the swollen leaf bases surrounding squat stems topped with feathery green leaves. Fennel is prized for its delicate aniseed flavour, and is delicious both raw in salads and cooked.

If you have a warm, sheltered garden, and can guarantee a frost-free site, fennel can be grown at home, but it is not an easy vegetable to cultivate successfully. It also needs a lot of attention, since the heads must be earthed up or encased in cardboard to ensure whiteness. It can however be bought readily from September through to early spring, most supplies being imported from warmer countries of Europe. Fennel freezes well, but after freezing does not have a good enough texture to be eaten as a salad vegetable. It can be frozen as below or in composite dishes, such as Chicken and Fennel Sauté (page 168), Fennel with Tomatoes and Garlic (page 176).

Selecting for freezing: Choose firm, tight heads with white leaf bases. The feathery green leaves should not be limp, nor the white parts brown or discoloured.

Preparation for freezing: Trim the top of the fennel (the feathery green parts can be frozen separately as a herb, see page 65). Scrub the outside leaves, then scrape them with a sharp knife to remove any strings. Cut each head into quarters.

To freeze: Blanch the quartered heads in boiling salted water for 3 to 5 minutes, according to size. Drain, cool rapidly in iced water, then drain again and pat dry with kitchen paper. Pack in usable quantities in polythene bags, seal, label and freeze for up to 6 months.

To thaw and serve: Cook from frozen in boiling salted water for about 7 minutes until tender, drain well and serve with a béchamel or cheese sauce, or with a mixture of other cooked vegetables. Fennel can be used from frozen in soups, stews and casseroles. If left to thaw until soft enough to slice thinly, it can also be stir-fried with other vegetables. If sparingly used, so its flavour does not mask that of other ingredients, it makes an interesting substitute for celery.

Kale

Kale, with its fibrous, dark green leaves which are often tightly curled, is a relation of the cabbage. Well able to withstand even the most severe of frosts, kale has been grown in Britain for centuries, especially in Scotland. It is one of the easiest of vegetables to grow, and will thrive even in quite poor soil. Good curly varieties are Fribor and Pentland Brig, while Thousand Headed is a good choice for plain-leaved kale. Seeds sown in April or May develop into plants with leaves ready for harvesting from early December onwards. The flavour of kale is best after the first frosts.

Selecting for freezing: Choose young kale leaves, and freeze them immediately after picking or purchase. The leaves should have a bright colour and show no signs of limpness or discoloration. Pick the young leaves from the top of the plant, working down the stem. Break off where they snap easily – do not cut.

Preparation for freezing: Working in a cool kitchen, pull the leaves off their stems with your hands, in the same way as you would prepare spinach, then wash the leaves thoroughly in iced water. Do not cut or break the leaves into smaller pieces.

To freeze: Blanch in boiling water for 3 minutes, drain, cool rapidly in iced water, then drain again very thoroughly and pat dry with kitchen paper. Pack in usable quantities in polythene bags, seal, label and freeze for up to 12 months.

To thaw and serve: Cook from frozen in boiling salted water for about 8 minutes until tender. Serve tossed in butter with plenty of black pepper, and a sprinkling of caraway seeds if liked.

Alternatively, shred or slice thinly while still frozen, then stir-fry on its own or with a mixture of other vegetables. Kale can be used as a substitute for spinach in many recipes, but it needs longer cooking.

Leek

Known in Egypt from the time of the Pharaohs, the leek has been cultivated in Britain since Saxon times and it is still the national emblem of Wales.

Homegrown leeks are available from autumn right through the winter until late spring, but they are generally at their best from November onwards. Leek growing competitions are highly popular in the north of England, but leeks can easily be grown anywhere in the country, since they are tolerant of frost. Seed sown in spring in well-drained soil germinates to produce plants which are collections of rolled leaves. These can be whitened by being earthed up like celery. Good varieties to choose for planting or for obtaining from pick-your-own farms are Musselburgh, Walton Mammoth, Royal Favourite and Winter Crop.

Leeks freeze reasonably well, and are a good standby to have in the freezer, but they do not retain their texture completely because of their high water content.

Selecting for freezing: Choose thin, young leeks and arrange to freeze them as soon as possible after they are bought or harvested. Look for firm produce with a fresh green colour and no trace of limpness. Avoid any leeks that have had their tops trimmed away and any that are very dirty.

Preparation for freezing: Trim away the root and the topmost green leaves (these can be used for soups and casseroles). Make several cuts lengthways down through the outer layers of leaves, then wash very thoroughly under cold running water to remove all grit. To ensure complete cleanliness, it often helps to stand the leeks upside down in a bowl of cold water for about 30 minutes to loosen the grit particles. The leeks should then be graded for size. Small ones can be left whole, larger ones cut into 2 cm/¾ inch slices or halved lengthways.

To freeze: Blanch whole, sliced and halved leeks in boiling water for 3 to 4 minutes, according to size. Drain, cool rapidly in iced water, then drain again and pat dry with kitchen paper. Pack in usable quantities in polythene bags, seal, label and freeze for up to 6 months.

To thaw and serve: Cook leeks from frozen in boiling salted water for 6 to 8 minutes until tender, according to size. Serve well drained as a vegetable accompaniment, either tossed in butter and black pepper or coated with a béchamel, cheese or tomato sauce. After cooking, leeks can also be used in pies, flans and quiches. Add leeks from frozen to soups, stews and casseroles; stir-fry sliced leeks from frozen.

Radish, Winter

Like other radishes, the winter ones are derived from plants native to Asia and long cultivated by the Chinese and Japanese. The winter radish is a huge size compared with its red summer relation. About 30 cm/ 12 inches long, and with a black skin, the winter radish has an excellent flavour and makes an unusual and interesting addition to winter salads. It can also be cooked and eaten as a hot vegetable accompaniment, tasting rather like a turnip. Available in shops from October onwards, winter radishes are also simple to grow, and seed planted in August will be ready by November. Black Spanish and Chinese Rose are good varieties.

Unlike summer ones, winter radishes can be frozen successfully, and are handy to have in the freezer when the ground is frozen and harvesting impossible.

Selecting for freezing: Choose firm, undamaged roots without blemishes. For ease of preparation, select roots without too many side shoots. If the leaves are still attached, they should be bright green and not limp.

Preparation for freezing: Trim the roots and wash them thoroughly, scrubbing to remove dirt. Peel thinly with a sharp knife, then grate or dice them.

To freeze: *Grated winter radish:* Pack in usable quantities in polythene bags, then seal, label and freeze for up to 6 months.

Diced winter radish: Blanch in boiling water for 2 minutes, drain, cool rapidly in iced water, then drain again and pat dry with kitchen paper. Pack in usable quantities in polythene bags, seal, label and freeze for up to 6 months.

To thaw and serve: *Grated winter radish:* Leave to stand in wrappings at room temperature for 3 hours, or until thawed. Pat dry with kitchen paper, then serve as a salad with mayonnaise or French dressing. It also makes an interesting addition to coleslaw, and combines well with French beans in a salad.

Diced winter radish: Cook from frozen in boiling salted water for about 8 minutes until just tender, then drain and serve with plenty of butter and black pepper, or mixed with mushrooms in a cream sauce.

Salsify and Scorzonera

These two oddly named root vegetables are native to Europe, where they have been widely cultivated for many centuries. Salsify is a white-skinned root commonly dubbed the 'vegetable oyster' because of its slightly fishy taste, while scorzonera is a black-skinned variation of the same plant.

Both salsify and scorzonera roots measure about 38 cm/15 inches in length, and are in season in winter. They are easy to grow from seeds planted in spring, and are resistant to frost. Mammoth is a good variety of salsify, while Russian Giant is the best scorzonera variety on the market.

The roots of these vegetables make an interesting change, and both freeze successfully – prepared as below or in made-up dishes, such as Salsify au Gratin (page 174), Curried Scallops with Salsify (page 166).

Selecting for freezing: Choose firm young roots with good shapes and no signs of blemish. Salsify should be white, while scorzonera should be black or purplish brown. Never buy shrivelled roots or any with wilted leaves attached – if the leaves are still present they should be fresh looking and green, with a greyish bloom. Handle the roots carefully, taking particular care if lifting them from the garden, because they will 'bleed' like beetroot if they are damaged.

Preparation for freezing: Trim off the leaves, if present, but be careful not to cut into the root. Scrub under cold running water, do not peel.

To freeze: Blanch the roots whole in boiling water for 2 minutes, drain well, then peel while they are still warm. Cut each root into 7.5 cm/3 inch pieces, either before or after peeling, whichever is easier. Alternatively, blanch by steaming for 2 minutes; this is particularly recommended for scorzonera. After blanching and peeling, leave to cool completely, then pack in usable quantities in polythene bags, seal, label and freeze for up to 6 months.

To thaw and serve: Cook salsify and scorzonera from frozen in boiling salted water (or a mixture of equal quantities of milk and water) for 5 to 8 minutes until tender. Serve tossed in butter with plenty of black pepper, or top with a béchamel sauce and breadcrumbs and finish off under the grill. Alternatively, after cooking, leave to cool, then serve cold in a lemony French dressing. Or thaw in their wrappings at room temperature for about 2 hours, then fry and serve on toast.

Freezing fennel and kale

CITRUS FRUIT

Although citrus fruits are available all year round, it is only in the winter months that these fruits really come into their own, when other seasonal and soft fruits are scarce and prohibitively expensive. All citrus fruits freeze well, and are worth their space in the freezer at this time of year when there is plenty of choice and their prices are competitively low. The different citrus fruits and the most suitable methods for freezing them are given below. They can also be frozen in made-up dishes, on their own, or combined with other citrus flavours as in Chilled Citrus Appetizer (page 165). Citrus Skate with Peppers (page 166) and Turkey St. Clements (page 168).

Selecting citrus fruit for freezing: Buy shiny, firm fruit which weigh heavy for their size – this indicates juiciness. Some varieties of citrus fruit have thicker skins than others, so size is not always the best indication of a good fruit.

Citrus fruit juices: All of these freeze well. Simply squeeze the juice by hand or use a juice extractor, then pour into rigid containers in usable quantities. Seal, label and freeze for up to 12 months. Thaw in container at room temperature for about 2 hours or in the refrigerator overnight.

A convenient way to freeze lemon, lime and orange juices is to pour them into ice cube trays, open freeze until solid, then turn out and pack cubes together in a polythene bag. They can then be used individually from frozen for flavouring hot dishes, both sweet and savoury.

Whole citrus fruit: Can be frozen for later use in marmalade-making and preserving – it is often useful to be able to pop the whole fruits into the freezer if you do not have time to deal with them when they are available. (Seville oranges, for example, have a very short season.) Simply wash the whole fruit, then wrap individually in foil or cling film, pack together in polythene bags, seal, label and freeze for up to 12 months. Thaw at room temperature for 1½ hours, then use as for fresh fruit.

Clementine/Mandarin/Satsuma/Tangerine

Grouped together because they are available in this country at the same time – just before and after Christmas – and because they are frozen in the same way, these miniature members of the citrus fruit family are individual nonetheless. Mostly imported from Italy, Spain and Israel, all these fruits are worth freezing because their season is so short, and their distinctive, sweet flavours make them a welcome change from the more usual orange.

Preparation for freezing: Peel, then separate into segments, removing pips if necessary.

To freeze: Pack segments in usable quantities in rigid containers, sprinkling each layer with sugar to taste. Or cover with a medium sugar syrup made from 350 g/12 oz sugar to 600 ml/1 pint water. Seal, label and freeze for up to 12 months.

To thaw and serve: Leave to stand in container at room temperature for about 2 hours, then use slightly iced in fruit salads.

Grapefruit

Native to the West Indies, most of the grapefruits imported into this country now come from America, South Africa, Israel and other Mediterranean countries. There are two main types: the white- or yellow-fleshed grapefruit, and the pink-fleshed grapefruit which is sweeter. Both are suitable for freezing and are convenient to use at breakfast since they can be frozen ready-prepared. High in Vitamin C, the grapefruit has increased in popularity in recent years as a slimming aid – a whole grapefruit contains as few as 30 calories. See also Grapefruit Sorbet (page 179).

Preparation for freezing: Peel fruit, removing all pith, then divide into segments.

To freeze: Pack segments in usable quantities in rigid containers, sprinkling each layer with sugar to taste. Or cover with a light sugar syrup made from 250 g/8 oz sugar to 600 ml/1 pint water. Seal, label and freeze for up to 12 months.

To thaw and serve: Leave to stand in container at room temperature for about 2 hours or in the refrigerator overnight. Serve for breakfast, or as a starter, or use in desserts.

Kumquat

The tiniest of all the citrus fruit, the kumquat is about the size of an olive. Native to China but now grown in the Middle and Far East and South America, the kumquat is a rare fruit in Britain, but you may find it in specialist markets. It is an extremely versatile fruit, like its relative the orange, with a bitter-sweet, piquant flavour which is both refreshing and thirst-quenching. It can be used in most recipes calling for oranges, but one of its advantages over the orange is that it can be eaten whole, including the skin. Its miniscule size also makes it ideal for fruit salads and preserves. Kumquat is excellent served with duck as a substitute for orange.

Preparation for freezing: Wash and leave whole or slice thickly (including skin).

To freeze: Open freeze whole fruit until solid, then pack in polythene bags. Pack slices in usable quantities in rigid containers, sprinkling each layer with sugar to taste. Or cover with a medium sugar syrup made from 350 g/12 oz sugar to 600 ml/1 pint water. Seal, label and freeze for up to 12 months.

To thaw and serve: Leave to stand in container at room temperature for 2 hours. Use whole fruit and dry pack in preserves and fruit salads. Serve sugar syrup pack as a dessert with pouring cream or ice cream, sprinkled with liqueur if liked.

Lemon/Lime/Orange

Both lemons and limes are native to India and South-East Asia, and are closely related. Although the lemon is more common in Britain, the lime is increasing in availability. The two fruits can be used interchangeably in most recipes – lime has a thinner green-coloured skin and the flesh is slightly more pungent in flavour than lemon, but these are the only differences. Limes are immensely useful for giving a sharp 'kick' to savoury meat and vegetable dishes. They also make sweet mousses and soufflés more 'exotic' than lemons. Limes are particularly good for marmalade-making, either alone or mixed with other citrus fruit. Slices of lime make an unusual alternative to lemon slices in garnishes and decorations. Lemons and limes have long been noted for their high Vitamin C content.

Both lemons and limes are immensely useful in the freezer, because they can be used in so many different dishes, both sweet and savoury. Lemons can be purchased in bulk from wholesalers at bargain prices, and are well worth buying for freezing.

Oranges originated in China and India, and are undoubtedly one of the most popular fruits in the world. Most of the oranges imported into Britain come from the Mediterranean countries, South Africa and North and South America. As one variety follows another, oranges are available all year round. From the large sweet seedless navel to the juicy Valencias, sweet Blood Oranges with their attractive pink flesh, and the bitter Sevilles for marmalade-making, all types of orange freeze well. Check with your retailer/wholesaler when your favourite variety is in season and buy in bulk at a reduced price.

See also Citrus Mousse (page 181), Iced Lime Soufflé (page 180), Lemon Lattice Flan (page 183), Crêpes Suzette (page 183), Date and Orange Pudding (page 184).

Preparation for freezing: Grate rind finely or peel off in thin strips with a cannelle knife or vegetable peeler, then cut into thin julienne shreds. Remove all pith, then slice lemons and limes thinly crosswise into rings and remove pips. If rind is not required separately, slices can be cut including the rind, according to taste. Slice oranges into rings without skin, or separate into segments, removing pith and pips.

To freeze: Wrap usable quantities of rind or strips of peel in foil or cling film, then pack together in polythene bags. Open freeze slices or segments until solid, then pack in polythene bags, seal, label and return to the freezer. Or pack slices or segments in usable quantities in rigid containers, sprinkling each layer with sugar to taste. Or cover with a light syrup made from 250 g/8 oz sugar to 600 ml/1 pint water. Seal, label and freeze. Rind, peel, slices and segments can all be stored in the freezer for up to 12 months.

To thaw and serve: Unwrap individual parcels of rind and peel and leave to stand at room temperature for a few minutes before using as a flavouring, garnish or decoration. Leave slices to stand in containers at room temperature for about 1 hour, then use as for fresh. Open frozen slices and segments can be taken straight from wrappings and are immensely useful for last-minute decoration, and for use in drinks.

Ugli Fruit

This fruit is a cross between a grapefruit and a tangerine, with loose, wrinkled skin tinged with green. Underneath its aptly named exterior, its flesh is sweet and juicy – and well worth eating. Ugli fruit imported from the Caribbean and Far East can be found in specialist greengrocers, markets and some good supermarkets throughout the winter: freeze some if you see them for use out of season.

Preparation for freezing: Peel, then separate into segments, removing all pith.

To freeze: Open freeze segments until solid, then pack in polythene bags, seal, label and return to the freezer for up to 12 months. Or pack segments in usable quantities in rigid containers, either sprinkling each layer with sugar to taste or covering the fruit slices with a light sugar syrup made from 250 g/8 oz sugar to 600 ml/1 pint water. Seal, label and freeze for up to 12 months.

To thaw and serve: Leave to stand in wrappings or container at room temperature for about 2 hours, then use as for fresh ugli fruit in fruit salads for example, and as a substitute for oranges in any recipe.

Coconut

Native to the tropics, particularly the Pacific, the fruit of the coconut palm is very versatile. Its milk is used as a drink, its flesh is eaten and its coir is used to make ropes and matting. But most important of all, the dried flesh of the coconut is used to make coconut oil for cooking, and margarine.

Coconuts are imported into Britain in the winter months, and are well worth buying for use in cooking because the flavour of fresh coconut flesh is far superior to that of dried or desiccated coconut, which is most commonly used in baking.

Fresh coconut is particularly useful in Indian and oriental dishes, especially for toning down fiery curries, and the 'milk' obtained by soaking grated coconut flesh in water is indispensable in Indonesian cooking. Since fresh coconuts are only in the shops and markets for a relatively short time each year, it is well worth freezing the flesh for use in such recipes – and for baking and dessert making. See also Apple and Coconut Pie (page 184).

Selecting for freezing: When choosing coconuts, hold the fruit in your hand, it should weigh heavy. Shake it and listen for the sound of milk inside – then you know it is reasonably fresh.

Preparation for freezing: Pierce a few eyes in the shell with a skewer or by hitting in a nail with a hammer, then pour off the liquid inside. Place the shell on a heavy surface or the floor and hit it several times with the hammer until it cracks open into several pieces. Scrape the flesh away from the shell (a curved grapefruit knife is a good tool for this). Grate or shred the flesh using a hand grater or food processor.

To freeze: Open freeze until solid, then pack in polythene bags. Seal, label and return to the freezer for up to 6 months.

To thaw and serve: Tip whole packs or large quantities of frozen coconut, into a colander and leave at room temperature for 2 hours, then use as fresh. Small amounts of coconut sprinkled over food will thaw in a few minutes.

Freezing grapefruit, oranges, lemons and limes

Cranberry

A native of North America, the cranberry was first discovered as an edible fruit by the Indians, who also used it as a medicine and as a colourful dye for their blankets and rugs. The fruit acquired the name 'crane berry', because its pink blossom looked like the heads of cranes.

Cranberries grow on vines and thrive best on a combination of sand and water. Some varieties come from northern Europe (most notably Finland), but the majority of cranberries on sale here are imported from North America. Since the fruit has a protective waxy coating, it travels extremely well. Harvested in the late autumn, cranberries arrive here in plenty of time for the Christmas season, to be served as the traditional accompaniment to roast turkey. They are extremely rich in Vitamin C.

Cranberries retain their flavour, texture and colour well in the freezer, and are well worth freezing because their season in the shops and markets is extremely brief. Their tart, acidic flavour makes it impossible to eat them raw, but they are excellent for jams and jellies, as well as the traditional cranberry sauce; they also make delicious fruit tarts and other desserts, and are the perfect 'sharp' accompaniment to rich meats such as pork and ham, duck and goose.

Selecting for freezing: Cranberries are usually sold in punnets or plastic bags rather than loose by the kg/lb. Look for bright red, shiny fruit with no trace of mould – imported fruit is perfect for freezing. Buy as soon as you see cranberries in the shops in November.

Preparation for freezing: Cranberries sold in plastic bags have already been washed and picked over prior to packing, so no further preparation is necessary. Tip out cranberries from punnets, wash and pick over, discarding any that are shrivelled or mouldy.

To freeze: _Whole cranberries:_ Unopened plastic bags of cranberries can be put straight into the freezer as they are; they will keep for up to 12 months. Open freeze cranberries from punnets until solid, then pack in polythene bags, seal, label and return to the freezer for up to 12 months.

Cranberry sauce: This is useful to have in the freezer ready-made, and is far superior to the commercial bottled brands. Cook whole cranberries with water and sugar (allowing 450 ml/¾ pint water and 500 g/1 lb sugar to every 500 g/1 lb cranberries). Boil until the cranberry skins pop, boil for a further 5 minutes, then cool quickly and pour into rigid containers in usable quantities. Seal, label and freeze for up to 12 months. If preferred, the sauce can be sieved before freezing to make a smooth purée.

To thaw and serve: _Whole cranberries:_ Leave to stand in wrappings at room temperature for 2 hours or reheat from frozen, then use as fresh in sauce, jam and jelly making and for all kinds of desserts.

Cranberry sauce: Thaw at room temperature as for whole cranberries, then use cold in mousses, sorbets, ice creams and other desserts. For serving and using hot, reheat from frozen in a heavy-based pan over the lowest possible heat, stirring frequently and adding a little water if necessary to prevent sticking.

Date

The date is the fruit of the date palm which thrives in desert conditions. Arab in origin, it grows prolifically in North Africa and is increasingly grown in America.

Most of the dates imported into Britain are the dried, compressed, 'block' or sugar-rolled varieties, but fresh dates are sometimes available in specialist greengrocers and markets especially around Christmastime. Fresh dates freeze exceptionally well, so are well worth storing away for future use when out of season. See also Date and Orange Pudding (page 184).

Selecting for freezing: Look for plump, moist fruits in specialist greengrocers and some delicatessens. Check freshness carefully because dates quickly become dry and shrivelled.

Preparation for freezing: Dates are best frozen without their stones. Either pierce the end of the date with a skewer and squeeze the fruit until the date stone pops out, or cut the date in half lengthways with a sharp knife and dig out the stone with the point of a knife. Select your method according to whether or not the dates are likely to be needed whole for future use (for example as stuffed dates).

To freeze: Pack in usable quantities in polythene bags, seal, label and freeze for up to 12 months.

To thaw and serve: Leave in wrappings at room temperature for 2 hours, then eat as fresh or use chopped in sweet and savoury salads. Alternatively stuff them with cream cheese mixtures, or use in baking according to individual recipes.

Freezing pineapples and mangoes

Lychee

Grown in China for over 2000 years, the lychee (also spelt litchi, leechee and lichi) is now so popular throughout the world that it is grown in many other tropical and sub-tropical countries. The majority of lychees imported into Britain are canned in syrup or dried (available from Chinese supermarkets), but fresh lychees from China, India and Pakistan, Africa and the USA are available in the winter. December, January and February are the most likely months to find them available. It is possible to grow lychees in hothouses and heated greenhouses in Britain, but the ones you see for sale will be imported.

Referred to as both a nut and a fruit, fresh lychees are encased in a brittle, knobbly-looking outer covering – the familiar fleshy white fruit is not visible unless the stallholder has cut a few open. This outer casing is rosy red when the fruit is on the tree, but once harvested it soon turns brown. The flesh inside is juicy and translucent with a large stone. The flavour of lychees is often likened to that of the muscat grape, with a slightly acid aftertaste. It is most often eaten as a dessert fruit, but it is also delicious in duck, pork and chicken dishes.

Fresh lychees are so unusual, and since they are not widely available all year round, it is a nice idea to freeze some – if only for their rarity value! They keep their texture and flavour well in the freezer if they are packed in a sugar syrup (as described below) and are useful for pepping up a plain fruit salad. They are also rich in Vitamin C.

Selecting for freezing: Look for nuts with a reddish-brown hue as an indication of freshness. If the outer casing is a dull brown, this is a sign that they have been kept too long and their flesh will not be so succulent. Stallholders usually sell them in clusters – they are not harvested individually because the shells are easily damaged.

Preparation for freezing: Lychees are very simple to prepare. Squeeze the fruit gently between your fingers until the outer casing or jacket cracks open, then peel it off with the fingertips. Squeeze out the central stone carefully.

To freeze: Pack whole stoned lychees in usable quantities in rigid containers and cover with a heavy sugar syrup made from 500 g/1 lb sugar to 600 ml/1 pint water. Leave 2 cm/¾ inch headspace, seal, label and freeze for up to 12 months.

To thaw and serve: Leave to stand in container in the refrigerator for about 1 hour, then serve slightly frosted with ice cream or as part of a fruit salad.

Mango

Native to India and discovered by the Chinese, the mango has been cultivated for more than 4000 years. It is now grown all over the world in tropical and sub-tropical climates. Surprising though it may seem, this tropical fruit is in fact the fruit of an evergreen tree, from the same family as the cypress pine.

There are numerous different varieties of mango and many shapes, colours and flavours. Weight varies between 250 g/8 oz and 750 g/1½ lb, although some varieties can be as heavy as 2 kg/4½ lb. Unripe, small green mangoes are the ones most often used in pickle and chutney making and in savoury Indian and Chinese dishes. The sweet, juicy ripe fruit is the one most frequently imported into this country for use as a dessert fruit.

Ripe mangoes freeze well in a sugar syrup (described below) and in dishes such as Singapore Spareribs (page 172). Their flavour is unusual in that it is somehow both sweet and acid at the same time, tasting like a cross between nectar and peach. All mangoes should be peeled before eating because the skin is tough, furry and unpalatable.

Selecting for freezing: Mangoes for freezing should be fully ripe, so avoid any fruit which has green skins. Ripe mangoes vary in colour from rosy red to orange, peach and yellow. If there are any unripe green patches on them simply keep them in a warm place until they turn colour. Mangoes are available from January right through to September. When buying, squeeze the stalk end gently if possible, it should yield slightly under pressure but not feel soft or squashy. Do not buy damaged or bruised fruit at bargain prices for freezing.

Preparation for freezing: Mangoes must be peeled and sliced, but this is not an easy task because the flesh has a habit of clinging closely to the stone. The easiest way to peel a mango is to score the flesh lengthways into 3 sections with a sharp knife, hold the fruit in one hand, grip the skin at the top with the fingers of the other hand, then peel the skin off in sections as when peeling a banana. Slice the fruit away from the stone as best you can, although some flesh is bound to be wasted.

To freeze: Pack slices in usable quantities in rigid containers and cover with medium sugar syrup made from 350 g/12 oz sugar to 600 ml/1 pint water with 2 teaspoons lemon juice added to prevent discoloration. Leave 2 cm/¾ inch headspace, seal, label and freeze for up to 6 months.

To thaw and serve: Leave to stand in container at room temperature for 1½ hours, then use in fruit salads or serve with ice cream.

Pineapple

One of the most attractive and delicious of all tropical fruits, the pineapple is native to South America, but it is now produced in tropical climates all over the world. Originally called ananas because it is the fruit of the ananas tree, the fruit was given its present name from the Spanish word for pine cone *pina*, which of course it resembles. Imported fresh pineapples are available all year round in Britain, but are more prolific and therefore more reasonably priced during the winter.

Pineapples are available canned in rings, slices, chunks, crushed and juice form, therefore freezing this fruit may not seem worthwhile. However, pineapples do freeze exceptionally well, and if they can be bought at a reasonable price (say in bulk from a wholesaler),

they are well worth the effort. The flavour of pineapple lends itself beautifully to all kinds of sweet and savoury dishes, but particularly pork and chicken. Freeze it in made-up dishes, or freeze it without sugar (as described below). Fresh pineapple juice has tenderizing qualities if used in a marinade for meat. Using pineapple juice in made-up dishes which are to be frozen is therefore a good idea.

Selecting for freezing: Freeze only ripe fruit, that is when the skin smells fragrantly sweet and is orange in colour with a slightly green tinge; if it is very orange it may have gone past its best. A good test of suitability for freezing (and eating) is to pull out one of the centre leaves from the crown – if it will come out quite easily then the fruit is just ready. Any pineapple that is too ripe and soft can be crushed (see below) for use in made-up desserts such as mousses, ice creams, sorbets, etc.

Preparation for freezing: Whole pineapples do not freeze successfully; they also take up less space in the freezer if the flesh is cut into rings or chunks, or is crushed. To peel a pineapple, first cut off its crown, then cut a 1.5 cm/½ inch slice from each end. Stand the fruit upright on a chopping board then, working from top to bottom, cut off the skin in strips, using a very sharp knife and a sawing action. Turn the fruit round as you work. When all the skin has been removed, turn the fruit on its side and use the point of the knife to gouge out the prickly 'eyes'. Work downwards, following the line of the strips.

Slice the fruit crossways into rings, then cut out the tough central cores. Leave as whole rings or cut into chunks, as wished. Crush pineapple by working it in an electric blender or food processor for a few seconds (with or without sugar, according to future use) – this is the best use for overripe pineapple or any pieces and juice leftover from slicing.

To freeze: *Pineapple rings:* These can be frozen in dry packs. Simply pack together in rigid containers, separating each ring with an interleaving sheet, grease-proof or cling film. Seal, label and freeze for up to 12 months.

Pineapple chunks: These can be frozen in dry sugar or syrup packs.

Dry sugar pack: Pack in usable quantities in rigid containers, sprinkling each layer with sugar and allowing 125 g/4 oz sugar for every 500 g/1 lb fruit. Seal, label and freeze for up to 12 months.

Sugar syrup pack: Pack in usable quantities in rigid containers and cover with a light sugar syrup made from 250 g/8 oz sugar to 600 ml/1 pint water. Leave 2 cm/¾ inch headspace, seal, label and freeze for up to 12 months.

Crushed pineapple: Pack in rigid containers, seal, label and freeze for up to 12 months.

To thaw and serve: Leave whole rings, chunks and crushed pineapple to stand in containers at room temperature for 3 hours. Use rings and unsweetened crushed pineapple as for fresh pineapple, in both sweet and savoury dishes – particularly the sweet-and-sour sauces of Chinese cooking. Use thawed sweetened pineapple in desserts and baking.

PHEASANT SOUP

Use the carcass of a pheasant left over from a roast for this soup, with the giblets for extra flavour, if available. Duck soup can be made in exactly the same way.

50 g/2 oz butter
125 g/4 oz back bacon, rinds removed, diced
250 g/8 oz chicken livers, trimmed and roughly chopped
2 onions, peeled and chopped
4 celery sticks, chopped
6 carrots, peeled and chopped
2 chicken pieces, total weight about 350 g/12 oz
1 pheasant carcass
1.2 litres/2 pints well-flavoured chicken stock
300 ml/½ pint dry red wine
1 bouquet garni
pinch of ground mace
salt and freshly ground black pepper
TO SERVE
4 tablespoons dry sherry
150 ml/¼ pint double cream
croûtons (see opposite page)

Melt the butter in a large pan, add the bacon and fry for 5 minutes until golden brown. Add the chicken livers, onions, celery and carrots and fry for a further 5 minutes, stirring frequently. Add the chicken pieces, pheasant carcass, stock, wine, bouquet garni, mace and salt and pepper to taste and bring to the boil. Lower the heat, cover and simmer for 2 hours.

Strain off the liquid from the soup into a bowl. Remove all skin, bones and cartilage from the chicken and pheasant and discard. Cut the meat into small pieces, add to the liquid with the bacon, liver and vegetables, then work to a purée in an electric blender or food processor. Leave to cool, then chill in the refrigerator until the fat has solidified on the surface of the soup. Lift off the fat and discard.

To freeze: Pour the soup into a rigid container leaving 2 cm/¾ inch headspace, seal, label and freeze for up to 3 months.

To thaw and serve: Leave to stand in container in the refrigerator overnight, or reheat from frozen in a heavy-based pan, stirring frequently to prevent sticking. Bring to the boil and simmer for 5 minutes, then stir in the sherry and boil rapidly for 1 minute. Remove from the heat, stir in the cream; taste and adjust the seasoning. Serve immediately, garnished with croûtons.

Serves 6 to 8

CURRIED ARTICHOKE SOUP

Jerusalem artichokes are in abundance in winter and therefore inexpensive. Parsnips can be used as an alternative, but they will give a stronger flavour. Croûtons can be served with this soup.

50 g/2 oz butter
2 large onions, peeled and finely chopped
1 garlic clove, peeled and crushed
1–2 teaspoons curry powder
25 g/1 oz plain flour
900 ml/1½ pints well-flavoured chicken stock
750 g/1½ lb Jerusalem artichokes, peeled and diced
½ teaspoon ground turmeric
salt and freshly ground black pepper
TO SERVE
1–2 teaspoons coriander seeds
150 ml/¼ pint double cream
2 tablespoons snipped chives

Melt the butter in a pan, add the onions and fry gently for 10 minutes until golden brown. Add the garlic and fry for a further 2 minutes. Stir in the curry powder, lower the heat and fry for 2 minutes, taking care that

the curry powder does not become brown.

Add the flour and cook for 2 minutes, stirring all the time. Gradually stir in the stock, bring to the boil, then lower the heat and add the artichokes, turmeric and plenty of salt and pepper. Cover and simmer for 20 to 25 minutes until the vegetables are soft.

Leave to cool slightly, then work to a purée in an electric blender or food processor. Cool completely.

To freeze: Pour the soup into a rigid container, leaving 2 cm/¾ inch headspace, then seal, label and freeze for up to 5 months.

To thaw and serve: Leave to stand in container in the refrigerator overnight or reheat gently from frozen in a heavy-based pan, stirring frequently to prevent sticking. Bring to the boil and simmer for 5 minutes. Stir in the coriander seeds and cream. Simmer for a further 1 minute, then pour into a warmed soup tureen or 6 individual bowls. Serve immediately, sprinkled with chives.

Serves 6

CROÛTONS

Cut bread into 5 mm–1 cm (¼–½ inch) cubes, or use small pastry cutters to make fancy shapes. Fry them in a little butter until crisp and golden all over.

Pheasant Soup; Mussel Soup; Curried Artichoke Soup

RAVIOLI BOLOGNESE

Pasta is easy to make, and freezes well, so make a large quantity and freeze in 500 g/1 lb amounts for tagliatelle and other dishes.

BOLOGNESE SAUCE
1 tablespoon olive oil
1 large onion, peeled and finely chopped
2 garlic cloves, peeled and crushed
350 g/12 oz lean ground beef
125 g/4 oz chicken livers, trimmed and diced
1 × 397 g/14 oz can tomatoes
150 ml/¼ pint dry red wine
1 tablespoon tomato purée
1 teaspoon each dried basil, oregano and marjoram
salt and freshly ground black pepper
PASTA
350 g/12 oz plain flour
4½ teaspoons salt
3 eggs, size 3–4
4 tablespoons olive oil
RAVIOLI FILLING
50 g/2 oz Gruyère cheese, grated
40 g/1½ oz lean ham, very finely chopped
25 g/1 oz Parmesan cheese, freshly grated
1 tablespoon chopped parsley
1 tablespoon olive oil
a little beaten egg
TO SERVE
freshly grated Parmesan cheese

Make the Bolognese sauce: Heat the oil in a pan, add the onion and garlic and fry gently for 5 minutes without browning. Increase the heat, add the beef and quickly brown well, then add the chicken livers and cook, stirring, for 2 minutes.

Add the tomatoes and their juice, the wine, tomato purée, herbs and salt and pepper to taste. Bring to the boil, lower the heat, cover and simmer for 45 minutes, stirring occasionally. Remove lid, increase the heat and boil vigorously for 5 to 7 minutes, until reduced.

Make the pasta: Sift the flour and 1½ teaspoons salt into a large bowl. Make a well in the centre, then add the eggs and add 1 tablespoon oil. Draw the flour gradually into the egg mixture. Knead well to give a firm elastic dough, adding a little water if it seems dry. Wrap in cling film and chill in the refrigerator for 40 minutes.

Make the ravioli filling: Cream together all of the ingredients until well mixed.

Divide the pasta in half; wrap one half again to prevent it drying out. Roll out the other half on a floured surface to a thin rectangle. Place heaped teaspoonfuls of the filling over the dough, spacing them at regular 5 cm/2 inch intervals. Roll out the remaining dough to a rectangle the same size. Brush all over with water, then place loosely over the filling, dampened side downwards. Press the pasta between the filling to seal, then using a pastry wheel, cut to make small squares of ravioli. Arrange the ravioli in a single layer on a floured surface and leave to dry for about 1 hour.

Add the remaining salt and oil to a large pan of boiling water. Add the ravioli and simmer for 5 to 7 minutes, or until they rise to the surface. Drain well and add to the Bolognese sauce. Cool quickly.

To freeze: Pack the ravioli and sauce in a rigid container, seal, label and freeze for up to 3 months.

To thaw and serve: Leave to stand in container at room temperature for 4 hours. Transfer to a pan and reheat very gently until bubbling, stirring carefully occasionally. Serve immediately, with Parmesan.

Serves 6

MUSSEL SOUP

Always use very fresh mussels, not frozen or canned ones for this tasty soup.

1 kg/2 lb fresh mussels, scrubbed, with beards removed
300 ml/½ pint dry white wine
6 shallots, peeled and chopped
4 garlic cloves, peeled and thinly sliced
1 tablespoon olive oil
3 leeks (white part only), thinly sliced
about 600 ml/1 pint water
2 tablespoons Patna rice
4 tomatoes, skinned, seeded and chopped
1 bouquet garni
salt and freshly ground black pepper
TO SERVE
3 tablespoons chopped parsley

Put the mussels (discarding any that are open), into a wide-based pan with the wine, shallots and half the garlic. Cover and cook until the shells open, discarding any that do not open. Remove the mussels with a slotted spoon and shell them. Strain the liquid through a muslin-lined sieve set over a measuring jug.

Heat the olive oil in a pan, add the leeks and remaining garlic and fry gently for 5 minutes without browning. Make up the strained mussel liquid to 1 litre/ 1¾ pints with water. Add to the leeks in the pan and bring to the boil, then add the rice and boil rapidly for 9 to 11 minutes, until the rice is tender.

Leave the soup to cool slightly, then work half to a purée in an electric blender or food processor. Stir the purée into the soup remaining in the pan, then add the tomatoes, bouquet garni and plenty of salt and pepper. Bring to the boil and simmer for 5 to 7 minutes, then discard the bouquet garni and stir in the shelled mussels. Simmer for a further 5 minutes, then remove from the heat and cool quickly.

To freeze: Pour the soup into a rigid container, leaving 2 cm/¾ inch headspace. Seal, label and freeze for up to 2 months.

To thaw and serve: Leave to stand in container in the refrigerator overnight, or reheat gently from frozen in a heavy-based pan, stirring frequently. Bring to the boil and simmer for 5 minutes, then stir in the parsley. Serve immediately, with French bread.

Serves 6 to 8

SCALLOPS AU GRATIN

Peeled Dublin Bay prawns can be used in place of the scallops if preferred, but this will make the dish more expensive.

450 ml/¾ pint dry white wine
1 onion, peeled and finely chopped
1 slice lemon peel
1 bouquet garni
6–8 large or 12–16 small scallops
250 g/8 oz small button mushrooms, trimmed
25 g/1 oz butter
25 g/1 oz plain flour
2 tablespoons sherry
150 ml/¼ pint double cream
1 tablespoon chopped parsley
salt and freshly ground black pepper
TOPPING
50 g/2 oz fresh breadcrumbs
2 tablespoons freshly grated Parmesan cheese
TO SERVE
25 g/1 oz butter
lemon or lime slices
fresh dill or parsley sprigs

Put the wine, onion, lemon peel and bouquet garni in a pan and bring to the boil. Cook rapidly until the liquid has reduced by at least half, then lower the heat and add the scallops and mushrooms. Simmer gently for 5 minutes.

Remove the scallops and mushrooms with a slotted spoon and drain on kitchen paper. Blend the butter and flour together to make a smooth paste (beurre manié), then whisk into the liquid in the pan a little at a time. Bring to the boil and simmer, stirring, until thickened. Add the sherry and cream, parsley and plenty of salt and pepper. Simmer until the sauce is thick and smooth, then stir in the scallops and mushrooms.

Divide the mixture equally between 6 to 8 individual dishes, mix together the breadcrumbs and Parmesan cheese and sprinkle over the top. Leave to cool.

To freeze: Cover the dishes with foil, then pack in polythene bags. Seal, label and freeze for up to 2 months.

To thaw and serve: Unwrap and leave to stand at room temperature for 2 to 3 hours. Dot with the butter and place under a preheated moderate grill for 8 to 10 minutes until heated through and golden brown. Serve hot, garnished with lemon or lime slices and dill or parsley sprigs.
Serves 6 to 8

GREEK PRAWNS

This recipe comes from the island of Crete. It is delicious served with sesame bread and chilled dry white wine.

1 tablespoon olive oil
1 onion, peeled and finely chopped
1 garlic clove, peeled and crushed
1 × 397 g/14 oz can tomatoes
150 ml/¼ pint dry white wine
1 teaspoon dried oregano
1 teaspoon dried marjoram
1 teaspoon dried mixed herbs
salt and freshly ground black pepper
6 saffron strands, soaked in 3 tablespoons boiling water for 20 minutes
2 tablespoons tomato purée
1 tablespoon Worcestershire sauce
large dash of Tabasco sauce
350 g/12 oz peeled prawns
TO SERVE
125 g/4 oz Gruyère cheese, grated
2 tablespoons freshly grated Parmesan cheese
1 lemon, sliced
6 whole prawns (optional)

Heat the oil in a pan, add the onion and garlic and fry gently for 5 to 7 minutes until lightly browned. Add the tomatoes and their juice, the wine, herbs and salt and pepper to taste. Bring to the boil and simmer, uncovered, for 20 to 25 minutes, until the sauce is thick, stirring occasionally.

Strain the liquid from the saffron into the pan and add the tomato purée, Worcestershire sauce and Tabasco; simmer for a further 5 minutes. Remove from the heat and stir in the prawns.

To freeze: Pour the prawn mixture into a rigid container, leaving 2 cm/¾ inch headspace. Cool quickly, then seal, label and freeze for up to 3 months.

To thaw and serve: Leave to stand in container in the refrigerator overnight, or at room temperature for 4 hours. Transfer to a pan and reheat gently for 7 to 10 minutes. Stir in the cheeses, then taste and adjust the seasoning. Spoon into 6 warmed individual serving dishes and garnish with lemon slices and prawns if using. Serve immediately.

Serves 6

POTTED STILTON

This is a traditional English recipe, which can be served on its own with hot buttered toast, or used as a stuffing for halved, peeled pears. As an alternative to Stilton, use Farmhouse Cheddar or Cheshire. If you have a food processor, the mixture can be made in minutes.

250 g/8 oz unsalted butter
125 g/4 oz creamy Stilton cheese, crumbled
250 ml/8 fl oz cream sherry or port
1 teaspoon Worcestershire sauce
pinch of cayenne pepper
dash of Tabasco sauce
rosemary sprigs
TO SERVE
hot buttered toast

Clarify half the butter: Put 125 g/4 oz butter in a pan and heat gently until it has melted. Strain the butter through a muslin-lined sieve set over a bowl.

Put the remaining butter in a bowl with the Stilton, sherry, Worcestershire sauce, cayenne and Tabasco. Beat well until the mixture is smooth and creamy, then press the mixture into 1 large dish or 4 to 6 individual dishes. Level the surface of the mixture and arrange rosemary sprigs on top. Pour over the clarified butter, then chill in the refrigerator until the butter has set.

To freeze: Cover the dish(es) with foil, then pack in polythene bag(s). Seal, label and freeze for up to 2 months.

To thaw and serve: Leave to stand in wrappings in the refrigerator overnight, or at room temperature for 3 to 4 hours. Unwrap and serve cold, with toast.

Serves 4 to 6

LEFT: Scallops au Gratin; Greek Prawns
RIGHT: Potted Stilton; Chilled Citrus Appetizer

CHILLED CITRUS APPETIZER

Any selection of citrus fruits may be used, according to taste and availability. Clementine segments can be used instead of kumquats for example.

250 g/8 oz granulated sugar
600 ml/1 pint water
juice of 1 lemon
3 large grapefruit
4 large oranges
4 large limes
125 g/4 oz kumquats, thinly sliced
TO SERVE
50 g/2 oz flaked almonds, toasted
50 g/2 oz pine nuts, toasted
crushed ice
fresh mint leaves

Put the sugar and water into a pan with the lemon juice. Heat gently until the sugar has dissolved, stirring constantly. Bring slowly to the boil, then simmer for 5 minutes. Remove from the heat and leave until cold.

Thinly pare the rind of 1 grapefruit, 1 orange and 2 limes. Cut into thin julienne strips, then blanch in boiling water for 5 minutes. Drain and cool.

Remove all the pith from these fruits, and the rind and pith from the remaining grapefruits, oranges and limes. Carefully cut the fruit into segments, squeezing any juice from the membrane. Mix with the kumquats in a rigid container. Pour over the sugar syrup, leaving 2 cm/¾ inch headspace, then add the julienne strips.

To freeze: Cover the container with the lid, seal, label and freeze for up to 3 months.

To thaw and serve: Leave to stand in container in the refrigerator overnight. Spoon into 6 individual dishes, top with the nuts, then surround the dishes with crushed ice. Garnish with mint and serve immediately.

Serves 6

WEST COUNTRY COD

Fresh cod gets an extra boost with an accompanying sweet apple and cider sauce. Serve with green beans and sauté potatoes.

4 cod steaks or cutlets, each 175–250 g/6–8 oz
300 ml/½ pint sweet cider
25 g/1 oz butter
salt and freshly ground black pepper
2 dessert apples
4 cloves
½ teaspoon paprika
1 tablespoon potato flour (fécule)
2 tablespoons cold water

Put the cod in a pan with the cider and butter and bring to the boil. Lower the heat and simmer gently for 8 to 10 minutes, until the fish is barely cooked. Remove the cod from the liquid with a fish slice and place in a single layer in a foil container. Sprinkle with salt and pepper.

Peel, halve and core the apples, then push 1 clove into the end of each half. Put the apples into the cider in the pan and poach gently until barely cooked. Lift out with a slotted spoon. With a sharp knife, make a series of cuts through the apples, leaving the end where the cloves are intact. Press with the hand to open the apples up like fans, then place 1 apple half on each piece of fish.

Boil the liquid in the pan until it is reduced by half. Mix the paprika and potato flour to a smooth paste with the water, then stir into the sauce. Cook, stirring until thickened, then pour around the fish. Cool quickly.
To freeze: Cover the container with the lid, seal, label and freeze for up to 3 months.
To thaw and serve: Leave to stand in container at room temperature for 2 hours. Remove the lid, then reheat in a preheated moderately hot oven (190°C/375°F/Gas Mark 5) for 30 minutes, basting once.
Serves 4

CURRIED SCALLOPS WITH SALSIFY

Scallops, one of winter's treats, combine well with salsify in a gently curried sauce. Serve with boiled rice and a green vegetable.

2 large carrots, peeled
175 g/6 oz salsify, peeled and cut into 5 cm/2 inch lengths
3 tablespoons plain flour
¾ teaspoon curry powder
salt and freshly ground black pepper
12 large scallops
4 tablespoons vegetable oil
300 ml/½ pint medium white wine
2 tablespoons double cream

Cook the carrots and salsify together in boiling water until just tender. Drain and leave to cool. Scoop the carrots into balls using a melon baller, or cut into small cubes.

Mix the flour and curry powder together with salt and pepper and use to coat the scallops; reserve any leftover flour. Heat the oil in a frying pan, add the scallops and fry for 1 minute on each side. Remove with a slotted spoon and transfer to a foil container.

Mix any leftover flour to a smooth paste with a little of the wine. Add to the pan with the remaining wine. Stir to dissolve the juices and sediment in the pan, then bring to the boil. Simmer, stirring, until the sauce thickens a little. Add any juice from the scallops in the container. Remove from the heat, add the carrots and salsify, then leave to cool a little. Stir in the cream, pour over the scallops and cool completely.
To freeze: Cover the container with the lid, seal, label and freeze for up to 1 month.
To thaw and serve: Leave to stand in container at room temperature for 2 hours, then put the container into a large pan and pour in enough boiling water to come one third up the sides of the container. Remove the foil lid, cover the pan and simmer for about 30 minutes, basting the scallops with the sauce once or twice. Serve hot.
Serves 4

CITRUS SKATE WITH PEPPERS

Oranges and peppers give interest to this variation upon the 'beurre noisette' theme, so traditional with skate.

4 pieces of skate, each 250–300 g/8–10 oz, skinned
300 ml/½ pint medium white wine
150 ml/¼ pint water
1 bay leaf
4 parsley stalks
salt and freshly ground black pepper
1 small yellow pepper, cored, seeded and cut into rings
1 small red pepper, cored, seeded and cut into rings
pared rind of 1 orange, cut into thin strips
juice of 1 orange
50 g/2 oz butter
TO SERVE
1 tablespoon chopped parsley

Put the skate into a pan with the wine, water, bay leaf, parsley stalks and salt and pepper to taste. Bring to the boil, then lower the heat and simmer gently for 12 to 15 minutes, until the fish is barely cooked. Remove the skate from the liquid with a fish slice and place in a foil container.

Discard the bay leaf and parsley stalks from the liquid in the pan. Add the pepper rings and strips of orange rind, bring to the boil and boil for 2 minutes. Remove the pepper and orange rind with a slotted spoon and sprinkle over the fish in the container. Pour off two thirds of the liquid in the pan; boil the remain-

ing third rapidly until it is reduced to 1 tablespoon. Remove from the heat and stir in the orange juice.

Melt the butter in a separate pan and heat until it turns golden brown. Immediately add the orange juice mixture with salt and pepper to taste. Cool a little, then pour over the skate. Cool completely.
To freeze: Cover the container with the lid, seal, label and freeze for up to 2 months.
To thaw and serve: Remove the lid, then reheat from frozen in a preheated moderately hot oven (190°C/375°F/Gas Mark 5) for 30 minutes, basting once or twice. Serve hot, garnished with chopped parsley.
Serves 4

HERBED SMELTS WITH CUCUMBER SAUCE

If you are lucky enough to find these delicate fish during their capricious season, it is worth freezing some for a later treat. Their delicate taste is complemented beautifully by the herbs and cucumber.

4 tablespoons chopped parsley
2 tablespoons snipped chives
8 tablespoons plain flour
salt and freshly ground black pepper
6 tablespoons milk
750 g/1 ½ lb smelts, cleaned
75 g/3 oz butter
2 tablespoons vegetable oil
1 small cucumber, peeled, seeded and cut into 1 cm/½ inch lengths
300 ml/½ pint dry white wine
2 × 142 ml/5 fl oz cartons soured cream

Mix the parsley, chives and flour together on a large flat plate with salt and pepper to taste. Pour the milk into a shallow bowl. Turn each smelt in the milk, then in the flour mixture until evenly coated.

Heat 50 g/2 oz butter and the oil in a frying pan, add the smelts a few at a time and fry for 1 minute on each side. Remove with a slotted spoon, drain on kitchen paper, then put in a foil container and cool quickly.

To make the sauce, melt the remaining butter in a clean pan, add the cucumber sticks and fry for about 30 seconds. Add the wine with salt and pepper to taste and bring to the boil. Remove from the heat, leave to cool slightly, then stir in the soured cream. Put into a separate foil container and cool quickly.
To freeze: Cover the containers with the lids, seal, label and freeze for up to 2 months.
To thaw and serve: Remove the lids and reheat both fish and sauce from frozen in a preheated hot oven (220°C/425°F/Gas Mark 7) for about 20 minutes. Separate the fish and stir the sauce, then reheat for a further 20 minutes. Serve hot.
Serves 4

Citrus Skate with Peppers; Herbed Smelts with Cucumber Sauce; Curried Scallops with Salsify

CHICKEN AND FENNEL SAUTÉ

Succulent pieces of chicken and fennel are
stir-fried together to make a tasty supper dish with
a Chinese flavour.

2 teaspoons cornflour
2 teaspoons sesame oil
1 tablespoon light soy sauce
1 teaspoon sugar
4 large chicken breasts, cut into 2.5 cm/1 inch squares
2 tablespoons soya oil
1 large head of fennel, sliced crosswise
1 garlic clove, sliced
60 ml/2 fl oz rice wine or dry sherry
1 tablespoon oyster sauce
1 tablespoon sesame seeds, toasted

Mix the cornflour, sesame oil, light soy sauce and sugar
together in a bowl until thoroughly blended. Add the
chicken and toss until evenly coated.

Heat the soya oil in a wok or a deep frying pan and
add the fennel and garlic. Stir-fry quickly over brisk
heat for 30 seconds. Remove from the pan. Increase
the heat, add the chicken to the pan and stir-fry for 1
to 2 minutes until tender. Replace the fennel and garlic,
add the wine or sherry and oyster sauce, and cook for
1 minute. Sprinkle with sesame seeds. Cool quickly.
To freeze: Transfer to a foil container, seal, label and
freeze for up to 2 months.
To thaw and serve: Leave to stand in container at
room temperature for 2 hours, then put the container
into a large pan and pour in enough boiling water to
come half way up the sides of the container. Remove
the foil lid, cover the pan and simmer for 15 to
20 minutes, stirring occasionally. Serve hot, with crisp
noodles or fried rice.
Serves 4

TURKEY ST. CLEMENTS

Oranges and lemons ring the changes in this dish using
cooked turkey or chicken. If you have poultry left over
at Christmas time, freeze it in this way to be eaten at a
later date.

625 g/1 1/4 lb boneless cooked turkey or chicken, cut
into 2.5 cm/1 inch cubes
2 teaspoons paprika
1/2 teaspoon salt
3 tablespoons olive oil
1 red pepper, cored, seeded and sliced
shredded rind and juice of 2 oranges
juice of 1 lemon
2 tablespoons honey
2 garlic cloves, peeled and crushed
25 g/1 oz flaked almonds (optional)
TO SERVE
2 tablespoons dark rum

Sprinkle the turkey with the paprika and salt. Heat the
oil in a flameproof casserole, add the turkey and fry
over brisk heat until browned on all sides. Remove
from the pan with a slotted spoon and place in a rigid
container.

Add the pepper to the pan and fry gently until
barely tender. Add the orange rind and juice, the
lemon juice, honey, garlic and flaked almonds, if using.
Cook, stirring, over low heat for 2 to 3 minutes until a
sauce forms, then pour over the turkey in the
container. Cool quickly.
To freeze: Cover the container with its lid, seal, label
and freeze for up to 3 months.

To thaw and serve: Leave to stand in container at
room temperature for 2 hours, then transfer to an
ovenproof serving dish and reheat in a preheated
moderately hot oven (200°C/400°F/Gas Mark 6) for
12 to 15 minutes or until very hot.

Just before taking the dish to the table, warm the
rum in a ladle or small pan, remove from the heat and
ignite. Pour over the turkey and serve immediately,
while still flaming.
Serves 4

RIGHT: Landlord's Goose; Farmhouse Pheasant
LEFT: Chicken and Fennel Sauté; Turkey St. Clements

FARMHOUSE PHEASANT

Pheasant and celeriac is a classic winter combination. This dish will serve 2 or 4, depending on appetites.

500 g/1 lb celeriac
1 oven-ready pheasant, weighing 850 g/1¾ lb
25 g/1 oz butter, softened
6 tablespoons full-bodied red wine, made up to
  300 ml/½ pint with chicken stock
salt and freshly ground black pepper
TO SERVE
parsley sprigs

Peel and halve the celeriac, then cut into thin slices. Immediately put the slices into a bowl and pour in enough boiling water to cover. Leave for 2 minutes, then drain and put into a small roasting tin.

Wipe the pheasant inside and out, then spread the skin with the butter. Place on the celeriac, pour in half the wine and stock and sprinkle liberally with salt and pepper. Roast in a preheated moderately hot oven (200°C/400°F/Gas Mark 6) for 35 minutes or until the pheasant is almost tender, turning it after 20 minutes.

Remove the pheasant and cut it into quarters. Put the celeriac into a rigid container with any liquid from the pan. Arrange the pheasant on top and pour over the remaining wine and stock. Cool quickly.

To freeze: Cover the container with the lid, seal, label and freeze for up to 3 months.

To thaw and serve: Leave to stand in container at room temperature overnight. Replace celeriac in base of roasting tin with pheasant on top, then reheat in a preheated moderate oven (180°C/350°F/Gas Mark 4) for 50 minutes, basting once or twice. Serve hot, garnished with parsley.
Serves 2 or 4

LANDLORD'S GOOSE

Rich fare for the festive season: brandy-soaked prunes and pâté to give goose an extra-special savour. Make sure that each portion includes some pâté and prunes.

1 × 5 kg/11 lb oven-ready goose
salt and freshly ground black pepper
500 g/1 lb smooth-textured liver pâté
250 g/8 oz stoned prunes, soaked in 4 tablespoons
  brandy
TO SERVE
watercress sprigs

Wipe the goose inside and out, dry well and season with salt and pepper. Spread the pâté evenly over the inside of the bird with your fingers. Put 4 prunes in the neck cavity; space the others in the body. Pour in any remaining brandy.

Truss the goose, tying its wings under its body. Stand it on a rack in a roasting pan and cover the neck end with foil. Roast in a preheated moderately hot oven (200°C/400°F/Gas Mark 6) for 1 hour. Remove the goose from the oven and prick the skin so that the fat runs, taking care not to cut into the flesh. Pour off the liquid from the pan into a basin and chill.

Reduce the oven temperature to moderate (160°C/325°F/Gas Mark 3) and roast for a further hour or until the juices run clear when the thickest part of the thigh is pierced with a skewer. Cool quickly. Remove the fat from the juices and pour them over the goose.

To freeze: Wrap the goose in foil, then overwrap in a polythene bag. Seal, label and freeze for up to 2 months.

To thaw and serve: Remove polythene bag and leave goose to stand in its foil wrapping at room temperature overnight. Loosen the foil wrappings, then reheat in a preheated moderately hot oven (190°C/375°F/Gas Mark 5) for 1 to 1¼ hours until the bird is heated through, basting occasionally. Serve hot, garnished with watercress. Serve the pan juices separately.
Serves 8

BRASSERIE PANCAKES

Meat-stuffed pancakes in a creamy sauce are equally good for a quick lunch, dinner or late-night supper.

500 g/1 lb veal or lamb's kidneys, skinned and cored
1 tablespoon vegetable oil
125 g/4 oz mushrooms, sliced
150 ml/¼ pint plus 2 tablespoons Madeira
1¼ teaspoons Worcestershire sauce
1 bay leaf
salt and freshly ground black pepper
1 thick slice cooked ham, about 125 g/4 oz, diced
1 teaspoon potato flour (fécule)
150 ml/¼ pint single cream
PANCAKES
125 g/4 oz plain flour
pinch of salt
1 egg, beaten
300 ml/½ pint milk and water mixed
1 tablespoon vegetable oil
vegetable oil for frying

Cut the kidneys into very thin slices. Heat the oil in a pan, add the kidneys and fry over moderate heat until browned on all sides. Stir in the mushrooms, then 150 ml/¼ pint Madeira, ¼ teaspoon Worcestershire sauce, the bay leaf and salt and pepper to taste. Bring to the boil, then lower the heat, cover and simmer very gently for 10 minutes. Remove from the heat and leave to cool.

Drain off the juices from the kidney mixture and reserve. Mix the kidneys with the ham, reserving a few cubes of ham for the garnish. Mix the potato flour to a smooth paste with the cream in a heavy-based pan, then add the reserved kidney juices with the remaining Worcestershire sauce. Heat gently until the sauce thickens, stirring constantly, then remove from the heat and set aside.

Make the pancakes: Sift the flour and salt into a bowl, make a well in the centre, then add the egg. Add half of the milk and water mixture gradually, beating vigorously to incorporate the flour. Beat in the remaining milk and water, then the oil. Pour the batter into a jug.

Heat a few drops of oil in a 20 cm/8 inch pancake pan or frying pan until very hot. Pour in one eighth of the batter and swirl around the pan until the bottom is covered evenly. Cook until the underside is golden brown then turn the pancake over and cook for a further 10 to 15 seconds. Slide out onto a plate lined with greaseproof paper and cover with another sheet of greaseproof paper. Continue in this way to make 8 pancakes, stacking them between sheets of greaseproof as they are cooked.

Combine the kidney and mushroom filling with half of the sauce and divide between the pancakes. Roll up the pancakes, enclosing the filling and put 4 pancakes in each of 2 foil containers. Add the remaining Madeira to the remaining sauce and pour over the pancakes. Sprinkle the reserved ham over the top. Leave until completely cold.

To freeze: Cover the containers with their lids, seal, label and freeze for up to 2 months.

To thaw and serve: Place the containers on a baking sheet and loosen the lids. Reheat from frozen in a preheated moderately hot oven (200°C/400°F/Gas Mark 6) for 30 minutes. Remove the container lids and reheat for a further 5 minutes. Serve hot, with a crisp green salad.

Serves 4

VEAL CHOPS VIVANDIÈRE

This interesting veal dish is given its title *vivandière* because it contains gin amongst its ingredients – *vivandière* is the name French troops gave their liquor suppliers!
Homemade light veal stock is most suitable for this dish, but a very light chicken stock may be used instead.

15 g/½ oz butter
1 tablespoon olive oil
25 g/1 oz pine nuts
4 veal chops, total weight about 850 g/1¾ lb
2 tablespoons gin
2 shallots, peeled and sliced
300 ml/½ pint stock
salt and freshly ground black pepper
1½ teaspoons potato flour (fécule)
150 ml/¼ pint double cream

Heat the butter and oil in a flameproof casserole, add the pine nuts and fry gently until lightly browned.

Remove the nuts with a slotted spoon and drain on kitchen paper. Add the chops to the pan and fry, turning once, until browned on each side. Remove from the heat and drain off all excess fat.

Warm 1 tablespoon gin in a ladle or small pan, pour over the veal chops off the heat and ignite. When the flames have died down, return to the heat and add the shallots, stock and salt and pepper to taste. Bring to the boil, then lower the heat, cover and simmer for 20 minutes or until the chops are tender. Transfer the chops to a rigid container with a slotted spoon.

Boil the liquid in the pan rapidly until reduced to half its volume. Mix the potato flour to a smooth paste with the cream, stir into the pan and heat gently until the sauce thickens, stirring constantly. Remove from the heat, stir in the remaining gin, then pour over the chops in the container. Cool quickly, then sprinkle with the browned pine nuts.
To freeze: Cover the container with its lid, seal, label and freeze for up to 2 months.
To thaw and serve: Leave to stand in container at room temperature for 2 hours, then transfer to a saucepan, cover and reheat gently for 35 minutes or until heated through. Serve hot.
Serves 4

BEEF LAGERFELDT

Beef cooked in lager makes a sustaining casserole; perfect for cold weather appetites, or supper after a day outdoors.

850 g/1¾ lb piece of beef (blade, skirt or chuck) cut 2.5 cm/1 inch thick
¼ teaspoon freshly grated nutmeg
2 tablespoons olive oil
25 g/1 oz butter
125 g/4 oz flat mushrooms, stalks removed
250 g/8 oz button onions, peeled
1 sprig lovage or 1 bay leaf
450 ml/¾ pint lager
1 tablespoon tomato purée
juice and finely shredded rind of 1 lemon
salt and freshly ground black pepper

Cut the beef into strips, about 7.5 cm/3 inches long and 1 cm/½ inch wide. Sprinkle with nutmeg. Heat the oil and butter in a heavy-based frying pan until foaming, then fry the meat in batches until evenly browned on all sides.

Remove the meat from the pan with a slotted spoon. Add the mushrooms and onions to the pan and fry until evenly browned, turning the flat mushrooms carefully. Remove from the pan and set aside.

Return the beef and onions to the pan, then add the lovage or bay, lager, tomato purée, lemon juice and rind. Bring to the boil, then lower the heat, cover and simmer for 1½ hours or until the meat is tender. Discard the lemon rind and lovage or bay if desired. Cool quickly.

To freeze: Transfer the meat and sauce to a rigid container, arranging the sautéed mushrooms on top. Seal, label and freeze for up to 3 months.
To thaw and serve: Leave to stand in container at room temperature for 2 hours, then transfer carefully to a flameproof serving dish. Reheat gently, stirring occasionally, for 35 to 40 minutes or until very hot. Serve immediately with buttered macaroni, noodles or boiled rice.
Serves 4 to 6

ROMAN BEEF

The 'leg of mutton' used here is a boneless well-flavoured cut of beef from the thick rib.
This frequently neglected cut of beef is cooked to melting tenderness, scented with clove and bay. It is frozen in the piece, but cut into slices before serving. If wished, the cooking liquid can be thickened with beurre manié or potato flour (fécule).

1.2 kg/2¼ lb piece 'leg of mutton' cut of beef
12–15 cloves
¾ teaspoon ground bay leaves
salt and freshly ground black pepper
1 tablespoon olive oil
300 ml/½ pint full-bodied red wine
450 ml/¾ pint beef stock
TO SERVE
chopped parsley

Stud the beef with the cloves and rub it all over with the ground bay leaves and salt and pepper. If necessary, tie into shape. Heat the oil in a large frying pan, add the beef and fry over brisk heat, turning until evenly browned on all sides. Transfer the beef to a flameproof casserole just large enough to hold it. Pour in the red wine.

Pour the stock into the frying pan and scrape up the sediment to deglaze, then pour over the beef. Bring to the boil, then lower the heat, cover and simmer for 1½ hours or until the beef is tender. Remove from the heat and cool quickly.

To freeze: Transfer the meat and liquid to a rigid container. Seal, label and freeze for up to 3 months.
To thaw and serve: Leave to stand in container at room temperature overnight, then reheat gently in a covered pan on top of the stove for about 35 minutes or until the beef is heated through. Remove the meat from the liquid and slice thinly. Arrange the slices on a warmed serving platter and pour over a little of the liquid. Sprinkle the beef with chopped parsley and serve immediately, with the remaining cooking liquid handed separately.
Serves 6

Beef Lagerfeldt; Veal Chops Vivandière; Roman Beef

SINGAPORE SPARERIBS

Spareribs with the distinctive taste of aniseed and the sharpness of fruit freeze well. Serve in bowls garnished with spring onion fans.

1 medium onion, peeled and chopped
1 garlic clove, peeled and chopped
3 tablespoons wine vinegar
1 tablespoon soy sauce
1 teaspoon sesame oil
¼ teaspoon aniseed or 5-spice powder
450 ml/¾ pint water
1.5 kg/3 lb Chinese- or American-style pork spareribs
1 medium mango, peeled and diced
1 small pineapple, peeled, cored and cut into 2.5 cm/
    1 inch fingers

Combine the onion, garlic, vinegar, soy sauce, oil, spice and water in a large pan, then add the spareribs. Bring to the boil, lower the heat, cover and simmer for 1 hour or until the spareribs are tender, turning them after 30 minutes.

Remove the pork from the pan, cut into separate ribs, then put into a rigid container. Boil the liquid in the pan until reduced to one third of its original volume. Taste for seasoning. Add the fruit and simmer for 2 to 3 minutes, then pour over the ribs. Cool quickly.

To freeze: Cover the container with the lid, seal, label and freeze for up to 3 months.

To thaw and serve: Leave to stand in container at room temperature for 2 hours. Transfer to a roasting pan and reheat in a preheated moderately hot oven (200°C/400°F/Gas Mark 6) for 50 minutes, making sure the ribs have separated and basting after 25 minutes. Serve hot.

Serves 4

LAMB AND BARLEY STEW

Barley and dried fruit add a creamy texture to this tasty lamb dish. Like many stews, it seems to improve in flavour after freezing and reheating.

1 tablespoon olive oil
850 g/1¾ lb boned shoulder of lamb, cut into 5 cm/
    2 inch cubes
25 g/1 oz pearl barley, soaked in cold water for
    2 hours
50 g/2 oz unsoaked dried apricots
few parsley stalks
25 g/1 oz sultanas
1 onion, peeled and sliced
1 garlic clove, peeled and crushed
450 ml/¾ pint light stock
1 tablespoon lemon juice
salt and freshly ground black pepper
TO SERVE
chopped parsley

Heat the oil in a frying pan, add the lamb in batches and fry until browned on all sides. Transfer to a flameproof casserole with a slotted spoon. Drain the pearl barley and add to the casserole, with the apricots, parsley stalks and sultanas.

Add the onion and garlic to the fat remaining in the frying pan and fry gently for 5 minutes without browning. Stir in the stock, lemon juice and salt and pepper to taste and bring to the boil, then pour over the lamb.

Place the casserole over a moderate heat and bring to the boil. Lower the heat, cover and simmer for 1 hour or until the lamb is tender, stirring occasionally. Remove from the heat and cool quickly.

To freeze: Transfer the stew to a rigid container, seal, label and freeze for up to 3 months.

To thaw and serve: Leave to stand in container at room temperature for 2 hours, then reheat gently in a covered pan on top of the stove for 45 minutes or until hot. Taste and adjust seasoning, then sprinkle with chopped parsley and serve hot.

Serves 4

PORK AND CABBAGE POTÉE

This half soup, half stew, from France will enliven any wintry evening. Serve with hot crusty bread.

1 bouquet garni
125 g/4 oz peeled chestnuts
850 g/1¾ lb boned pork shoulder, weighed after fat
    trimmed
1 large potato, peeled and quartered
2 medium onions, peeled and quartered
4 medium carrots, peeled
1 tablespoon tomato purée
2 tablespoons white wine vinegar
600 ml/1 pint light stock
salt and freshly ground black pepper
2 bay leaves
250 g/8 oz red cabbage, thinly sliced
TO SERVE
175 g/6 oz black pudding, skinned and sliced (optional)

Put the bouquet garni, chestnuts, pork, potato, onions, carrots, tomato purée, wine vinegar, stock, plenty of salt and pepper and the bay leaves into a large flameproof casserole. Bring to the boil, lower the heat, cover and simmer for 1½ hours or until the pork is tender.

Add the cabbage, increase the heat and cook for a further 5 minutes. Remove from the heat and cool quickly.

To freeze: Transfer to a rigid container, seal, label and freeze for up to 3 months.

To thaw and serve: Leave to stand in container at room temperature overnight, then reheat gently in a covered pan on top of the stove for 40 minutes or until hot. Add the black pudding, if using, and simmer for a further 5 minutes. Cut the pork into thick slices before serving.

Serves 4

BACHELOR'S FLAN

This is a useful savoury flan to keep as a standby in the freezer.

PASTRY
125 g/4 oz plain flour
pinch of salt
50 g/2 oz butter
25 g/1 oz grated Parmesan cheese
about 1 tablespoon iced water
FILLING
1 teaspoon vegetable oil
250 g/8 oz pork chipolata sausages
125 g/4 oz back bacon, rinds removed, chopped
1 medium onion, peeled and sliced
125 g/4 oz potato, peeled and cut into 1 cm/½ inch
*   cubes*
freshly ground black pepper
250 g/8 oz boneless cooked chicken, shredded
2 eggs
1 egg yolk
150 ml/¼ pint double cream

Make the pastry: Sift the flour and salt into a bowl. Rub in the butter until the mixture resembles fine breadcrumbs. Stir in the Parmesan cheese and enough water to mix to a fairly stiff dough. Turn the dough onto a floured surface, knead lightly until smooth, then roll out and use to line a 20 cm/8 inch loose-based flan tin or flan ring placed on a baking sheet. Chill in the refrigerator for 30 minutes.

For the filling: Heat the oil in a frying pan, add the sausages and fry until cooked. Remove from the pan with a slotted spoon and drain on kitchen paper. Add the bacon to the pan, fry until cooked, then remove and drain on kitchen paper. Add the onion and fry for 5 minutes without browning, then remove and drain. Add the potato, sprinkle with ½ teaspoon salt, increase the heat and fry until brown and crisp. Drain on kitchen paper.

Put the potato in the pastry case. Cover with the sausages, bacon and onion. Sprinkle the chicken over the top. Mix the eggs, egg yolk and cream together with salt and pepper to taste and pour into the flan. Cover with foil, then bake in a preheated moderately hot oven (200°C/400°F/Gas Mark 6) for 20 minutes. Remove the foil and bake for a further 5 minutes until the filling is golden brown and just set. Leave to cool.

To freeze: Open freeze the flan until solid, then remove carefully from the flan tin and wrap in foil. Seal, label and return to the freezer for up to 1 month.

To thaw and serve: Unwrap and place on a baking sheet. Reheat from frozen in a preheated moderate oven (180°C/350°F/Gas Mark 4) for about 1 hour. Serve hot.

Serves 4

ABOVE: Pork and Cabbage Potée; Lamb and Barley Stew
OPPOSITE: Singapore Spareribs

SALSIFY AU GRATIN

This dish makes an unusual accompaniment to roast and grilled meats. As an alternative, black-skinned scorzonera may be used instead of salsify. It has white flesh, like salsify, and its flavour is almost identical.

1.25 kg/2½ lb salsify
juice of 1 lemon
salt
SAUCE
40 g/1½ oz butter
1 onion, peeled and finely chopped
40 g/1½ oz plain flour
450 ml/¾ pint milk
125 g/4 oz mature Cheddar cheese, grated
2 tablespoons freshly grated Parmesan cheese
1 teaspoon French mustard
4 tablespoons double cream
2 egg yolks
freshly ground white pepper
TOPPING
3 tablespoons dried white breadcrumbs
25 g/1 oz Gruyère cheese, grated
TO SERVE
25 g/1 oz butter
50 g/2 oz button mushrooms, trimmed

Scrape the skins from the salsify, then cut the flesh into 5 cm/2 inch lengths. Drop these immediately into a pan of cold water to which the lemon juice has been added, to prevent discoloration. Add salt, bring to the boil and cook for 12 to 15 minutes, until just tender.
Make the sauce: Melt the butter in a pan, add the onion and fry gently for 5 minutes without browning. Add the flour and cook for a further 2 minutes, stirring all the time. Gradually stir in the milk, bring to the boil, then lower the heat and simmer for 2 minutes, stirring constantly. Add the Cheddar and Parmesan cheeses and the mustard. Blend the cream and egg yolks together in a bowl, stir in a little of the hot sauce, then stir back into the sauce in the pan. Cook for 1 minute without boiling, then remove from the heat and season with pepper to taste.

Drain the salsify well, then fold into the sauce. Spoon the mixture into a lightly greased foil container or ovenproof dish. Leave to cool.
For the topping: Combine the breadcrumbs and Gruyère cheese and sprinkle over the salsify.
To freeze: Cover the container or dish with the lid or foil, then seal, label and freeze for up to 3 months.
To thaw and serve: Remove the lid or foil and leave to stand in container at room temperature for 4 hours. Bake in a preheated moderately hot oven (200°C/400°F/Gas Mark 6) for 30 minutes, until bubbling and golden brown.

Meanwhile, prepare the garnish. Melt the butter in a pan, add the mushrooms and fry gently until just tender. Arrange the mushrooms at each end of the dish and serve immediately.
Serves 4 to 6

BRAISED CELERY WITH SHERRY

This tasty celery dish is an excellent accompaniment for roast or grilled meat, and casseroles.

25 g/1 oz butter
1 small onion, peeled and finely chopped
1 garlic clove, peeled and crushed (optional)
2 heads celery, trimmed, quartered and cut into
    13 cm/5 inch lengths
1 × 425 g/15 oz can consommé
150 ml/¼ pint dry sherry
1 bouquet garni
salt and freshly ground black pepper
15 g/½ oz butter, softened
15 g/½ oz plain flour
TO SERVE
1 tablespoon snipped chives or chopped parsley

Melt the butter in a pan, add the onion and cook for 8 to 10 minutes until lightly browned. Stir in the garlic, then place the celery on top and pour over the consommé and sherry. Add the bouquet garni and salt and pepper to taste. Bring to the boil, then lower the heat, cover and simmer for 40 minutes, until the celery is just tender.

Remove the celery from the pan, using a slotted spoon, and discard the bouquet garni. Put the celery in a rigid container. Work the butter and flour together to a smooth paste (beurre manié). Bring the liquid in the pan to the boil, then add the beurre manié a little at a time. Cook for 1 to 2 minutes, whisking vigorously until the sauce has thickened. Spoon the sauce over the celery.
To freeze: Cool quickly, then cover the container with the lid. Seal, label and freeze for up to 3 months.
To thaw and serve: Leave to stand in container in the refrigerator overnight, or at room temperature for 2 to 3 hours, then transfer the mixture to a pan and reheat gently until hot. Taste and adjust the seasoning, then serve immediately, sprinkled with the chives or chopped parsley.
Serves 4 to 6

BRAISED RED CABBAGE WITH CHESTNUTS

This piquant dish is a delicious accompaniment to roast poultry, pork and gammon.

I tablespoon olive oil
125 g/4 oz lean streaky bacon, rinds removed, chopped
2 large onions, peeled and sliced
I kg/2 lb red cabbage, trimmed and cut into I cm/ ½ inch slices
4 carrots, peeled and sliced
500 g/I lb Bramley or other tart cooking apples, peeled, cored and roughly chopped
2 garlic cloves, peeled and sliced
pinch of ground cloves
pinch of freshly grated nutmeg
salt and freshly ground black pepper
I bouquet garni
150 ml/¼ pint dry red wine
24 whole chestnuts, skinned
TO SERVE
150 ml/¼ pint well-flavoured beef stock
125 g/4 oz streaky bacon, rinds removed, crisply fried and crumbled

Heat the oil in a pan, add the bacon and onions and fry gently for 5 minutes without browning.

Arrange the cabbage, bacon and onions, carrots, apples and garlic, in layers in a deep ovenproof dish, seasoning each layer with cloves, nutmeg and salt and pepper to taste. Put the bouquet garni in the centre of the casserole, then pour over the wine.

Cover and cook in a preheated moderate oven (160°C/325°F/Gas Mark 3) for I hour. Remove from the oven and stir in the chestnuts, cover and return to the oven for a further I to I ½ hours, until the vegetables are tender.

To freeze: Transfer the mixture to a rigid container, leaving 2 cm/¾ inch headspace. Cool quickly, then seal, label and freeze for up to 3 months.

To thaw and serve: Leave to stand in the refrigerator overnight, then transfer to a large pan and pour in the stock. Cover and heat gently, stirring occasionally, then remove the lid and boil rapidly until the stock has evaporated, stirring all the time to prevent sticking. Taste and adjust the seasoning, then spoon into a warmed serving dish. Serve immediately, topped with the crisply fried bacon.

Serves 4 to 6

TO SKIN CHESTNUTS

Place a few at a time in a pan of boiling water. Boil for 4 minutes then drain. Protecting your hand with a glove or cloth, and using a sharp knife, peel off the shell and furry inner skin while the chestnuts are still hot.

LEFT: Carrot Purée; Braised Celery and Sherry
RIGHT: Braised Red Cabbage with Chestnuts; Winter Cabbage and Apples

WINTER CABBAGE AND APPLES

For contrast, use green-skinned apples with red cabbage, red-skinned apples with white or green cabbage.

I tablespoon olive oil
I onion, peeled and finely chopped
I small firm cabbage, trimmed and cut into I cm/ ½ inch slices
4 red or green apples, cored and sliced
finely grated rind and juice of I lemon
I tablespoon soft brown sugar
salt and freshly ground black pepper
150 ml/¼ pint well-flavoured chicken stock
TO SERVE
25 g/I oz flaked almonds, lightly toasted

Heat the oil in a pan, add the onion and fry gently for 5 minutes without browning. Add the cabbage and mix well. Add the apples, lemon rind and juice and the sugar, and season well with salt and pepper. Pour over the stock and bring to the boil, then lower the heat, cover and simmer for 40 to 45 minutes, stirring occasionally.

To freeze: Transfer the mixture to a rigid container, leaving 2 cm/¾ inch headspace. Cool quickly, then seal, label and freeze for up to 3 months.

To thaw and serve: Leave to stand in container in the refrigerator overnight, or at room temperature for 2 to 3 hours. Transfer to a heavy-based pan and simmer gently for 5 to 7 minutes until very hot. Serve immediately, sprinkled with the toasted almonds.

Serves 4 to 6

CARROT PURÉE

This is a good method of cooking and serving old winter vegetables such as celeriac, turnips, Brussels sprouts and swedes, which can so often be woody.

Cook 2 or 3 vegetables in this way and serve them together as an attractive main course accompaniment.

I kg/2 lb carrots, peeled and diced
150 ml/¼ pint chicken stock
75 g/3 oz butter
salt and freshly ground black pepper
3–4 tablespoons double cream
TO SERVE
25 g/I oz butter

Put the carrots and stock into a pan and bring to the boil. Lower the heat, cover tightly with a lid and simmer for 10 to 15 minutes, until the carrots are very tender. Remove the lid, increase the heat and boil rapidly for 2 to 3 minutes, until most of the liquid has evaporated. Remove from the heat and stir in the butter. Cool slightly, then work the carrots in an electric blender or food processor until smooth. Season with salt and pepper to taste and stir in the cream.

To freeze: Transfer to a rigid container. Cool completely, then seal, label and freeze for up to 3 months.

To thaw and serve: Leave to stand in container in the refrigerator overnight, or at room temperature for 2 to 3 hours. Melt the butter in a heavy-based pan, stir in the carrot purée and cook gently until hot. Taste and adjust the seasoning, then serve immediately.

Serves 6

POTATO GALETTE

75 g/3 oz butter
3 onions, peeled and sliced
2 leeks, trimmed and sliced
500 g/1 lb potatoes, peeled and diced
salt
1 egg, beaten
125 g/4 oz mature Cheddar cheese, grated
50 g/2 oz Gruyère cheese, grated
freshly ground black pepper
4 tablespoons dried white breadcrumbs
2 tablespoons freshly grated Parmesan cheese
TO SERVE
spring onions

Melt the butter in a pan, add the onions and fry over moderate heat for 15 to 20 minutes golden brown. Lower the heat, add the leeks and cook for 5 minutes.

Meanwhile, cook the potatoes in boiling salted water for 10 to 12 minutes until tender. Drain well, then work through a coarse sieve. Add the onions and leeks to the potatoes, then add the Cheddar and Gruyère cheeses and pepper to taste. Mix well.

Spoon the mixture into a lightly greased foil container or ovenproof dish and level the surface. Leave to cool, then sprinkle over the breadcrumbs and Parmesan cheese.

To freeze: Cover the container or dish with the lid or foil, then seal, label and freeze for up to 3 months.

To thaw and serve: Remove the lid or foil and leave to stand in container at room temperature for 3 to 4 hours. Bake in a preheated moderately hot oven (200°C/400°F/Gas Mark 6) for 30 to 35 minutes until golden brown. Serve immediately, garnished with spring onions.
Serves 4 to 6

JACKET POTATOES WITH CREAMED GARLIC

Jacket potatoes freeze well and are quickly reheated. They are a great time saver.

---

6 large even-sized potatoes, scrubbed
20 garlic cloves
125 g/4 oz butter
1 tablespoon plain flour
300 ml/½ pint milk
salt and freshly ground black pepper
4 tablespoons double cream
4 tablespoons chopped parsley
3 tablespoons freshly grated Parmesan cheese
TO SERVE
parsley sprigs

Prick the potatoes all over with a fork and bake in a preheated moderately hot oven (200°C/400°F/Gas Mark 6) for 1½ hours or until tender.

Meanwhile put the unpeeled garlic in a pan, cover with water, bring to the boil and simmer for 2 to 3 minutes. Drain, remove the skins and crush the garlic.

Melt the butter in a pan, add the crushed garlic and cook gently for 10 minutes without browning. Add the flour and cook for 2 minutes, stirring. Gradually stir in the milk, bring to the boil, then lower the heat and simmer for 2 minutes, stirring constantly. Season well with salt and pepper and stir in the cream. Remove from the heat.

Cut the potatoes in half lengthways. Scoop out the flesh and add to the sauce. Work to a purée in an electric blender or food processor. Stir in the parsley. Pile the potato mixture back into the skins. Leave to cool, then sprinkle over the cheese.

To freeze: Open freeze the potatoes until solid, then pack in a single layer in a rigid container. Seal, label and freeze for up to 4 months.

To thaw and serve: Reheat from frozen in a preheated moderately hot oven (200°C/400°F/Gas Mark 6) for 35 to 40 minutes, or leave to stand in container at room temperature for 2 to 3 hours, then bake for 15 to 20 minutes. Serve hot, garnished with parsley.
Serves 6

WINTER VEGETABLE CASSEROLE

Any selection of winter vegetables may be used for this meal-in-itself casserole. The important thing is that the dish should be colourful, with plenty of different textures.

---

2 tablespoons olive oil
3 large onions, peeled and quartered
2 garlic cloves, peeled and thinly sliced
1 × 397 g/14 oz can tomatoes
150 ml/¼ pint dry white wine
1 small or ½ large celeriac, peeled and diced
4 celery sticks, trimmed and cut into 5 cm/2 inch lengths
6 carrots, peeled and quartered
salt and freshly ground black pepper
1 green pepper, cored, seeded and sliced
2 leeks, trimmed and cut into 5 cm/2 inch lengths
few cauliflower florets
1 tablespoon tomato purée
2 teaspoons dried mixed herbs
TO SERVE
175 g/6 oz plain flour
pinch of salt
75 g/3 oz butter
2 tablespoons freshly grated Parmesan cheese
125 g/4 oz mature Cheddar cheese, grated
2 tablespoons chopped parsley

Heat the oil in a large pan, add the onion and garlic and fry gently for 5 minutes without browning, taking care not to break up the onions. Stir in the tomatoes with their juice, and wine, then add the celeriac, celery, carrots and salt and pepper to taste. Cover and simmer for 20 minutes. Stir in the green pepper, leeks, cauliflower, tomato purée and herbs and simmer for a further 10 minutes.

To freeze: Transfer to a rigid container, leaving 2 cm/¾ inch headspace. Cool quickly, then seal, label and freeze for up to 4 months.

To thaw and serve: Leave to stand in container in the refrigerator overnight, or at room temperature for 5 hours, then transfer to a casserole or ovenproof dish.

To make the topping, sift the flour and salt into a bowl. Rub in the butter until the mixture resembles fine breadcrumbs, then stir in the cheeses and parsley. Sprinkle over the vegetable mixture. Bake in a pre-heated moderately hot oven (200°C/400°F/Gas Mark 6) for 35 to 40 minutes, until golden brown. Serve hot.
Serves 4 to 6

FENNEL WITH TOMATOES AND GARLIC

This accompaniment is delicious served with fish.

---

6 heads fennel, trimmed and cut lengthways in half if large
TOMATO SAUCE
1 tablespoon olive oil
1 large onion, peeled and finely chopped
3 garlic cloves, peeled and thinly sliced
1 × 397 g/14 oz can tomatoes
150 ml/¼ pint dry white wine
2 teaspoons dried mixed herbs
dash of Tabasco sauce
salt and freshly ground black pepper
TO SERVE
125 g/4 oz streaky bacon, rinds removed, crisply fried and crumbled

---

To make the sauce: Heat the oil in a pan, add the onion and garlic and fry gently for 10 minutes until translucent. Stir in the tomatoes with their juice and remaining sauce ingredients, adding salt and pepper to taste. Bring to the boil. Lower the heat, cover and simmer for 30 minutes. Remove lid, increase the heat and cook rapidly for a further 10 minutes, until the sauce is thick.

Meanwhile, cook the fennel in a pan of boiling salted water for 7 to 8 minutes until just tender. Drain well.
To freeze: Cool the fennel and sauce quickly. Arrange the fennel in a lightly greased foil container or ovenproof dish and spoon over the sauce. Seal label and freeze for up to 3 months.

To thaw and serve: Leave to stand in container or dish at room temperature for 2 to 3 hours, then reheat, uncovered, in a preheated moderate oven (180°C/350°F/Gas Mark 4) for 35 to 40 minutes, until hot. Sprinkle the bacon on top and serve immediately.
Serves 4 to 6

Fennel with Tomatoes and Garlic; Jacket Potatoes with Creamed Garlic; Potato Galette; Winter Vegetable Casserole

LEMON ICE CREAM

A simple ice cream with a fresh flavour and a smooth texture. For a special occasion, scoop it into these little basket-shaped biscuits; for an everyday dessert, serve it plain. The biscuit mixture makes about 16 baskets – more than you will need for this ice cream – but they can be used for other ices, whips or fruit fools.

ICE CREAM
4 egg yolks
150 g/5 oz caster sugar
finely grated rind and juice of 2 lemons
300 ml/½ pint single cream
300 ml/½ pint double cream
BISCUIT BASKETS
40 g/1½ oz plain flour, sifted
75 g/3 oz caster sugar
3 egg whites
25 g/1 oz butter or margarine

Make the ice cream: Put the egg yolks, sugar and lemon rind in a bowl and beat until thoroughly blended. Bring the single cream just to the boil in a pan, remove from the heat and gradually stir into the egg yolk. Transfer to the top of a double boiler, or a heat-proof bowl over a pan of simmering water, and cook, stirring constantly, until the custard is thick enough to coat the back of a spoon. Stir in the lemon juice, strain into a bowl and leave to cool, stirring occasionally to prevent a skin forming.

Whip the double cream until it will stand in soft peaks, then fold in the cold custard. Pour into a rigid container, cover and freeze for 2 to 3 hours until half-frozen.

Make the biscuit baskets: Place the flour and sugar in a bowl and mix well. Add the egg whites and butter or margarine, and beat thoroughly until smooth.

Place dessertspoonfuls of the mixture well apart on greased and floured baking sheets and spread them thinly to form 13 cm/5 inch rounds. Bake, one tray at a time, in a preheated moderately hot oven (200°C/400°F/Gas Mark 6) for 4 to 5 minutes until golden at the edges. (It is important not to bake too many biscuits at once or they will set before you have time to mould them.)

Leave the biscuits to cool slightly, then scrape them off the baking sheets with a sharp knife and place each one right side down over the base of an inverted glass. Mould the biscuits to give wavy edges, leave to set, then remove carefully. Repeat with the remaining trays of biscuits.

Remove the half-frozen ice cream from the freezer and stir well.

To freeze: Seal the ice cream container, label and return to the freezer for up to 3 months. Pack the biscuit baskets in rigid containers, carefully fitting them into one another. Seal, label and freeze for up to 6 months.

To thaw and serve: Unpack the biscuits and leave to stand at room temperature for 30 minutes. Transfer the ice cream to the refrigerator 20 minutes before serving to soften. Scoop into the basket-shaped biscuits to serve.

Serves 6

CHESTNUT ICE CREAM

This ice cream can be served simply scooped into individual dishes or moulded and decorated for an impressive dessert. For the latter, freeze the ice cream in a 1 kg/2 lb loaf tin lined with foil. To serve, unmould and decorate with piped whipped cream and chocolate curls.

1 × 439 g/15½ oz unsweetened chestnut purée
4 tablespoons brandy
175 g/6 oz caster sugar
450 ml/¾ pint double cream
2 egg whites
CHOCOLATE SAUCE
175 g/6 oz plain chocolate, chopped
150 ml/¼ pint water
125 g/4 oz sugar
TO SERVE
chocolate curls (optional)

Put the chestnut purée, brandy and 50 g/2 oz of the sugar in a bowl and beat well until smooth. Whip the cream until it will stand in soft peaks, then fold into the chestnut purée.

Whisk the egg whites until stiff, then gradually whisk in the remaining sugar. Continue whisking until the mixture is very stiff. Fold into the chestnut mixture, then turn into a rigid container.

Make the chocolate sauce: Put all the ingredients in a pan and heat very gently until the chocolate has melted and the sugar dissolved. Simmer uncovered for 10 minutes, then remove from the heat and leave to cool.
To freeze: Pour the sauce into a rigid container. Seal, label and freeze both containers for up to 3 months.
To thaw and serve: Leave the sauce to stand in container at room temperature for 2 hours. Transfer the ice cream to the refrigerator 20 minutes before serving to soften. Stir the chocolate sauce well. Scoop the ice cream into individual dishes, pour over the sauce and decorate with chocolate curls, if desired.
Serves 8

GRAPEFRUIT SORBET

A very sharp, fresh sorbet – ideal to serve at the end of a rich meal.

450 ml/¾ pint water
125 g/4 oz caster sugar
thinly pared rind and juice of 2 grapefruit
1 egg white

Heat the water, sugar and grapefruit rind gently in a pan, stirring until the sugar has dissolved. Boil rapidly for 5 minutes, then remove from heat and stir in the grapefruit juice. Strain into a rigid container, cool, then cover and freeze for 2 to 3 hours until half-frozen.

Remove from the freezer and turn into a bowl.

Whisk the egg white until stiff, then whisk into the half-frozen grapefruit mixture.

To freeze: Return the sorbet to the container, seal, label and return to the freezer for up to 2 months.
To thaw and serve: Transfer to the refrigerator 10 minutes before serving to soften. Scoop into chilled glasses and serve immediately.
Serves 4 to 6

BOMBE NOËL

A rich vanilla ice cream mixed with glacé fruits and nuts soaked in brandy make a less filling alternative to the traditional Christmas pudding.

125 g/4 oz glacé cherries, chopped
50 g/2 oz candied angelica, chopped
50 g/2 oz crystallized pineapple, chopped
50 g/2 oz preserved stem ginger, drained and chopped
75 g/3 oz seedless raisins
4 tablespoons brandy
3 egg yolks
75 g/3 oz caster sugar
300 ml/½ pint single cream
150 ml/¼ pint double cream
75 g/3 oz chopped almonds, toasted
TO SERVE
6 tablespoons double cream, whipped

Put the chopped cherries, angelica, pineapple, ginger and raisins in a bowl. Pour over the brandy and leave to macerate for 1 hour.

Put the egg yolks and sugar in a bowl and beat until thoroughly blended. Bring the single cream just to the boil in a pan, remove from the heat and stir gradually into the yolk mixture. Transfer to the top of a double boiler or a heatproof bowl over a pan of simmering water and cook gently, stirring constantly, until the custard is thick enough to coat the back of a spoon. Strain into a bowl and leave to cool, stirring occasionally to prevent a skin forming.

Whip the double cream until it will stand in soft peaks, then fold in the cold custard. Pour into a rigid container, cover and freeze for 2 to 3 hours until half-frozen. Remove from the freezer and stir in the macerated fruits with the brandy, and the almonds. Spoon into a 900 ml/1½ pint foil pudding basin and level the surface.

To freeze: Cover basin with foil, then wrap in a polythene bag. Seal, label and freeze for up to 3 months.
To thaw and serve: Unwrap the basin and invert onto a serving plate. Rub with a cloth wrung out in very hot water until the bombe drops out. Pipe the cream in a border around the base of the bombe, then place in the refrigerator for 30 minutes before serving to soften.
Serves 6 to 8

ABOVE: Bombe Noël
OPPOSITE: Grapefruit Sorbet; Lemon Ice Cream; Chestnut Ice Cream

ICED LIME SOUFFLÉ

A very impressive way to serve an ice cream for a dinner party. Make sure the foil band fits very tightly or the mixture will ooze out before it freezes.

finely grated rind of 3 limes
juice of 4 limes
4 eggs, separated
175 g/6 oz caster sugar
300 ml/½ pint double cream
TO SERVE
6 tablespoons double cream, whipped
½ lime, thinly sliced

Tie a double band of foil around a 900 ml/1½ pint soufflé dish to stand 5 cm/2 inches above the rim.

Put the lime rind in a bowl with the egg yolks and 125 g/4 oz sugar and whisk until thick and mousse-like. Heat the lime juice in a small pan, pour over the egg mixture and whisk until thoroughly incorporated.

Whisk the egg whites until stiff, then gradually whisk in remaining sugar. Whip the cream until it will stand in soft peaks, then fold into the lime mixture. Fold in the egg whites. Spoon into the dish and level the surface.
To freeze: Open freeze, then wrap in a polythene bag. Seal, label and return to freezer for up to 3 months.
To thaw and serve: Remove the paper carefully, then decorate with whipped cream and lime slices. Transfer to refrigerator 30 minutes before serving to soften.
Serves 8

ICED ADVOCAAT SOUFFLÉS

These delicious iced desserts are best served with crisp wafer biscuits or macaroons, to contast their rich, creamy texture.

2 egg whites
50 g/2 oz caster sugar
300 ml/½ pint double cream
6 tablespoons Advocaat
finely grated rind of 1 lemon
TO SERVE
6 split almonds, toasted
6 tablespoons double cream, whipped (optional)

Tie double bands of foil tightly around the outside of 6 ramekins to stand 2.5 cm/1 inch above the rims.

Whisk the egg whites until stiff, then gradually whisk in the sugar. Whip the cream with the Advocaat and lemon rind until it will stand in soft peaks, then fold into the meringue.

Spoon into the ramekins and level the surfaces. Chill in the refrigerator for about 30 minutes or until set.

To freeze: Open freeze the soufflés until solid, then stand in a rigid container. Seal, label and return to the freezer for up to 3 months.

To thaw and serve: Remove the foil carefully, then decorate with whipped cream if using, and split almonds. Place in the refrigerator 15 minutes before serving to soften.

Serves 6

SOUFFLÉ CHINOIS

3 eggs, separated
50 g/2 oz caster sugar
300 ml/½ pint milk
15 g/½ oz (1 envelope) powdered gelatine, dissolved
    in 4 tablespoons water
250 ml/8 fl oz double cream
50 g/2 oz preserved stem ginger, drained and
    chopped, with 2 tablespoons syrup reserved
TO SERVE
2 tablespoons finely chopped almonds, toasted
150 ml/¼ pint double cream, whipped
preserved stem ginger slices

Tie a band of foil very tightly around a 1 litre/1¾ pint soufflé dish to stand 5 cm/2 inches above the rim.

Put the egg yolks and sugar in a bowl and beat until thoroughly blended. Bring the milk to the boil in a pan, remove from the heat and gradually stir into the yolk mixture. Transfer to the top of a double boiler, or a heatproof bowl over a pan of simmering water, and cook gently, stirring constantly, until the custard is thick enough to coat the back of a spoon. Remove from the heat and stir in the gelatine liquid. Strain into a bowl and cool, stirring occasionally to prevent a skin forming.

Whip the cream with the ginger syrup until it will stand in soft peaks. When the custard is beginning to set, fold it into the cream with the chopped ginger. Whisk egg whites until stiff. Carefully fold 2 tablespoons into the custard mixture to lighten it, then fold in the remainder. Spoon into the soufflé dish and level the surface. Chill in the refrigerator for 1 hour or until set.

To freeze: Open freeze the soufflé until solid, then wrap in a polythene bag. Seal, label and return to the freezer for up to 3 months.

To thaw and serve: Unwrap and leave in refrigerator overnight. Remove foil carefully and press almonds around the sides. Decorate with the cream and ginger.

Serves 6 to 8

CITRUS MOUSSE

3 eggs, separated
125 g/4 oz caster sugar
finely grated rind and juice of 2 oranges
finely grated rind of 1 lemon
juice of 2 lemons
15 g/½ oz (1 envelope) powdered gelatine, dissolved
    in 3 tablespoons water
300 ml/½ pint whipping cream
TO SERVE
orange rind shreds, blanched and drained

Put the egg yolks, half the sugar and the orange and lemon rinds in a bowl and whisk until thick and creamy. Heat the orange and lemon juices in a pan, then gradually stir into the yolk mixture. Transfer to the top of a double boiler, or a heatproof bowl over a pan of simmering water, and cook gently, stirring constantly, until the custard is thick enough to coat the back of a spoon. Remove from the heat and stir in the gelatine liquid, then strain into a bowl and leave to cool.

Whisk the egg whites until stiff, then whisk in the remaining sugar. Whip the cream until it will stand in soft peaks. When just beginning to set, fold the cold custard and the meringue mixture into the cream. Turn into a freezerproof glass bowl.

To freeze: Cover with cling film, wrap in a polythene bag, seal, label and freeze for up to 3 months.

To thaw and serve: Remove the polythene bag and leave to stand in the refrigerator overnight. Decorate with the orange shreds before serving.

Serves 6 to 8

Iced Lime Soufflé; Iced Advocaat Soufflés; Citrus Mousse

APPLE AND MINCEMEAT PANCAKES

Serve these rich brandy-flavoured pancakes with vanilla ice cream or whipped fresh cream.

PANCAKES
125 g/4 oz plain flour
pinch of salt
1 egg, beaten
1 tablespoon vegetable oil
300 ml/½ pint milk
vegetable oil for shallow frying
FILLING
250 g/8 oz dessert apples
25 g/1 oz butter or margarine
250 g/8 oz mincemeat (see page 194)
1 tablespoon brandy
TO SERVE
25 g/1 oz chopped almonds, toasted

Make the pancakes: Sift the flour and salt into a bowl. Make a well in the centre and add the egg. Add the oil and half of the milk gradually, beating vigorously to incorporate the flour. Beat in the remaining milk and pour into a jug. Leave to stand for 30 minutes.

Pour a few drops of oil into a 15 cm/6 inch pancake pan or omelet pan and place over high heat. When the pan is very hot, pour in a generous tablespoon of the batter and swirl around the pan until the bottom is covered evenly. Cook until the underside is golden brown, then turn the pancake over and cook for a further 10 to 15 seconds. Slide out onto a plate lined with greaseproof paper and cover with another sheet of paper. Continue in this way to make 12 pancakes, stacking them interleaved with greaseproof paper as they are cooked. Leave to cool.

Make the filling: Peel, core and chop the apples. Melt the butter or margarine in a small heavy-based pan, add the apples, cover and cook gently, stirring occasionally, for 10 to 12 minutes until the apples are tender. Remove from the heat, add the mincemeat and brandy and stir well. Leave to cool.

Divide the filling evenly between the pancakes and roll up, enclosing the filling.

To freeze: Open freeze the pancakes until solid, then stack in a rigid container. Seal, label and freeze for up to 3 months.

To thaw and serve: Transfer the pancakes to a shallow ovenproof serving dish. Cover with foil and reheat from frozen in a preheated moderate oven (180°C/350°F/Gas Mark 4) for 20 to 25 minutes until heated through. Remove the foil, sprinkle with the almonds and serve hot.
Serves 6

APPLE AND DATE PANCAKES

Make the pancakes as above. Prepare the filling as above, omitting the mincemeat and using 500 g/1 lb dessert apples. Cook the apples as above, adding 25 g/1 oz brown sugar, 75 g/3 oz stoned, chopped dates and ¼ teaspoon ground mixed spice.

OPPOSITE: Lemon Lattice Flan
BELOW: Apple and Mincemeat Pancakes; Crêpes Suzette

CRÊPES SUZETTE

The classic Crêpes Suzette can be made very quickly with crêpes from the freezer. Make the orange sauce while the crêpes are thawing and they will be ready to serve within 20 minutes. If the crêpes are frozen in a stack as suggested here, you need only thaw as many as you need.

CRÊPE BATTER
125 g/4 oz plain flour
pinch of salt
1 tablespoon caster sugar
2 eggs, beaten
1 tablespoon vegetable oil
250 ml/8 fl oz milk
vegetable oil for shallow frying
ORANGE SAUCE TO SERVE
50 g/2 oz butter
50 g/2 oz caster sugar
finely grated rind and juice of 2 oranges
2 tablespoons Cointreau or other orange-flavoured
  liqueur
2 tablespoons brandy

Make the crêpes: Sift the flour and salt into a bowl and make a well in the centre. Add the sugar, eggs, oil and a little of the milk and beat vigorously to incorporate the flour. Beat in the remaining milk, then pour into a jug. Leave to stand for 30 minutes.

Pour a few drops of oil into a 15 cm/6 inch pancake pan or omelet pan and place over high heat. When the pan is very hot, pour in a generous tablespoon of the batter and swirl around the pan until the bottom is covered evenly. Cook until the underside is golden brown, then turn the crêpe over and cook for a further 10 to 15 seconds. Slide out onto a plate lined with greaseproof paper and cover with another sheet of paper. Continue in this way to make 12 crêpes, stacking them interleaved with greaseproof paper as they are cooked. Leave to cool.

To freeze: Place the stack of crêpes in a polythene bag, seal, label and freeze for up to 4 months.

To thaw and serve: Unwrap the crêpes, spread out individually and leave to stand at room temperature for 20 minutes. Meanwhile, make the orange sauce. Melt the butter in a frying pan, add the sugar, orange rind and juice and heat until bubbling.

Dip each crêpe into the sauce, fold into quarters, then place in a warmed serving dish. Add the liqueur and brandy to the pan, heat gently, then remove from the heat and ignite. Pour the flaming sauce over the crêpes and serve immediately.

Serves 4 to 6

VARIATION

For a quick and simple dessert, pancakes can be reheated from frozen. Unwrap them, spread them out on a baking sheet, cover with foil and heat in a moderately hot oven (200°C/400°F/Gas Mark 6) for 10 minutes. Serve sprinkled with lemon juice and sugar.

LEMON LATTICE FLAN

A rich lemon curd tart which is best served warm with single cream, but any that is left over can be eaten cold.

RICH SHORTCRUST PASTRY
250 g/8 oz plain flour
150 g/5 oz butter or margarine
1 tablespoon caster sugar
1 egg yolk
1–2 tablespoons iced water
FILLING
125 g/4 oz butter or margarine
125 g/4 oz caster sugar
finely grated rind and juice of 2 lemons
4 egg yolks
125 g/4 oz ground almonds
120 ml/4 fl oz double cream
TO SERVE
1 egg yolk, mixed with 1 teaspoon water

Make the pastry: Sift the flour into a bowl. Rub in the butter or margarine until the mixture resembles fine breadcrumbs. Stir in the sugar. Add the egg yolk and enough water to mix to a fairly stiff dough.

Turn the dough onto a floured surface and knead lightly until smooth. Roll out and use to line a 20 cm/8 inch fluted flan ring placed on a baking sheet.

Reserve the trimmings. Chill the flan and trimmings in the refrigerator for 30 minutes.

Prick the base of the dough and line with foil and baking beans. Bake 'blind' in a preheated moderately hot oven (200°C/400°F/Gas Mark 6) for 15 minutes, then remove the foil and beans and return the flan to the oven for a further 5 minutes. Leave to cool.

Make the filling: Cream the butter or margarine, sugar and lemon rind together until light and fluffy. Beat in the egg yolks thoroughly, then beat in the almonds and lemon juice. Add the cream and mix well. Turn into the pastry case and level the surface.

Roll out the reserved pastry trimmings and cut into narrow strips. Use these to make a lattice pattern over the filling, moistening the edges of the pastry with water so that the lattice will adhere.

To freeze: Open freeze the flan until solid, then carefully remove from the flan ring. Wrap in cling film and overwrap in a polythene bag. Seal, label and return to the freezer for up to 3 months.

To thaw and serve: Unwrap and return to the flan ring placed on a baking sheet. Brush the pastry lattice with the egg glaze, then bake from frozen in a preheated moderately hot oven (200°C/400°F/Gas Mark 6) for 15 minutes. Reduce the oven temperature to moderate (180°C/350°F/Gas Mark 4) and bake for a further 20 to 25 minutes until golden brown. Leave to cool slightly, then remove from the flan ring. Serve warm.

Serves 6 to 8

STEAMED CHOCOLATE PUDDING

If you prefer, the pudding may be steamed from frozen, in which case it will take 2 hours. If you are making the treacle pudding in the variation, do not put golden syrup in the bottom of the basin as it can cause the mixture to become soggy in the freezer.

175 g/6 oz self-raising flour
2 tablespoons cocoa powder
125 g/4 oz butter or margarine
125 g/4 oz caster sugar
2 large eggs, beaten
3 tablespoons milk
TO SERVE
125 g/4 oz plain chocolate, chopped
25 g/1 oz soft brown sugar
2 tablespoons water

Sift the flour and cocoa together. Cream the butter or margarine and sugar together until light and fluffy. Beat in the eggs a little at a time, adding 1 tablespoon flour and cocoa mixture after each addition. Carefully fold in the remaining flour and cocoa with a metal spoon, then fold in the milk.

Spoon the mixture into a greased 1.2 litre/2 pint foil or freezerproof pudding basin and level the surface. Cover with oiled foil, making a pleat across the centre to allow the pudding to rise. Secure the foil around the rim with string. Place the basin in a steamer and steam for 1½ to 2 hours. Remove from the steamer and leave to cool.

Make the sauce: Put the chocolate, sugar and water in a small heavy-based pan and heat gently until the sugar has dissolved. Pour into a rigid container and leave until cold.

To freeze: Wrap the pudding in a polythene bag, seal, label and freeze for up to 4 months. Cover the sauce container with its lid, seal, label and freeze for up to 4 months.

To thaw and serve: Unwrap the pudding and leave to stand at room temperature for 4 hours. Leave the sauce to stand in its container for 1 hour.

Steam the pudding for 45 minutes and reheat the sauce in a small heavy-based pan, stirring frequently. Turn the pudding onto a serving dish, pour over the sauce and serve immediately.
Serves 4 to 6

STEAMED TREACLE PUDDING

Prepare and freeze the pudding as above, omitting the cocoa powder and 1 tablespoon of the milk. Make a syrup sauce, instead of the chocolate sauce, by heating 4 tablespoons golden syrup with 1 tablespoon water, just before serving.

STEAMED FRUIT PUDDING

Prepare the pudding as above, omitting the cocoa powder and 1 tablespoon milk. Fold in 125 g/4 oz mixed dried fruit alternately with the flour, then cook as above. Serve with custard.

DATE AND ORANGE PUDDING

3 oranges
125 g/4 oz dates, stoned and roughly chopped
125 g/4 oz butter or margrine
125 g/4 oz soft brown sugar
2 eggs, beaten
125 g/4 oz self-raising flour, sifted
1 tablespoon hot water
15 g/½ oz flaked almonds

Finely grate the rind from the oranges, then peel and cut them into segments, discarding all of the pith. Mix the rind of 1 orange with the dates and orange segments. Spoon into a 1.2 litre/2 pint pie dish.

Cream the butter or margarine, sugar and remaining orange rind together until light and fluffy. Beat in the eggs a little at a time, adding 1 tablespoon flour after each addition. Fold in the remaining flour, then the hot water.

Spoon the mixture over the fruit and spread to the edges. Sprinkle with the almonds, place on a baking sheet and bake in a preheated moderate oven (180°C/350°F/Gas Mark 4) for 35 to 40 minutes until golden. Leave to cool.
To freeze: Cover with foil and overwrap in a polythene bag. Label and freeze for up to 4 months.
To thaw and serve: Unwrap and reheat from frozen in a preheated moderate oven (180°C/350°F/Gas Mark 4) for 20 minutes. Serve warm with cream.
Serves 6

APPLE AND COCONUT PIE

A warming winter pudding with a crunchy coconut topping. Desiccated coconut can be used in place of freshly grated coconut.

25 g/1 oz butter or margarine
750 g/1½ lb cooking apples, peeled, cored and sliced
2 tablespoons soft brown sugar
1 teaspoon dried mixed spice
125 g/4 oz dates, stoned and roughly chopped
TOPPING
1 egg white
50 g/2 oz demerara sugar
50 g/2 oz fresh coconut, finely grated

Melt the butter or margarine in a pan and add the apples, sugar and spice. Cover and cook over a very low heat, stirring occasionally, for 10 to 12 minutes. Stir in the dates and place in a 900 ml/1½ pint pie dish.

Whisk the egg white until stiff, then gradually whisk in the demerara sugar. Fold in the coconut. Spread the coconut meringue over the fruit, using a fork to form a rough surface.

Bake in a preheated moderate oven (180°C/350°F/Gas Mark 4) for 20 to 30 minutes until the topping is golden. Leave to cool.

To freeze: Cover with foil and overwrap in a polythene bag. Label and freeze for up to 4 months.
To thaw and serve: Unwrap, remove the foil and reheat the pie from frozen in a preheated moderate oven (180°C/350°F/Gas Mark 4) for 20 minutes. Serve warm with pouring cream.
Serves 4 to 6

GINGER VACHERIN

Meringue can be varied by flavouring with coffee or chocolate, or with brown sugar which will give it a caramel flavour. The whipped cream filling can be flavoured with 1 tablespoon Tia Maria or rum, rather than ginger; and the ginger decoration can be replaced with grated chocolate.

GINGER MERINGUE
5 egg whites
300 g/10 oz caster sugar
2 teaspoons ground ginger
FILLING
450 ml/¾ pint double cream
50 g/2 oz preserved stem ginger, drained and thinly sliced, with 2 tablespoons syrup reserved
TO SERVE
4 tablespoons double cream, whipped
8 thin slices preserved stem ginger

Line 3 baking sheets with non-stick silicone paper or baking parchment. With a pencil, draw a 20 cm/8 inch circle on each piece of paper.

Make the ginger meringue: Whisk the egg whites until stiff, then whisk in 3 tablespoons of the sugar with the ground ginger. Carefully fold in the remaining sugar with a metal spoon. Spoon into a piping bag fitted with a 1 cm/½ inch plain nozzle and pipe over the circles marked on the paper. Bake in a preheated very cool oven (110°C/225°F/Gas Mark ¼) for 2 hours until crisp. Peel the paper carefully off the meringue rounds, then place on a wire rack and leave to cool.

Make the filling: Whip the cream with the ginger syrup until it will stand in soft peaks, then fold in the sliced ginger. Sandwich the meringue rounds together with the ginger and cream filling.

To freeze: Open freeze the vacherin until solid, then place carefully in a rigid container. Seal, label and freeze for up to 3 months.

To thaw and serve: Remove from the container, place on a serving plate and leave to stand in the refrigerator for 8 hours. Pipe rosettes of whipped cream around the edge and decorate with the ginger slices. Serve as soon as possible.
Serves 8

Date and Orange Pudding; Apple and Coconut Pie; Steamed Chocolate Pudding

COFFEE RING CAKE

A useful cake to have in the freezer as it can be frozen completely finished and only needs to be thawed before it is ready to serve. Coffee powder – not granules – must be used.

175 g/6 oz butter or margarine, softened
175 g/6 oz caster sugar
3 eggs, beaten
175 g/6 oz self-raising flour, sifted
50 g/2 oz ground hazelnuts, toasted
2 tablespoons strong black coffee
COFFEE FUDGE ICING
50 g/2 oz butter
2 tablespoons milk
1 tablespoon instant coffee powder
250 g/8 oz icing sugar, sifted
TO SERVE
25 g/1 oz plain chocolate, broken into small pieces

Grease a 23 cm/9 inch ring mould and dust very lightly with flour.

Cream the butter or margarine and sugar together until light and fluffy. Beat in the eggs a little at a time, adding 1 tablespoon flour after each addition. Fold in the remaining flour with the ground hazelnuts, then fold in the coffee powder.

Turn the mixture into the prepared mould and bake in a preheated moderate oven (180°C/350°F/Gas Mark 4) for 40 minutes until the cake springs back when lightly pressed. Turn out onto a wire rack and leave to cool.

For the icing: Heat the butter gently in a pan with the milk and coffee powder until melted. Add the icing sugar and beat well until smooth and glossy. Leave to cool until the icing thickly coats the back of a spoon, then pour over the cake and spread with a palette knife to cover it completely.

Melt the chocolate in a heatproof bowl over a pan of hot water. Put the warm chocolate into a greaseproof piping bag, leave to cool slightly, then snip off the tip. Drizzle the chocolate across the cake, then leave to set.

To freeze: Open freeze the ring cake until solid, then place in a rigid container, seal, label and freeze for up to 2 months.

To thaw and serve: Place on a serving plate and leave to stand at room temperature for 3 to 4 hours until thawed before serving.
Serves 8

FRANGIPANE FINGERS

These are very quick to thaw, so are ideal to have in the freezer for unexpected tea-time guests.

250 g/8 oz plain flour
pinch of salt
125 g/4 oz butter
2–3 tablespoons water
6 tablespoons apricot jam
TOPPING
125 g/4 oz butter
125 g/4 oz caster sugar
2 eggs, beaten
2 tablespoons plain flour, sifted
125 g/4 oz ground almonds
few drops of almond flavouring
50 g/2 oz flaked almonds
a little icing sugar

Grease a 30 × 20 cm/12 × 8 inch Swiss roll tin, line with greaseproof paper, then grease the paper.

Sift the flour and salt into a bowl. Rub in the butter until the mixture resembles fine breadcrumbs. Stir in enough water to mix to a fairly stiff dough. Turn the

dough onto a floured surface, knead lightly until smooth, then roll out and use to line the prepared tin. Spread the jam over the pastry, then chill in the refrigerator for 15 minutes.

For the topping: Cream the butter and sugar together until light and fluffy, then beat in the eggs a little at a time, adding 1 tablespoon flour after each addition. Stir in the ground almonds and flavouring, then spread over the jam, smoothing it evenly to the edges. Sprinkle the almonds on top.

Bake in a preheated moderately hot oven (190°C/ 375°F/Gas Mark 5) for 25 to 30 minutes until golden. Cool in the tin for a few minutes, then turn out carefully onto a wire rack, remove the paper and turn the cake the right way up. Leave to cool, then sift icing sugar lightly over the top and cut into 16 fingers.

To freeze: Pack the fingers in a rigid container, separating the layers with interleaving sheets or foil. Seal, label and freeze for up to 4 months.

To thaw and serve: Place on a serving plate and leave to stand at room temperature for 15 to 20 minutes. Serve as soon as possible.

Makes 16 fingers

CHERRY AND ALMOND CAKE

This cake has an unusual crunchy almond topping. It can be cut into sections before freezing and separated with foil so that you can take a few pieces out of the freezer at a time.

TOPPING
50 g/2 oz plain flour
25 g/1 oz butter or margarine
50 g/2 oz soft brown sugar
50 g/2 oz split almonds, chopped
½ teaspoon ground cinnamon
CAKE MIXTURE
175 g/6 oz butter or margarine, softened
175 g/6 oz caster sugar
3 eggs, beaten
250 g/8 oz self-raising flour, sifted
250 g/8 oz glacé cherries, halved
50 g/2 oz ground almonds
about 2 tablespoons milk

Grease a deep 20 cm/8 inch loose-bottomed round cake tin, line the base with greaseproof paper, then grease the paper.

Make the topping: Sift the flour into a bowl. Rub in the butter or margarine until the mixture resembles fine breadcrumbs. Stir in the sugar, almonds and cinnamon.

For the cake mixture: Cream the butter or margarine and sugar together until light and fluffy. Beat in the eggs a little at a time, adding 1 tablespoon flour after each addition. Fold in the remaining flour, then fold in the cherries, almonds and enough milk to give a soft dropping consistency.

Turn the mixture into the prepared tin, level the surface and sprinkle the topping over the mixture.

Bake in a preheated moderate oven (160°C/325°F/ Gas Mark 3) for 1½ to 1¾ hours, or until a skewer inserted in the centre comes out clean. Leave to cool for 3 minutes, then remove from the tin and carefully peel off the lining paper. Cool on a wire rack.

To freeze: Wrap the cake in a polythene bag, seal, label and freeze for up to 4 months.

To thaw and serve: Unwrap, place on a serving plate and leave to stand at room temperature for 3 to 4 hours. Serve as soon as possible.

Serves 8

CHOCOLATE WALNUT CAKE

A luscious, sticky chocolate cake containing ground walnuts, which help keep it very moist.

175 g/6 oz plain chocolate, broken into small pieces
2 tablespoons water
125 g/4 oz butter or margarine, softened
125 g/4 oz caster sugar
4 eggs, separated
2 tablespoons cornflour
175 g/6 oz shelled walnuts, ground
TO SERVE
150 ml/¼ pint double cream, whipped
8 walnut halves

Grease a 20 cm/8 inch loose-bottomed cake tin, line with greaseproof paper, then grease the paper.

Melt the chocolate with the water in a heatproof bowl over a pan of hot water. Remove from the heat. Cream the butter or margarine and sugar together until light and fluffy. Beat in the egg yolks one at a time, adding the cornflour with the last 2 yolks. Beat in the chocolate, then the walnuts.

Whisk the egg whites until fairly stiff, then carefully fold 1 tablespoon into the cake mixture to lighten it. Fold in the remaining whites with a metal spoon.

Turn the mixture into the prepared tin and level the surface. Bake in a preheated moderate oven (160°C/ 325°F/Gas Mark 3) for 1 hour 10 minutes or until the cake springs back when lightly pressed in the centre. Leave in the tin for 5 minutes, then remove from the tin and carefully peel off the paper. Turn the cake the right way up, place on a wire rack and leave to cool.

To freeze: Wrap the cake in a polythene bag, seal, label and freeze for up to 4 months.

To thaw and serve: Unwrap, place on a serving plate and leave to stand at room temperature for 4 hours. Spread half the cream evenly to the edges of the cake and mark with a palette knife. Pipe the remaining cream in a border around the edge. Decorate with the walnuts. Serve as soon as possible.

Serves 8 to 10

ABOVE: Cherry and Almond Cake
OPPOSITE: Coffee Ring Cake; Chocolate Walnut Cake

FRUITY FINGERS

These individual cakes are very useful to store in the freezer: they can be taken out one at a time when required, and only take about 30 minutes to thaw.

200 g/7 oz plain flour
1 teaspoon ground mixed spice
½ teaspoon ground nutmeg
175 g/6 oz butter or margarine, softened
175 g/6 oz soft brown sugar
4 eggs, beaten
250 g/8 oz currants
250 g/8 oz sultanas
75 g/3 oz seedless raisins
75 g/3 oz glacé cherries, quartered
1 tablespoon orange juice
ALMOND PASTE
250 g/8 oz ground almonds
125 g/4 oz caster sugar
125 g/4 oz icing sugar
2 teaspoons lemon juice
3 drops almond flavouring
1 egg, beaten
2 tablespoons warmed, sieved apricot jam

Grease a 28 × 18 cm/11 × 7 inch baking tin, line the base and sides with greaseproof paper, then grease the paper well.

Sift the flour and spices together. Cream the butter or margarine and sugar together until light and fluffy. Beat in the eggs a little at a time, adding 1 tablespoon flour after each addition. Fold in the remaining flour with the fruit and orange juice.

Turn the mixture into the prepared tin and level the surface. Bake in a preheated moderate oven (160°C/325°F/Gas Mark 3) for 30 minutes, then reduce the temperature to cool (150°C/300°F/Gas Mark 2) and bake for a further 40 to 50 minutes until a warmed fine skewer inserted into the centre comes out clean. Turn out onto a wire rack, carefully peel off the paper, turn the cake the right way up and leave to cool.

Make the almond paste: Put the almonds and sugars in a bowl and stir well to mix. Make a well in the centre, add the lemon juice, flavouring and egg and mix to a firm paste. Turn onto a surface sprinkled with icing sugar and knead lightly until smooth. Roll out to a 28 × 18 cm/11 × 7 inch rectangle.

Turn the cake upside down and brush the top with the warm apricot jam. Lay the almond paste on top and roll the surface lightly until smooth. Trim edges with a sharp knife and mark a diamond pattern on the top. Place under a preheated hot grill for a few minutes until golden. Cool, then cut into 20 to 24 fingers.

To freeze: Pack the fingers in a rigid container, separating the layers with interleaving sheets or foil. Seal, label and freeze for up to 4 months.

To thaw and serve: Remove from the container and leave to stand at room temperature for about 30 minutes. Serve as soon as possible.

Makes 20 to 24 fingers

JAMAICAN RUM GÂTEAU

This light sponge cake, soaked in dark rum and covered with coffee butter cream, makes a lusciously rich gâteau.

4 eggs
175 g/6 oz caster sugar
125 g/4 oz plain flour
2 tablespoons instant coffee powder
1 tablespoon vegetable oil
4 tablespoons dark rum
BUTTER ICING
250 g/8 oz butter, softened
500 g/1 lb icing sugar, sifted
2 tablespoons coffee and chicory essence
TO SERVE
chocolate curls

Grease two 20 cm/8 inch sandwich tins, line the bases with greaseproof paper, then grease the paper.

Put the eggs and sugar in a bowl and whisk with an electric beater until thick and mousse-like. Sift the flour with the coffee powder and carefully fold into the egg mixture with a metal spoon. Fold in the oil.

Divide the mixture equally between the prepared tins and level the surface. Bake in a preheated moderately hot oven (190°C/375°F/Gas Mark 5) for 20 minutes until the cakes spring back when lightly pressed in the centre. Turn out onto a wire rack and carefully peel off the lining paper. Turn the cakes the right way up and leave to cool. Sprinkle both cakes with the rum.

Make the butter icing: Cream the butter with half the icing sugar. Add the coffee essence and remaining icing sugar and beat thoroughly until smooth.

Sandwich the cakes together with about one quarter of the icing and place on a board or plate. Spread three quarters of the remaining icing over the top and sides of the cake, smoothing the top evenly with a palette knife. Press chocolate curls onto the icing around the sides. Spoon the remaining icing into a piping bag fitted with a fluted nozzle and pipe a border around the edge. Decorate the top with chocolate curls.

To freeze: Open freeze the gâteau until solid, then pack carefully in a rigid container. Seal, label and return to the freezer for up to 1 month.

To thaw and serve: Remove from the container, place on a serving plate and leave to stand at room temperature for 3 to 4 hours. Serve as soon as possible.
Serves 8

VARIATION

Bake the mixture for about 20 minutes in a 33 × 23 cm/13 × 9 inch greased and lined Swiss roll tin. Turn out on to a sheet of greaseproof paper sprinkled with sugar. Peel off the lining paper and roll up the cake in the paper. Leave to cool. Unroll, peel off the paper and spread over two thirds of the filling. Roll up again. Decorate with the remaining filling. Freeze as above.

ORANGE CAKE

A basic Victoria sandwich mixture flavoured with fresh orange freezes well with its filling, but for a perfect finish the glacé icing topping must not be added until the cake has thawed.

175 g/6 oz butter or margarine, softened
175 g/6 oz caster sugar
finely grated rind and juice of 1 orange
3 eggs, beaten
175 g/6 oz self-raising flour, sifted
BUTTER ICING
50 g/2 oz butter, softened
125 g/4 oz icing sugar, sifted
1 tablespoon orange juice
GLACÉ ICING TO SERVE
175 g/6 oz icing sugar
1–2 teaspoons orange juice
finely grated rind of 1 orange
orange rind shreds, to decorate

Grease two 18 cm/7 sandwich tins, line the bases with greaseproof paper, then grease the paper.

Cream the butter or margarine, sugar and orange rind together until light and fluffy. Beat in the eggs a little at a time, adding 1 tablespoon flour after each addition. Fold in the remaining flour, then fold in the orange juice.

Turn the mixture into the prepared tins and level the surface. Bake in a preheated moderate oven (180°C/350°F/Gas Mark 4) for 20 to 25 minutes until the cakes spring back when lightly pressed in the centre. Turn onto a wire rack, carefully peel off the lining paper, turn the cakes the right way up and leave to cool.

Make the butter icing: Cream the butter with half the icing sugar. Add the orange juice and the remaining sugar and beat thoroughly until smooth. Sandwich the cold cakes together with the icing.

To freeze: Wrap the cake in a polythene bag, seal, label and freeze for up to 4 months.

To thaw and serve: Unwrap the cake, place on a serving plate and leave to stand at room temperature for 3 to 4 hours.

Meanwhile make the glacé icing. Sift the icing sugar into a bowl, then gradually beat in the orange juice until the icing thickly coats the back of a spoon. Beat in the orange rind, then immediately pour the icing over the top of the cake. Spread to the edges and allow to drizzle over the sides. Blanch the orange shreds in boiling water for 1 minute, drain and cool thoroughly, then use to decorate the top of the cake. Serve as soon as possible.
Serves 8

Orange Cake, Fruity Fingers, Jamaican Rum Gâteau

NUTTY CHOUX RINGS

These may be filled with almond-flavoured crème patissière (pastry cream) if preferred.

CHOUX PASTRY
50 g/2 oz butter or margarine
150 ml/¼ pint water
65 g/2½ oz plain flour, sifted
2 eggs, lightly beaten
25 g/1 oz blanched almonds, chopped
TO SERVE
175 ml/6 fl oz double cream
2 tablespoons Tia Maria or other coffee-flavoured
   liqueur
icing sugar, for sifting

Make the choux pastry: Put the butter or margarine and water in a pan and bring to the boil. Remove from the heat and immediately beat in the flour all at once. Continue beating until the mixture leaves the sides of the pan. Cool slightly, then add the eggs a little at a time, beating vigorously between each addition until the mixture is thick, smooth and shiny.

Spoon the dough into a piping bag fitted with a 1 cm/½ inch plain nozzle and pipe ten 7.5 cm/3 inch circles on dampened baking sheets, spacing them well apart. Sprinkle the almonds on top of the rings.

Bake in a preheated hot oven (220°C/425°F/Gas Mark 7) for 10 minutes, then reduce the temperature to moderately hot (190°C/375°F/Gas Mark 5) and bake for a further 20 minutes until well risen and golden brown. Make a slit in the side of each choux ring with the point of a sharp knife, then leave to cool on a wire rack.

To freeze: Open freeze the choux rings until solid, then pack in a rigid container, seal, label and return to the freezer for up to 6 months.

To thaw and serve: Place the rings on a baking sheet and reheat from frozen in a preheated moderate oven (180°C/350°F/Gas Mark 4) for 10 to 15 minutes. Transfer to a wire rack, carefully split each ring in half and leave to cool.

Whip the cream with the coffee liqueur until it will stand in soft peaks. Spoon into a piping bag fitted with a 1 cm/½ inch fluted nozzle and pipe into the bottom halves of the rings. Replace the tops. Sift the sugar lightly over the choux rings and serve immediately.
Makes 10

OPPOSITE: Mince Pies
BELOW: Chelsea Buns; Nutty Choux Rings

CHELSEA BUNS

Originally made in the famous Bun House in Chelsea in the 18th century, homemade Chelsea buns are so much more delicious than any of the commercial varieties. If reheated from frozen, they taste as good taken from the freezer as they do freshly baked.

15 g/½ oz fresh yeast
120 ml/4 fl oz lukewarm milk
350 g/12 oz plain flour
½ teaspoon salt
1 teaspoon ground mixed spice
75 g/3 oz butter or margarine, melted
1 large egg, beaten
75 g/3 oz caster sugar
FILLING
50 g/2 oz butter or margarine, melted
75 g/3 oz demerara sugar
175 g/6 oz sultanas
2 teaspoons ground mixed spice
TO SERVE
4 tablespoons caster sugar
4 tablespoons water

Cream the yeast with a little of the milk and leave in a warm place for 10 minutes until frothy. Sift the flour, salt and spice into a warm bowl. Add the melted butter or margarine, the yeast mixture, egg, sugar and remaining milk, and mix to a soft dough.

Turn the dough onto a floured surface and knead for 8 to 10 minutes until smooth and elastic. Place in a clean bowl, cover with a damp cloth and leave to rise in a warm place for 2 hours or until doubled in bulk.

Turn the dough onto a floured surface and knead again for 2 to 3 minutes, then roll out to a 30 cm/12 inch square.

For the filling: Brush the melted butter or margarine over the dough, then sprinkle with the demerara sugar, sultanas and spice. Roll up like a Swiss roll, ending with the join underneath. Cut into 12 equal pieces and place, cut side downwards, in rows in a greased 18 × 28 cm/7 × 11 inch baking tin. Cover loosely with foil and leave to prove in a warm place for about 40 minutes until almost doubled in size.

Bake in a preheated moderately hot oven (200°C/400°F/Gas Mark 6) for 20 to 25 minutes until golden. Transfer to a wire rack and leave to cool.

To freeze: Wrap the buns in a single layer in foil, then pack in a polythene bag. Seal, label and freeze for up to 3 months.

To thaw and serve: Remove the polythene bag and place the foil package on a baking sheet. Reheat from frozen in a preheated moderately hot oven (190°C/375°F/Gas Mark 5) for 15 minutes until hot. Meanwhile, make the glaze. Heat the caster sugar and water gently in a small pan until the sugar has dissolved, then boil for 2 minutes.

Unwrap the buns and place on a wire rack. Brush them with the glaze and serve while still warm.
Makes 12

MINCE PIES

It is useful to prepare mince pies in advance and store them in the freezer a few weeks before Christmas to save any last minute rush.
To serve immediately, without freezing, bake as below but for only 15 minutes.

RICH SHORTCRUST PASTRY
250 g/8 oz plain flour
150 g/5 oz butter or margarine
1 tablespoon caster sugar
1 egg yolk
1–2 tablespoons cold water
FILLING
250 g/8 oz mincemeat (see page 194)
1 tablespoon brandy
TO SERVE
milk, to glaze
icing sugar

Make the pastry: Sift the flour into a bowl. Rub in the butter or margarine until the mixture resembles fine breadcrumbs. Stir in the sugar and egg yolk and enough water to mix to a fairly stiff dough. Turn the dough out onto a floured surface, knead lightly until smooth, then divide in half.

Roll out one piece of pastry fairly thinly and cut out 12 rounds using a 6 cm/2½ inch fluted cutter. Roll out the other piece of pastry a little thinner than the first and cut out twelve 7.5 cm/3 inch rounds with a fluted cutter. Use the larger rounds to line 12 patty tins.

For the filling: Mix the mincemeat with the brandy and divide equally between the patty tins. Moisten the edges of the pastry cases, place the smaller rounds on top and press the edges together firmly to seal. Make a small hole in the centre of each pie.

To freeze: Open freeze the pies until solid, then remove from the tins and pack in a rigid container. Seal, label and freeze for up to 3 months.

To thaw and serve: Return the pies to the patty tins and brush with milk. Bake from frozen in a preheated moderately hot oven (200°C/400°F/Gas Mark 6) for 20 to 25 minutes until golden brown. Transfer to a wire rack to cool. Sprinkle with icing sugar and serve while still warm.

Makes 12

GRANARY BREAD

If you do not have time to thaw the loaves at room temperature, they may be quickly reheated wrapped in foil in a preheated moderately hot oven (200°C/400°F/Gas Mark 6) for 30 minutes.

25 g/1 oz fresh yeast
900 ml/1 ½ pints lukewarm water
1 kg/2 lb granary flour
500 g/1 lb wholemeal flour
1 tablespoon salt
2 tablespoons malt extract
2 tablespoons vegetable oil
1 tablespoon cracked wheat

Cream the yeast with a little of the water and leave in a warm place for 10 minutes until frothy. Mix the flours and salt together in a warm bowl, make a well in the centre, then pour in the yeast mixture with the malt extract and oil. Mix to a soft dough.

Turn the dough onto a floured surface and knead for 8 to 10 minutes until smooth and elastic. Place in a clean bowl, cover with a damp cloth and leave to rise in a warm place for 2 hours or until doubled in bulk.

Turn the dough onto a floured surface and knead again for 2 to 3 minutes. Divide into 3 equal pieces and shape each into an 18 cm/7 inch round, flatten slightly and place on greased baking sheets. Brush with water and sprinkle with the cracked wheat. Cover loosely with foil and leave to prove in a warm place for about 30 minutes until almost doubled in size.

Bake in a preheated hot oven (220°C/425°F/Gas Mark 7) for 30 to 35 minutes or until the bread sounds hollow when tapped underneath. Transfer to a wire rack and leave to cool.

To freeze: Pack the loaves individually in polythene bags. Seal, label and freeze for up to 6 months.

To thaw and serve: Remove the polythene bags and leave to stand at room temperature for 2 to 3 hours.

Makes three 500 g/1 lb loaves

GRANARY ROLLS

Divide the risen dough into 30 equal pieces, then shape (see below). Prove and bake the rolls as above, but for only 15 to 20 minutes. Freeze, thaw and serve as above, leaving the rolls to stand for 1 to 2 hours.

Twists: Divide each piece in half and roll into 2 strips. Twist them together, pinching the ends to seal.

Clover Leaves: Divide each piece into three and form into balls. Dampen one side of each ball and press the dampened sides together.

Knots: Roll into a long strip and tie in a knot.

SAVOURY SCONE ROUND

It is particularly useful to store scones in the freezer otherwise they soon turn stale after they are made.

This savoury scone round is an excellent standby because it can be reheated very quickly from frozen for an instant snack or tea-time treat.

250 g/8 oz self-raising flour
½ teaspoon salt
1 teaspoon dry mustard
pinch of cayenne pepper
50 g/2 oz butter or margarine
125 g/4 oz Cheddar cheese, grated
1 teaspoon dried mixed herbs
120–150 ml/4–5 fl oz milk
a little extra milk, to glaze

Sift the flour, salt, mustard and cayenne pepper together into a bowl. Rub in the fat until the mixture resembles fine breadcrumbs. Reserve 1 tablespoon of the cheese; stir the remainder into the rubbed-in mixture, with the herbs. Add enough milk to mix to a soft dough.

Turn the dough onto a floured surface, knead lightly, then shape into an 18 cm/7 inch round and place on a lightly floured baking sheet. Score the scone round with a sharp knife into 8 sections, brush the top with a little milk to glaze and sprinkle with the reserved grated cheese.

Bake in a preheated moderately hot oven (200°C/400°F/Gas Mark 6) for 15 to 20 minutes until golden brown. Transfer the round to a wire rack and leave to cool.

To freeze: Wrap in a polythene bag, seal, label and freeze for up to 4 months.

To thaw and serve: Unwrap the scone round, place it on a baking sheet and reheat from frozen in a preheated moderate oven (180°C/350°F/Gas Mark 4) for 15 minutes until golden. Transfer the round to a wire rack and leave to cool slightly. Serve warm, split and thickly buttered.

Serves 8

BLOOMER LOAVES

As a variation, these loaves may be sprinkled with poppy seeds instead of salt crystals. To thaw them quickly, reheat, wrapped in foil, in a preheated moderately hot oven (200°C/400°F/Gas Mark 6) for 30 minutes, removing the foil for the last 10 minutes.

25 g/1 oz fresh yeast
900 ml/1½ pints lukewarm water
1.5 kg/3 lb strong white plain flour
1 tablespoon salt
2 tablespoons vegetable oil
coarse salt crystals, for sprinkling

Cream the yeast with a little of the water and leave in a warm place for 10 minutes until frothy. Sift the flour and salt into a warm bowl. Make a well in the centre, then pour in the yeast mixture with the remaining water and oil. Mix to a soft dough.

Turn the dough onto a floured surface and knead for 8 to 10 minutes until smooth and elastic. Place in a clean bowl, cover with a damp cloth and leave to rise in a warm place for 2 hours or until doubled in bulk.

Turn the dough onto a floured surface and knead again for 2 to 3 minutes. Divide in half and shape each piece into a long fat sausage. Using a sharp knife, make 7 to 8 deep diagonal cuts at regular intervals along the top of each loaf. Place on floured baking sheets, cover loosely with foil and leave to prove in a warm place for about 30 minutes until almost doubled in size. Brush with water and sprinkle with the salt crystals.

Bake in a preheated hot oven (220°C/425°F/Gas Mark 7) for 30 minutes or until the bread sounds hollow when tapped underneath. Cool on a wire rack.

To freeze: Pack the loaves individually in polythene bags. Seal, label and freeze for up to 6 months.

To thaw and serve: Remove the polythene bags and leave to stand at room temperature for 3 to 4 hours.

Makes 2 large bloomer loaves

COTTAGE ROLLS

Divide the risen dough into 30 equal pieces, then break each piece into two-thirds and one-third portions. Roll each portion into a ball. Dampen the top of the large ball, put the smaller one on top and push the handle of a wooden spoon through the centre to secure them.

Prove and bake as above, but for only 20 minutes. Thaw for 1 to 2 hours before serving.

CHRISTMAS FARE

CELEBRATION TURKEY

MINCEMEAT AND APPLE JALOUSIE

Christmas comes but once a year – and if you're the cook you'll think it's just as well! Having family and friends for Christmas is fun, but it puts an enormous strain on the host and hostess, especially if you happen to be working during the week leading up to Christmas. Catering for any number of guests over a period of several days demands plenty of organization beforehand. Shopping and cooking simply can't be put off until the last minute, and this is where your freezer will really come into its own.

Plan your menus several weeks before and make out shopping lists, including all meals from breakfast through to evening snacks and drinks. Try to choose a fair amount of dishes which can be prepared well in advance, then pack them away in the freezer ready to simply thaw or heat through and serve.

Christmas cake and pudding are not worth freezing; they keep so well, that there is no need for them to take up valuable freezer space. However, be sure to freeze several batches of Mince Pies (see page 191) which are always useful if unexpected guests drop in – they can be reheated from frozen in only 20 minutes. Bread and rolls can be made or bought and frozen in advance to avoid pre-Christmas queues at the baker's, and the inconvenience of running out of bread when all the shops are shut. (Remember not to put crusty rolls and French bread in the freezer for much more than a week or their crusts will flake off.)

Frozen turkeys are a good buy, especially the self-basting 'butterball' variety, and are well worth making freezer space for, up to several months ahead, both to avoid last-minute disappointment and to help spread the cost of Christmas. You can also save time and effort later by preparing stuffings and savoury sauces beforehand and storing them in the freezer.

An even better idea is to order a succulent fresh hen bird from your butcher well in advance of Christmas, then to bone, stuff and freeze it as in this Celebration turkey, ready to go straight in the oven on Christmas morning. Remember to leave enough time for it to thaw – 36 to 48 hours. A boned turkey takes far less freezer and oven space than a whole bird, the carving is effortless, and the inclusion of ham and extra minced turkey (available all year round at most large supermarkets) makes for a veritable feast. The turkey bones can be used to make a rich stock and frozen for later use in warming soups.

Mincemeat and Apple Jalousie is another old-time favourite – a combination of grated apple, mincemeat and cinnamon surrounded by crisp, yet melt-in-the-mouth, puff pastry. It makes the ideal dessert for those of your guests who find Christmas pudding too rich and heavy. Bombe Noël (see page 179) is another light alternative to the traditional pudding.

Boned celebration turkey is excellent for busy people with limited freezer and oven space, and being fully prepared for roasting 2 to 3 weeks ahead of Christmas it reduces any last-minute panics. If you are unsure of boning the turkey yourself, ask your butcher if he will do it for you. Boneless turkey meat for mincing is widely available from supermarkets.

1 × 7 kg/15 lb oven-ready hen turkey
salt and freshly ground black pepper
125 g/4 oz (4 slices) cooked ham
125 g/4 oz fresh breadcrumbs
finely grated rind of 1 small lemon
250 g/8 oz fresh spinach, blanched, drained and chopped
1.5 kg/3 lb boneless turkey meat, minced
25 g/1 oz butter
75 g/3 oz large button mushrooms, trimmed
TO SERVE
50 g/2 oz butter, softened

Bone the turkey, except for the wings and drumsticks: Lay the bird, breast down, on a board. Using a small sharp knife, make a slit down the centre of the back, starting at the neck end. Scrape the flesh away from the rib cage down to the leg and wing joint and cut through the sinews, holding the wings and legs in place. Finally work the flesh away from the breast bone, taking care not to cut through the skin, and remove the carcass.

Place the turkey skin down and sprinkle the flesh liberally with salt and pepper. Arrange the ham slices over the turkey flesh. Mix together the breadcrumbs, lemon rind and spinach with salt and pepper to taste. Spread over the ham, then cover with the minced turkey, stuffing it into the tops of the legs.

Melt the butter in a small pan, add the mushrooms and fry lightly. Arrange down the centre of the stuffing and pour the butter and juices on top. Fold up the sides of the turkey to make a compact shape. Hold the edges together, using 2 or more skewers along the join, or sew together, using a trussing needle and string. Turn the bird up the right way and pat into shape.

To freeze: Wrap in foil, then overwrap in a polythene bag. Seal, label and freeze for up to 3 weeks.

To thaw and serve: Remove polythene bag and leave turkey to stand in its foil wrapping at room temperature for 36 to 48 hours. Unwrap, place on a rack in a roasting tin and spread with the softened butter. Roast in a preheated moderate oven (160°C/325°F/Gas Mark 3) for 3½ hours or until the juices run clear when the thickest part of the thigh is pierced with a skewer. Baste with the fat in the pan every 30 minutes.

Leave the turkey to stand for about 15 minutes. Meanwhile remove excess fat from the pan juices and use to make gravy. Carve the turkey crossways into slices. Serve hot, with the gravy, Brussels sprouts, roast potatoes and baked parsnips.
Serves 16 to 20

For a festive occasion, buy the best quality mincemeat which usually has rum or brandy in it, or – better still – make your own (see below). Use puff pastry, made with 200 g/7 oz flour (see Tarte Française – page 140). If serving immediately, without freezing, a 400 g/14 oz frozen packet puff pastry can be used (bake as below). Serve with whipped or clotted cream.

400 g/14 oz fresh puff pastry (total weight)
500 g/1 lb cooking apples
8 tablespoons mincemeat
1 teaspoon ground cinnamon
1 egg, lightly beaten
1 tablespoon caster sugar

Cut the pastry in half. Roll out one piece of pastry on a lightly floured surface to a 30 × 23 cm/12 × 9 inch rectangle. Place on a baking sheet lined with a large sheet of foil and set aside.

Peel and core the apples, then grate them into a bowl. Add the mincemeat and half the cinnamon and stir well to mix. Spread this mixture over the pastry on the baking sheet, to within 2.5 cm/1 inch of the edges. Brush the edges with beaten egg.

Roll out the remaining piece of pastry to the same size rectangle as the first, then place over the filling. Press the edges firmly to seal, then knock up and flute. Brush all over the pastry rectangle with more beaten egg. With a sharp knife, make several slashes widthways in the pastry, right through to the filling. Mix the caster sugar and remaining cinnamon together, then sprinkle over the top of the jalousie.

To freeze: Open freeze the jalousie on the baking sheet until solid, then remove from the sheet and wrap in the foil. Seal, label and return to the freezer for up to 1 month.

To thaw and serve: Unwrap the jalousie and place on a dampened baking sheet. Bake from frozen in a preheated moderately hot oven (200°C/400°F/Gas Mark 6) for 20 minutes or until the pastry is puffed up and golden. Serve the jalousie warm or cold, cut into squares or slices.
Serves 6 to 8

TO MAKE MINCEMEAT
Mix together 350 g/12 oz raisins, 125 g/4 oz finely chopped, peeled apples, 50 g/2 oz chopped candied peel, 175 g/6 oz currants, 125 g/4 oz sultanas, 75 g/3 oz shredded suet, ¼ teaspoon ground mixed spice, the finely grated rind and juice of 1 lemon, 250 g/8 oz soft brown sugar and 3 tablespoons rum or brandy. Cover and leave to stand overnight.

The quantity will make about 1 kg/2 lb of mincemeat. Any amount that is not used immediately can be frozen for up to 1 month in small containers. Thaw at room temperature for about 3 hours.

Celebration Turkey: Mincemeat and Apple Jalousie

Reference Section

HOW TO FREEZE CUTS OF VEAL

VEAL	CUTS	PREPARATION	PACKAGING	STORAGE TIME	THAWING
Joints (for roasting/slow roasting/pot roasting/ poaching/braising)	Leg divided into 3 joints (Cushion, Silverside and Thick Flank), Loin (sold on the bone and boned and rolled), Best End (Ribs), Breast (boned and rolled), Shoulder (boned and rolled), Neck (including Middle Neck and Best End of Neck), Flank (rolled).	As for Preparation of Beef Joints (opposite).	As for Packaging of Beef Joints (opposite).	12 months	Thaw as for Beef Joints (opposite). Small boned and rolled joints under 1.5 kg/3 lb and all joints on the bone can be cooked from frozen for approximately twice usual time until 77°C/170°F is registered on meat thermometer. *Do not cook boned and rolled joints from frozen.*
Chops, Cutlets, Escalopes and Medaillons (for grilling/frying/ sautés/braising)	Fillet End of Leg cut into escalopes and medaillons, Loin divided into chops, Loin Fillet sliced into medaillons, Best End Ribs and Middle Neck divided into cutlets.	Trim any bone ends and surplus fat. Beat out escalopes until very thin.	As for Packaging of Beef Steaks (opposite).	12 months	Thaw chops as for Beef Steaks (opposite). Escalopes and medaillons can be sautéed quickly in butter from frozen.
Slices and Cubes (for braising/casseroling/ pies/stewing)	Boneless slices and cubes from Knuckle and Shin, Shoulder, Breast, Neck and Flank (Pie Veal). Leg meat on the bone (known as Osso Buco).	As for Preparation of Beef Slices and Cubes (opposite).	As for Packaging of Beef Slices and Cubes (opposite).	3 months	As for Thawing of Beef Slices and Cubes (opposite).
Minced Veal	Boneless meat from Shoulder and Flank.	As for Preparation of Minced Beef (opposite).	As for Packaging of Minced Beef (opposite).	3 months	As for Thawing of Minced Beef (opposite).

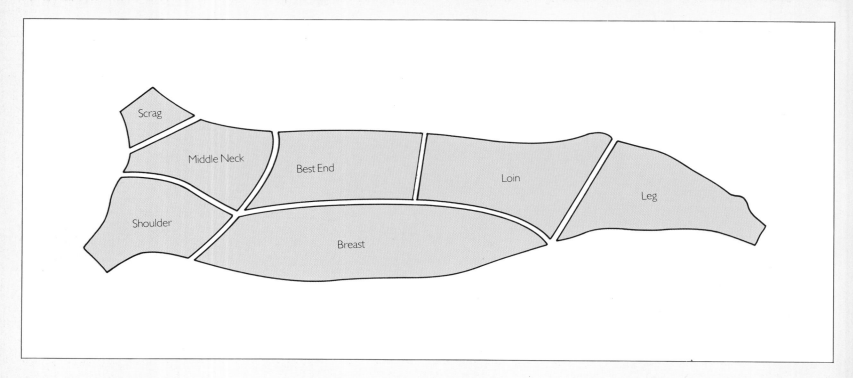

HOW TO FREEZE CUTS OF BEEF

BEEF	CUTS	PREPARATION	PACKAGING	STORAGE TIME	THAWING
Joints (for roasting/slow roasting/pot roasting/braising)	*Forequarter* Foreribs, Back Ribs, Thick and Thin Ribs – on bone or as boned and rolled joints. Brisket is boned and rolled. *Do not* freeze salted brisket. *Hindquarter* Sirloin (including wing ribs – on or off the bone), Fillet, Rump, Top Rump (thick flank), Topside, Aitchbone cut, Silverside. Top Rump, Topside and Silverside are rolled.	Saw off any protruding bone ends and remove surplus fat. Pad bones with foil. Do not stuff boned and rolled joints.	Wrap individual joints in cling film or foil, then overwrap in polythene bags. Exclude all air and seal.	12 months	Thaw in wrappings at room temperature for 6 to 8 hours per kg/3 to 4 hours per lb, then cook as fresh. Small joints under 1.5 kg/3 lb and on the bone can be cooked from frozen for approximately twice usual time until 74°C/165°F is registered on meat thermometer. *Do not* cook boned and rolled joints from frozen.
Steaks (for grilling/frying/barbecuing)	*Forequarter* Forerib Steaks on the bone. *Hindquarter* T-bone (including Fillet), Porterhouse (on the bone), Sirloin (boneless), Fillet, Rump.	Remove surplus fat. Do not cut more than 2.5 cm/1 inch thick. Pad any protruding bones with foil.	Wrap individually in cling film or foil or interleave, then pack together in polythene bags. Exclude all air and seal.	12 months	Thaw in wrappings at room temperature for 2 to 3 hours or in refrigerator overnight, then cook as fresh. Or grill/fry thin steaks from frozen; allow extra time and brush with oil.
Slices and Cubes (for braising/casseroling/pies/stewing)	*Forequarter* Boneless meat from Thick and Thin Ribs, Blade, Chuck, Clod, Neck, Shin, Brisket, Flank. *Hindquarter* Top Rump, Leg, Flank.	Trim off surplus fat, sinews and gristle. Cut into 2.5 cm/1 inch thick slices or cubes if not already cut.	Pack in usable quantities in polythene bags, exclude all air and seal.	8 months	Thaw slices and cubes in wrappings at room temperature until pieces separate, then cook as fresh, allowing a little extra time and using thawed juices.
Minced Beef	*Forequarter* Boneless meat from Thick and Thin Ribs, Clod, Neck, Flank. *Hindquarter* Flank.	Only freeze lean Minced Beef. Leave loose or shape into burgers/meatballs/patties, etc. (Minced Chuck from forequarter is excellent for these.)	Pack loose mince in usable quantities in polythene bags; exclude all air and seal. Open freeze burgers, etc., then interleave and pack in bags.	3 months	Partially thaw loose mince in wrappings in refrigerator, then cook as fresh, stirring to prevent sticking. Cook burgers, etc. from frozen.

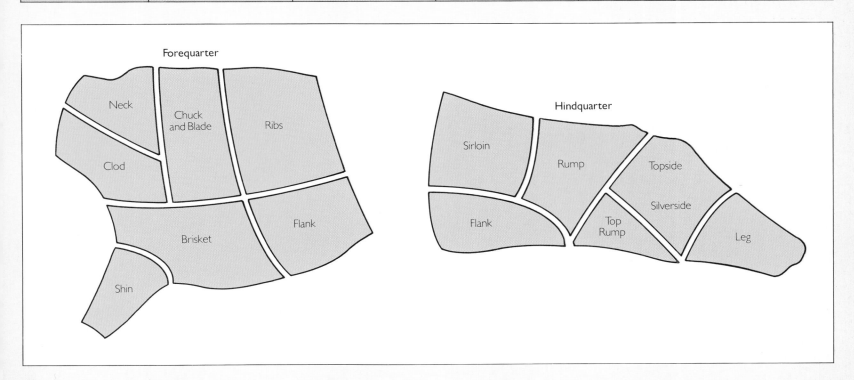

HOW TO FREEZE CUTS OF LAMB

LAMB	CUTS	PREPARATION	PACKAGING	STORAGE TIME	THAWING
Joints (for roasting/slow roasting)	Shoulder (whole and halved), Breast, Leg (whole and halved), Loin (whole and halved into Best Loin and Chump End), Saddle (both loins joined together by backbone), Best End of Neck, Crown Roast and Guard of Honour (two Best Ends tied together).	To facilitate carving and economize on freezer space, Shoulder, Breast and Leg may be boned, rolled and tied (but do not stuff before freezing). Ask butcher to chine Loin, which can also be boned if wished. Saw off any protruding bone ends and remove surplus fat. Pad bones with foil.	Wrap individual joints in cling film or foil, then overwrap in polythene bag. Exclude all air and seal.	12 months	Thaw in wrappings at room temperature for 6 to 8 hours per kg/3 to 4 hours per lb, then cook as fresh. Small joints under 1.5 kg/3 lb and on the bone can be cooked from frozen for approximately twice usual time until 85°C/185°F is registered on meat thermometer. *Do not* cook boned and rolled joints from frozen.
Chops/Cutlets/Steaks (for grilling/frying/barbecuing)	Breast cut into 2.5 cm/1 inch riblets. Fillet End of Leg cut into 1 to 2.5 cm/½ to 1 inch thick steaks. Loin divided into loin and chump chops. Best End of Neck divided into cutlets; large cutlets boned to make noisettes.	Trim off bone ends, surplus skin and fat. Pad bones with foil.	Wrap individually in cling film or foil or interleave, then pack together in polythene bags, exclude all air and seal.	12 months	Thaw in wrappings at room temperature for 2 to 3 hours, or in refrigerator overnight, then cook as fresh. Alternatively grill/fry from frozen, allowing extra time and brushing liberally with oil.
Cubes and Pieces (for casseroling/pies/sautés/stewing)	Boneless cubes from Shoulder and Leg. Middle Neck and Scrag chopped into serving-sized pieces (including bones) by butcher.	Trim off surplus fat, sinews and gristle. Cut boneless meat into 2.5 cm/1 inch cubes if not already cut.	Pack cubes in usable quantities in polythene bags, exclude all air and seal. Pack bony pieces in rigid containers and seal.	8 months	Thaw in wrappings at room temperature until pieces separate, then cook as fresh allowing a little extra time and using thawed juices.
Minced Lamb	Boneless meat from shoulder.	As for Preparation of Minced Beef (page 197).	As for Packaging of Minced Beef (page 197).	3 months	As for Thawing of Minced Beef (page 197).

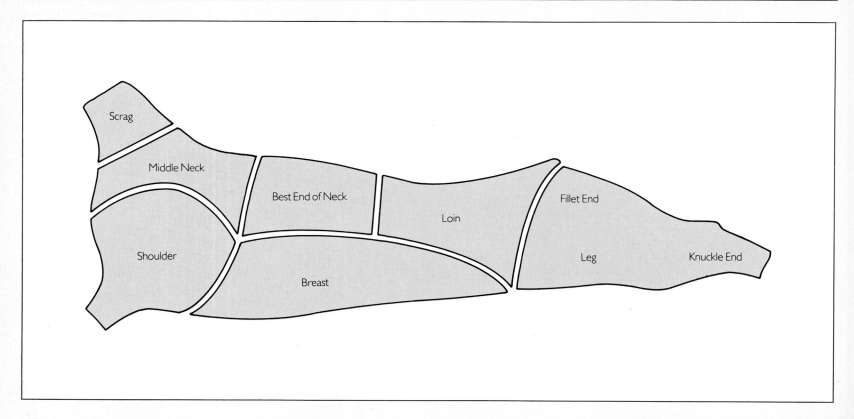

HOW TO FREEZE CUTS OF PORK

PORK	CUTS	PREPARATION	PACKAGING	STORAGE TIME	THAWING
Joints (for roasting/pot roasting)	Leg (can be whole but usually cut into Fillet End and Knuckle End), Loin (sold on the bone or boned, rolled and tied; divided into Foreloin, Middle Loin and Chump End), Belly (sold on and off the bone; divided into Thick and Streaky Ends), Shoulder or Neck End (including Spare Rib and Blade; can be boned and rolled), Hand and Spring (Hand can be boned and rolled).	Saw off any protruding bone ends and remove surplus fat. Leave skin on for crackling if liked. Pad bones with foil. Roll and tie boneless meat if not already done by butcher, but do not stuff. Pork crown roast can be made by tying together 2 Foreloins.	Wrap individual joints in cling film or foil, then overwrap in polythene bag. Exclude all air and seal.	9 months 6 months (Belly)	Thaw in wrappings at room temperature for 6 to 8 hours per kg/3 to 4 hours per lb, then cook as fresh until 87°C/190°F is registered on meat thermometer. *Do not* cook pork joints from frozen.
Chops/Steaks/ Escalopes/Rashers/ Spareribs (for grilling/frying/ roasting/barbecuing)	Leg Fillet, Eye of Loin and Tenderloin cut into thin slices or escalopes. Loin divided into Foreloin chops (from Rib or Neck End), Middle Loin chops and Chump chops. Belly cut into rashers or boned to provide Spareribs. Shoulder cut into Sparerib chops.	Trim off bone ends and surplus fat. Leave skin on for crackling if liked. Pad bones with foil.	Wrap individually in cling film or interleave, then pack together in polythene bags, exclude all air and seal.	9 months 6 months (Belly)	Thaw in wrappings at room temperature for 2 to 3 hours, or in refrigerator overnight, then cook as fresh. Alternatively grill/fry from frozen, allowing extra time and brushing liberally with oil.
Cubes (for casseroling/pies/ sautés/stewing)	Boneless cubes from Leg, Tenderloin, Shoulder (Sparerib), Hand.	As for Preparation of Lamb cubes and pieces (opposite).	As for Packaging of Lamb cubes and pieces (opposite).	9 months	As for Thawing of Lamb Cubes and Pieces (opposite).
Minced Pork	Boneless meat from shoulder.	As for Preparation of Minced Beef (page 197).	As for Packaging of Minced Beef (page 197).	3 months	As for Thawing of Minced Beef (page 197).

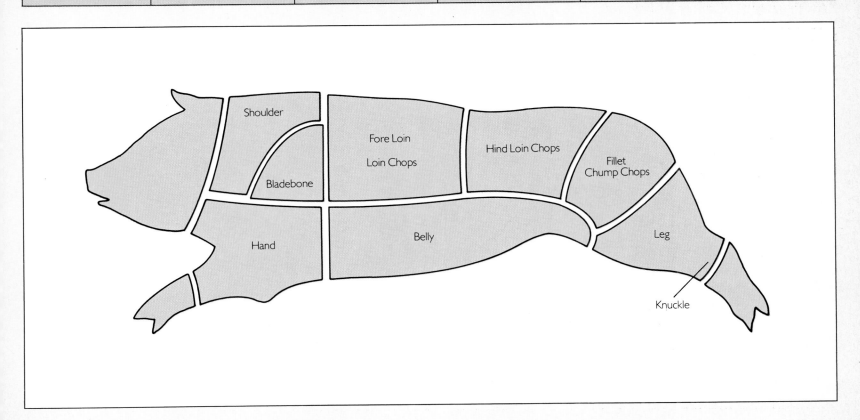

HOW TO FREEZE FISH AND SHELLFISH

FISH	PREPARATION	PACKAGING	STORAGE TIME	THAWING
White Fish Bass, Bream, Brill, Carp, Cod, Coley, Flounder, Grey Mullet, Haddock, Hake, Halibut, Plaice, Red Mullet, Rock Salmon (Huss), Skate, Sole, Turbot, Whiting	Freeze within 24 hours of catching. Gut and clean, remove scales and fins. Cut off heads and tails and remove skin if wished. Leave whole if small, cut into steaks or fillets if large. Rinse under cold running water and pat dry with absorbent paper.	Wrap individual whole fish in cling film, then overwrap in polythene bags. Exclude all air and seal. Interleave steaks and fillets, then pack together in bags.	3 months	Thaw whole fish in wrappings in refrigerator overnight, then cook as fresh. Cook steaks and fillets from frozen as for commercially frozen fish.
Oily Fish Eel, Herring, Mackerel, Salmon, Salmon Trout, Sprat, Trout, Whitebait	Freeze within 24 hours of catching (Mackerel within 12 hours). Gut and clean, remove scales and fins. Leave whole with heads and tails on if wished, or cut off heads and tails, split open and bone. Whole Salmon can be cut into steaks. Rinse under cold running water and pat dry with absorbent paper.	As for White Fish (above). Whole Salmon can also be ice glazed (see page 11).	2 months	Thaw whole fish in wrappings in refrigerator for about 1 hour, then cook as fresh allowing extra time. Cook boned fish and steaks from frozen allowing extra time.
Smoked and Cured Fish Buckling, Finnan Haddie, Haddock, Kipper, Mackerel, Salmon, Trout	Only freeze freshly smoked/cured fish, not fish that has been previously frozen and thawed. Leave whole with heads and tails on if wished, or cut off heads and tails, split open and bone. Remove skin if wished. Fillets of smoked/cured fish need no preparation for freezing.	As for White Fish (above).	3 months	Thaw in wrappings in refrigerator for about 1 hour, then cook as fresh smoked fish allowing extra time. If serving cold, thaw in wrappings in refrigerator overnight.

SEASONAL AVAILABILITY OF WHITE FISH   ○ Available   ● At its best

	JAN	FEB	MAR	APR	MAY	JUNE	JULY	AUG	SEP	OCT	NOV	DEC
BASS					○	○	○	○	○			
BREAM	○	○	○				○	○	○	○	○	○
BRILL				○	○	○	○					
CARP	○	○	○				○	○	○	○	○	○
COD	●	●	●	○	○	○	○	○	○	●	●	●
COLEY	○								○	○	○	○
FLOUNDER		○	○	○	○	○	○	○	○			
GREY MULLET				○	○	○	○	○	○	○		
HADDOCK	○	○									○	○
HAKE	●	○	○	○		●	●	●	●	●	●	●
HALIBUT	○	○	○	○				○	○	○	○	○
PLAICE	○	○	○	○	●	●	●	●	●	●	●	●
RED MULLET				○	○	○	○	○	○	○		
ROCK SALMON (HUSS)	●	●	●	●	●	○	○	●	●	●	●	●
SKATE	○	○	○	○						○	○	○
SOLE, DOVER	○					○	○	○	○	○	○	○
SOLE, LEMON	○	○	○									○
TURBOT	○	○	●	●	●	●	●	●	○	○	○	○
WHITING	●	●	○	○	○	○	○	○	○	○	○	●

SEASONAL AVAILABILITY OF OILY FISH	○ Available				● At its best							
	JAN	FEB	MAR	APR	MAY	JUNE	JULY	AUG	SEP	OCT	NOV	DEC
EEL	○	○		○	○			○	○	○	○	○
HERRING	○	○	○	○	○	●	●	●	●	○	○	○
MACKEREL	●	●	●	○	○	○	○	○	○	●	●	●
SALMON		○	○	○	○	○	○	○				
SALMON TROUT			○	○	○	○	○					
SPRAT	○	○	○						○	○	○	○
TROUT	○	○	○	○	○	○	○	○	○	○	○	○
WHITEBAIT			○	○	○	○	○	○				

SHELLFISH	PREPARATION	PACKAGING	STORAGE TIME	THAWING
Cockle, Mussel, Oyster, Scallop	Freeze on day of catching as soon as possible after boiling and cooling in the usual way. Open shells and remove fish. Retain juices. Wash fish in salted water (2 tablespoons salt to 600 ml/1 pint water) then drain thoroughly.	Pack fish and juices in usable quantities in rigid containers with crumpled greaseproof paper between surface of liquid and lid.	1 month	Cook from frozen allowing very little extra cooking time or fish will be tough. To serve oysters raw, thaw in container in refrigerator overnight then eat as soon as possible after thawing.
Prawn, Shrimp, Scampi (Dublin Bay Prawns)	Freeze on day of catching as soon as possible after boiling and cooling in the usual way. Twist off heads leaving tails in shell. Wash in salted water as Cockle, etc. (above), then drain thoroughly. Prawns may be cooked in boiling salted water for 2 to 4 minutes then drained and cooled before freezing.	Pack in usable quantities in polythene bags.	1 month	Cook raw fish from frozen as Cockle, etc. (above). Thaw cooked prawns in wrappings in refrigerator for 2 to 3 hours then serve cold or cook as for fresh prawns.
Crab, Lobster	Freeze only absolutely fresh fish as soon as possible after boiling and cooling in usual way. Leave meat in shell or remove according to personal preference and future use.	Wrap fish in shell tightly in cling film then overwrap in polythene bag. Crab can be frozen 'dressed' in shell or white and dark meat frozen in separate rigid containers. Lobster meat can also be removed from shell and packed in containers.	1 month	Thaw in wrappings in refrigerator for 6 to 8 hours then eat or use as fresh.

SEASONAL AVAILABILITY OF SHELLFISH	○ Available				● At its best							
	JAN	FEB	MAR	APR	MAY	JUNE	JULY	AUG	SEP	OCT	NOV	DEC
COCKLE	○	○	○	○	○	○	○	○	○	○		○
MUSSEL								○	○	○	○	
OYSTER	○	○	○	○					○	○	○	○
SCALLOP	○	●	●							○	○	○
PRAWN	○	○	○	○	○	○	○	○	○	○		○
SHRIMP	○	●	●	●	●	●	●	●	●	●	○	○
SCAMPI (DUBLIN BAY PRAWNS)	○	●	●	●	●	●	●	●	●	●	○	○
CRAB	○	○	○	○	●	●	●	●	○	○	○	○
LOBSTER	○	○	○	●	●	●	●	●	○	○		○

HOW TO FREEZE POULTRY

POULTRY	PREPARATION	PACKAGING	STORAGE TIMES	THAWING
Whole Capon, Chicken, Duck, Goose, Guinea Fowl, Poussin, Turkey.	Choose young plump birds. Pluck and hang if necessary, within 24 hours of killing. Draw and wash poultry thoroughly inside and out. Dry then truss. Do not stuff poultry before freezing. Reserve giblets separately, discarding sac from gizzard.	Pad protruding bones with foil, then wrap whole birds individually in foil and overwrap in polythene bags. Pack giblets in rigid containers or polythene bags, keeping livers separate for use in pâtés, etc.	Capon, Chicken, Poussin } 12 months Duck, Goose } 4 to 6 months Guinea Fowl – 6 months Turkey – 8 months Giblets – 3 months	All whole birds **must** be thawed completely before cooking to avoid risk of salmonella poisoning. Thaw Chicken, Guinea Fowl and Poussin in wrappings in refrigerator for 24 to 36 hours according to size. Thaw Goose, Turkey and Capon in wrappings at room temperature for up to 72 hours according to size. As a guide, a 4 kg (9 lb) bird will take approximately 36 hours; a 6 kg (14 lb) bird – about 48 hours; a 9 kg (20 lb) bird – about 60 hours. Thaw giblets in container in refrigerator for 12 hours.
Halves and Joints/ Portions (From Poultry as above)	Buy jointed poultry, or cut up whole birds at home into halves and joints such as wings, legs, thighs, drumsticks, breasts. Wash and dry thoroughly and remove any protruding bones.	Pad any protruding bones with foil, then wrap individual pieces in foil and pack together in polythene bags.	As for whole birds (above).	Thaw in wrappings in refrigerator for up to 15 hours according to size, or cook from partially frozen, allowing extra time until thoroughly cooked through.

HOW TO FREEZE DAIRY PRODUCE

DAIRY PRODUCE	PREPARATION	PACKAGING	STORAGE TIME	THAWING
Butter	Freeze very fresh butter as soon as possible after purchase.	Freeze in 225 g/½ lb quantities. Leave in original packs and overwrap in foil or a polythene bag.	3 months (salted) 6 months (unsalted)	Remove overwrapping and thaw in refrigerator for 4 hours or at room temperature for 2 hours; use quickly.
Cheese Hard (Cheddar, Cheshire, Edam, etc.); Soft (Brie, Camembert, Mozzarella, etc.); Blue (Stilton, Danish, etc.); Cream Cheese	Cut hard cheese into 225 g/½ lb blocks. Freeze only mature soft cheeses – cut into usable quantities. Only freeze cream cheese that contains at least 40% butterfat.	Wrap hard and soft cheeses in foil or cling film, then overwrap in a polythene bag. For grated cheese, grate in the usual way and pack in polythene bags.	3–6 months (depending on freshness at time of freezing)	Thaw hard and cream cheeses in wrappings in refrigerator overnight. Whisk cream cheese before using. Thaw soft cheese for 24 hours in refrigerator, then 24 hours at room temperature. Use grated cheese from frozen. Use cheeses soon after thawing.
Cream	Only very fresh cream, containing at least 40% butterfat, should be frozen. Chill, then whip lightly with 1 teaspoon sugar.	Pack in usable quantities in rigid containers, leaving 2 cm/¾ inch headspace.	3 months	Thaw in container in refrigerator for 8 hours. Whip again before using, for sweet dishes.
Eggs	Only freeze very fresh eggs. Do not freeze in shells or hard-boiled. To freeze whole eggs, whisk lightly, then add ½ teaspoon salt or 1 teaspoon sugar to every 3 eggs. For yolks, add ¼ teaspoon salt or ½ teaspoon sugar to every 3 yolks. Or freeze egg yolks individually in ice cube trays. Freeze egg whites in usable quantities, or individually in ice cube trays.	Pour whole eggs, egg yolks or egg whites into rigid containers. For cubes, open freeze until solid, then pack in polythene bags.	6 months	Transfer whole eggs, yolks and whites to a bowl and thaw for at least 1 hour at room temperature. Use as soon as possible.

HOW TO FREEZE GAME

GAME	PREPARATION	PACKAGING	STORAGE TIME	THAWING
Game Birds (Grouse, Partridge, Pheasant, Pigeon, Quail, Snipe, Squab, Woodcock)	Hang if necessary, then pluck, draw and wash thoroughly inside and out. Dry then truss if necessary. *Do not stuff.* Reserve giblets separately, discarding sac from gizzard.	Pad protruding bones with foil, then wrap whole birds individually in foil and overwrap in polythene bags. If the game is very high use several bags and seal each one tightly. Pack giblets in rigid containers or polythene bags, keeping livers separate for use in pâtés, etc.	6 months 3 months	All game birds **must** be thawed thoroughly before cooking and cooked **immediately** after thawing. Thaw Grouse, Partridge, Pheasant and Pigeon in wrappings in refrigerator for up to 24 hours according to size. Thaw Quail, Snipe, Squab and Woodcock in wrappings in refrigerator for 12 to 15 hours according to size. Thaw giblets in container in refrigerator for 12 hours.
Halves and Joints/ Portions	Cut suitable sized game birds into halves and joints. Wash and dry thoroughly and remove any protruding bones.	Pad any protruding bones with foil, then wrap individual pieces in foil and pack together in polythene bags.	6 months	Thaw in wrappings in refrigerator for up to 15 hours according to size, then cook immediately.
Game Animals (Hare, Leveret, Rabbit, Venison)	Hang if necessary. Skin Hare, Leveret and Rabbit, then draw and wash thoroughly inside and out in lightly salted water. Dry thoroughly, then leave whole or halve and joint according to personal preference and future use. Venison is butchered and prepared for the freezer in a similar way to Beef (page 197).	Pack Hare, Leveret and Rabbit as for whole game birds and halves and portions/joints above. Pack Venison cuts as for Beef cuts (page 197).	Hare Leveret } 6 months Rabbit Venison – 12 months	Thaw Hare, Leveret and Rabbit at room temperature for up to 18 hours according to size. Thaw Venison as for Beef (page 197).

SEASONAL AVAILABILITY OF GAME	○ Available		● At its best									
	JAN	FEB	MAR	APR	MAY	JUNE	JULY	AUG	SEP	OCT	NOV	DEC
GROUSE								●	●	●	○	○
HARE	●	●	●						○	●	●	●
LEVERET	●	●	●									
PARTRIDGE	○								○	●	●	○
PHEASANT	○									○	●	●
PIGEON	○	○	○	○	○	○	○	●	●	●	○	○
QUAIL	○	○	○	○	○	○	○	○	○	○	○	○
RABBIT	○	○	○							○	○	○
SNIPE	○								○	○	●	○
SQUAB				○	○							
VENISON	○				○	○	○			○	○	○
WOODCOCK	○									○	●	●

INDEX

ACKNOWLEDGMENTS

Photography by Paul Williams
Food prepared by Clare Ferguson, Carole Handslip
and Caroline Ellwood
Photographic Stylist: Penny Markham